THE ARMENIAN PEOPLE FROM ANCIENT TO MODERN TIMES

VOLUME I

Also by Richard G. Hovannisian

ARMENIA ON THE ROAD TO INDEPENDENCE
THE REPUBLIC OF ARMENIA *(4 volumes)*
THE ARMENIAN GENOCIDE: History, Politics, Ethics *(editor)*
THE ARMENIAN HOLOCAUST
THE ARMENIAN GENOCIDE IN PERSPECTIVE *(editor)*
THE ARMENIAN IMAGE IN HISTORY AND LITERATURE *(editor)*
ISLAM'S UNDERSTANDING OF ITSELF *(editor)*
ETHICS IN ISLAM *(editor)*
THE PERSIAN PRESENCE IN THE ISLAMIC WORLD *(editor)*
THE THOUSAND AND ONE NIGHTS IN ARABIC LITERATURE AND
    SOCIETY *(editor)*

THE ARMENIAN PEOPLE FROM ANCIENT TO MODERN TIMES

VOLUME I

The Dynastic Periods:
From Antiquity
to the Fourteenth Century

Edited by Richard G. Hovannisian

Professor of Armenian and Near Eastern History

University of California, Los Angeles

St. Martin's Press
New York

THE ARMENIAN PEOPLE FROM ANCIENT TO MODERN TIMES, VOLUME I
Copyright © Richard G. Hovannisian, 1997. All rights reserved. Printed
in the United States of America. No part of this book may be used or
reproduced in any manner whatsoever without written permission except
in the case of brief quotations embodied in critical articles or reviews.
For information, address St. Martin's Press, 175 Fifth Avenue, New
York, N.Y. 10010.
ISBN 0-312-10169-4

Library of Congress Cataloging-in-Publication Data

The Armenian people from ancient to modern times / edited by Richard
    G. Hovannisian.
        p.   cm.
    Includes bibliographical references and index.
    Contents : v. 1. The dynastic periods—from antiquity to the
fourteenth century — v. 2 Foreign dominion to statehood—the
fifteenth century to the twentieth century.
    ISBN 0-312-10169-4 (v. 1). — ISBN 0-312-10168-6 (v. 2)
    1. Armenia—History. 2. Armenians—History. I Hovannisian,
Richard G.
DS175.A715   1997
956.62—dc21   97-5310
                                                                  CIP

Design by Acme Art, Inc.
First edition: September, 1997
10 9 8 7 6 5 4 3 2 1

CONTENTS

LIST OF MAPS AND DYNASTIC TABLES

MAPS

DYNASTIC TABLES

INTRODUCTION

Richard G. Hovannisian

The history of the Armenian people is long, complex, and in many ways epic and heroic. Emerging as an organized state by the middle of the second millennium B.C., Armenia lay at the ancient crossroads of orient and occident on the highland located between the Mediterranean, Black, and Caspian seas. The Armenian plateau became the buffer and coveted prize of rival empires: Assyrian, Mede, Achaemenian, Parthian, Sasanian, Arab, Seljuk, and Mongol from the south and east, and Seleucid, Roman, Byzantine, and Crusader from the west. Through all the turbulence, however, the Armenians created a rich and colorful culture and defensive mechanisms for survival. Even during long periods of foreign dominion, internal religious and socioeconomic structures allowed them to preserve their distinct way of life.

The dynastic era of Armenian history extended, with interruptions, over a time span of some two thousand years. The pre-Christian period, spanning more than one thousand years, was characterized by strong interchanges with Persian and Hellenistic civilizations. The Ervandian (Orontid), Artashesian (Artaxid), and Arshakuni (Arsacid) dynastic families held sway during this epoch, which for a brief historic moment even gave rise to an Armenian empire in the first century B.C.

The adoption of Christianity as the religion of state at the beginning of the fourth century A.D. introduced a new period that had a profound effect on the spiritual and cultural life and the political orientation of the Armenian realm. Although untold suffering would befall the Armenians in the name of their religion, the fusion of Armenian faith and patriotism provided a powerful defensive weapon in the unceasing struggle for national survival.

The underpinning of Armenian society, before and after the conversion to Christianity, was the military-feudal *nakharar* class—often unruly, divisive, ambitious, and vain, but also valiant and heroic. So long as the *nakharars* remained strong and able to rally against external threats and challenges, the continuum of Armenian life was maintained whether or not an Armenian monarch reigned. Hence, in the long span between the end of the Arshakuni dynasty in the fifth century and the restoration of monarchy under the Bagratunis (Bagratids) in the ninth century, the *nakharars* and the Church provided the structures essential for the continuation of traditional society and a national existence.

The fall of the last major Armenian kingdom on the great plateau in the eleventh century gave rise to an expatriate kingdom in the region of Cilicia, which is bounded by the northeastern corner of the Mediterranean Sea. There, the successive royal families of the Rubenians, Hetumians, and Lusignans came into close contact with the Crusader states and Europe. In face of the threat posed by resurgent Muslim powers, attempts were made to overcome the dogmatic and hierarchical differences separating the Armenian Apostolic, Greek Orthodox, and Roman Catholic churches. Armenian art, architecture, and literature flourished during this period. These and other themes are presented in detail in the first volume of this history.

The fall of the Cilician kingdom late in the fourteenth century left only isolated pockets of semiautonomous Armenian life: Zeitun in Cilicia, Sasun in the heart of the Armenian plateau, and Karabagh (Artsakh) along the eastern perimeter of that highland. Armenia came under the domination of rival Muslim dynasties: the Turkmen Aq Qoyunlu and Kara Qoyunlu, the hordes of Tamerlane, the Safavids and Qajars of Persia, and the Ottoman Turks, who captured Constantinople in the mid-fifteenth century and extended eastward into both Cilicia and Armenia proper during the next century.

Thereafter, the subject Armenians existed as a religious-ethnic minority with the legal status of second-class citizens. Because of the segregated nature of Muslim-dominated societies and the quasi-theocratic foundation of certain Islamic states, the Armenian Church was accorded jurisdiction in internal civil and religious matters. In return, the church hierarchy was held responsible for the conduct of all members of the ethnic community, their payment of taxes and fulfillment of other obligations, and their loyalty and devotion to the reigning sultan or shah. In the Ottoman Empire, this system was undermined by political, economic, and social decay, especially in the eighteenth and nineteenth centuries and by the infiltration of intellectual and political currents inspired by the Enlightenment and the French Revolution. These developments raised serious questions about the relationship between ruler and ruled and about the ability and even desirability of maintaining the status quo in a moribund empire.

The winds of change also affected the Armenian community *(millet)*, first through an intellectual revival and ultimately through plans and pressure for reforms both within and for the community. The articulation of Armenian social and political programs reached the table of international diplomacy at the Congress of Berlin in 1878, but the failure of the powers to resolve the so-called "Armenian Question" was to lead to the eventual elimination of the Ottoman Armenians and their removal from most of their historic lands. The widespread massacres of 1894-1896 were followed by the Cilician pogroms of 1909 and ultimately by the Armenian Genocide beginning in 1915 and culminating in 1922 with the burning of Smyrna and the final Armenian exodus from Cilicia. The "Young Turk" regime, on which reform-minded Armenians had placed so much hope, became in fact the catalyst for the annihilation of the Ottoman Armenians.

The eastern reaches of the Armenian plateau were spared this calamity only because Russian rule had been established there during the nineteenth century. Despite discriminatory practices and the arbitrariness of Romanov governors and bureaucrats, the Russian Armenians made significant organic progress during the century of tsarist rule. Like the Ottoman Armenians, they experienced an intellectual renaissance, which was strongly influenced by European social, political, and economic thought. By the outbreak of World War I in 1914, there were nearly as many Armenians living in the Russian Empire as in the Ottoman Empire. They became the fastest-growing and most affluent element in Transcaucasia, the region extending from the Black Sea to the Caspian Sea south of the Caucasus Mountains.

World War I, the Armenian Genocide, and the Russian revolutions and Civil War shattered the Armenian infrastructures in both the Ottoman and Russian empires. By the end of the world war in 1918, most Armenians either had been killed or displaced. Yet, there was cause for great excitement and anticipation. The European Allied Powers, assisted by the United States of America, had defeated the German Empire and its ally, the Ottoman Empire, and were publicly committed to the restoration and rehabilitation of the Armenian people. But the first modern experiment in Armenian independence lasted less than three years, from 1918 to the end of 1920. The reluctance of the Allied Powers to sustain their pledges with armed force and the collaboration of the Turkish Nationalists led by Mustafa Kemal Pasha and of Soviet Russia led by V.I. Lenin crushed the Republic of Armenia.

That which remained of historic Armenia, an area of less than 12,000 square miles, was transformed into Soviet Armenia and a part of the Union of Soviet Socialist Republics. Seven decades of Soviet rule were characterized by heavy centralization and coercion and the attempted suppression of many traditional ways. Yet, that critical period also gave rise to the contemporary Armenian—literate, highly skilled, adept in the arts, and resourceful individually for self and family and collectively for the preservation of national traits and ideals under creative guises.

The rapid collapse of the Soviet Union in 1991 brought another opportunity for Armenian independence, albeit only on this small, landlocked portion of the ancient and medieval realms. Many of the problems besetting the first Armenian republic quickly resurfaced, including an enervative and disruptive territorial dispute with and economic blockade by the neighboring Azerbaijani republic. Moreover, the aspiration to democracy and the setting up of a framework of democratic institutions have grated roughly against the daily reality of political inexperience and perpetuation of some of the worst abuses of the Soviet system. Critical to the welfare of the new republic is its relationship with the numerous, generally able and affluent, and potentially invaluable communities of the Armenian diaspora. These and related issues are addressed in the second volume of this study.

No comprehensive history of the Armenian people exists in the English language. Many monographs on specific subjects have appeared in recent years, but the ambitious undertaking to present the entire span of Armenian history has awaited this endeavor. Those who teach Armenian history have had little choice but to resort to selected readings from sundry sources in place of a cohesive textbook, and general readers seeking a reliable history of Armenia written in English have often been disappointed with the results. It was to meet this long-standing need that seventeen specialists in various disciplines of Armenian studies were drawn together as contributors to this two-volume work.

Any publication with multiple authors is likely to have chronological and topical gaps, as well as significant differences in organization, style, and attention to detail in the individual chapters. This work is not an exception. It would have been desirable, moreover, to incorporate chapters on art and architecture, music and theater, and other aspects of culture that are important reflectors of the spirit and soul of a people.

Fortunately, a number of excellent monographs and illustrated volumes have been published in English on these subjects. A bibliography of the works cited in the two volumes is included in each of them.

The transliteration of Armenian personal and place names into the Latin alphabet is not consistent in the chapters that follow. As individual authors have strong personal preferences, the editor has in general respected those sentiments. Chapters 3 through 8 in volume I use the modified Hübschmann-Meillet system, which for the uninstructed English reader will not always seem phonetic. The system uses a single character, often with diacritical marks, to represent a single Armenian letter; thus *Mušeł* rather than *Mushegh,* and *Xoranac'i* rather than *Khorenatsi.* And the traditional rendering of "ian" as the suffix of Armenian family names has been altered to "ean"; thus, *Mamikonean* rather than *Mamikonian.* To assist readers unfamiliar with this system, the editor has added the phonetic form after the initial use of the term. A table comparing the Hübschmann-Meillet system with modern Eastern Armenian and modern Western Armenian pronunciations, without diacritical marks, follows this introduction. By and large, the transliteration system used in these volumes is based on the sounds of Classical and modern Eastern Armenian; thus *Trdat* rather than *Drtad,* and *Khachatur Abovian* rather than *Khachadour Apovian.* Exceptions are made in the case of names with a widely accepted alternative form; thus *Boghos Nubar* rather than *Poghos Nupar,* and *Hagop Baronian* rather than *Hakob Paronian.* Moreover, in chapters 5 and 6 of Volume II, a mixed system is used, so that the names of Western Armenian intellectual, political, and clerical figures appear in Western Armenian pronunciation, whereas the names of Eastern Armenian personages are shown in Eastern Armenian pronunciation; thus *Krikor Odian* rather than *Grigor Otian,* but *Grigor Artsruni* rather than *Krikor Ardzruni.*

The preparation of this history has been long and difficult, and the challenges and responsibilities facing the editor have been formidable. A single author may have provided greater consistency in style and content but could not have offered the expertise or most recent findings relating to all periods or topics. The editor wishes to commend the authors for their contribution, cooperation, and forbearance. Robert Hewsen has meticulously produced the useful maps in the two volumes, and Simon Winder, formerly of St. Martin's Press, enthusiastically initiated the long publication process. It is hoped that this collective study will bring the reader the rich historical and cultural heritage, and an appreciation of the continuing saga, of the Armenian people.

TRANSLITERATION SYSTEMS FOR ARMENIAN

Armenian Letter	Hübschmann-Meillet	Eastern Armenian	Western Armenian
Ա ա	a	a	a
Բ բ	b	b	p
Գ գ	g	g	k
Դ դ	d	d	t
Ե ե	e	e	e
Զ զ	z	z	z
Է է	ē	e	e
Ը ը	ĕ	e	e
Թ թ	tʻ	t	t
Ժ ժ	ž	zh	zh
Ի ի	i	i	i
Լ լ	l	l	l
Խ խ	x	kh	kh
Ծ ծ	c	ts	dz
Կ կ	k	k	g
Հ հ	h	h	h
Ձ ձ	j	dz	tz
Ղ ղ	ł	gh	gh
Ճ ճ	č	ch	j
Մ մ	m	m	m
Յ յ	y	y or h	y or h[1]
Ն ն	n	n	n
Շ շ	š	sh	sh
Ո ո	o	o or vo	o or vo[2]
Չ չ	čʻ	ch	ch
Պ պ	p	p	b
Ջ ջ	ǰ	dj or j	ch
Ռ ռ	ṙ	r	r
Ս ս	s	s	s
Վ վ	v	v	v
Տ տ	t	t	d
Ր ր	r	r	r
Ց ց	cʻ	ts	ts
Ւ ւ	w	u	u
Փ փ	pʻ	p	p
Ք ք	kʻ	k	k
Օ օ	ō	o	o
Ֆ ֆ	f	f	f

1. Pronounced as "h" at beginning of a word; often silent when the final letter of a word.
2. Pronounced as "vo" at beginning of a word.

1

THE GEOGRAPHY OF ARMENIA

Robert H. Hewsen

The influence of geography on the course of history has been recognized since the time of the ancient Greeks, but there have been few countries in the world where geography has played a more important role than it has in Armenia. This role, in fact, has been decisive to the point where the destiny of the Armenian people may be said to have been largely predetermined by the location of the Armenian homeland and by the nature of its terrain. The frequent invasions, the long periods of foreign domination, the difficulty of national leaders to unite against the common foe, the rugged nature and tenacious character of the Armenian people all become clear when seen against the background of the remarkable plateau on which they have always dwelled.

Physical Geography

Location and Natural Frontiers

Situated in the temperate zone, Armenia occupies the central-most and highest of three landlocked plateaus that, taken together, form the northern sector of the Middle East. On the west, the Anatolian plateau, built largely of limestone beds, rises slowly from the lowland coast of the Aegean Sea to attain a maximum average height of 3,000 feet. In Armenia this rise increases dramatically, to an average of 3,000 to 7,000 feet. Thereafter, the elevation drops off rapidly to the much lower Iranian plateau, which averages only 2,000 to 5,000 feet above sea level. The Armenian plateau is not only higher but differs in character from those on either side of it, for it is not only mountainous but hydrologically more complex. Within the plateau itself, elevations vary sharply. The Plain of Erzerum and the basin of Lake Sevan both reach 6,000 feet, while Erevan, situated at the lowest point on the plateau, is only 3,227 feet above sea level. The ranges average 10,000 feet and peaks over 12,000 are common. Mount Ararat (Armenian Masis), at nearly 17,000 feet, is the highest point, not only of Armenia but of the whole of West Asia. To the south lie the lowland steppes of the Arab world—Syria and Mesopotamia; to the north, the trenches and plains of South Caucasia—West Georgia, East Georgia, and Azerbaijan—backed by the great wall of the Caucasus range running diagonally between the Black and the Caspian seas and cutting Armenia off from the harsh winds of the Eurasian plain. Strategically placed so that it dominates the lower plateaus and lowlands to every side of it, Armenia has never been isolated and has been a crossroads for traders and invading armies since ancient times.

Although the Armenian plateau is sharply defined on the east, the northwest, and the south, its natural frontiers are much less clear in the west, where it descends gradually toward Anatolia; in the southeast, where it opens wide toward Iran; and in the north, where the mountains of northern Armenia become those of southern Georgia and where the two peoples have fought and mingled for more than 2,000 years.

Apart from the fact that the natural frontiers of Armenia are not as sharp as they might be, at least five other factors have made it difficult to determine exactly where Armenia begins and ends and greatly complicate the "Armenian question" in modern times. First of all, the Armenians, at least as we know them today, were not the original inhabitants of the plateau. The Urartian state, which existed there prior to the coming of the Indo-European-speaking "Armen" tribes from the west, was a federation of many peoples united under the kings of Van, most but not all of whom were absorbed by the Armens to form the modern Armenian people. Second, it took these newcomers a very long time to assimilate those of the proto-Armenian peoples of the plateau whom they did absorb. The Khaldians and Mardians, for example, are still heard of in Roman times, and the Urtaeans, Khoyts, and Sasunites

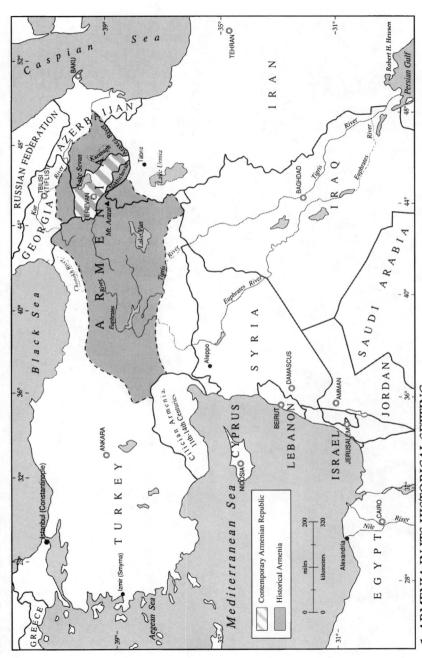

1. ARMENIA IN ITS HISTORICAL SETTING

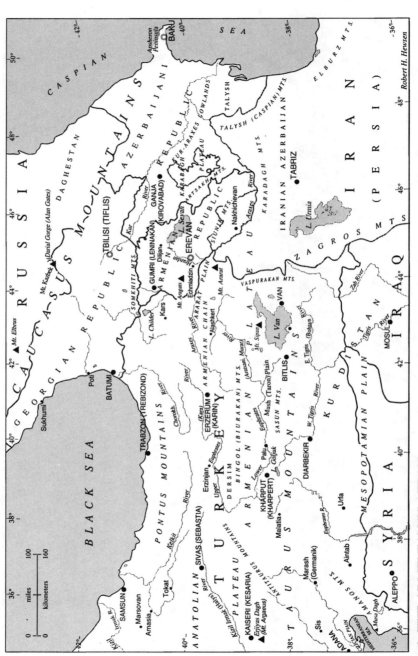

2. THE ARMENIAN PLATEAU

Robert H. Hewsen

even later. Third, the Armenians, from a very e;
share the plateau with later arrivals—Kurds, Pe
Turks—and many Armenians who gave up Christ.
have been absorbed by these Muslim peoples. Fourt.
the traditional lands of the Armenian monarchy wer(
century A.D. and most of these regions remained under
after. Finally, for over a thousand years the Armenian p(
gradually but continuously driven from their homeland.   ..ucess,
which began with transfers of population by the Byzantin~s and which
culminated in the great deportations of 1915 to 1922, created a situation
where, even before World War I, the Armenians were a minority in much
of Armenia, while today they occupy barely a tenth of the territory that
belonged to the Armenian kings in ancient times.

Despite these factors—and they are all important ones—it can be
said that historical Armenia is more or less the region located between
latitudes 38 and 48 degrees and longitudes 37 and 41 degrees, with a total
area of approximately 238,000 square miles. Thus it is a little larger than
Great Britain (228,000 square miles). Clockwise, its neighbors are the
Georgians on the north, the Azerbaijani Turks on the east, the Iranians on
the southeast, the Kurds in the south, the Arabs of Syria and Mesopotamia
on the southwest, and the Anatolian peoples, long ago absorbed by the
Turks, who live to the west. All of these peoples have influenced the
Armenians and have played a significant role in their history.

The Terrain

Armenia is mountainous country, surrounded by great mountain chains
on every side and crossed by lesser ranges that link the major ones
together. Within this framework, the Armenian tableland contains a
number of smaller plateaus set a different altitudes, the regions of Karin
(Erzerum) and Erznga (Erzinjan) being the highest. Apart from these
lesser plateaus, the ranges and their spurs divide Armenia into a number
of small but well-defined districts ranging from broad plains such as
those of Erzerum, Erzinjan, Kharpert (Kharberd, Kharput), and Mush,
to small valleys and narrow gorges such as those that characterize the
northern and eastern parts of the plateau.

In appearance Armenia is a land of harsh and rugged grandeur
more like the American Southwest than like the Rocky Mountain states
or Switzerland. There is little rainfall, forests are rare, and without
irrigation the rich but stony soil is barren.

ountains

Too often and too easily invaded to be called a natural fortress, as is often done, Armenia is best described as a large oval obstacle buttressed by mountain chains to the north and south and crisscrossed by other chains that cover the plateau and obscure its sharply rising escarpment. The mountains on the north are generally known as the Pontus Mountains, extending 680 miles and averaging 60 to 95 miles in width; those on the south as the Taurus or Tsul (the latter being the Armenian translation of the Greek *tauros,* "bull"), extending 930 miles and, with its ramifications, averaging 95 miles wide. South of the Pontus Mountains but facing the Taurus is the Anti-Taurus Range. South of these but farther east and extending through the center of Armenia stretch the Central or Armenian Mountains, which have different names in their different sectors and which turn abruptly south at Mount Ararat to form the Zagros Range that separates both Turkey and Iraq from Iran. On the north, where the Pontus Mountains turn inland, they become the Lesser Caucasus separating Armenia from Georgia and terminating in the Artsakh or Karabagh Range. Lake Sevan, thrust up like a great bowl above the rest of the plateau, is surrounded clockwise by the Areguni, Sevan, Vardenis, and Gegham mountains. Geologically, all of these ranges are mainly composed of limestone and igneous rocks, such as trachyte, porphyry, augite, feldspar, melaphyre, basalt, quartz, granite, obsidian, and tufa. Like all the great ranges of Asia, these formations are the result of the buckling of the earth's crust as it cooled and shrank eons ago.

Owing to these flanking ranges, the approach to Armenia is long and arduous and limited to only a few perennial routes. Only after crossing these ranges and noting the far less lengthy descent on their inner side do travelers become aware that they have ascended a tableland with a considerable elevation of its own, an island, as it were, overlooking the entire Middle East and hence having an extraordinarily strategic position whose importance cannot be overestimated. Before the coming of mechanized warfare and aircraft, whatever power dominated the Armenian plateau was in a position to dominate the Middle East. Most of the wars in this part of the world for the past 2,000 years were fought for its possession. Centrally located, whether for invasion routes or for paths of trade, Armenia has been both the victim and the beneficiary of its geographic location.

The Rivers

Six of the major Armenian rivers quickly leave the plateau, but one of them, the Araxes (Armenian Araks), flows more than halfway across the tableland before beginning its final descent to the sea. Watering the great Ararat plain and passing by so many of the great cities of Armenian antiquity, it is the only true river of Armenia and, as "Mother Araxes," has become, like Mount Ararat, a national symbol to the Armenian people.

The Araxes rises on the northeastern slopes of the Biurakan Mountains, nine miles south of Karin and passes through the plains of Pasen and Alashkert, both more than 5,000 feet above sea level. It then flows through the plain of Ararat, where it forms the boundary first between the former Soviet Union and Turkey and then between the former Soviet Union and Iran. The descent from the plain of Karin to that of Ararat involves a drop of some 5,000 feet, and the cascades and shallow bed of the river, as well as the narrow wooded gorges through which it must pass, make it unnavigable, although it has been utilized for irrigation since time immemorial. The broad plain of Ararat, however, leaves room for a more leisurely course, and here the river flows through a luxuriant and fertile region similar to central California. From earliest times this valley has been the center of Armenian life and remains so to this day, if only in its eastern half. Here, between Masis and Mount Aragats, lies the richest part of Armenia, and here in this plain have lain its various capital cities—Armavir, Ervandashat, Artashat, Vagharshapat, Dvin, Ani, and Erevan, as well as the important towns of Ervandakert and Nakhichevan. Here, too, at the site of Vagharshapat, is found the great monastery of Echmiadzin, the spiritual and administrative center of the Armenian Church.

Of the other major rivers originating in Armenia, only the Euphrates flows to any extent within Armenia itself. Here it consists of two arms, the Western or Upper Euphrates (Armenian Eprat; Turkish Kara) and the Eastern or Lower Euphrates (Armenian Aratsani; Turkish Murat). Both of these rivers flow westward through a series of fertile plains, the upper arm through those of Erzerum and Erzinjan; the lower through those of Bagrevand, Manazkert, Taron, Palu, and Kharpert. Then, after joining at Kaben Maden (Armenian Lusatarich), where a great dam creating a vast lake has been constructed in recent years, the combined Euphrates pierces the Taurus through a spectacular canyon, flowing down through the lowlands of Mesopotamia and eventually to the Persian Gulf.

The Tigris, likewise, flows into the Persian Gulf. Formed by the merger of several streams running south from the Taurus, it is a river of southern Armenia only. In the north, the chief river is the Chorokh or Voh, which carves out the wide valley of Khaghtik or Sper before entering the Black Sea. The Kur, which flows into the Caspian Sea and is the chief river of Georgia and Azerbaijan, also rises in Armenia, as do the Kizil Irmak or "Red River" (Armenian Alis; Greek Halys), the Yesil (Armenian Ris; Greek Iris), and the Kelkit (Armenian Gayl Get ["Wolf River"]; Greek Lycus), the three largest rivers of Anatolia. Among the smaller rivers of Armenia are the Akhurian, a tributary of the Araxes flowing from Lake Tseli (Turkish Çildir) past the ruins of the medieval city of Ani and forming part of the present frontier between Turkey and the Armenian Republic; the Hrazdan or Zangu, which flows from Lake Sevan past Erevan and whose hydroelectric stations provide much of the electricity for Armenia; the three rivers of Siunik: the Arpa, the Vorotan, and the Hakera; and the three main rivers of Artsakh: the Trtu (Terter), the Khachen, and the Gargar. To the north, Armenia is drained by a number of smaller rivers flowing down to the Kur: the Debed, Aghstev, Zakam, and others; in the south, by mountain streams feeding the Tigris: Bitlis, Bohtan, Batman, and others. None of the Armenian rivers is navigable and none is particularly well stocked with fish. The landscape of Armenia is old; the rivers have cut deep gorges and ravines through the soft fields of congealed lava, and waterfalls are rare. Although rainfall is scanty, the snowcapped peaks yield an abundant supply of water, especially in spring, when countless, rushing torrents feed the rivers, each cutting a tiny valley or gorge of its own, the fundamental geographic units of the Armenian plateau.

The Lakes

One of the most remarkable features of the Armenian plateau is the number and size of its lakes. In fact, most of the lakes of Western Asia are to be found on the Armenian plateau. The three largest, though not as large as Lake Erie, are all five to six times larger than Lake Geneva and lie some five times higher. Each of the three has its own character, and each now lies in a different country.

Lake Sevan (Classical Armenian Gegham or Gegharkuni) is the smallest, deepest, and highest of the Armenian lakes. Lying at an altitude of 6,279 feet, it is 45 miles long, 24 miles wide, and originally covered an area of some 550 square miles. Its average depth is from 174 to 600 feet. Some twenty-three streams enter the lake but it has only a single outlet, the Hrazdan, which, tumbling down some 3,300 feet in a distance of 65 miles, flows past Erevan to enter the Araxes River. Greatly reduced in size after 1948 as part of a vast hydroelectric scheme to harness its waters for the production of electricity, its level has dropped by some 50 feet. Attempts made in the last years of Soviet rule to restore the level by diverting a number of additional mountain streams to enter the lake have not been very successful, and pollution brought in by such waters has resulted in the destruction of much of the marine life of the lake, including the famous *ishkhan* "prince" fish, a kind of trout formerly much esteemed in Soviet Armenia. The lake possessed a single island, also known as Sevan, now a peninsula because of the lowering of the level of its waters.

Lake Van (Classical Armenian Bznuniats Dzov ["Sea of Bznunik"] or less often Rshtuniats Dzov ["Sea of Rshtunik"]) lies at an altitude of 5,360 feet, is 80 miles long and 40 miles wide, and is the deepest of the three lakes, having an average depth of some 5,643 feet. A number of streams enter Lake Van, the largest of which is the Arest, but it has no outlet. Evaporation of its waters is the sole means by which the lake level is stabilized. This has resulted in the waters having become charged with borax and hence undrinkable, but the lake still contains a solitary species of fish, the *tarekh (Cyprinus tarachi),* which was formerly caught and salted for export. Surrounded by mountains and dominated by the volcanic peak of Mount Nekh-Masik or Sipan, Lake Van is one of the loveliest lakes in the world. At the western end of the lake, a large lava flow from Mount Nemrud blocks what may well have been an egress once connecting the lake to the Bitlis River, which would have given it an outlet to the Tigris. A curious feature of Lake Van is the well-attested phenomenon whereby its waters periodically rise on one side while lowering on the other. Obviously due to a geological tilting of its basin, this is why it is rare to find two identical figures for the depth of its waters. As a result of this fluctuation, of the seven islands known to have once existed in the lake, three—Dzipan, Tokean, and Ardzke—are now submerged, as are much of the ruins of the old town of Arjesh. The four remaining islands in the lake are Lim, Arter, Aghtamar, and Ktuts. There used to be monasteries on all of them, but only the famous tenth-century cathedral of the Holy Cross on Aghtamar, one of the great masterpieces of world architecture, survives.

Lake Urmia (Classical Armenian Kaputan Dzov ["Blue Sea"]) lies some 4,000 feet above sea level, extends 100 miles from north to south,

and is 24 miles wide with an area of 1,800 square miles. The largest of
the three Armenian lakes and the only significant body of water in Iran,
its area is deceptive, for Lake Urmia is extremely shallow—more a
lagoon than a lake—averaging only 15 to 15.7 feet and nowhere more
than 44 feet in depth. Subject to the same process of desiccation that has
affected the Caspian Sea, Lake Aral, and other bodies of water in Central
Asia, Lake Urmia was originally much larger. Today surrounded by
marshes, quicksands, and salt flats, the towns of Urmia, Maragha, and
even Tabriz, which once stood on its shores, now lie many miles away.
Having no outlet, the lake is extremely alkaline, and its waters are almost
as lifeless as those of the Dead Sea. The lake supports neither fish nor
mollusks, and only a few crustaceans live in it. Among its many islands,
Shahi was the largest but is now a peninsula. On Shahi, the Mongol
emperor Hulegu Khan built a fortress to contain his treasures and there
he was buried in 1265.

Lake Tseli (Turkish Çildir), Lake Gaylatu (Turkish Balik), Lake
Archishak (Turkish Ercek) and Lake Dzovk (whose Turkish name,
Gölcük ["Little Sea"], is a translation of the Armenian) are four of the
lesser lakes of Armenia, many of which are filled with reeds that form
the homes of an astonishing variety of water fowl and other bird life.

The Climate

The elevation of most of Armenia neutralizes its location in the
temperate zone. The high mountains deprive it of the effects of the
cooling breezes from the Black, Mediterranean, and Caspian seas in
the summer and of the hot winds coming from the Mesopotamian
lowlands in winter. The climate is thus continental, harsh and given to
extremes, with long, cold, dry winters (averaging 21 to 50° Fahrenheit
in January with extremes of minus 22° Fahrenheit) and short, hot, dry
summers (averaging 64 to 70° Fahrenheit in July with daytime highs
of 100° or more). Erevan is colder than Moscow in January, and in
Erzerum the winters can be extremely bitter and accompanied by
severe blizzards. Its climate tends to make Armenia a westerly extension of the great desert lands of Central Asia, and, in spite of the natural
fertility of its rich volcanic soil, its fields are generally untillable
without intensive irrigation. Less than twenty inches of rain falls each
year in the central part of the tableland, while the Plain of Ararat
receives less than ten. The perennial problem of irrigating the soil is
best observed in the vicinity of Van, where the local peasants still make

use of the canal built by the Urartian king Menuas in the eighth century B.C. Although this tendency to aridity can be quite severe, it is mitigated by the fairly abundant snow, which, though neither frequent nor especially heavy, results in an enormous quantity of water flowing down from the mountains each spring, feeding both the major rivers and the great lakes. For all its severity, the Armenian climate is healthy and bracing, neither damp in winter like England or the Pacific Northwest, nor humid in summer like much of the eastern United States. The cold is brisk and invigorating in winter, and the heat of a summer day is always followed by a refreshing coolness at night. The Armenian climate has produced a rugged peasantry and has contributed to the hardiness and longevity of the population. It has influenced the construction of housing, determined the cycle of annual occupations, and led to the disaster of more than one military expedition that chose the wrong season in which to venture upon the high plateau. We even hear of an Armenian king—Tiran I—who perished in a sudden snowstorm while traveling across the high plateau.

Seismic Activity

The Armenian Mountains were highly volcanic in the geological past and most of its peaks, including Mount Ararat, Mount Aragats (Turkish Alagöz or Alakiaz), Mount Sipan, and Mount Sarakn (Turkish Nemrud), are extinct volcanos. While none of these has been active within historical memory, Armenia is still very much the product of the volcanic activity of its remote past. The plains have been flooded with lava, which congealed and has long since disintegrated into a rich volcanic soil, while obsidian (volcanic glass) and tufa (a lightweight volcanic stone) are still major natural resources. As in many volcanic areas of the world, mineral springs abound in Armenia, and earthquakes are common and frequently severe. The Ararat fault, consisting of two lines: Erzinjan-Ararat and Dvin-Siunik-Tabriz, runs through the very center of the country, and quakes along this fault have wreaked havoc in Armenia. The famed church of Zvartnots was destroyed by an earthquake in the tenth century and major earthquakes struck Dvin in 839, 862, and 892, and Tabriz in 858 and 1043. One at Erzinjan took some 12,000 victims in 1168; another killed about 32,000 people in 1457; and another about 30,000 in 1481. Earthquakes completely destroyed the city in 1784 and again in 1939 after which it was rebuilt on a slightly different site; nevertheless, it was badly damaged in yet another tremor in March 1992. Two especially severe quakes occurred in Taron in August 1650; another, on the night of June 20, 1840, centered at Mount Ararat, engulfed a monastery, a chapel, and the entire village of Akori, all swept into the great ravine on the eastern face of the mountain. In 1931 an earthquake centered in Zangezur destroyed the monastery of Tatev; another at Kars in 1935 destroyed twenty-five villages and took 2,000 lives. In July 1966 another at Varto killed 2,477 people. A severe earthquake struck Gumri (then Leninakan) in 1926 and another on December 7, 1988, destroyed the city and the neighboring town of Spitak, taking somewhere between 25,000 and 50,000 lives and leaving some 200,000 people homeless. More than any invader, these visitations have been responsible for the destruction of the historical monuments that were erected over the centuries upon the high plateau. While churches and monasteries were usually rebuilt, the castles, fortresses, and civil structures, once leveled, were usually quickly pillaged for building stone by the local peasants, a process that still goes on in historically Armenian lands under Turkish rule.

Natural Resources

Flora

Because of the lack of rainfall, Armenia largely presents a stark and barren appearance except around the towns and villages, where irrigation transforms the countryside into a natural garden. Trees are rare and forests are found only on the exterior slopes of the mountains facing the Black Sea and the Mediterranean, except in northern Armenia and in Karabagh, where some rich forests survive. Most of the trees probably were cut down in the remote past to provide fuel in winter, so much so that *tesek* (dried animal dung mixed with chopped straw) became the standard fuel in Armenia, as it still is in the villages from Anatolia through Central Asia. The trees that do exist are largely the poplar, the aspen, and the oak, as well as all the various fruit trees that can be induced to grow at these elevations. Small but delicious apples, pears, peaches, plums, apricots, and cherries, as well as all sorts of melons, are staples of Armenian horticulture, along with the vine whose grapes provide heavy sweet wines and rich cognacs. The flowers of Armenia are the rose, violet, lily, and jasmine.

Fauna

Armenia is a paradise for hunters, and, in ancient and medieval times, the kings and nobles devoted themselves to the chase above all other leisure activities. The wild goat, wild sheep, wolf, fox, mountain lion, deer, antelope, jackal, bear, lynx, and, above all, the *varaz,* or wild boar, were hunted. Among the smaller animals is the rodent known to the Romans as the *Sora armenica* (Armenian mouse), which is still called the ermine. Among the domestic animals, cattle, buffalo, donkeys, mules, goats, and sheep—especially the fat-tailed variety of the latter— are the most common. Camels, not native to the plateau but once common as beasts of burden, are now unusual. Pigs are also rare; as everywhere else in the Middle East, lamb is the meat of choice. In former times, wild horses, now extinct, were native to Armenia. Large herds were cultivated for the benefit of the mounted aristocracy, and Strabo (1961, 10.14.9) tells us that 20,000 foals per year were exported to Persia as part of the annual tribute. The birds of Armenia are astonishingly varied. In the marshes of the Plain of Erzerum, some 170 species have been identified, among them the eagle, vulture, falcon, pheasant, pigeon, grouse, partridge, hawk, egret, bustard, wild goose, wild duck, quail, pheasant, francolin, heron, swan, ibis, stork, and crane. The last, the beloved *grunk,* has become yet another national symbol for the Armenian people, the Armenian bird par excellence. The insects of Armenia are the scorpion, tarantula, the mosquito, and the fly. The last was particularly noxious and was brought under control in Erevan only in the 1960s.

Agriculture

Two different and not always compatible economies have traditionally been practiced in Armenia, the lowlands being given over to farming and the highlands to herding and stockbreeding. Transhumance or seminomadism is still common, herdsmen spending the winters in the lowlands and taking their flocks to the mountains for summer pasture after the heat has burned the plains dry. The Armenians generally have tended to practice agriculture, leaving the herding of flocks to the mountain people, especially the Kurds. The conversion of the Armenians to Christianity and the Kurds to Islam only added a religious aspect to what was already a fundamental difference in the ways of life of the two peoples. The best farmlands are found in the irrigated plains and valleys, where cereals, cotton, orchards, vineyards, and, more recently, tobacco, have been cultivated, while in the unirrigated lower slopes, wheat and barley are grown and goats and sheep are grazed for their milk, cheese, wool, and hides. Silk cultivation was widely practiced in the regions of Erevan and Gandzak (Ganja), and rice is grown in the valley of the Araxes. Vegetables raised include beans, sugar beets, cabbages, onions, and, more recently, potatoes. Above all, Armenia is famous for its fruits. Small in size but extremely tasty and full of juice, its melons, grapes, pomegranates, peaches, pears, apples, cherries, figs, and apricots form an important part of the Armenian diet. The apricot is believed to have originated on the Armenian plateau and was known to the Romans as the *prunus armenicus* (the Armenian plum). The hot, dry summers are especially well suited to the growing of grapes, and Armenia produces excellent cognacs and many varieties of heavy, sweet wines, as well as some lighter wines and rosés.

Mineral and Other Resources

Armenia is rich in minerals and, if little has been done to exploit its resources in the western regions, enough progress was made in Soviet Armenia to give some idea of the treasures that lie beneath the soil. Copper is found at Alaverdi in the north and at Kapan in Zangezur, and Armenia was the third largest producer of this mineral in the USSR. Molybdenum, iron, zinc, lead, tin, silver, and gold are also found, as well as such building stones as limestone, pumice, basalt, marble, and volcanic tufa. The last, a lightweight, easily worked material, is especially abundant. Found in various colors—red, black, cream, pink, and lavender—tufa has been used for construction purposes from remote antiquity. A major project in the Soviet period was the harnessing of the Hrazdan River for hydroelectric purposes, and by 1970 six power stations had been constructed along its precipitous course. More such stations have been built along other rivers in the republic, and it is not too much to say that water power is not only the greatest resource of Armenia but has the greatest potential for the country's future. Many rivers on the plateau beyond the borders of the Armenian republic are also suitable for the development of the tableland, and this accounts for the great number of dams with their attendant reservoirs that have been erected on the Turkish side of the frontier. Although Armenia's mineral resources were little exploited in earlier times, gold and silver mines were worked, quarries exploited, the sodas of the lakes utilized for cleansing agents, and the deposits of the extensive salt flats collected. Another natural resource appreciated in antiquity and much cultivated in the Soviet period is the variety of mineral springs and thermal waters, whose curative properties are highly regarded. Several such spas exist in the mountains north and south of Lake Sevan—Dilijan, Arzni, and Jermuk in particular—but they are found as far west as the Euphrates and they abound in the Plain of Karin (Erzerum).

Historical Geography

Traditionally, Greater Armenia consisted of fifteen "provinces": Upper Armenia, Fourth Armenia, Aghznik, Turuberan, Mokk, Korjaik, Parskahayk, Vaspurakan, Siunik, Artsakh, Paytakaran, Utik, Gugark, Tayk, and Ayrarat. While all of these "provinces" existed at one time or another, they never existed all at once, and most had different origins and organizations as well. Siunik and Mokk, for example, were two separate principalities, while Fourth Armenia, so-called to distinguish it from the three Armenias comprising Lesser Armenia west of the Euphrates, consisted of five Armenian principalities, composed of six separate districts, that, acquired by the Romans in 298, were reorganized into a single Byzantine province in 536. Gugark was a military zone organized to protect Armenia from invasion from the north; Ayrarat originally consisted of the royal domains in the center of the country. Nine of these territories were lost in 387, most of them forever; three others—Vaspurakan, Turuberan, and Tayk—emerged only after the Byzantine-Persian partition of Armenia in 591, when the districts of which they were comprised passed under Byzantine control. Paytakaran, a completely alien land, left the Armenian orbit in 387, as did Korjaik, originally the kingdom of Gordyene, a foreign state that had belonged to Armenia for only about 250 years and whose territory was completely Kurdish in population even before the deportations of 1915.

Actually, Armenia consisted not of large provinces but of nearly 200 small districts large and small. Some of these, such as Vanand and Shirak, formed separate principalities on their own. Some, such as Nakhichevan, Vostan Hayots, and Vostan Dunoy, were the municipal territories of Armenian cities (i.e., Nakhichevan, Vagharshapat, and Dvin). Some, such as Aghiovit and Karin, belonged to the royal family; others, such as Hashtiank, were assigned to the support of junior members of the ruling house; still others, such as Khoyt or Sanasunk, were in the possession of semi-independent mountain tribes. Ekeghiats, Daranaghli, and Derjan, among others, were originally great temple-states belonging to the pagan religious establishment and in the fourth century passed to the Armenian Church. Most of these districts, however, were component parts of large principalities consisting of many districts in the possession of a single princely house. Siunik, with twelve districts, was the largest of these—virtually a state within the state; Tayk and Mokk were two others; Aghbak, the original domain of the Artsruni family, was another. Of particular interest are the four military zones, each called a *bdeshkutiun* Aghznik, Korjaik, Gugark, and Nor Shirakan, whose princes were charged with the duty of protecting the Armenian kingdom from foreign invasion. Formed perhaps as early as the first century B.C., these viceroyalties functioned for 300 to 400 years.

Lying west of Greater Armenia and separated from it by the Euphrates was Lesser Armenia (Pokr Hayk), which, as far as we can tell, was never a part of the kingdom of Greater Armenia but always formed a separate Armenian state of its own with Ani-Kamakh and later Nikopolis as its capital. Annexed by the Romans in A.D. 72, Lesser Armenia remained a part of the Romano-Byzantine Empire for 1,000 years, following its own line of development quite different from that of Greater Armenia. Its people were Roman citizens, for example, and belonged to the Catholic Church until the Byzantine Church broke with Rome in 1054, taking the Byzantine Armenians with it. Although its history unrolled quite outside that of Greater Armenia, Lesser Armenia is significant because so many Armenians from Armenia proper settled there after 1021. Moreover, many Western Armenians in the diaspora originated in this region, which, besides Sivas, includes such later Armenian centers as Malatia, Agn, Divrig, Arabkir, and others.

Over the centuries the political organization of Greater Armenia changed repeatedly. Principalities merged, divided, changed hands or were lost to Armenian control. In the ninth to the eleventh centuries, a number of new Armenian kingdoms emerged on the tableland, their lands made up of groupings of earlier small districts. Later, under Persian, Turkish, and Russian rule, new provinces were established with their own divisions and subdivisions, a few of which correspond to the earlier Armenian lands. In the Ottoman Empire, Turkish Armenia was comprised of six large provinces called *vilayets,* divided into *sanjaks* (counties), and *kazas* (districts). In the Persian Empire, large semi-independent provinces called *khanligs* (khanates) under hereditary khans (governors) existed, divided into districts *(mahals)* some of which were held by independent or autonomous Armenian chieftains called *meliks*. In Tsarist times, Russian Armenia consisted of the *gubernia* (province) of Erevan, divided into *uezds* (counties) and subdivided into *ushchatoks* (districts), with Karabagh *(Artsakh)* being assigned to the neighboring province of Elisavetpol. Soviet Armenia consisted of thirty-nine small districts called *shrjans* (Russian *raiony*) corresponding to the counties of an American state. In 1995 these were combined into eleven larger units called *marzers* by the new republic. Karabagh, set apart from Soviet Armenia and placed within the Azerbaijani Soviet Republic as the *Nagorno* (Highland)–Karabakh Autonomous Province, consisted of five (later six) districts, that now, since January 6, 1992, form the Republic of Nagorno-Karabakh or Lernayin Gharabagh (NKR).

This then is Hayastan, the Armenian homeland, high, arid, and harsh, but beautiful in a stark and rugged way. In the words of H.F.B. Lynch, the noted British naturalist and traveler, and perhaps the foreigner who knew the country best, it is "a spacious plain, quite treeless, but clothed with warm and delicate hues, and framed in the distance by mountains of great individuality" (Lynch, 1901, vol. 1). A land of inspiring vistas, rich in wildlife and natural resources, dotted with crumbling castles and ruined churches, and capable of arousing deep emotions in the people who live there, it is a land that has seen the coming of Assyrians, Persians, and Kurds; Romans, Byzantines, and Turks; Scythians, Georgians, Russians, and Medes; the Ten Thousand Greeks of Xenophon's army, the Mongol hordes of Timur, the soldiers of the Red Army, and the forces of NATO. The stage has been set. It will be worthy of the heroic and terrible events that will be played out upon it.

FOR FURTHER INFORMATION

For the sources of, or more information on, the material in this chapter, please consult the following (full citations can be found in the Bibliography at the end of this volume).

Borisov, 1965.   Lydolph, 1970.
Gregory, 1968.   Mathieson, 1975.
Halasi-Kun, 1963.   Pitcher, 1972.
Hewsen, 1978-79, 1992.   *Soviet Armenia,* 1972.
Hughes, 1939.   Toumanoff, 1963.
Le Strange, 1939

2

THE FORMATION OF THE ARMENIAN NATION

James Russell

Introduction: The Armenia of Darius

The first historical reference to the Armenians appears in the rock-cut inscription of 518 B.C. of the Achaemenian Persian king Darius I at Behistun, on the main road from Babylon to the Median capital Ecbatana (modern Iranian Hamadan). Only a generation before, in 550, Cyrus II (the Great) had defeated Astyages of Media, whose kingdom had previously held dominion over Armenia, and had carried his conquests far beyond western Iran—to Mesopotamia in the southwest and to central Asia and the Punjab in the east. Darius seems to have seized power in a dynastic struggle, during which the various satrapies, or provinces, of the newly formed empire took the opportunity to rebel. Armenia was among them. In the Behistun inscription it is called *Armina* in Old Persian, but *Urashtu* ("Urartu") in the Babylonian version cut alongside. Urartu had been the principle power on the Armenian plateau centuries before. Darius sent a faithful Armenian subject, Dadarshi, to Armenia to fight on his behalf, and battles were joined at places named Zuzahya, Tigra, Uyama, and Autiyara. Later in the same inscription, Darius mentions an Armenian named Arkha, son of Haldita, who claimed to be the son of the last Babylonian king, whom Cyrus had overthrown. Some have suggested that this Arkha bears as a name what was in fact his title: Armenian *arka* ("king").

The Greek historian Herodotus, a Persian subject who describes the peoples and events of the age, mentions the Armenians as "Phrygian colonists" who "in their language speak very much like Phrygians" (Herodotus, 1954, book 7.77). In their dress and in their names, the Armenians of his time also had much in common with the Iranian Medes, cousins of the Persians. The later Greek writer Xenophon describes Armenia in detail in his *Anabasis,* or "March Up-Country," the chronicle of the retreat of a detachment of Greek mercenaries from an unsuccessful campaign involving the Persian royal succession in 401 B.C. In Xenophon's largely fictional *Cyropaideia* (The Education of Cyrus), the Persian king has an Armenian childhood friend named Tigran, later an Armenian royal name. (And there is a place called Tigra mentioned in the Behistun inscription.)

These first firm references to the Armenians are an introduction into the intricacies of the problem of Armenian origins, with references to Urarteans (Urartians), Babylonians, Phrygians, Medes, and Persians—some of them neighbors, others inhabitants of the Armenian plateau itself—each of whom seems to hold part of the solution to the puzzle of Armenian identity. It will be necessary to examine the linguistic, historical, and religious links between the Armenians and each of these ancient civilizations to determine the extent to which they contributed to forming the Armenian people. The Armenians begin to speak at length for themselves in historical records only after the invention of the Armenian alphabet by St. Mesrop in the fifth century A.D. Much of the material on Armenian origins and antiquities related by the historian Movses Khorenatsi (Moses of Khoren), however, is exceedingly ancient and must be evaluated in the light of other archaeological, linguistic, and mythological data. Khorenatsi probably lived long after the conversion of the Armenian people to Christianity, yet the wealth of archaic material he preserves is testimony to the great conservatism of Armenian culture. The question of ethnic migrations and "native" inhabitants of the Armenian plateau also must be addressed, and this will involve the data afforded by language.

The Prehistory of the Armenian Language

Armenian is an Indo-European language. Much of the core of its vocabulary is related to other languages of this family, such as English,

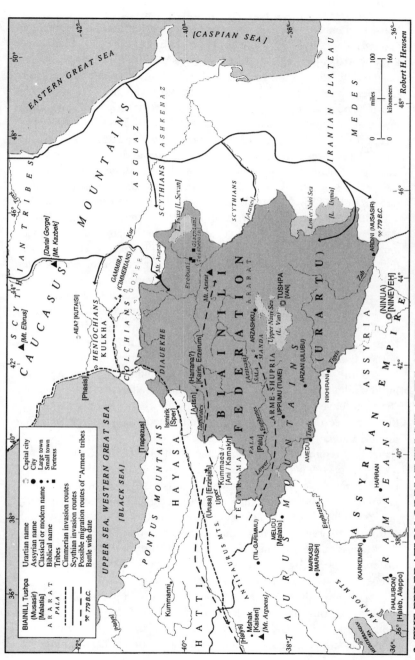

3. THE FEDERATION OF BIAINILI (URARTU), NINTH – SIXTH CENTURIES B.C.

Robert H. Hewsen

Sanskrit, Persian, and Russian. The words for mother and father, *hayr* and *mayr,* are obviously cognates to English, once the particular sound laws of Armenian are recognized—in this case, that -*t*- is lost between vowels and that initial *p*- (English *f*-) becomes an *h*-. Some Indo-European bases are harder to recognize. For example, Armenian *erku* ("two") and *erkayn* ("long") do not outwardly resemble words of similar meaning in other Indo-European languages; but it has been established that proto-Indo-European **dw*- becomes *erk*- in Armenian, so Greek *duo* ("two") and *dweron* ("far") are in fact cognates to the Armenian words. Such great changes would indicate that the Armenians separated at a very early stage from their closest Indo-European cousins (the proto-Greeks, it has been surmised), when they migrated to eastern Anatolia.

It is possible that the word in Armenian for "Armenian," *hay,* is the result of the loss of an intervocalic -*t*-, as in the cases just described, and comes from an original form **Hati-yos,* ("Hattian"). This indicates that the Armenians adopted the name of the great Hittite nation over whose lands they passed in their eastward migrations from southeastern Europe. Perhaps their migration was even connected to the crisis and decline of the Hittite Empire. Certain Armenian terms of religious connotation have cognates in Hittite and in Phrygian, signifying the conservation of very archaic beliefs. Such linguistic affinities are important data in determining the origins of the Armenian people.

Some words in Armenian appear to be related to other languages, but if similar words appear in different language families and cannot be shown to have been borrowed, they must be classified only as "areal," that is, reflecting the culture of a common geographical area, in which diverse language groups have long coexisted. The Armenian word for wine, *gini,* cognate to English "wine" and Greek *oinos,* for example, seems to be related also to Georgian (Caucasian) *gvini* and Hebrew (Afro-Asiatic) *yayin.* Another example is Armenian *kamurj,* Greek *gephyra,* Hebrew *gesher,* all meaning "bridge." Although the early Armenian languages developed in some isolation from the other Indo-European tongues, the Armenians shared with their other neighbors of the Mediterranean basin the economic and cultural features that bridge differences of religion and language—even as Turkish, Armenian, Greek, and Arab cuisine today are very similar.

Other words in Armenian, still, are loans from neighboring languages of various periods. The word *dzov,* "sea," for example, comes from Urartean *sue.* Urartean, which seems to have been related to the modern Caucasian languages, was probably already dead long before the birth of Christ, but the word survives, in Hebrew form, as Ararat, the name by which the Bible knows the mountainous land where Noah's ark rested. The Urarteans called themselves Biaina, a name that survives in Armenian Van; Urartu seems to come from an Assyrian word meaning "high place." The word for "sea" is a fairly basic one, which replaced the proto-Armenian Indo-European term, so one can assume the Armenians had already fully assimilated *dzov* at a very early date. In the Behistun inscription discussed earlier, the name of Armenia is still represented in Babylonian as "Urartu," and one Armenian is named Haldita, a word that probably means "servant of Haldi." Haldi was the chief divinity of the Urartean pantheon, so it is possible that Haldita's parents had been worshippers of the Urartean god. The Armenian words for plum, apple, and mulberry *(salor, khndzor,* and *tut),* fruits native to the Armenian plateau, are also from the non-Indo-European Hurro-Urartean. Had the Armenians been living in Anatolia as long as the Hurro-Urarteans, probably they would have had native, Indo-European words for these fruits. More likely, they settled and learned the names of these fruits from the older, settled population who cultivated them.

It is also sometimes possible to assign loan words in Armenian from the same language family to different periods; this helps us to establish the cultural ties Armenians maintained over time with neighbors belonging to these language families. The Armenian place name *Til* comes from a Semitic word for "hill" and may be a relic of Assyrian trading settlements along the upper Euphrates in the second millennium B.C., but *selan* (now pronounced *seghan*), "table," from Semitic *shulhan,* probably came into Armenian only with the introduction of Syriac Christianity around the third century A.D. Armenian ties with the Semitic world to the south were evidently ancient. Many Armenian terms having to do with trade (e.g., *shuka,* "market"; Syriac *shuqa*) are Semitic, as are later Christian terms (e.g., *kahana,* "priest"). Much of the vocabulary of Armenian comes from Parthian, testimony to the extent to which Armenia was permeated by the political and religious institutions of pre-Islamic Iran. And, as suggested, the oldest identifiable stratum of loan words comes from the Anatolian civilizations, both Hittite and Hurro-Urartean, with which the proto-Armenian colonists first came into contact.

To sum up, the evidence of language allows us to construct a tentative model of Armenian origins. Related Phrygian and Armenian populations in the middle of the second millennium B.C. crossed from southeastern Europe into Anatolia. The people whose descendants became the Armenians were the ones who moved the farthest eastward. The latter took their ethnic name from the Hattian people whose state they overran. They settled down, learning the words for some local fruits and other everyday items from the native Hurro-Urarteans. Other aspects of their culture had the common Mediterranean stamp. They interacted in trade with the Assyrians to the south; from the south, too, Christianity was to come to the country many centuries later. As the Iranian states of the Medes, then the Persians, on the east, became the dominant force in the region, Armenian language and culture acquired the additional riches of that civilization.

Just as ancient civilizations reflect through language a process of continuous cross-fertilization, so racial characteristics also become shared with the interaction of peoples in areas like the ancient Near East. Thus, when one speaks of the ancient Armenians, what is meant is a people identifying themselves as such, their main common denominator usually being the Armenian language. Racial characteristics cannot be paired with language, except in conditions of extreme physical and cultural isolation. The Armenians emerged from a complex process of cultural interaction, as the inheritors of a rich and ancient mixture of civilizations—and the same can be said of virtually all their neighbors.

Migrations: Phrygians, Mushki, and the "Classical" and "Revisionist" Hypotheses

With the theory of multiple proto-Armenian Indo-European migrations onto the Armenian plateau as early as the beginning of the second millennium B.C. one must consider another hypothesis, advanced in recent years, that suggests the earliest Indo-European speakers themselves were natives of the Armenian plateau; so that in the case of the Armenians, at least, no mass migration to their present home from elsewhere ever took place. Finally, there is the approach to Armenian origins that is, without the strictest controls, unscientific, though it has its supporters. This is to take at face value the genealogies proposed by the historian Movses Khorenatsi and beginning with Hayk, the descendant of Noah and the titanic progenitor of the Armenian (Hay) people. These lists are, for the most part, a mixture of mythologies and biblical traditions. The latter reflect the view of any pious medieval man that whatever is true must find an explanation somehow within the pages of Scripture. Khorenatsi's rich narrative does contain material of what seems to be genuine historical value, and his tales provide evidence of a world view that is likely to have existed among medieval Armenians contemplating themselves and their destiny.

Following Herodotus, scholars have sought to link the earliest Armenians with the Phrygians. A people whose language belonged to the Eastern branch of Indo-European, the Phrygians invaded the Anatolian peninsula from Thrace around the thirteenth century B.C. and destroyed the empire of the Hittites. This is the "classical" hypothesis of Armenian origins. The "Hittite" or Hattic language spoken in central Anatolia belonged to the Western branch of Indo-European. All Indo-European languages belong to one or another of two branches, conveniently termed "Eastern" and "Western" Indo-European. These are separated by certain sound changes common to the languages of either branch.

The earliest "Eastern" Indo-Europeans seem to have lived also to the north of their "Western" cousins, so one might visualize the movement of these languages southward from an original home in the South Russian steppes and Central Asia in two successive waves: the ancestors of the Hittites in the first; the Phrygians and Armenians in the second, moving from the north of the Black Sea down into Thrace and across the Hellespont into Anatolia. Migrations southward out of Asia are common in history and are generally the product of changes in climate.

In the mid-second millennium B.C., "Western" Indo-European Luwians and Hittites lived in western and central Asia Minor. As one moved eastward onto what later came to be called the Armenian plateau, the Hurrian and Urartean languages predominated. These belonged to the Caucasian family. It is logical that the Armenian language and culture would bear traces of both groups, and this is, in fact, the case. Herodotus links the Armenians with the Phrygians, but "Phrygian" is a Greek term. Contemporary records call the invaders Mushki, and a part of Thrace, whence they came, was called Mysia. It is the source of the biblical proper name Meshekh and the name of the Cappadocian capital Mazaka (Armenian Mazhak; Greek Caesarea; modern Turkish Kayseri, in central Anatolia). The Mushki, or proto-Armenians, would appear to have adopted for themselves the name of the great, defeated empire of the Hittites, which they would have pronounced *hatiyos;* thereby the familiar Armenian word *hay* ("Armenian") develops. Historically, such adoption of the name of another people has many precedents. With the fall of the Hittites, the Luwians of southwestern Anatolia likewise adopted their name. The word *armina* in Persian would come from the name of the region of Arme-Shupria, west of Van, where Mushki seem to have concentrated.

This "classical" hypothesis takes into account the complex picture of Indo-European migration and culture just sketched. It was challenged many years ago by Armenian scholars who would see the origin of the word *hay* in the name of the region Hayasa, in northern Armenia, and would regard the Armenians as the aboriginal inhabitants of the region. Several learned non-Armenians have in recent years attacked the "classical" hypothesis as a whole. They do not regard Armenian as a Hurro-Urartean language, but they do consider it a language essentially native to Anatolia, developing in the context of other Indo-European tongues attested there from the second millennium B.C. In support of their hypothesis, they use not only the data of linguistics, but the most recent advances in archaeology, to suggest that certain agricultural skills were developed in Armenia by the Indo-Europeans and then taken elsewhere. People speaking Indo-European languages were responsible for the transfer. Indo-Europeans have traditionally been associated with a semi-nomadic life and with horse-breeding. Proponents of the "revisionist" school challenge this association, linking the proto-Indo-Europeans rather with farming. Archaeological studies indicate to them that the cultivation of grains began in Anatolia and radiated from there, as, they propose, did the Indo-Europeans.

The "revisionist" hypothesis represents an original challenge to long-accepted assumptions and needs to be tested and examined by experts in the various facets of Indo-European studies. Most reject it. Whichever theory one is inclined to accept, it is, at least, indisputable that there were Armenians in Armenia by the late second millennium B.C., speaking their own language. They interacted there with the Urarteans, who have left written records and monuments of material culture.

Biainili-Urartu: History

The Urartean people spoke a language related to those of the modern Caucasus, and, as noted, an Armenian of the sixth century B.C. bore the Urartean name Haldita. The indigenous languages of the Armenian plateau, such as Urartean, probably survived well into the Hellenistic age, for the Greek geographer Strabo reports that it was only after the conquests of Artaxias (Artashes) I in the early second century B.C. that the Armenians became "of one language" (Strabo, 1961, 11.14.5).

The Urarteans gradually united the various petty kingdoms of the Armenian plateau from the thirteenth century B.C. onward. These in many ways resemble the *nakharar*doms of later Classical and medieval Armenia, and, as in later eras, it seems to have been the threat of a neighboring great power, Assyria in this instance, which served as the spur to political unity. From their center at Van (where stood the Urartean capital Tushpa), the Urarteans gradually expanded their power to the east. In the ninth century B.C., Urartu, led by King Aramu, conquered tracts in Media. In the eighth century B.C., the fortress-cities of Teishebaini (Armenian Karmir Blur) and Erebuni (Arin Berd) were established, in what is now Erevan, by King Argishti II. His successor, Rusa II, concentrated on consolidating Urartean power in the west. The kings of Urartu left abundant religious and political inscriptions in stone, in a cuneiform script. Urartean culture and domination extended also over much of what is now northwestern Iran—King Ishpuini occupied the region of Lake Urmia around 820 B.C.—and by the early eighth century B.C., Urartu was able to challenge and defeat the great power of the day, Assyria.

But this predominance was short-lived. The mighty Assyrian monarch Tiglath-Pileser III (ruled 745-28 B.C.) invaded the heartland of Urartu, laying siege to Tushpa itself. The country suffered from the incursions of the Cimmerians (Gomer in the Bible; Armenian Gamirk) and of the Scythians, a North Iranian nomadic nation of the steppes. Their memory is preserved in the Armenian place name Shakashen ("Abode of the Sakas," i.e., Scythians), in words like Armenian *hskay,* "giant," literally "a good saka," and in names like that of the epic hero Paroyr Skayordi "son of the Saka," who is listed by Movses Khorenatsi as one of the progenitors of the Armenians. Armenian tradition thereby commemorates events that occurred a thousand years before the Armenians preserved a script to record them. The Bible calls the Scythians by the name Ashkenaz, from a misspelling of Ashguza; and Greek Skythos comes from the latter. In Armenian tradition, the Armenians are called the sons of Askanaz; so these North Iranian nomadic people, too, contributed to the rich fabric of the formation of the Armenian nation, albeit with the intrusion of biblical legends about the same events. As Urartu faced the power of Assyria to the south and the incursions of nomads from the north, a third power was on the rise.

Around the eleventh century B.C., Iranians began migrating westward from Central Asia into the lands that are now Iran and Afghanistan. One Iranian people, the Medes, begin to appear in Assyrian records of the ninth century B.C.; and in 612 B.C., acting in alliance with Babylon, the Median king Cyaxares conquered and destroyed the Assyrian capital, Nineveh. Urartu itself fell in around 585, but Median domination was short-lived. In 559, Cyrus the Great (Kurush), king of the Persians, southern cousins of Medes, overthrew his father-in-law, the Median king known to Herodotus as Astyages. Armenian tradition regards the Mede as a tyrant. Khorenatsi calls him Azhdahak, a monstrous serpent-man, and claims an Armenian king named Tigran helped Cyrus defeat him. Xenophon's *Cyropaideia* names an Armenian prince, Tigran, as one of Cyrus's childhood friends, so perhaps Khorenatsi draws these fictional details from a common tradition. The memory of the last Mede as a tyrant, though, seems to be a genuine survival of the era of Cyrus, who presented himself everywhere as a just liberator. With Cyrus, Armenia enters the Achaemenian Empire and the cultural orbit of Iran.

Biainili-Urartu: Culture

Urartu is notable not only for its political history as a major power of the ancient Near East but for its culture as well. Urartean was written first with a crude system of pictograms. Later, probably because the demands of writing became more complex, the cuneiform writing general to ancient Mesopotamia and its neighbors was adapted to Urartean, and approximately 400 inscriptions have been discovered in this script. Most of these deal with royal building projects and religious dedications. Sealings of papyrus indicate that the Aramaic alphabet and language might have been employed for correspondence, as in later Artaxiad (Artashesian) Armenia in the second century B.C. This is not unlikely, as alphabetic Aramaic and Phoenician are known in ancient Anatolian inscriptions. Expressions such as "By the will of Haldi" *(Haldini ishmasini)* in royal inscriptions seem to have been adapted by the Achaemenians to their own purposes in the sixth century, so it is possible to speak of limited Urartean literary influence on an important neighboring culture. The title "great king" was used by the Urarteans before its employment in the Iranian state; and this, too, may indicate the continuation of Urartean political forms in a later age.

Other important achievements are evident in Urartean architecture. In the stepped tomb of Cyrus at Pasargadae with its pitched roof, and the finely dressed stonework of Persepolis, some scholars have discerned the influence of Urartean architectural styles and techniques.

A relief in the palace of the Assyrian king Sargon depicts the Urartean temple of Haldi at Ardini, called in Assyrian Musasir, which was sacked during his campaign of 714 B.C. against Urartu. The building has a hexastyle portico and triangular pediment. Shields hang from the walls and columns, and the door is flanked by two great urns. Here is, very likely, an Anatolian prototype of Classical Greek temple architecture. Urartean fortresses were impressively massive in scale, and Assyrian reliefs show windowed, crenelated towers.

It is sometimes difficult, in the absence of identifying inscriptions, to distinguish between Urartean, Archaemenian, and Assyrian works of art. But some pieces are nonetheless distinctive. Metallurgy probably originated on the mineral-rich Armenian plateau, where objects worked in metal dating back to 9500 B.C. have been found; and the Urarteans have left us cast, embossed, and etched bands; buckles; harness pieces; horse bits; helmets; candelabra; and other work in copper and bronze. There are depictions of men and horses (the latter also found finely worked in the round, indicating a long acquaintance with the animal), and of a curious symbol, probably of victory, of an embrasure with an upright spear rising from the center. The Scythians are said to have worshipped a sword thrust into a mound, probably with martial intent, given their preoccupation with war in most regions outside their homeland. Of obvious religious significance are pictures and figurines of the gods Haldi, Teisheba, and Shivini (the Sun god, surmounted by an Assyrian adaptation of the Egyptian winged disk of the Sun-god Re). There is also a bone figurine of a goddess, and at Karmir Blur were found statuettes of a fish-man and a scorpion-man. At Alishar was discovered a bronze statuette of a bird with a human head and torso, strongly reminiscent of the Harpies of Greek art. In a scene known throughout the ancient Mesopotamian world, figures are shown on either side of the Tree of Life, making offerings. The Tree of Life, Armenian *tsarrn kenats,* continued to be revered in medieval Armenian folk songs, and two figures are shown holding it, in a drawing in one manuscript.

The Urartean component in the Armenian heritage is evident, not only from Urartean loans for words such as lake, plum, quince, brick, slave, mint, and pomegranate, which would have entered Armenian soon after the initial settlement, but from the evidence of historical geography, where Armenian preserves old Urartean place names over the entire extent of the Armenian plateau: Van, from Biaina; Tosp, from Tushpa; Erevan, from Erebuni; Garni, from Giarniani; Andzit, from Enzite; the river Aratsani, from Arzani; and Manazkert and Arjesh, from the names of the Urartean kings Menuas and Argishti. Armenians perpetuated old Urartean settled sites, notably Van.

Movses Khorenatsi attributes to the legendary Assyrian queen Shamiram (Semiramis) the ancient Urartean irrigation canal of Artamet, near Van, and other relics of Urartean antiquity that cluster about the ancient capital and its environs are celebrated in Armenian tradition (Mouses Khorenats'i, 1978, vol. 1, p. 16). For centuries to come, storms on lake Van were explained as a battle between the god Vahagn (Iranian Verethraghna) and undersea serpents called *vishaps*. Khorenatsi has preserved a stanza of pagan poetry describing the birth of the sun-like god from a reed in the sea, following the travail of heaven and earth. This song appears to contain features going back to the Indo-European past of the proto-Armenians, since it resembles an episode in the Indian Vedic literature, but the legend of the serpent-slaying itself, despite the Zoroastrian names and accretions, seems to be an Urartean inheritance, or combination of influences for such exploits belong to the weather-god Teisheba, Hurrian Teshub.

On the cliff sides of the great rock of Van, the Urarteans carved blind portals called "gates of the god," before which offerings were made. Though the Urartean religion waned, the sacred character of these portals was remembered, and later Zoroastrian Armenian mythology named one of these the Gate of Mithra *(Mheri durrn),* The Armenian epic of Sasun, still recited orally, warns that the grotto of Pokr Mher, Little Mithra, will open only at the end of time. This popular Iranian god of justice, associated in Armenia with apocalypse and the Sun, was believed to dwell in a dark cave, where he held the globe of the heavens and was served by a raven. Here are several elements—Anatolian and Iranian commingled together—of the later Roman religion of Mithraism; and it is most probable that the cult originated in Armenia and was brought to the West by Roman legions who served in the country in the first century A.D. Some of the elements of Mithraism may survive in the West to this day in the legendry and the initiatory rituals of the Freemasons.

In some cases, noble families of Urartean lineage may have existed continuously for thousands of years, into medieval and modern Armenia. The Artsruni dynasty of Vaspurakan, whose descent is traced in legend to two brothers who fled from Assyria, may derive its name from Urartean *artsibini* ("eagle"). The eagle, *artsiv* in Armenian, was the totemic animal of the Artsrunis. In a legend, the progenitor of the Artsrunis is said to have been abandoned as a child but rescued by an eagle, which nurtured the infant in its eyrie.

Another ancient Anatolian survival in Armenian legend with interesting connections to other cultures of the Mediterranean area is the myth of Tork Angelea or Tork of Angl, related by Khorenatsi (1978, vol. 2, p. 8). The historian claims to have heard an oral saga in which Tork "would strike with his hands granite rocks in which there was no fissure and crack them, as he desired, into big and little pieces." He also threw stones the size of hills at enemy ships on the Black Sea to a distance of eight stadia. Angl is a place in southwestern Armenia (modern Egil, Armenian Angegh Tun), known to the Hittites as Ingalava, but Khorenatsi gives us a folk etymology of *an-gel* as "of ferocious mien" *(dzhnahayiats)*. It was long ago recognized that the Armenian Tork is the weather-god of Asia Minor, Tarkhu, whose name means "victor."

Angegh Tun was a royal necropolis of several ancient Armenian dynasties. According to Khorenatsi, Tork is descended from Paskam, grandson of Hayk, the eponymous ancestor of the Armenians (Movses Khorenats'i, vol. 1, p. 23). Khorenatsi says Tork used to scratch pictures of eagles and other designs on stone tablets with his sharp fingernails (Movses Khorenats'i, vol. 2, p. 8). Armenians would have seen such images on stone, notably the Hittite double eagle, which has had such a long history in subsequent European heraldry. This seems to be an aetiological legend to explain the mysterious carvings, and a grain of truth is preserved in their attribution to a Hittite god inherited by Armenian religion.

The name of Tarkhu/Tork means "conqueror," from a root meaning "go, traverse," hence "overcome." The name of the god appears to be present in Tarchon (Latin Tarquin), the name of the violent Etruscan hero. The Etruscans, ancient inhabitants of Italy, are said by Herodotus to have come from Lydia in Asia Minor; and the only known relative of their mysterious language is attested in a single inscription from Lemnos, not far from the Anatolian mainland. Hesychius explained an Etruscan word pronounced *truna* as "rule, primacy," a word perhaps from the same root as Tarkhu. Another word for ruler, found in Greek but non-Hellenic in origin, is *tyrannos,* English "tyrant," perhaps related to Lydian *tern,* "army." So the Armenian god has Hittite-Mesopotamian ancestry, an Italian relative in the Tarquin of Classical mythology, and possibly a distant echo, through Greek, in the political vocabulary of modern English.

The Legendary Beginnings: Hayk and Bel

It has been suggested that the Armenians, a people speaking an Indo-European language related to those of the Phrygians and early Greeks, settled in eastern Anatolia. Their own name, *hay,* may have been adopted from that of the great Hittite Empire whose former lands they traversed. The name by which the Persians and most later peoples (through the Greeks) knew them, *armina,* comes probably from the fastness of Arme-Shupria where first they became established. The name by which their southern, Semitic neighbors—Assyrians, Babylonians, Hebrews—knew them, *urashtu, uruatri, ararat* (or *urarat* in a rare biblical variant), comes from that of the Urarteans. The Armenians intermarried over the ages with the various peoples of Urartu, as the ancient origins of the Artsrunid house, for example, would seem to indicate, as do the Urartean names borne by Armenians that Darius mentions in his victory inscription at Behistun; and they inherited many Urartean place names and words for the fruits and natural features of the land. Struggle against powerful states to the south has been a continuous feature of Armenian historical experience. The national epic of Sasun crystallized around a saga of heroic resistance to the Muslim Arab caliphate in the eighth century A.D. Movses Khorenatsi's tale of the war between Tigran the Armenian and Azhdahak the Mede (the latter a kind of dragon-man), and the larger-than-life confrontation between the Armenian Arshak and the Sasanian Shahbuhr II (Armenian Shapuh) in the *Epic Histories* of Pavstos Buzand (P'awstos Buzand, 1989) reflect the continuing rivalry between Armenia and Iran.

Similarly, the legend of Hayk and Bel commemorates an earlier struggle. Hayk is the mighty archer who is the eponymous, "name-giving" ancestor of the *hay* "Armenian" people. His opponent, Bel, is the ancient Assyrian *baal,* a word for a god meaning simply "lord," who is meant to embody all that is oppressively alien. The contest of Hayk and Bel, related by Movses Khorenatsi, seems to preserve a memory of the wars between the Armenians and Assyria. It has become in the Armenian consciousness something more important: the paradigm of the just resistance of a small people to the tyranny of a great empire. Hayk is a hero on a human scale. Armenian tradition calls the Milky Way the "Trail of the Straw-Thief," for the Armenian god Vahagn, probably a stand-in for Hayk on a cold night once stole kindling for his people from the heavenly woodshed of the mighty Bel.

The legend of Ara and Semiramis, found in Khorenatsi, seems also to be a relic of that same conflict. The mighty Assyrian queen Semiramis

(Armenian Shamiram) conceived a passion for the Armenian king Ara *geghetsik,* "the Beautiful," but he rejected her advances. She pursued him, he was killed in battle by her army, and she placed his lifeless body in an upper room of her palace so that supernatural dogs called *aralezk,* "Ara-lickers" or "take and lick," might come and lick him back to life. In Movses Khorenatsi's account, which one imagines is colored by his disdain for pagan stories of miracles, the *aralezk* do not come, and the body disintegrates. Shamiram displays to the wondering crowd another of her lovers who looks like Ara. Khorenatsi liked to find rational explanations for ancient myths; in this, he merely followed the Greek euhemerist approach to history. But he does portray Ara as a good and faithful family man, dedicated to his nation; Shamiram is an imperious nymphomaniac. In later Armenian history, the contest between the Armenian Christian hero Vardan Mamikonian and the Mazdean Persian tyrant Yazdagerd II also takes on the character of a battle between virtue and iniquity, chastity, and voluptuousness.

The legend of Ara and Shamiram has a definite religious component, beyond its significance as a historical parable. It evidently reflects the pre-Christian belief that certain men might visit the underworld and return. Ara appears in the *Republic* of Plato as Er, son of Armenios, who is killed in battle, travels in spirit down to Hades, and then returns to his body. The idea of spirit-travel may have been one of the earliest Iranian beliefs to be shared in Armenia. It is the core of the Zoroastrian book of the righteous Viraz, and later echoes of it, transmitted through Islamic Arab literature, probably influenced the thirteenth-century Italian poet Dante, who in his *Inferno* travels to the underworld and returns safely to earth. In Armenia, as elsewhere in the ancient Near East, there was practiced the cult of a young god who is driven mad by a lustful mother or stepmother. He mutilates himself, dies, and is reborn in the springtime. In Greece, it is the tale of Hippolytus and Phaedra; in Iran, of Siyavush and Sudabeh; in Phrygia, of Cybele and Attis. Ara and Shamiram present the Armenian variant. This is why the lust of the Assyrian queen figures so prominently, aside from its didactic importance.

The two legends just discussed seem to be Armenian in essence. In the first section of his *History,* Khorenatsi deals with many others, although much of this material is drawn from Greek and Syriac histories and mythical works, often blended with either Iranian mythological figures or with anachronistic Armenian characters. An example is the legend of the contest of Tigran and Azhdahak. The former is almost

certainly Tigran II, the Great, the Artaxiad king of Armenia in the first
century B.C. who briefly created an empire stretching from the Caucasus
mountains and Media in the northeast to Lebanon in the southwest. He
is pitted against the Median tyrant Azhdahak, whose name, as noted, is
that of a three-headed dragon-man tyrant of the Zoroastrian sacred
book, the *Avesta*. Azhi Dahaka (Azhdahak) became for Iranians the
exemplar of inhuman tyranny and misrule. This king, according to
Herodotus, was in fact overthrown by a younger man who created a
great empire, just as Tigran did. But the man was Cyrus, the founder
of the Persian Empire, and once this is realized, all the details fall into
place. Khorenatsi has presented a garbled tale, but one of interest.
Again, there is the example of the brave, young Armenian hero
struggling against an alien tyrant. But here, the old story of Cyrus, with
a mythological component introduced, has been adapted to Tigran.
Since the Persian Sasanian dynasty also adapted the Cyrus legend to
the early life of Ardashir I, their own founder, it seems likely that we
are dealing with royal propaganda of the first century B.C. rather than
with an older legend going back to the beginnings of the Armenians,
nearly a millennium earlier.

The Beginning of the Historical Era of Armenia

The Armenian plateau at the time of its conquest by the Achaemenian
kings of Iran in the second half of the sixth century B.C. was inhabited
by a mixture of peoples, probably with a predominance of Urarteans and
Armenians, whose appellations were used interchangeably at Behistun
to identify the country. It is likely, though, that the Armenian-speakers
developed the strongest dynastic and cultural ties to the Iranians, becoming thereby the dominant population to which the other ethnic groups
were gradually assimilated. Until the conversion of the Armenians to
Christianity, with its Byzantine and Syrian cultural and political links,
Armenia was to remain in the Iranian cultural orbit almost exclusively.

But it would seem that some greater diversity persisted on the
plateau. A few tantalizing monuments, in addition to persistent proper
names, may indicate that Hittite and ancient Semitic culture survived.
To the west of Armenia, at Arebsun near Nevshehir, there are several
bas-reliefs in what has been described as "Neo-Hittite" style, which
seem to depict a myth of the creation of the world. Scratched onto the
same stones are a number of inscriptions in Aramaic, the Semitic

language used throughout the ancient period for official purposes in Armenia, Iran, and elsewhere in the Near East. They sum up well both the diversity and the interpenetration of linguistic, artistic, religious, and ethnic influences in the region where the Armenian nation emerged. A rich and archaic world of which the Armenians, both adaptable and tenacious, are now the sole survivors, their language and legendry the inheritance of both a continuous and limpid Indo-European tradition of extreme antiquity and all that rich mixture gained along the way.

FOR FURTHER INFORMATION

For the sources of, or more information on, the material in this chapter, please consult the following (full citations can be found in the Bibliography at the end of this volume).

Arutyunian, 1970.

Azarpay, 1968.

Balcer, 1984.

Bauer-Manndorff, 1984.

Diankonoff, 1985, 1985.

Fontenrose, 1959.

Forbes, 1983.

Herodotus, 1954.

Jahukian, 1987.

Lukenbill, 1989.

Mallory, 1989.

Meillet, 1936.

Movses Khorenats'i, 1978

Olmstead, 1948.

Piotrovsky, 1967.

Renfrew, 1987.

Russell, 1982, 1987a, 1987b,
    1984, 1987, 1989.

THE ERUANDID (ERVANDIAN)/ORONTID DYNASTY

The dates are approximative and still debated. All dates are B.C.

Ervand (Orontes) I, c.401-c.344
Ervand (Orontes) II, c.344-331
Mithranes, 331–before 317
Ervand (Orontes) III, before 317–c.260
Samus, c.260
Xerxes, after 228–c.212
Ervand (Orontes) IV, c.212-c.200

3

THE EMERGENCE OF ARMENIA

Nina Garsoïan

The Fall of Urartu and the Persian Conquest

The political situation prevailing in Anatolia and particularly on the Armenian highlands altered radically with the beginning of the sixth century B.C. as the Urartian Empire, which had survived the downfall of its mighty Assyrian rival, disappeared in its turn, somewhere in the first two decades of the new century.

We cannot date the Urartian collapse with absolute accuracy. A passage from the Book of Jeremiah (51:27) attests to its survival as late as the fourth year of King Zedekiah of Jerusalem (594 B.C.) when it calls upon "Ararat [Urartu], Menni and Askenaz" to rise against "Babylon." An alliance is confirmed by the contemporary *Babylonian Annals* (pp. 13-20), which noted the collaboration of Urartu with the newly come Indo-Iranian tribesmen, Scythians (Askenaz) as well as Medes, in the capture of the Assyrian capital of Nineveh in 612 B.C. Excavations of the north Urartian capital of Tešebaini (Teshebaini)/Karmir Blur in the suburbs of modern Erevan show with amazing precision that the destruction of this site came swiftly and unexpectedly under a rain of arrows, whose three-pronged bronze heads identify them as belonging to Urartu's former Scythian allies (Piotrovskii, 1967, p. 24). The inhabitants of Tešebaini fled headlong, abandoning weapons, jewels, and household goods, or died in the fire that ravaged the citadel. The blow evidently fell in late July or August since excavators observed that the granaries had already been filled with the new harvest but the wine jars were still empty awaiting the vintage and charred remains of late summer flowers could be identified in the ruins. The date of the catastrophe, however, can be given as lying between 594 and 590 B.C., a period during which the main Urartian capital, Rusaxinili on Lake Van, also fell to the Medes pressing in from the East. The various portions of the far-flung Urartian possessions obviously could not have been overwhelmed all at once, but everything was apparently over by 585, since there is no longer any mention of Urartu in the treaty dividing Asia Minor along the Halys River between the Median conqueror Cyaxares and the king of Lydia (a treaty whose date is set beyond question by its association with the eclipse of the sun observed on May 28 of that year) (Herodotus, tr. Godley, I. 103; vol. I, pp. 134/35). Little more than one generation later, the conquering Medes gave way to a still more powerful Indo-European group, the Persians, whose empire was to stretch from Central Asia across Asia Minor to the shores of the Aegean Sea for more than two centuries.

The Persian Empire (594–331 B.C.)

With the disappearance of Urartu and the establishment of the Persian Achaemenid Empire, our knowledge of the history of the Armenian plateau enters into a long period of darkness. The Urartian inscriptions with their extensive political and socioeconomic information now fall silent, as do those of neighboring Assyria and Babylonia. When the Armenians finally came to record their own history more than a millennium later, only a dim and inaccurate memory survived of their distant past. Archaeology, so generous in its evidence for the Urartian period, has inexplicably failed until now to provide material for the era of the Persian domination, not only in the still-untouched regions of Anatolia, but even in the well-surveyed sites of the Armenian Republic. Thus, the existing sources of information for the earliest Armenian period are reduced to a few Achaemenid royal inscriptions, the most important and famous of which is the one set up ca. 520 B.C. at the order of Darius the Great on the cliff at Behistun near Hamadan, where the name "Armina" is recorded for the first time. The far more extensive Greek records of Herodotus and Xenophon do not begin earlier than the mid to late fifth century, a century after the Persian conquest.

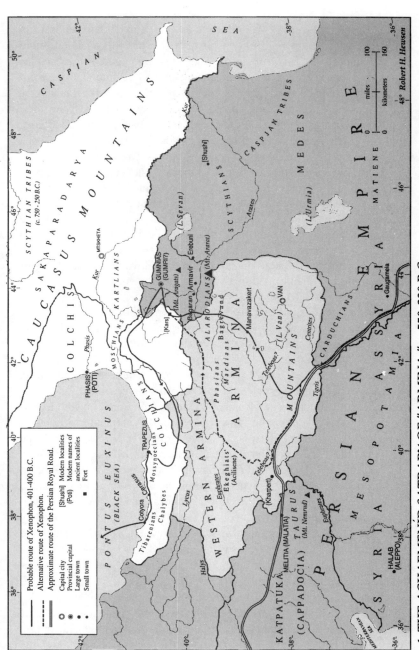

4. *THE ACHAEMENID SATRAPY OF "ARMINA," c. 550–330 B.C.*

Despite the scantiness of information, which precludes a reconstruction of most of the internal political history of the period, some of its more significant aspects can be observed. The lands conquered by the Persians were in no sense homogeneous and the newly come Armenians were but one of a multitude of tribes among whom they cannot have been a majority at first. The Urartians were by no means exterminated despite their political disintegration. Some sites, such as Tešebaini, were abandoned, but the persistence of other place names such as Biaina/Van or Tušpa (Tushpa)/Tosp indicate a surviving population with a continuing memory. In the trilingual Behistun inscription of the late sixth century, the Semitic Akkadian and Elamite versions still use the name "Uraštu" for the land called "Armina" in the Indo-European Old Persian text. According to Herodotus (Herodotus, tr. Godley, III. 93-94, vol. II, pp. 120/1-122/3), the Persian administration may have distinguished between its Thirteenth Satrapy or Province, which included the "Armenoi," and the Eighteenth, to which belonged the Alarodians or Urartians. However, the accuracy of his administrative information has been questioned. Later in the fifth century, Xenophon (*Anabasis,* IV iii, 4-5, vol. II, p. 24/5) reports that the "Armenoi" were still distinct from the "free Khaldaioi/Chaldaeans," who must have been the worshippers of the supreme Urartian god, Khaldi. In the north, the presence of Saka or Scythian tribes is attested by the survival of such place names as Šakašēn, Šakak'ar, and Šakē (Shakashen, Shakakar, and Shake). Indeed, a memory of the link between the Scythians and the Armenoi is underscored in the genealogies compiled by the Armenian historian Movsēs Xorenac'i (Movses Khorenatsi), who identified the first Armenian king crowned by the Medes (presumably at the time of their conquest of the plateau) as *"Mer Paroyr orti Skayortoy"* that is to say, "Our Paroyr, the son of the son of the Saka" (Movses Khorenats'i, I. 21-22, pp. 108, 110). The "White Syrians" of the western, Cappadocian border may have been survivors of the earlier Assyrian colonies and so added a Semitic element to the Hurrian Urartians and varied Indo-European–speaking groups in the area. Some of the tribes can be localized by the names they left to regions of medieval Armenia, as in the case of the "Saspires" and "Utioi" (Herodotus, tr. Godley, I. 104; III, 93-94; IV, 37; vols. I, 134/5; II, pp. 120/1-122/3, 236/7) in northern Sper, and Utik', or the Kardukhoi found by Xenophon (*Anabasis,* III. v, 15; IV, iii, 1; vol. I, pp. 490/1, II, pp. 24/5) in the southern district later known as Korduk'. Thus, the tribal and linguistic multiplicity of the Armenian highlands throughout the Achaemenid period is undeniable, and the Armenoi at first occupied only the southwestern portion of the plateau. Nevertheless, the name "Armina" given to the entire region in the Old Persian version of the Behistun inscription suggests that these "Armenoi" were gradually gaining a dominant position by the end of the sixth century B.C. and that this preponderance had been accepted by the Persian authorities.

The Persian Empire laid an administrative framework over this diversity. The authority of the Achaemenid King of Kings was supreme, as was that of the satrap within his province. The main line of communications from the Persian capitals of Susa and Persepolis to Sardis in western Asia Minor, the Royal Highway, ran for fifteen resting stages through southern Armenia (Herodotus, tr. Godley, V. 52; vol. III, pp. 56/5-58/9). As part of the empire, the "Armenoi" contributed a yearly tribute of 400 silver talents as well as the horses for which the region was famous, and they served in the Persian army. Despite these obligations, however, the position of the country was by no means unfavorable. The inclusion of the entire Armenian plateau inside the heartland of the Persian Empire kept it within a single political and cultural sphere and preserved it from the opposing external tensions that were to characterize most of its subsequent history. At the same time the customary tolerance of the Achaemenid authorities toward the various peoples of their empire, as long as the peace was kept and the tribute paid, fostered the development of local institutions that flourished in general peace and prosperity.

To be sure, the great rebellion of 522 B.C., marking the inauguration of Darius the Great's reign throughout the Persian Empire, was serious enough to require at least three campaigns to subdue "Armina" alone, although even here an Armenian named Dadaršiš (Dadarshish) commanded the Persian army. But, thereafter, the country appears to have been satisfied with its distant rulers. Armenians served in the army led by Xerxes against Greece in 480 B.C. (Herodotus, tr. Godley, VII. 73; vol. III, p. 384/5) and supplied a contingent of 10,000 for the Persian war against Cilicia in 368. At the very end of the Achaemenid Empire in 331 B.C., the Armenian infantry and armored cavalry still loyally defended Darius III in his last stand against Alexander the Great at the Battle of Gaugamela (Arrian, III. viii, 5; xi, 7; vol. I, pp. 246/7, 256/7).

The internal life of the country during the period of Persian rule is revealed to us in unexpected detail through the account of the Greek general Xenophon who in 401 led the "ten thousand" survivors of his army across the Armenian plateau from Mesopotamia to the Black Sea and recorded his experience in a work known as the *Anabasis,* or "The March Up-Country." Xenophon (*Anabasis,* III. v, 17; vol. I, p. 490/1), who observed a subdivision of the Armenian-inhabited area into Armenia, which he called "a large and prosperous province," and Western Armenia, ruled by a different satrap, a simple agricultural and tribal society, relatively peaceful despite some local strife, and amazingly wealthy for the times. Apparently no cities were to be found in the land, with the single exception of Gumnias in the north, whose location is uncertain although its identification with modern Leninakan/Giumri has been suggested (Manandyan, 1965, p. 27), and the recent excavations at Armawir (Armavir) on the Araxes River show no settlement between the early Urartian foundations and the later Hellenistic center on that site. The population lived primarily in strongly fortified villages with turreted houses or occasionally in underground dwellings, to protect themselves from the winter cold. A palace for the satrap is mentioned in one place (Xenophon, *Anabasis*, IV. iv. 2; vol.II, p. 18/9), but the villages were ruled by apparently autonomous village elders, and probably consisted for the most part of blood relatives since the village chiefs considered themselves responsible for the welfare of their kinsmen (Xenophon, *Anabasis,* IV. v, 32; vol. II, p. 56/7). The main occupations of the natives were agriculture, rather than trade, and stock raising, both of cattle and of the renowned "Nesaean" horses of the region. The Greeks marveled at the plentiful supplies and sumptuous fare of the country and Xenophon (*Anabasis,* IV. v, 25, 31; vol. II, pp. 54/5-56/7), does not tire of listing the "lamb, kid, pork, veal, and poultry, together with many loaves of bread, some of wheat and some of barley," served at a single meal with a much appreciated local form of beer.

The natives seemingly spoke among themselves a language different from Persian, which was reserved for official purposes, but in the absence of any other dominant influence the country was profoundly Iranized. The Armenians shared the typical Iranian social structure based on the tribe, clan, and family as well as the vocabulary for similar titles and institutions, for example:

Old Persian	Armenian	English
tauma	tohm	house
zantu/zana	azg	clan
xšathra (khshathra)	ašxarh (ashkharh)	country, realm
vith-puthra	sepuh	junior member of a ruling house

If the identification of the tribute-bearers depicted on the great staircase of the Persian capital at Persepolis is correct, the Armenians wore Iranian dress (Median rather than Persian) with knee-length tunics, trousers gathered at the ankle, and characteristic headdresses tied in the back. The Aramaic script of the Persian chancellery was used in writing at least at the end of the period. Most important, the religion attributed to the Armenians reflected the growing Zoroastrianism of the Persian court, although it is difficult to date the time at which beliefs and cults made their first appearance. The Greek geographer Strabo (XI. xiv, 16; vol. V, p. 340/1), writing at the very beginning of the Christian era, informs us that the customs of the Medes, Persians, and Armenians were the same "because their countries are similar" and that "the sacred rites of the Persians one and all are held in honor by both the Medes and the Armenians; but those of Anaïtis are held in exceptional honor by the Armenians who have built temples in her honor in different places and especially in Akilisēnē." This identification of the great goddess of the Zoroastrian pantheon, Anahita the Lady, with the western Armenian district of Akilisēnē (Armenian Ekełeac'/Ekeghiats) is borne out by later classical sources, which call this region "Anaetica" or "Anaïtis" and by the *Armenian History* attributed to Agat'angełos' (Agathangelos) description of the destruction of her great temple at Erēz (modern Erzincan) in the same district (Agathangelos, 1976, #809, pp. 346/7-348/9). The worship of Anahita may have entered Armenia later, perhaps after the period of the Achaemenids, who themselves record her cult officially only in the second half of the dynasty, and her rites at Erēz appear to have been contaminated by Semitic practices such as temple prostitution. However, the places of worship and sacrifice called "Iazonia" by Strabo (XI. iv, 8; vol. V, p. 230/1) were mistakenly associated by him with the Greek tale of Jason and the Argonauts, since their name (derived from the Avestan *yaz-* Old Persian *yad,* Middle Iranian *yaštan/yashtan* "to worship, consecrate") clearly indicates their Iranian origin. The horse sacrifices associated with the cult of the Zoroastrian sun-god Mithra, also observed by Strabo (XI. xiv, 9; vol. V, p. 330/1), are confirmed by Xenophon (*Anabasis,* IV. v, 24, 34/5; vol. II, pp. 52/3, 56/7) for the earlier Achaemenid Armenia and are now illustrated by the splendid silver-gilt bowls, decorated with the figure of a horse raising his forefoot in reverence before a fire altar, recently uncovered near the Georgian capital of Tbilisi. Thus, the Iranian character of Armenian paganism can undoubtedly be traced as far back as the Achaemenid period.

In spite of its Iranization, Armenia was not merely a docile portion of the Achaemenid Empire. As we have seen, the natives used their own language and their land was identified as a separate unit called Armenia by both the Persian chancellery and contemporary Greek authors. Moreover, the position of Armenia in the Persian Empire was distinguished by special honor. The Armenian satrap Tiribazos was characterized by Xenophon (*Anabasis,* IV. iv, 4; vol. II, p. 38/9) as "a friend of the King . . . the only man permitted to help the King mount his horse," and extensive ties of kinship through blood and marriage linked the rulers of Armenia with the household of the King of Kings. This close connection is all the more interesting since, as far as we can judge from the scanty evidence, these rulers of Armenia, as we shall see, appear not to have been foreign governors imposed from outside, but rather native dynasts, since their names "Orontes" (Eruand) and "Tigranes," first recorded by Xenophon at the end of the fifth century, were to reappear subsequently as identifiably Armenian royal names. Thus, as early as the Achaemenid period of the sixth–fifth centuries B.C., we can trace the coalescence of an Armenian entity emerging from the earlier fragmented tribal pattern of the region and controlling an increasing portion of the plateau; an entity with its own language and identity, despite its cultural Iranization, and with the nucleus of a ruling house.

Alexander the Great and His Successors (331–188 B.C.)

The formidable thrust of Alexander the Great through most of Western Asia and the lengthy struggle of his successors to dominate the Near East had relatively little direct influence on the Armenian plateau, although with the removal of the semblance of unity provided by the overall Persian administration, the Armenian lands began to fragment into new units. Greater Armenia east of the Euphrates River preserved its identity in the northeast, but west of the river, the lands of Armenia Minor gradually united into a separate kingdom associated with Pontus in the north and Cappadocia to the west. Similarly, the kingdom of Sophēnē linked with Mesopotamia and Syria to the south probably emerged in the southwestern portion of the plateau in the latter part of the third century B.C., although the date is still disputed. Even so, we must remember that Alexander himself never set foot in the Armenian highlands despite legendary allegations to the contrary, and the sparse references to Armenia in the classical sources dealing with this period clearly suggest that Armenia and its neighbors usually lay beyond the reach of the new Macedonian conquerors, even if Armenia was occasionally compelled to recognize their overlordship.

In 331 B.C. a governor was sent by Alexander to rule Armenia (Arrian, III. 16, 5; vol I, p. 276/7) and another is known to have been there in 323-321, but even at this early date soon after Alexander's victory over Persia, the murder by the natives of the representative whom he had sent to supervise the gold mines of Sper on the northwest border of Armenia suggests that Macedonian authority was little respected in the region. There is no mention of Armenia among the lands divided by Alexander's successors in their treaty of 321, and by 316 Armenia was again ruled by a satrap named Orontes, who may be the one who had led the Armenia contingent defending the last Achaemenid king at the Battle of Gaugamela some fifteen years earlier, or his successor namesake. The later Roman historian Appian ("The Syrian Wars," IX. 55; vol. II, p. 208/9), writing in the second century A.D. claimed that Armenia had become a province belonging to Alexander's general Seleukos I (who had obtained the eastern share of the conqueror's empire) and Seleukos probably was in Armenia in the last year of the fourth century, but the information that the ruler of Armenia in alliance with his Cappadocian neighbor had driven out the Macedonian and "recovered his original domain" suggests that Seleukos probably accepted the autonomous status of the region. The royal title attributed by later sources to the ruler of Armenia may well mean that Armenia stepped almost at once out of the hands of Seleukos and his successors. One more effort was made by the Seleucids at the end of the third century B.C. to reimpose Macedonian rule on all the Armenian lands. The southwestern region known as Sophēnē (Armenian Cop'k'/Dzopk), which by then formed a separate unit, was attacked in 272 by King Antiochos III (Polybius, VIII. 23; vol. III, pp. 504/5-506/7), presumably in retaliation for the failure of Sophēnē to pay the expected tribute. The land was overrun, the local ruler paid a considerable indemnity of 300 talents of silver and 1,000 horses and mules, but then was murdered and Sophēnē was reintegrated into the Seleucid realm. Antiochos may then have turned northward to attack Armenia proper; nevertheless, by 188 B.C. both Armenia and Sophēnē were firmly in the hands of local rulers whom Strabo (XI. xiv, 15; vol. V, p. 336/7) called "Artaxias" and "Zariadris," and not even the subsequent capture of "King Artaxias" by Antiochos IV seems to have hindered the autonomy of the region. In short, despite the occasional attempts of the Seleucids to control their northern border, local dynasts already present under the Achaemenids continued to maintain their rule over their native territories.

The Native Dynasties:
Eruandids (Orontids) and Artašēsids (Artashesids)

Foreign authors observing Armenia from afar could gain only a fragmentary and external impression of what they considered barbaric lands only occasionally brought into the sphere of the civilized world. Beneath this superficial image, however, signs of a far more coherent and continuous native tradition can be detected. Weaving together the scattered information of the often-distorted notices in classical sources together with the semilegendary and chronologically confused Armenian tradition preserved in the *History of Armenia* of the later historian Movsēs Xorenac'i and the newly discovered epigraphic material (both at Armawir in the valley of the Araxes and on Nemrud Dagh in southwestern Kommagēnē), the Armenian historian Hakob Manandyan (1965) began to trace the presence in Armenia of a forgotten dynasty going back to the fifth century B.C.; a native dynasty to which he gave the name of Eruandid or Orontid, from the most common name of its rulers.

Manandyan observed the repeated references by classical sources to dynasts variously named Orontes, Orontas, Aroandes, Ardoates, Aruandes, ruling in Armenia between 401 and ca. 190 B.C. These variants appear to be Greek distortions of a single unfamiliar foreign name known in Armenia under the form Eruand, derived from the Iranian *auruand/auruant,* "mighty, hero." Manandyan (1965; pp. 36-38) linked these observations to the tale of the Armenian King Eruand, recorded out of chronological sequence in Book II of Movsēs Xorenac'i's *History* (II. 37-46, pp. 178-187). The discovery at the beginning of this century of a Greek inscription near Armawir (in which a "King Orontes" is mentioned) reinforced the hypotheses of the presence of a ruler of that name in Greater Armenia. Finally, the conclusion of Movsēs Xorenac'i's tale (II. 46, pp. 185-187) with King Eruand's defeat and death at the hand of his own soldiers in the war against his successor King Artašēs (Artashes) (Greek Artaxias) seemed to coincide remarkably with Strabo's statement (XI. xiv, 15; vol V, p. 336/7) that the last dynast of Armenia before the coming of Artaxias had been named Orontes, and with another of the Armawir inscriptions, which mourned the death in battle of a ruler linked with Armenia and killed by his own soldiers.

Both the interior chronology of Movsēs Xorenac'i and the reading of the Armawir inscriptions are still open to considerable disagreement, but the existence of a local Armenian dynasty, probably of Iranian origin, as indicated by both Strabo and Movsēs Χorenac'i as well as by the derivation of the Eruandid name, has now received additional corroboration. In the middle of the last century B.C. Armenia's neighbor, King Antiochos of Kommagēnē, inscribed upon his splendid funerary monument on Nemrud Dagh a list of the ancestors through whom he claimed descent from the Achaemenid kings (Toumanoff, 1963, pp. 277-94). These lists support and extend our knowledge of the Orontid/Eruandid dynasty, since they not only include the Orontes known to Xenophon in 401, but push our knowledge back to the grandfather, still named Orontes, of Xenophon's contemporary and incidentally identify Alexander's governor Mithranes as a member of the same family. Consequently, even though gaps in our knowledge still preclude the establishment of a continuous line down to the last Eruand/Orontes of Movsēs Χorenac'i and Strabo at the beginning of the second century B.C., it is already evident that the Eruandids were neither chance leaders nor appointed governors. They were powerful dynasts able to raise sizable military contingents who probably achieved royal status at the very end of the fourth century, when both the Greek authors and the Nemrud Dagh inscription begin to style "Orontes" king rather than satrap. At first, these dynasts recognized the overlordship of the Achaemenids with whom they intermarried, and occasionally that of the Seleucids, but after Alexander's conquests, the replacement of the Persians and Macedonians in 331 B.C. did not break the Eruandid control of their native land.

The accession in 188 B.C. of Artašēs/Artaxias as King of Greater Armenia has usually been taken to mark a new era in the history of Armenia, and presumably, therefore, the end of the Eruandid rule over the country. Strabo asserted that Artaxias and his colleague Zariadris were:

> generals of [the Seleucid King] Antiochos the Great . . . and these generals ruled the country, since it was turned over to them by the King; but when the King was defeated, they joined the Romans and were ranked autonomous, with the title of King.(Strabo, XI. xiv, 15; vol V, p. 336/7)

A new Artaxiad or Artašēsid dynasty then descended from this Artaxias/Artašēs. It was to rule Armenia until the dawn of the Christian era and reach its zenith in the last century B.C. with Tigran II the Great. However, newly uncovered evidence now suggests that the "new" Artaxiad dynasty was not descended from a Seleucid general alien to

Armenia, as Strabo had mistakenly assumed, but that it could trace its
ancestry back to the preceding Eruandid house.

This thesis is supported by the very names: Artaxias/Artašēs and
Zariadris/Zareh given by Strabo to his presumed Seleucid generals, since
they are Irano-Armenian and not Greek in origin. Furthermore, the most
common royal name in the Artaxiad dynasty, Tigran/Tigranes, far from
being introduced by it into Armenia, had been attributed by Xenophon
(*Cyropaedia*, III. i, 7, vol I, p. 220/1) to the "eldest son" of the Armenian
king in the days of his own contemporary Orontes some two centuries
earlier, and Movsēs Χorenac'i (I. 22, p. 111) listed "Tigran" after
"Eruand" among the most ancient Armenian kings. Finally, the most
telling evidence for the association of the Artašēsids with their Eruandid
predecessors was provided by inscriptions on boundary stones discovered
near Lake Sevan and particularly the one more recently come to light near
Tat'ew in the northeastern Armenian district of Zangezur. These inscriptions written in the official Aramaic script of the Persian chancellery speak
of "Artašēs, the son of Zareh" and "Artašēs, the Eruandid King, the good
[king] the son of Zareh . . . " (Perikhanian [1966], p. 18) As such, they
provide documentary evidence that Artašēs/Artaxias himself had officially claimed to be an Eruandid and give greater credibility to a question-
able later Armeno-Georgian tradition that Artašēs was the brother of King
Eruand. The identity of the name of Strabo's contemporary ruler of
Sophēnē, Zariadris/Zareh, with that of Artašēs' father in the inscription
suggests that he too belonged to the same house, especially since he is
known to have had a descendant called "Artanes" by Strabo, (XI. xiv, 15;
vol V, p. 336/7) whose name is probably one more Greek corruption of
the name Eruand. Thus, the evidence of the Sevan and Zangezur inscriptions, as well as that of classical and Armenian sources, support an
Eruandid connection for both Artašēs and Zareh and consequently the
absence of a clear dynastic break in Armenia at the beginning of the second
century B.C. We cannot yet trace the interrelations of the various subdivisions of the Eruandids, and both Artašēs and Zareh probably belonged to
collateral lines since neither saw fit to establish himself in the Eruandid
capital, but branches of the earlier house apparently survived in Sophēnē
and in neighboring Kommagēnē, as well as in Greater Armenia.

The Prosperity of Armenia under the Early Artašēsids

The Armenian tradition of attributing to Artašēs a major role in the
consolidation and organization of the Armenian realm appears to be

grounded in fact. The king failed in his attempt to absorb Sophēnē, and he was even briefly captured in 165 B.C. in the last attempt of the Seleucids to reassert their authority over Armenia, but his hold over Greater Armenia does not seem to have been shaken. On the contrary, we learn from Strabo (XI. xiv. 5, pp. 322/3-324/5) that Artašēs, together with Zariadris/Zareh of Sophēnē, extended his realm on all sides by wresting considerable territories from the tribes that still possessed them: Kaspianē/Kazbkʻ and Basropeda/Vaspurakan in the southeastern portion of the highlands and eastward through Azerbaijan as far as the Caspian Sea; Gogarēnē/Gugarkʻ north of Lake Sevan to the Kura River and the borders of modern Georgia; Karenitis/Karin, Xerxēnē or Derxēnē/Derǰan (Terjan) and Akilisēnē/Ekełeacʻ in the west, around the south of present-day Erzerum, and finally Taronitis/Tarōn in the south. The contemporary Roman historian Polybius called him "the ruler of the greater part of Armenia."

Artašēs founded a new city as a capital for his expanded realm, Artašat/Artaxata, or more properly Artaxiasata, "the joy of Artašēs," which Strabo (XI. xiv. 6, p. 324/5) calls "a beautiful settlement and the royal residence of the country." The city was laid out on a peninsula of nine hills at the junction of the Araxes and Mecamor (Metsamor) rivers, thus showing that Artaxias already controlled the central valley of the Araxes. The city contained a citadel on the height later called Xor Virap (Khor Virap) and was protected by extensive fortifications and a moat. Recent excavations have revealed a major urban center with paved streets, public buildings, baths, shops, and workshops of various craftsmen. Artašat's position favored its participation in the great commercial development stimulated by the coming of the Greeks, and it rapidly became a major junction point between the trade route along the valley of the Araxes leading outward to Bactria and India and the one running northward to the Black Sea (Manandyan, 1965, pp. 44-52). The considerable number of Greek coins dating from this period found on the territory of the Armenian Republic testify to the prosperity brought to this region by its transit trade.

The boundary stones bearing Artašēs' inscriptions found in Zangezur and near Lake Sevan bear tangible witness of Xorenacʻi's assertion that the king had personally supervised the apportioning and ordering of the Armenian lands. One in particular records the presence of royal fisheries established on the shores of Lake Sevan. Unfortunately, no description of the interior life of the country such as was provided by Xenophon has survived from Hellenistic Armenia, but a reference to a royal "coronant" in the Zangezur inscription (Perikhanian, p. 18) shows that this office, which was to be of major importance in medieval Armenia, already existed at this early date, and other officials may also have been present at the Artašēsid court. Perhaps most significant of all is the observation of Strabo (XI. xiv, 5, vol V. p. 324/5) that the unification of the various districts under Artašēs and Zareh had led the population of Greater Armenia and Sophēnē to "speak the same language." The Armenization of the entire area was progressing apace.

The Rise of Greek Culture in Armenia

As we have already seen, the political consequences of Alexander's conquests in the East were relatively superficial in Armenia. The attendant cultural break was to prove far more significant and lasting, as the impact of Greek/Hellenistic traditions shattered the cultural hegemony of Iran in the East. The present state of the evidence does not permit us to date with precision the path of Hellenization in Armenia, and some of its manifestations may have appeared only considerably later. By the third century B.C., however, it had unquestionably reached Sophēnē, which lay closest to the centers of Seleucid culture, and from there it seeped into Eruandid Greater Armenia as well, bringing with it new practices and institutions.

The most characteristic institution of the Greek world, the city-state, with a name usually commemorating its founder in the Hellenistic period—as did the multiple Alexandrias and Seleucias of the East—manifested itself unmistakably in the Armenian lands as Arsamosata (Aršamašat [Arshamashat]) on the Euphrates, Eruandakert, Zarehawan, Zarišat (Zarishat), and especially Artašat (Artashat) on the Araxes, thus flattering the pride of Arsames (Aršam) of Sophēnē as well as those of the Eruandids and Artašēsids. These cities introduced a new and alien element into the rural and tribal world of the plateau described by Xenophon. The closed agricultural economy was transformed by its contact with Hellenistic international commerce, and local coinage appeared for the first time in the area. Both the silver coinage of Sophēnē and of the Artašēsids, bearing the portrait of the king and Greek inscriptions, followed standard Greek models, and some of the Artašēsid kings officially proclaimed themselves "Philhellenes" on their coins.

The Greek parchment contracts discovered near the village of Avroman in the Zagros Mountains show the familiarity of the native population with the Greek language, Greek law, and the Seleucid calendar in a region bordering on Armenia. This situation is paralleled in the heartland of the Araxes Valley by the Greek inscriptions from Armawir, among which can be found a listing of the Macedonian months and references to the Greek classics such as Hesiod and Euripides. According to Movsēs Xorenac'i (II. 40, p. 182), Eruand founded the city of Bagaran to place there the statues of the "idols" he had brought from Armawir and which were subsequently transported to Artašat by Artašēs, who is said to have also brought bronze statues of the Greek gods Zeus, Artemis, Herakles, and Apollo to Armenia from the west. Xorenac'i's (II, 12, 77, pp. 148, 225) claim that Eruand and Artašēs had established in Armenia shrines served by priests and supported by large estates including numerous slaves seems substantiated by a fragmentary inscription at Armawir recording the dedication of four horses with a chariot and a small statue. Excavations at Armawir and Artašat are only beginning, but they have uncovered objects of unmistakable Hellenic type.

Despite this onslaught of Hellenism, however, Iranian culture remained deeply rooted on the Armenian plateau. The names of all the Eruandid and Artašēsid kings are Iranian in origin. The Armawir inscriptions are unquestionably written in Greek, but their haphazard placement on the face of two rocks brings them close to the level of graffiti, whereas the Aramaic of the Persian chancellery is reserved for the official inscriptions of Artašēs in Zangezur and elsewhere. Artašēsid dignitaries such as the royal coronant known to Xorenac'i (II, vii, p. 136), belong in an Iranian and not a Greek world, as does the Zoroastrian pantheon of Ahura-Mazda, Mithra, Anahita, and Vahagn, even though they seem to have been identified at times with their Greek equivalents in accordance with the syncretism fashionable throughout the Hellenistic world. The very name of the Eruandid holy city of Bagaran, composed of the Iranian *baga* "god" and the suffix of place *-aran,* points to the Iranian antecedents of such "divine places," and we find numerous additional examples, such as Bagrewand, Bagawan, Bagayaṙič (Bagaharich), in Armenia. The excavations of Artašat have brought up clay plaques bearing the representation of the Iranian "heroic rider" as well as statuettes of Greek type. Perhaps the most tangible examples of the hybrid cultural traditions developing through most of Transcaucasia are to be found at present on the borders of Armenia: in the south at Nemrud Dagh, where King Antiochos of Kommagēnē (Commagene) traced his ancestry to both the Achaemenids and Alexander the Great, and is shown receiving his investiture from the Greek Herakles as well as the Iranian Mithra; and in the north at the excavations near Tbilisi, where purely classical silver vases lay in graves side by side with the Iranian horse bowls of the Mithraic cult, and the epitaph of the young wife of a local magnate was written in both Greek and Aramaic.

The new Greek elements unquestionably enriched the culture of the Armenian highlands, and Armenia prospered in the Hellenistic period as it became a part of the wider Mediterranean world. Hellenization presented no direct threat in the early Artašēsid period, and the combination of Iranian and Greek traditions helped to produce an increasingly complex and sophisticated Armenian civilization. Nevertheless, from this time on the Armenians would never find themselves again inside a united homogeneous world. As Armenia slowly proceeded in the last centuries preceding the Christian era to the status of a "buffer state," the opposing cultural and more ominously political pressures of the Mediterranean and Oriental worlds eventually increased, threatening at times its unity and its identity.

Armenia under Tigran the Great (95–55 B.C.)

The threat of foreign domination was still distant from Armenia in the second and first centuries B.C. and the temporary absence of external pressures favored the rise of local ambitions. The Seleucids, increasingly embroiled in family quarrels, were in no position to assert their authority outside their diminishing realm. The renaissance of Iran under the new Parthian dynasty of the Arsacids was still being consolidated. Rome had not yet fully committed itself to the tumultuous struggle for power in the Near East into which it was being reluctantly drawn, though its antagonism to the Seleucids could already help local rulers, such as Artašēs and Zareh, to free themselves from the suzerainty of King Antiochos III. The growing resentment of the Oriental population toward their western conquerors, which was soon to explode in the general massacre of Romans in the East in 88 B.C., could be exploited. Conditions were ripe for a bid for power in Armenia.

Not much is known concerning the period between the reign of Artašēs I and the accession of Tigran II in Armenia. The contradictory genealogies of narrative accounts have been clarified by the numismatic evidence, so that it is now clear that Artašēs I was succeeded by two of his sons: Artawazd (Artavazd) I, followed by Tigran I, the father of the

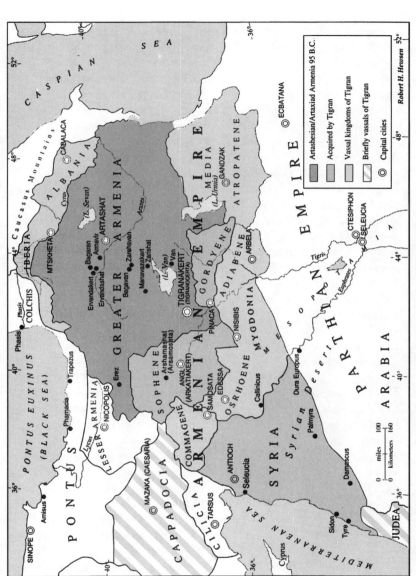

5. *THE EMPIRE OF TIGRAN THE GREAT, FIRST CENTURY B.C.*

future Tigran II the Great. Artawazd I was defeated in the first Parthian attack on Armenia at the end of the reign of the Arsacid king Mithradates I (128-88 B.C.) and forced to surrender his nephew as a hostage, but nothing is known of the reign of Tigran I beyond a few copper coins that have now been attributed to him and support the claim of the Roman historian Appian ("The Syrian Wars," viii, 48, p. 196/7) that Tigran the Great and the king his father had borne the same name. Sources are plentiful, on the contrary, for the reign of Tigran II in which the Artašēsid dynasty reached its zenith, but our knowledge of it derives almost exclusively from Roman writers invariably hostile to a ruler who had posed a major threat to Roman power in the East. They often present a distorted image requiring rectification, and they are only partly complemented by Tigran's extensive coinage and the imperfect memories preserved in Armenian accounts composed many centuries later.

To obtain his release at his father's death in 95 B.C. Tigran II was compelled to return to Parthia "seventy valleys" (Strabo, XI, xiv, 15, p. 338/9), probably those conquered by Artašēs I in the direction of Azerbaijan, but immediately upon his accession he returned to Artašēs' expansionist policy. His first move was to absorb the neighboring kingdom of Sophēnē, which his grandfather had failed to conquer, thus consolidating most of the Eruandid lands under his power. So far, Artašēsid policy had attracted little attention from the West, but Tigran's next move brought him into conflict with Roman interests. The marriage alliance concluded by him with his northwestern neighbor, King Mithradates VI of Pontus, whose kingdom included the lands of Armenia Minor, led Tigran to support his father-in-law's attempt to annex the adjacent Kingdom of Cappadocia. Provoked by this attack on one of its clients, the Roman Senate sent the general Sulla to drive Mithradates' young son from Cappadocia and to conclude in 92 B.C. an agreement with King Mithradates II of Parthia that first set the Euphrates River as the boundary between the Roman and Iranian worlds.

Armenia's first encounter with the Romans was inconclusive. The Pontic candidate was soon replaced on the Cappadocian throne, but for some two decades thereafter Tigran did not participate in the bitter conflict opposing Pontus to the Roman state, although he may have renewed his treaty of alliance with Mithradates VI. His attention was focused on the more threatening Parthian Empire to the east of Armenia. Making the most of Parthia's temporary weakness at the death of Mithradates II and of the distracting attacks of Central Asiatic nomads on its eastern border, Tigran began the reconquest of the territories ceded at his accession. A series of campaigns between 88 and 85 B.C. carried the Armenian armies to the gates of the Arsacid summer residence at Hamadan in Media, extending the Artašēsid Empire over the principalities of Atropatēnē, Gordiēnē, Adiabēnē, Osrhoēnē, and Mygdonia in modern Iranian Azerbaijan and Mesopotamia, in a series of victories that justified Tigran's assumption of the Achaemenid title of King of Kings, which appears on his coins after 85 B.C.

If Tigran's Parthian campaigns were in part a retaliation for the earlier humiliation of Armenia by the Arsacids, his southern conquests were not altogether his own initiative. Weary of the anarchy caused by the constant quarrels of the Seleucids, a Syrian party offered to crown the new conqueror of the East. Turning southward, Tigran annexed Kommagēnē, the Cilician plain, northern Syria, and coastal Phoenicia, and perhaps imposed his overlordship on the Kingdom of Judea, although these campaigns probably proved more difficult than some sources imply. In 84-83 he apparently occupied the Syrian capital of Antioch, as is evidenced by the silver tetradrachms bearing the king's portrait on one side and on the other the fortune of the city represented by a woman wearing a turreted crown and holding the palm of victory. Even hostile Roman authors admit that Syria enjoyed thirteen years of peace under Tigran's rule. His empire now stretched from the Mediterranean to the Caspian Sea.

The Roman republic, occupied by the continued war with Mithradates of Pontus (Appian, "The Mithridatic Wars") and troubled by internal party strife, did not interfere with Tigran's conquests directed against the Parthians and the Seleucids. The Armenian King of Kings was consequently left free to organize his multinational and multicultural empire. No uniform pattern seems to have been imposed on the new territories, all of which paid tribute and supplied military contingents. The Greek cities kept their institutions and some even struck their own coinage. Four vassal kings were in perpetual attendance on Tigran's person, if Plutarch ("Lucullus," XXL, 5, p. 536/7) is to be believed, but as a rule the conquered territories merely acknowledged his suzerainty and preserved their internal autonomy with a few exceptions. Tigran's brother was installed in the important city of Nisibis, which controlled the East–West trade route through Mesopotamia. Nomadic Arabs were resettled in the area to assist in the transport of goods over the Euphrates. In general, massive shifts of population are characteristic of this reign, and a persistent Armenian tradition attributes the settlement of a Jewish population in the cities of Greater Armenia to the policy of Tigran the

Great. A general named Magdates or more correctly Bagdates ruled over the Syrian territories. The figures given by ancient writers for the Armenian armies are unquestionably inflated, but they indicate a powerful war machine largely composed of heavily armored cavalry and experienced in siege warfare.

Since the old Artašēsid capital of Artašat on the Araxes was too remote for the government of the extended empire, Tigran II chose a location far to the south in the early seventies for the new capital to which he gave his name. The site of Tigranakert/Tigranocerta continues to be disputed, since it cannot yet be confirmed by archaeological evidence. We learn from Appian ("The Mithridatic Wars," XII. 84, pp. 398/9) that the city was surrounded by (turreted?) walls fifty cubits (22 meters) high, the base of which was filled with stables and contained a citadel. A palace with "large parks, hunting grounds and lakes," as well as "a strong fortress" were erected nearby and the city also contained a theater. To fill this new capital Tigran forcibly removed the population from the cities of Mesopotamia, Cilicia, and particularly Cappadocia, which he had invaded again in 78 B.C. Strabo and Appian probably exaggerate grossly when they speak of the population of twelve destroyed Greek cities or of the 300,000 Greeks moved from Mazaka (later Caesarea/Kayseri) in Cappadocia (Strabo, XI. xiv, 15; XII. ii, 9; vol. V, pp. 338/9, 366/7. Appian, "The Mithridatic Wars," X. 67, pp. 364/5), but Appian insists that the city was "founded on an ambitious scale" and Plutarch adds that "the city was also full of wealth . . . since every private person and every prince vied with the King in contributing to its increase and adornment" (Plutarch, "Lucullus," xxvi, 2, pp. 552/3). The wealth and power of Tigran, increased by his control of the great cities of Syria and Phoenicia and of the transit trade through Mesopotamia, had become legendary by the days of Movsēs Xorenac'i:

> Who among true men and those who appreciate deeds of valor and prudence would not be stirred by his memory and aspire to become such a man? He was supreme among men and by showing his valor he glorified our nation. Those who had been under a yoke he put in a position to subject and demand tribute from many. He multiplied the stores of gold and silver and precious stones, of garments and brocades of various colors, both for men and women, with the help of which the ugly appeared as wonderful as the handsome, and the handsome were altogether deified at the time . . . The bringer of peace

and prosperity, he fattened everyone with oil and honey . . . over all
alike he spread the mantle of his care. (Movses Khorenats'i, I. 24,
pp. 113-14)

This is again an undoubted exaggeration, nevertheless, even Plutarch
admitted ("Lucullus," xxi, 2, pp. 536/7), albeit ungraciously, that "the
King . . . had become pompous and haughty in the midst of his great
prosperity," and the almost contemporary Roman historian Velleius
Paterculus (II. xxxiii, 1, pp. 120/1) conceded that Tigran II was the
"greatest of Kings."

Armenia's increased contact with the more Hellenized regions of
Syria and Pontus as a result of Tigran's conquests and alliances also bore
fruit. The Armenian court was profoundly Hellenized under the influence of its queen, Cleopatra of Pontus, and Greek rhetoricians and
philosophers were welcomed as guests and advisors of the royal family.
A troupe of Greek actors was summoned to inaugurate the theater built
at Tigranakert (Plutarch, "Lucullus," xxix, 4, pp. 566/7). Greek was
probably the language of the court, since Tigran's son and heir Artawazd
II wrote, in Greek, tragedies, orations, and historical works, some of
which were still known in the second century A.D., and Euripides'
famous play *The Bacchae,* was performed at his sister's wedding to the
Parthian heir (Plutarch, "Crassus," xxxiii, pp. 420/1, 422/3).

The brilliance of this Hellenic culture should not blind us, however, to the survival of the Iranian tradition that helped preserve Armenia
from the total assimilation of Cappadocia or Pontus. Both Tigran's title
of King of Kings and the pearl tiara with the star of divinity in which he
is invariably represented on his coins belong to the Persian world. It is
not certain whether the four kings attending Tigran at all times were the
ancestors of the great marcher lords, the *bdešxs* (*bdeshkh*s), so familiar
to the fifth century A.D. Armenian authors, but the court ceremonial was
Iranian and the presence of a vassal nobility is an element alien to the
Classical world. The pleasure gardens and the hunting preserves laid out
at Tigranakert (Appian, "The Mithridatic Wars," xii, 67, pp. 398/9) are
precisely the "paradises" (Armenian *partēz*) enjoyed by the Arsacid
nobility in Iran and subsequently recorded repeatedly in Armenia. We
know little of the structure of the country outside the court, but the
familiarity of the Roman author of the first century A.D., Pliny the Elder
(*Natural History,* VI. x, 27; vol. II, pp. 356/7), with the "120 strategies"
composing Armenia one century later suggests that the social pattern of
great autonomous families each controlling its own lands, so character-

istic of medieval Armenia and the Parthian realm but unknown to the Roman system, was already developing in Tigranid Armenia. Thus, the philhellenism of the Armenian court does not seem to have set deep roots, nor did it impress the Romans, who invariably viewed Tigran with hostility as a haughty and arrogant Oriental monarch.

The peace imposed by Tigran II did not prove long-lasting, as the imperialist party in the Roman Senate decided to put an end to the drain of the Mithridatic wars and impose its own solution on the East. Tigran delayed the opening of hostilities to the maximum, but late in 71 B.C. Appius Claudius, the legate of the Roman general Lucullus, brought an ultimatum to Antioch. Insolently addressing Tigran as "King" rather than by his official title of King of Kings, Appius Claudius demanded the surrender of the defeated King Mithradates VI of Pontus, who had taken refuge in Armenia. War followed soon upon Tigran's refusal to surrender his father-in-law (Plutarch, "Lucullus," xxi, pp. 534/5, 538/9). In the spring of 69 B.C. Lucullus, who had succeeded in winning over some of Tigran's vassals, suddenly crossed the Euphrates near Melitēnē and marched across Sophēnē directly on Tigranakert. Unprepared to meet this unexpected attack, Tigran withdrew from the capital to join forces with Mithradates and summon his vassals, most of whom seem to have still obeyed. An attempt to raise the siege of the capital succeeded in rescuing the king's treasure and his harem, but the main Armenian army was severely defeated by the Romans near the city. Betrayed by its Greek garrison, Tigranakert finally fell to the besiegers. The enormous booty found in the still unfinished ten-year-old city, even after the removal of the royal treasury, amazed its conquerors, according to Plutarch (Plutarch, "Lucullus," XXX, 2-4, pp. 566/7; Strabo XI, xiv, 15; vol. V. pp. 338/9); Appian, "The Mithridatic Wars," XII pp. 402-3), and provides an additional index of the wealth of Armenia in this period.

The fall of Tigranakert marked the end of Tigran's control of Kommagēnē, Syria, and Mesopotamia, except for Nisibis, as his vassals turned their allegiance to Rome. Even so, the core of the Armenian kingdom was still untouched. Supported by Mithradates and his own son-in-law, the king of Atropatēnē, Tigran harried the Romans while Lucullus struggled to make his way northward to the old capital of Artašat. Sapped by the absence of supplies along the way and delayed by Armenian guerrilla activity, the Romans reached the plateau at the beginning of winter as roads became impassable. The threat of mutiny forced Lucullus to turn back to Mesopotamia, where he succeeded in capturing Nisibis (Plutarch, "Lucullus," xxxi-xxxii, pp. 572/3, 578/9).

Meanwhile, Mithradates reentered Pontus, and Tigran had already begun the reconquest of territories north of the Tigris and in Cappadocia when Lucullus was recalled to Rome in 67 B.C.

Unfortunately for Armenia, the Roman decision to subdue the East remained unaltered, and the new general Pompey counted on victory to support his bid for power at Rome. The first blow fell in 66 B.C. on Mithradates, who was defeated and fled northward to the eastern shore of the Black Sea. Tigran the Great, faced with the rebellion of his sons Zareh and Tigran the Younger, did not participate at first. But as the younger Tigran took refuge with his father-in-law, the king of Parthia, Armenia soon found itself attacked on all sides.

The Parthian king failed in his attempt to capture Artašat, whose fortifications withstood his assault, but the younger Tigran then turned for help to Pompey, whom he guided to his father's capital in the hope of being rewarded with the throne. Unable to save Artašat, and in order to prevent its sharing the fate of Tigranakert, Tigran II agreed to make his submission to Pompey from whose hands he received back the royal diadem, thus acknowledging the Roman protectorate over Armenia. The peace of 66 B.C. stripped Tigran of all his conquests in Syria, Phoenicia, Mesopotamia, Atropatēnē, Cilicia, Kommagēnē and even Sophēnē, reducing his realm to Greater Armenia proper. A formidable indemnity of 6,000 talents plus additional gifts to each of the Roman soldiers was required of Armenia, and the younger Tigran, to whom Sophēnē had first been offered but who continued to prove untrustworthy, was sent with his family to Rome to be displayed in Pompey's triumph (Plutarch, "Pompey," xxxiii, pp. 202/3-204/5). In spite of this, the situation was by no means desperate. Pompey proclaimed Tigran II a friend of the Roman people, thus halting any further attacks on the Armenian heartland, which remained untouched, and even returned to him considerable territories in Mesopotamia. Still bearing the title of King of Kings, acknowledged to him by Pompey, in spite of the objections of Parthia, Tigran II ruled peacefully for another decade before dying in extreme old age in 56 or 55 B.C.

The far-flung empire of Tigran the Great was probably not viable, since no cohesive framework held together such disparate elements as the Greek cities and the eastern principalities with varying languages and customs. Hellenized and urban Syro-Mesopotamia had little in common with the essentially rural and tribal Armenian plateau. If the surviving references to Arabs and Jews are correct, the transit trade through Armenia remained primarily in foreign hands. No allegiance tied the forcibly moved population to Tigran. The imported Greek garrison of Tigranakert betrayed it to the Romans, and the displaced groups went home at the first opportunity. But in any case, the beneficial vacuum of power that had favored the rise of Tigran II no longer existed by the middle of the first century B.C. Instead, the revived power of the Parthian Arsacid and Roman imperialism faced each other across the Euphrates and in Mesopotamia in an endemic war that was to last for centuries. The time was past for local initiatives throughout the East, and Armenia did not have the power base to take on the two world powers on either side. Nevertheless, the forty-year reign of Tigran the Great may well have provided the interval of peace needed for the development of Greater Armenia and the nexus of clan relationships that were to preserve the Armenian identity in the troubled years to come.

The End of the Artašēsid Dynasty (55 B.C.–A.D. 6)

Tigran II's son and successor, Artawazd II (55-34 B.C.), tried to make the best of Armenia's new position as a buffer state and to preserve his equilibrium in the repeated campaigns of Rome against Parthia. He offered the support of the Armenian cavalry to the Roman general Crassus in 53 and sought to advise him against the dangerous southern route, which took the Romans to the disastrous defeat of Carrhae in Mesopotamia. He then gave his sister in marriage to the Parthian heir and participated in raids against the Roman province in Syria from 42 to 40 B.C. The letters of Cicero, who was proconsul of Cilicia in 51 B.C., show that the Romans had become suspicious of Artawazd's intentions. These suspicions greatly intensified with Marc Antony's campaign in the East in 37 B.C. during the last throes of the Roman civil war. The withdrawal of the Armenian army, which had first accompanied Antony on his unsuccessful campaign to Atropatēnē, was viewed as a betrayal, although the returning Romans were received and supplied in Armenia, and Antony's vengeance was not long delayed. After an attempt to lure Artawazd to Egypt in 35 B.C., Antony marched on Artašat the following year and finally succeeded in bringing the Armenian king to his camp. The Romans occupied and looted Armenia (Dio, XLIX. 39-41; vol. V, pp. 420/1, 424/5), and Artawazd with most of his family was carried as a captive to Egypt (where Antony celebrated his triumph, commemorated by a coin bearing a representation of the Armenian royal tiara and the legend ANTONI ARMENIA DEVICTA) and eventually executed (Strabo,

XI. xiv, 15; vol V, pp. 338/9-340/1). His kingdom was bestowed on Alexander Helios "the Sun," Antony's six-year-old son by the Egyptian queen Cleopatra VII, while one of Artawazd's sons, the future Artašēs II, fled to Parthia. The memory of Artawazd's disappearance to Egypt lingered on in the folk memory of the Armenian people in the legend recorded by Movsēs Xorenac'i (II. 61, pp. 203-4) that partly confused him with his treacherous brother Tigran the Younger. In it, Artawazd had been cursed by his father for his undutiful behavior and consequently was held prisoner by the *k'aǰ (kadj)* inside the "free Masis," yet Armenia still awaited his ultimate return.

The fate of the Artašēsid dynasty was all but settled with the death of Artawazd II, although Antony's son Alexander Helios never set foot in Armenia and some six Artašesids ruled briefly over the next generation, still claiming sovereignty on their coinage. Supported by the Parthians, Artawazd's son Artašēs II was reinstated in Armenia for ten years and avenged his father's death by the massacre of the Roman garrisons found in the country. But at his murder in 20 B.C., the Armenian crown became for all purposes a mere stake in the quarrels of the Roman emperor Augustus with the Parthians, and Armenia broke up into pro- and anti-Roman parties. To use Augustus' own words in his political testament:

> In the case of Greater Armenia, though I might have made it a province after the assassination of King Artaxes [Artašés II], I preferred, following the precedent of our fathers, to hand that kingdom over to Tigranes [Tigran III, 20-8/6 B.C.], the son of King Artavasdes [Artawazd III], and grandson of King Tigranes, through Tiberius Nero who was then my stepson. And later, when the same people revolted and rebelled, and was subdued by my son Gaius, I gave it over to King Ariobarzanes the son of Artabazus, King of the Medes, to rule [A.D. 2-4], and after his death to his son Artavazdes [Artawazd IV, A.D. 4-6]. When he was murdered I sent into that kingdom Tigranes [Tigran V, ca. A.D. 6], who was sprung from the royal family of the Armenians. (*Res Gestae Divi Augusti,* V. xxvi, pp. 390/1)

The account of Augustus is slightly simplified since it omits Tigran III's brother Artawazd III [5-2 B.C.], but it amply shows the interference of Rome in the internal affairs of Armenia. On their side, the Parthians supported the opposition party, which briefly succeeded in placing Tigran III's son, Tigran IV, on the Armenian throne on two separate occasions (8-5 B.C. and 2 B.C.–A.D. 1), together with his sister-wife Erato, who, on the basis of numismatic evidence, seems to have ruled again with Tigran V (ca. A.D. 6) as well. The autonomy of the Artašēsid dynasty was clearly at an end. Artawazd III might still style himself King of Kings on his coins, although the economic situation of Armenia apparently no longer permitted silver coins but only copper, but for a time at least, the gold issue of Augustus bearing the legend ARMENIA CAPTA was probably closer to reality.

FOR FURTHER INFORMATION

For the sources of, or more information on, the material in this chapter, please consult the following (full citations can be found in the Bibliography at the end of this volume).

Adontz, 1970.   Dandamaev and Lukonin, 1988.
Bedoukian, 1978.   Der Nersessian, 1969.
The Cambridge History of Iran   Hewsen, 1983, 1984.
Chaumont, 1982.   Manandyan, 1963, 1965.
Chronicles of the Chaldoean   Perikhanian, 1967.
    Kings, 1961.   Russell, 1987.
Dandamaev, 1990.   Toumanoff, 1963, 1966.

THE ARTAŠĒSID (ARTASHESIAN)/ARTAXIAD DYNASTY

All dates are B.C. unless otherwise indicated. Some dates are approximative and still in doubt. Names in brackets are not members of this dynasty.

Artašēs (Artashes)/Artaxias I, 188-c.165?

Artawazd (Artavazd) I

Tigran I

Tigran/Tigranes II, 95-55

Artawazd (Artavazd) II, 55-34

[Alexander Helios]

Artašēs (Artashes) II, c.30-20

Tigran III, 20-8/6

Tigran IV, 8-5

Artawazd (Artavazd) III, 5-2

Tigran IV and Erato, 2 B.C.–A.D. 1?

[Ariobarzanes, A.D. 2-4]

Artawazd (Artavazd) IV, A.D. 4-6

Tigran V and Erato, c.A.D. 6-14

4

THE ARŠAKUNI DYNASTY
(A.D. 12–[180?]–428)

Nina Garsoïan

The First Two Centuries

The chaos that marked the end of the Artašesid dynasty in Armenia did not abate with its disappearance, and the rivalry of Rome and Iran for the control of the highlands strategically placed between them was to continue for centuries. Even so, Greater Armenia fared better than its neighbors in that it succeeded in preserving its identity and institutions as a dependent kingdom with some internal autonomy instead of being totally annexed by the Romans, reduced to the status of province, and gradually assimilated, as was to be the fate of all the adjacent kingdoms of Syria, Kommagēnē, Cappadocia, Pontus, Sophēnē, and even of the lands of Armenia Minor west of the Euphrates River at which the emperor Augustus set the eastern border of the Roman Empire.

Our knowledge of the events or even the chronology of Armenia during this complicated period remains fragmentary in the extreme, confused, and still highly debated. The main sources of information continue to be the occasional references in classical authors, the most important of whom are the Roman historians Tacitus, Dio Cassius, and Ammianus Marcellinus writing between the second and fourth centuries in the Christian era. These can occasionally be supplemented by coins and a few inscriptions whose damaged state makes them difficult to date and gives the possibility for widely differing interpretations. In the third century, the royal inscriptions of the Sasanian kings of Persia, as well as those of the contemporary Zoroastrian high priest, are indispensable material, but they too are far from being as extensive and explicit as one might wish. The Armenians must still wait until the late fifth century for the records, notorious for the confusion of their chronology, of their own past, which was already growing dim with time. The archaeological evidence for this period remains to date scant. Consequently, very little is known of the internal life of the country during the first three centuries of the Christian era except by inference from later sources, as we shall see, and even its political framework still contains many gaps and problems.

The Arsacids in Armenia

The first appearance in Armenia of the Parthian Arsacid (Armenian Aršakuni/Arshakuni) dynasty, which was eventually destined to hold the undisputed crown of the country, dates as early as A.D. 12 when a member of this family, the King of Kings Vonones, driven from Parthia for his pro-Roman tendencies, managed to cling to the Armenian throne. This was, however, but a fleeting claim, since Vonones was expelled by the Romans some three years later. In A.D. 18, the heir of the emperor Tiberius solemnly crowned at Artašat a Pontic prince named Zeno who took at his accession the name Artaxias/Artašēs, more acceptable to his new subjects (Tacitus, II. lvi, vol. II, pp. 474/5), whose tastes he shared, and reminiscent of their former kings. Zeno/Artašēs seems to have reigned undisturbed until his death in A.D. 35, but the Parthian king had no intention of relinquishing the Arsacid claim to Armenia, on which he repeatedly, if unsuccessfully, attempted to impose his sons. The Roman candidates, who form what might be called a brief Iberian or Georgian interlude beginning in A.D. 37 on the Armenian throne, were only a little more successful. The Parthian king Vologeses (Armenian Vałaršak [Vagharshak]) set out to install his younger brother Tiridates/Trdat on the throne of Armenia, which he considered to have been "once the property of his ancestors, now usurped by a foreign monarch in virtue of a crime," (Tacitus, XII, l; vol. III, pp. 388/9) and he occupied the two capitals of Artašat and Tigranakert without opposition from the native population, which generally seems to have preferred the Parthians to the Romans insofar as we can judge. An Armenian

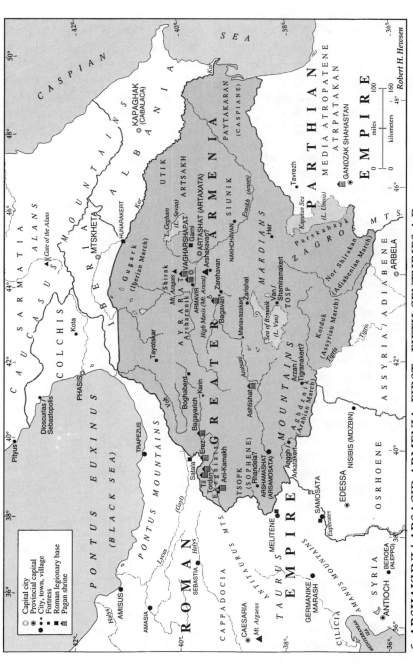

6. ARSHAKUNI / ARSACID ARMENIA, FIRST - FIFTH CENTURIES A.D.

Robert H. Hewsen

revolt compelled the Iberian prince supported by the Romans to flee
northward to Iberia, abandoning his pregnant wife whom, according to
Tacitus, he stabbed and threw into the Araxes to prevent her capture by
the enemy, but who was rescued and received at Artašat with royal
honors by Trdat (Tacitus, XII. li; vol III, pp. 388/9-390/1). The Iberian
prince was put to death by his own father a few years later (Tacitus, XIII.
xxxvii; vol. IV, pp. 60-61), and the "Iberian interlude" came to an end
after less than two decades.

By 53 the Parthian Arsacid control of Armenia seemed assured,
but the scales turned once again, and Trdat I was to wait more than ten
years for the undisputed enjoyment of his throne. New Roman legions
were sent to Syria and the East at the accession of the emperor Nero
in 54 under the command of the empire's best general, Corbulo, and
two client states were set up in Sophēnē and Armenia Minor to assist
in the encirclement of Greater Armenia. Negotiations may have been
attempted by the Parthians, but late in 57 Corbulo moved his troops
into winter quarters near Karin/Erzerum and Armenia's neighbors
were encouraged to harry its borders. In the spring Corbulo marched
directly on the Armenian capital undeterred by Armenia guerrillas.
Horrified by the capture of the fortress of Volandum/Olane (Armenian
Ołakan [Oghakan]) and the execution of its entire adult population,
Artašat opened its gates to the Romans only to be set on fire and razed
to the ground (Tacitus, XIII. xli; vol. IV, pp. 70/1), though Trdat
himself could not be captured and fled eastward. Tigranakert surrendered in its turn in the following spring of 59 (Tacitus, XIV. xxiv; vol.
IV, pp. 146/7-148/9). Nero triumphantly celebrated Corbulo's victories. A new Roman candidate from the royal house of Judea, who may
have had a trace of Artašēsid (Artashesid) blood, was installed at
Tigranakert under the protection of a Roman garrison; and Armenian
border districts were distributed to allied rulers in Pontus, Iberia,
Kommagēnē and Armenia Minor.

Despite this serious setback, the Parthian Arsacids did not abandon
their Armenian claim. Trdat was formally crowned king of Armenia by
his brother before the approving Parthian magnates. The Roman garrison was forced to withdraw from Tigranakert with its candidate, although the Parthians failed to take the city. The Romans were now
considering a policy of outright annexation of Armenia, even though the
Arsacids were showing their willingness to negotiate, when the inepti-
tude of the new Roman commander Paetus altered the situation and
helped to bring about a compromise. Trapped in the southern fortress of

Rhandeia, not far from modern Kharput (Kharpert), Paetus was compelled to surrender and to agree to evacuate Armenia in 62. Negotiations began anew the following year, and the continued willingness of the Arsacids to compromise in the face of another Roman army once more commanded by Corbulo finally brought the conflict to a close in 63. Again at Rhandeia, Trdat I laid down his diadem before an effigy of Nero and agreed to go to Rome in order to receive it back from the emperor in person (Tacitus, XV. xv-xvi; vol. IV, pp. 238/9-240/1. CD, LXII; vol. VIII, pp. 120/1, 126/7). The so-called Compromise of Rhandeia provided a solution tolerable for both sides. A junior branch of the Parthian Arsacid/Aršakuni house would reign in Armenia, but it would receive its crown from the Roman emperor. Rome's choice of candidates was limited by the obligation to choose a member of the Arsacid house.

The long journey of Trdat I to Rome and the magnificent ceremonies of his coronation by Nero struck the imagination of the contemporaries who have left detailed accounts. Following Zoroastrian practices, the Armenian king traveled by land so as not to pollute the sea. He was accompanied by his wife, wearing a gold helmet to cover her face instead of a veil, by some 3,000 Parthian cavalry, by a Roman contingent, and by Magian priests (CD, LXII, vol. VIII, pp. 138/9-140/1). In 66 he finally reached Italy and was received at Naples by Nero to whom he did homage and who organized gladiatorial games in his honor. The coronation took place in Rome, which had been entirely "decorated with lights and garlands" for the occasion (CD, LXII, vol. VIII, pp. 138/9-140/1). At daybreak Nero in triumphal dress, attended by the Senate and surrounded by the army on parade, seated himself on the rostra before the crowd that filled the Forum. Trdat knelt before him and again acknowledged vassality in terms that contained the formula proclaiming the supernatural attributes of the Iranian sovereign, of which this seems to be the first occurrence known to date:

> Master . . . I have come to thee, my god, to worship thee as I do
> Mithras. The destiny thou spinnest for me shall be mine, for thou art
> my *Fortune and my Fate*. (Dio, LXII; vol. VIII, pp. 142/43)

Highly pleased, Nero then placed the diadem on Trdat's head and proceeded to entertain him in the theater of Pompey, which had been entirely covered with gold for the occasion and shaded from the sun by purple curtains stretched overhead, "so that people gave to the day itself the epithet of 'golden.'" The festivities continued with banquets, and Trdat may in turn have initiated Nero into certain Magian rites, if we are to believe their contemporary Pliny the Elder. At Trdat's departure, Nero presented him with 2,000,000 sesterces and, more important, with the permission to rebuild the destroyed capital of Artašat. Trdat I raised the capital again with the help of artisans given to him by Nero; and renamed it Neroneia in honor of the emperor (Dio, LXII; vol. VIII, pp. 146/7).

We know very little of Trdat's reign after his coronation. The Armenian sources are curiously silent, ignoring even his name, although the memory of the installation of a junior Aršakuni in Armenia by his brother the Parthian king and the subsequent ordering of the kingdom has been preserved in Xorenac'i's account, which however confuses and alters the names of the protagonists. We know of a new barbarian invasion of Armenia raiding down through the Caucasian passes, in which Trdat I barely escaped capture in 72 or 73, and perhaps of a war with Iberia, if an Aramaic inscription found near Tbilisi has been correctly read. Trdat probably also repaired the fortress of Gařni, where he erected a building for his sister-queen. The famous Greek inscription found at Gařni in 1945 refers to Trdat as "the sun" and as "supreme ruler of Greater Armenia." Unfortunately, the damaged state of the inscription permits widely differing readings, which are far from resolved. A parallel passage of Movsēs Xorenac'i states that

> Trdat completed the construction of the fortress of Gařni in hard and dressed blocks of stone cemented with iron [clamps] and lead. Inside, for his sister Khosrovidukht, he built a shaded residence with towers and wonderful carvings in high relief. And he composed in her memory an inscription in the Greek script. (Movses Khorenats'i, II. 90, p. 247)

But this confuses the situation by attributing the activity to Trdat III in the third/fourth century. On the basis of building techniques and pale-ography, most scholars have preferred Trdat I, but the controversy is not yet at an end. Meanwhile, Armenia Minor was definitely set on a separate path of de-Armenization as the emperor Vespasian incorpo-rated it in 72 into the Roman province of Cappadocia-Galatia.

Although the coronation of 66 is usually given as the inauguration of Aršakuni rule over the country, Armenian history enters a particularly obscure period after the disappearance of any reference to Trdat I in the sources ca. 75. The main problem, as usual, is the total inadequacy of the information on the classical side, especially in the third century, when the Roman Empire itself was plunged into chaos. Compounding this difficulty, Armenian historians improbably record only three or even two kings for the span of a century and a half between 145 and 325. Finally, both classical and Armenian sources know of a King Sanatruces/Sanatruk associated by the Armenians with the martyrdom of the apostle Thaddeus and presumably buried in the royal necropolis of the Armenian Arsacids at Ani-Kamax (Ani-Kamakh) on the upper Euphrates. Unfortunately, Sanatruk has been made to appear and disappear like the Cheshire cat at various dates, some scholars have further confused matters by mistakenly identifying his opponent as the Roman emperor Septimus Severus (193-211) instead of Trajan's governor of Armenia, L. Catilius Severus (ca. 116/7). Reconstructions of Armenian history in this period consequently disagree greatly.

Certain scholars have proposed this Sanatruk as the successor of Trdat between 75 and 110, but this hypothesis, for which there is no explicit evidence, has been categorically rejected by others. The first secure information we possess dates from the attempt of the emperor Trajan (98-117) to break the "Compromise of Rhandeia," and impose total Roman control on Armenia. The Armenian king at the time was presumably an Aršakuni and the son of the Parthian king. He was deposed in 113, "inasmuch as he had been satisfactory neither to the Romans nor the Parthians" (Dio, LXVIII, vol. VIII, pp. 394/5), and replaced on the Armenian throne by another son of the Parthian ruler who voluntarily came to meet Trajan not far from Erzinjan, expecting to receive back "the kingdom as Tiridates had received it from Nero." Trajan, however, replied that "he would surrender Armenia to no one, for it belonged to the Romans and was to have a Roman governor." The Armenian king was permitted to depart, but was murdered by his escort on the way, and Armenia was annexed outright for the first time. Trajan's coins for 115/6 celebrate this new status with the legend ARMENIA ET MESOPOTAMIA IN POTES-TATEM P[OPULI] R[OMANI] REDACTAE, claiming that Armenia had been "returned" to the Roman people. Inscriptions attest the presence of Roman troops at Artašat (Artashat). Armenia was fused with Cappadocia and Armenia Minor in one large province governed by L. Catilius Severus, while its financial administration was entrusted to another Roman official, and the XV Legion Apollinaris was probably moved to Satala/Satał (Satagh) in northeastern Armenia Minor as an advance base for the control of Greater Armenia.

This violation of Armenia's autonomy proved extremely brief. Even before Trajan's death in 117 the Armenians were in revolt, perhaps under the elusive Sanatruk, whom a number of sources link with this period. In any case, the new emperor Hadrian returned to the earlier compromise formula. "The Armenians were permitted to have their own king, whereas under Trajan they had a governor" (*The Scriptores Historiae Augustae,* vol. I, pp. 66/7). This king, apparently under another Arsacid known to Dio Cassius as "Vologeses the son of Sanatruces" (Dio, LXVIII; vol. VIII, pp. 418-19) and as Vałarš (Vagharsh) to Movsēs Xorenac'i, was to reign from 117 to 138/40. He evidently extended his rule to all of Greater Armenia, since the cities of Vałaršapat (Vagharshapat) (called Kainē Polis "New City" by the Greeks), Vałaršawan (Vagharshavan), and Vałaršakert (Vagharshakert) are clearly his foundations. Armenia evidently prospered under his rule, but toward its end it suffered from another Ibero-northern attack, against which the king appealed to Rome for help, and was forced to buy the invaders off. According to Xorenac'i, Vałarš may even have died in battle against them.

With the final deterioration of Roman sources, even the names of the Armenian kings are often unknown. Thus, between 140 and 144 a coin of the emperor Antonius Pius proclaiming REX ARMEN[IIS] DATUS does not identify the Roman candidate "granted" to Armenia. Some twenty years later, a Roman army responding to a catastrophic Parthian raid drove out of Armenia a ruler with the unmistakably Iranian Aršakuni (Arshakuni) name of Pacorus/Bakur. He is also known from an inscription at Rome dedicated by "Aurelius Pacorus King of Greater Armenia" to the memory of his brother "Aurelius Merithates" [Mihrdat, or gift of Mithra], where the twin cultural currents of contemporary Armenia are particularly well illustrated by the Latin-Iranian names of the two brothers. In 164 the Romans reoccupied Artašat (Artashat), installed a garrison at Vałaršapat/Kainē Polis (where it remained at least twenty years, according to inscriptions found there), and crowned a certain Sohaemus, usually known as a prince of Emesa (Homs) in Syria, but also identified by a contemporary author as "an Achaemenid and an Arsacid, born a king of royal ancestors." Sohaemus had to be restored at least once by the Romans, and we have no idea of the length of his reign, but the compromise formula of Rhandeia was seemingly still operative in Armenia after one century and the Aršakuni usually in possession of the throne, which they seem to have occupied continually from 180 to 428 except for a brief break between 252 and 278/9.

Relying increasingly on the later and complicated Armenian sources, the Armenian historian Manandyan (followed by Cyril Toumanoff [1969] but opposed by some other scholars) identified in 180 the presence on the Armenian throne of another Arsacid, Vologeses/Vałarš (Vagharsh) II, who then moved to Iran, where he ruled the Parthian empire in 191 as Vologeses IV, leaving Armenia to his son Xosrov (Khosrov) I. In Toumanoff's tempting but by no means universally accepted reconstruction of Armenian history in this period, Xosrov I (whom Armenian sources confused with his more famous grandson Xosrov II) was the anonymous king whom classical authors show first as a neutral in 193, then as sending gifts and hostages to the Roman emperor Septimus Severus on his great campaign to the Parthian capital of Ctesiphon in 197/8. He would also presumably be the still-anonymous Armenian king whose detention with his family by the Romans provoked a major uprising in Armenia from 214 to 216, and his name may be recorded in an Egyptian inscription that speaks of "Xosrov the Armenian." The Armenian crown was then granted by the Romans in 216/7 to Trdat/Tiridates II on the eve of the Sasanian revolution in Iran, which was to alter radically the situation in the East.

Armenia Under the Sasanians (224–298)

The overthrow of the last Parthian king of Iran, Artawan V, by the Sasanian usurper Ardašir (Ardashir) I (ca. 224) radically broke the compromise status quo of Rhandeia between Rome and Iran and inaugurated centuries of intensified warfare between them. More critically for Armenia, it turned its Aršakuni (Arshakuni) rulers from kinsmen of the Iranian Parthian royal house into its avengers, so that the earliest Armenian fifth-century account of Armenian Christianization, attributed to Agat'angełos (Agathangelos), significantly presents the war between Ardašir and Xosrov of Armenia in terms of a blood feud. Xosrov

> . . . attempted to eradicate, destroy completely, extirpate and over-
> throw the Persian Kingdom and aimed at abolishing its civilization
> . . . in order to seek vengeance for the blood of Artavan.
> (Agathangelos, #19, pp. 36/7)

The hostility of the Armenian Aršakuni to the Persian usurpers drove Armenia closer to Rome, breaking the Compromise of Rhandeia and subjecting the country to Sasanian attacks and at times to outright conquest.

The famous account of Agat'angełos accepted by Armenian tradition is simple and clear: Alarmed by the victories of Xosrov, Ardašir incited a Parthian noble named Anak to murder the Armenian king, promising to return his own domain as a reward. Anak went to Armenia, won Xosrov's trust, treacherously murdered him, and was then slain with his entire family by the outraged Armenian nobles. Only two infants were saved from the slaughter: Xosrov's son, carried to safety on Roman territory, and one of Anak's sons (also rescued by a faithful nurse), the future Gregory the Illuminator. Meanwhile "the Persian King came and imposed his own name on Armenia." (Agathangelos, #24-36, pp. 42/3, 50/1) This epic tale is straightforward and deeply moving, but it unfortunately covers a multitude of problems. Scholars have long struggled to give a rational explanation for the history of third-century Armenia in which only two abnormally long reigns (that of Xosrov K'aǰ [Kadj] "the brave" and of his son Trdat the Great) are recorded by Armenian sources, a task made still more difficult by the need to account for the claims made in the royal Sasanian inscriptions. To resolve the chronological improbability of the two reigns spanning over a century, Toumanoff (1969) has sought to separate individuals subsumed under one and the same name but revealed as different individuals by irreconcilable features. For example, after Xosrov's murder, in the words of Agat'angełos, the fleeing Trdat was carried as an infant to Rome; yet according to Greek sources, he was the father of grown sons. (Moreover, an alternate Armenian tradition, reported by the historian Ełišē [Eghishe], claimed that Xosrov of Armenia had been murdered by his brothers and not by Anak the Parthian). Toumanoff therefore added a generation of two brothers: Xosrov II (279/80-287) and Trdat III (287-293) between Trdat II to whom he assigns the dates (216/7-252), following the account of Cassius Dio noted earlier, and Trdat (IV) the Great.

The Roman-Persian wars of the third century give a framework for this hypothetical reconstruction. The Persian campaign of the emperor Alexander Severus, whose army crossed in 231/2 through "Armenia which seemed to favor the Roman cause," allows a glimpse of the situation in the Armenian Aršakuni kingdom (presumably under Trdat II). Under the next emperor, contingents of Armenian archers still served in the Roman army as "friends and allies." But the situation altered radically with the accession of the new Sasanian King of Kings, Šāhpur I (240-270), who recorded his successive victories over Rome on his great trilingual inscription found near Persepolis and on monumental reliefs depicting the humiliation of the Romans, as the pendulum now swung radically over to the Persian side.

For the first time in 244, Šāhpur I crushed the Romans near Baghdad at Mizikē (renamed Pērz-Šāhpur, "Victory of Šāhpur" in commemoration) and obtained an enormous indemnity from the emperor, Philip the Arab. More pertinently, Šāhpur's inscription continues: "Then Caesar secondly lied and did wrong to Armenia. And we upon the Romans' empire made an attack and the Romans' force of 60,000 at Barbalissus slaughtered." This second campaign of 252/3 was followed by the annihilation of the Romans in Carrhae in 260 and the capture of the emperor Valerian himself. The mid third century unquestionably marked the Persian hour in the East. On the basis of Šāhpur's claim that Armenia had been injured "for the second time" in 252, historians have set the beginning of the Persian domination over the Armenians after the first victory at Mizikē, especially since later Greek sources asserted that Philip the Arab had been forced to surrender Armenia. Trdat II's reign thereafter presumably ended with his, after the second disaster at Barbalissus in 252/3, while his sons turned to Iran.

In the face of Rome's helplessness, Šāhpur had no reason to hold back. A Sasanian army overwhelmed the garrison city of Satala/Satał west of the Euphrates, although Armenia Minor remained a Roman province. Far more damagingly,

> the country of Armenia, and Georgia, and Albania and Balakasan until forward to the Alan's [Darial] pass [in the Caucasus] Shahpuhr King of Kings with horses and men of his own visited with pillaging and firing and havoc. (Sprengling, 1953, p. 52)

In place of the exiled Aršakuni, Šāhpur set his own son Hormizd-Ardašir over Armenia, whose special title of *"wuzurg Arminan šah,"* "great king of Armenia" (which distinguished him from the ordinary kings of other regions) appears both on the Sasanian victory inscription and on his own coin preserved in St. Petersburg. When Hormizd-Ardašir left to succeed his father in 272, his brother Narseh took over the Armenian throne, which he kept until 293. Thus, Greater Armenia had been incorporated into the Persian empire, although Hormizd-Ardašir's title shows that even the Sasanians clearly recognized the special privileged position Armenia had enjoyed in the Iranian world as far back as the early days of the Achaemenids.

The Sasanian domination of Greater Armenia proved brief. Their internal difficulties after the death of Šāhpur I ca. 270 and the contemporary revival of Rome under the emperors Aurelian (270-275) and Probus (276-282) gradually re-created the former equilibrium in the East. This eventually led to the restoration in Armenia of the Aršakuni heir Trdat the Great under the emperor Diocletian (284-305), but the details and especially the chronology of this restoration are still highly debatable. Classical sources date the return of Roman prestige in Armenia as early as the emperor Aurelian. The ruler of the country, however, was still the Sasanian Narseh, who sought peace from the emperor Probus as early as 278/9. Toumanoff gives considerable importance to these negotiations, which, in his opinion, marked both the return of an Aršakuni king (Trdat II's son Xosrov II) to the western part of Greater Armenia and a first partition of the country, with Xosrov II ruling the western or Roman portion while the Sasanian Narseh kept the eastern or Persian part. It is not impossible that classical writers overlooked such a restoration and a partition of Armenia. It coincides with Xorenac'i's statement that the Aršakuni had returned after twenty-six years of Persian rule (278/9 minus 252/3 equals 27/6) and with his memory that "Probus. . . making peace with Ardashir divided our land and dug ditches to mark the frontier," (Movses Khorenats'i II. 77, pp. 224-25) a memory also preserved in Agat'angełos, who, however, attributed this activity to the Persian king, who "had ditches dug to fix the frontier." (Agathangelos, #36 p. 50/1). This hypothetical reconstruction solves many problems and is consequently very attractive, but tells nothing of the terms of Probus's treaty.

When the Sasanian, Narseh, finally ascended the Persian throne in 293, the inscription of Paikuli in the province of Fars celebrating this event recorded two important details: Narseh returned to "Ērānšahr" from Armenia, and he received, among others, the congratulations of "Tirdat the King." Many scholars have identified this ruler with Trdat "the Great," restored to his father's throne in 287 ("the third year of Diocletian," according to some Armenian sources). But (on the basis of Ełišē's claim [Ełišē, iii, p. 123] that Xosrov II had been murdered by his brother) Toumanoff has preferred to follow Manandyan in placing Xosrov II's death in 287, followed by the king's replacement in western Armenia by his murderous brother, whom he calls Trdat III. Meanwhile, eastern Armenia still continued to acknowledge Sasanian overlordship. Finally, Toumanoff sees the return of Xosrov II's son Trdat IV to Armenia in 298/9 as part of the reorganization of the East dictated to Narseh by the victorious Diocletian at the so-called Peace of Nisibis.

The date of 298/9 for Trdat the Great's restoration ending all Sasanian rule over Armenia is very tempting. It coincides with some of the Armenian chronologies. Under the terms of the Peace of Nisibis, the southern districts of Armenia known to the contemporary classical world as the "Satrapies" or "Nations" (Latin *gentes,* Greek *ethne*): Sophēnē/Cop'k', Ingelēnē/Angełtun, Arzanēnē/Ałjnik' (Aghdznik) , (Korduēnē/ Korduk' and Zabdikēnē/Cowdek'(Tsovdek), whose territories included the ancient Eruandid and Artašēsid kingdom of Sophēnē, were returned by Persia to the Roman sphere of influence. They received the status of *"civitates foederatae liberae et immunes,"* that is to say, free territories enjoying total internal autonomy and only coordinating their foreign policy with the empire, a status underlined by the regalia of their hereditary rulers (Procopius, "Buildings," III. i, 17-23; vol VII, pp. 182/3-184/5): a cloak embroidered in gold and fastened with a jeweled brooch, a silk tunic ornamented with gold, and most important of all, the imperial red shoes symbolic of sovereignty. The simultaneous return to Greater Armenia of its Aršakuni heir educated from childhood by the Romans would have been entirely logical and would have reestablished there too the normal autonomy of the kingdom and the balance of power achieved at Rhandeia. Unfortunately, the chaotic and mutually contradictory chronologies of the Armenian sources and the absence of additional contemporary evidence permit no definite conclusions to date, and all reconstructions, no matter how attractive, must still remain provisional.

The Social Structure and Culture of Armenia Under the Aršakuni

Even though the tormented political history of Armenia cannot yet be coherently reconstructed, a highly individual and identifiable Armenian entity with its own life and institutions is recorded in the Aršakuni period. Our main source of information are the anonymous *Epic Histories,* usually called *History of Armenia,* composed in the late fifth century and mistakenly attributed to P'awstos Buzand. The obvious familiarity of these *Epic Histories* with the great families that were to dominate medieval Armenia and their description of institutions and customs shows them as so deeply rooted that they must obviously have had a long history behind them. Indeed some of the features of the characteristic social structure of the country can be glimpsed in the *Annals* of Tacitus and can be traced back as far as the Artašēsids and Eruandids. Despite the Roman protectorate exercised over Aršakuni Armenia, this characteristic social structure was unmistakably Iranian. Tacitus (II. lvi; vol. II, pp. 474/5) had already shrewdly observed that Zeno of Pontus wisely changed his name at his accession to the more acceptable Artašēs, and that he shared his subjects' taste for the hunt and for banquets, the only two diversions suitable for a nobleman in the Iranian world. Linguistic studies have already shown such a close connection between Armenian and Middle Persian vocabulary that the two societies must have been in immediate and continuous contact. In fact, much of the lost Middle Parthian terminology can be reconstructed from the Armenian loan words.

The central institution of this world, the kingship, was hereditary in the Aršakuni house. *The Epic Histories* repeatedly cite exhortations to the Armenians that they should die for their "own true lords" *(bnik teark'),* the Aršakuni, and deny that even their sins might make them unfit for the crown. The Aršakuni possessed the "supernatural glory," the *xwarrah* or *p'aṙk',* distinguishing the king in the Iranian tradition and protecting his country even after his death. This belief embodied the formula *baxt u p'aṙk',* "fortune and fate or rather glory," used by Trdat I at his coronation by Nero (Garsoïan, 1976, pp. 39-40), as we have seen, is also found in *The Epic Histories'* accounts of the Persian attempt to steal the bones of the Aršakuni kings from their tomb at Ani-Kamax in Daranałik' (Daranaghik) so as to carry the protection of their *baxt* and *p'aṙk'* away from Armenia (P'awstos Buzand, IV, xxiv, pp. 157-58). Hailed as *Helios,* "the sun," in the Gaṙni inscription, the Armenian king thus shared the status of the Persian king "brother of the sun and the moon" and this equality was underscored by the protocol of the Persian court, which stipulated that on ceremonial occasions the Kings of Persia and Armenia should wear identical robes and diadems and share the same couch (P'awstos Buzand, IV. xvi, p. 146).

Below the ruler, society was divided into the three great estates of the Iranian world. First came the magnates variously known as *mecameck'* *(metsametsk), gahereck' (gaheretsk), tanutērk', naxarars,* or *nahapets* to the Armenians, and called *megisthanes* or *nobiles* by Tacitus. All *naxarars* were theoretically equal insofar as they belonged to the same social class (although there are occasional references to "seniors" *[awag]* and "juniors" *[krtser]),* but they were ranked in a rigid order of precedence according to the "cushion or throne" *(barj,* [bardz], *gah)* that they occupied at court. Most senior among them were the four great *bdešxs* *(bdeshkhs)* guarding the borders of Armenia: in Arzanēnē/Ałjnik', the Arabian March; Korduk', the Assyrian March; Adiabēnē/Heydab or Nor Širakan, the Median March, to the south; and Gogarēnē/Gugark', the Iberian March, in the north. These may perhaps go back to the four vassal kings perpetually attending Tigran the Great, and were known under the form *vitaxa* or *pitiarch* in both classical and Iberian sources, as well as in the bilingual inscription found near Tbilisi. The second estate consisted of the junior nobility or *azat*s, "free men" or better, "knights" who usually held conditional land tenures *(xostaks/khostaks)* granted by the magnates in exchange for cavalry service in the *naxarar*'s military contingent. Finally, the mass of the population consisted of the *an-azat* "non-noble" *ŕamik,* who included both the relatively rare artisans and traders and the "peasants" *šinakan (shinakan)* who were the overwhelming majority. Slaves *(struk),* usually prisoners of war, are mentioned especially on temple estates, but were apparently not as common as elsewhere. The fourth estates of the Sasanians, the *dpir*s or "clerks," does not seen to have been fully developed in Aršakuni Armenia. A royal chancellery with *dpir*s is known to have existed, since the learned Maštoc' (Mashtots) was one of them (Koriwn, iii, p. 27), but it does not seem to have evolved into a separate estate, perhaps because these duties were usually performed by clerics.

The magnates, usually dwelling in remote and inaccessible fortresses, were unquestionably the dominant class of this period. The great autonomous families *(tun),* first noted by Pliny the Elder in the 120 administrative districts or "strategies" into which Armenia was divided in the first century A.D. (Pliny, *Natural History,* VI, x, 27; vol. II, pp. 356/7), jealously preserved their rights and prerogatives. Their heads, *tēr* or *tanutēr,* (lord of the house), had sovereign administrative and judicial power within their domains, and they led the military contingent of their *tun* in battle. Their power was hereditary within the clan though not invariably in direct line of descent. Particularly characteristic of Aršakuni Armenia is the fact that the *tanutēr* was only the temporary administrator of the unalienable and indivisible possessions, both inherited *(hayrenik')* and granted *(pargewagank'),* of his eternal family "past, present and future" held jointly by all members of the house, and he ruled with the advice and assistance of the other male members of the family or *sepuh*s. Later conciliar lists indicate that each clan even had its own bishop, who was the family representative in religious matters.

The hallmarks of this aristocratic society were: first, precedence, the *gah,* strictly set according to a "Rank List," or *Gahnamak,* of which no contemporary examples are known, but whose existence is clearly implied, and of which later copies have survived (this precedence probably related to the size of the military contingent of each house recorded in the "Military List," or *Zornamak*); second, the hereditary offices, which belonged absolutely to certain houses. Thus the *sparapetut'iwn, (sparapetutiun),* or "supreme command of the army" was invariably held by the Mamikonean (Mamikonian) house, according to *The Epic Histories* (P'awstos Buzand, IV. ii, pp. 107-8). The office of *t'agadir,* or "coronant," already recorded in the second century B.C. Zangezur inscription of Artašēs I (Perikhanian, 1966, p. 18), belonged to the Bagratuni together with the title of *aspet,* or "commander of the cavalry." The Gnuni were *hazarapets,* "seneschals," set over the peasantry, and the office of *mardpet,* "keeper of the royal treasures and fortresses," is also recorded in the Armenian sources. After the conversion of Armenia, the patriarchate became the hereditary office of the house of St. Gregory the Illuminator until its extinction, although this ran counter to general Christian customs and canon law. The king himself was but the *tanutēr* of the Aršakuni clan, whose hereditary office was the kingship, and as such only the first among his equals.

The *naxarars* owed to the king military services *(carayut'iwn/tzarayutiun)* in time of war but inherited their rank and insignia *(gah* and *patiw/pativ).* No homage has been recorded in Aršakuni Armenia but "oaths of fidelity" *(uxt)* are known. The Aršakuni rulers constantly sought to reduce their turbulent magnates to the level of royal "officials," or *gorcakalk'* (gortsakalk). Nevertheless, they were never able to achieve the centralization of their Sasanian neighbors. The king was forced by custom to seek the counsel of the *naxarars* on all important occasions. As early as A.D. 18 Tacitus observed that Zeno/Artašēs had been crowned "before the consenting nobles." This council opposed the king on occasion and even met in his absence. Land personally forfeited by a *naxarar* returned to his *tun,* which kept its possessions as long as a single male heir, no matter how remote, survived. In the absence of a male, the nearest female heir transmitted them to her husband's *tun,* as was the case of the patriarchal lands carried at the death of St. Sahak I by his daughter to her husband Hamazasp Mamikonean. The king at best ratified the succession of a *tanutēr* to the prerogatives of his house, and the allegiance of the *sepuhs* went to their *tanutēr* rather than the king. The inalienable nature of the hereditary office, irrespective of the capacity of the holder to perform its duties, is clearly illustrated in *The Epic Histories'* account of the granting of the *sparapetut'iwn* to Artawazd Mamikonean, even though he was a small child quite incapable of commanding the army, because it was his father's office "and no other adult could be found in that clan" (P'awstos Buzand, III. xi, p. 81). The most that the king could do to contain the arrogance of the "lords with contingents and banners" was to keep them under his eye at court and await the opportunity to extirpate some troublesome clan to the last infant. This tug of war between the king and the centrifugal tendencies of the magnates unquestionably sapped the authority of the crown and made it vulnerable. Yet the strength and permanence of the *tun* forged a social structure capable of surviving even in moments of political eclipse and the decentralized character of the society diminished its chances of total annexation.

We know very little of the lower classes of society. The cities populated by the natives and a large proportion of Jews survived until the mid-fourth century according to the Armenian sources, although no new ones seem to have been founded after Vałaršapat (Vagharshapat), except for the shift of the capital from Artašat to nearby Duin (Dvin). The Aršakuni preferred to create great hunting preserves of the Iranian type in which they built their palaces. The only royal attempt to create a new urban center met with disaster, and the tales of "God's wrath" falling upon it, killing and dispersing its "brigand" population (P'awstos Buzand, IV. xii-xiii, pp. 134-35, 137-38), reveal the latent hostility of the contemporary society. Artašat and later Duin prospered from their position on the transit trade route through the valley of the Araxes, but the magnates kept to their distant strongholds and even the king preferred his camp and hunting preserves to his capital. Like all parafeudal societies, Aršakuni Armenia was highly suspicious of urban centers. Villages and towns—*gewł* (geugh) and *awan*—under *gełjapet*s (geghjapet) and *dasapet*s were far more common, and some rights were recognized to the ramik, who occasionally appear at councils alongside the nobility. Like medieval serfs, the *šinakan* owed their lord taxes *(hark)*, of which the best known are *sak* and *baž (bazh)*, probably land and poll taxes, and work *(bekar)* similar to the western corvée; their military service was usually limited to the auxiliary infantry.

The religion of Aršakuni Armenia perpetuated the Greco-Iranian syncretism of earlier times, though some obviously Semitic gods such as Baršamin, Nanē, and Astłik (Barshamin, Nane, and Astghik), were also worshipped (Agathangelos, #784, 786, 809, pp. 322/3, 326/7,

348/9). The shrines of these gods were supported by vast temple estates, some surrounded by fortifications, served by a hereditary caste of priests called *k'urm,* and having military contingents of their own and up to 500 slaves. The most famous of these shrines were those of Zeus/Aramazd at Ani-Kamax, Hephaistos/Mihr at Bagayařič (Bagaharich), Apollo/Tir at Erazamoyn, and especially those of the "Golden Mother" Artemis/Anahit at Erēz and Hephaistos/Vahagn at Aštišat in Tarōn (Agathangelos, #778, 785-86, 790, 809, pp. 316/7, 324/5-328/9, 346/7-348/9). The Iranian aspect of these syncretic deities tended to dominate as a stronger Zoroastrian current seems to have swept Armenia in the third century, probably as a result of the Sasanian rule. Trdat the Great invoked for his realm the blessings of Aramazd, Anahit the Lady, and Vahagn on the eve of its Christianization (Agathangelos, #127, pp. 138-39). The setting up of a fire temple at Bagawan and the destruction of the statues placed there by Vałaršak recorded by Movsēs Xorenac'i (II. 77, pp. 224-25), also seem to herald a shift from the Greek aniconic tradition. The zeal of the Sasanian high priest Kartir establishing and fostering fire temples, "wherever the horses and men of the King of Kings arrived" (Sprengling, 1955, pp. 51-52) and specifically in Armenia, is amply attested by his inscriptions. Traces of Zoroastrian beliefs and customs, sun worship, and especially the practice of consanguineous marriages lingered on long after the Christianization of the country.

A bicultural tradition also affected other aspects of society. Artašat/Neroneia was rebuilt on a classical model with the help of artisans brought from Rome, and a classical building erected at Gařni, yet most noble families claimed direct Iranian descent: the royal Aršakuni from their Parthian ancestors, the patriarchal house of St. Gregory "Part'ew" from the great Iranian clan of Sūrēn, the Kamsarakan from the second clan of the Karēn. The dynastic names repeated from generation to generation in a certain house: Trdat, Xosrov, Aršak, Varazdat, Vramšapuh among the Aršakuni; Vardan, Vahan, Vasak, Vač'ē (Vache), Artawazd and Hamazasp Mamikonean; Meružan Arcruni (Meruzhan Artsruni), Bat Sahařuni; and even the royal Sasanian name Nersēs/Narseh among the descendants of St. Gregory, are all of Iranian origin. Armenian education and eventually the church liturgy were conducted in both Greek and Syriac until the fifth century. Greek learning was deep enough in Armenia for an Armenian to have taught philosophy in Athens during the fourth century. Yet Iranian oral epic tradition with its tales of gods and heroes, carried by *gusan*s, or minstrels, throughout the land, was familiar to late written sources despite all the efforts of the church to destroy it.

Multiple other examples of Greek influence on Aršakuni Armenia can be found. On balance, however, here as elsewhere in the East, the tide of Hellenism was ebbing. The hereditary character of the Armenian monarchy alone suffices to demonstrate that, true to their ancestry, the Aršakuni stood east of the watershed separating the Iranian from the classical world where to the very end the emperor constitutionally—if mostly fictionally—remained an elected magistrate deriving his authority from the mandate of the sovereign people. Similarly the survival of the great *tun*s with their unalienable hereditary offices cannot be reconciled with the system of appointed civil servants developed in the Roman imperial world.

The Christianization of Armenia

The conversion of Armenia to Christianity was probably the most crucial step in its history. It turned Armenia sharply away from its Iranian past and stamped it for centuries with an intrinsic character as clear to the native population as to those outside its borders, who identified Armenia almost at once as the first state to adopt Christianity.

The Armenian traditional account of this event related in the various versions of "Agat'angełos" is a familiar one: Gregory, the son of Anak the Parthian, was saved from the massacre of his family following the murder of King Χosrov *Kaĵ* and brought up as a Christian in Caesarea of Cappadocia. He returned to Armenia as an adult and served King Trdat until his refusal to sacrifice to Anahit led to his prolonged tortures and incarceration in the pit of Χor Virap (Khor Virap). Miraculously saved after a vision sent to Trdat's sister Χosroviduxt (Khosrovidukht), Gregory was raised from the pit and healed the king, who had been turned into a wild boar for his sins. He preached the true faith to the Armenians and erected shrines to the other Armenian martyrs, the virgin saints Hrip'simē and Gayanē, at Vałaršapat on the spot indicated to him in a vision as the place of descent to earth of God's "only begotten Son," Ēĵmiacin (Echmiadzin). St. Gregory was then sent back to Caesarea with a brilliant retinue of magnates and consecrated there by the archbishop Leontios during a great ecclesiastical council. Upon his return to Armenia, St. Gregory baptized the king and the nation in the Euphrates, destroyed the pagan shrines, and set up churches in their place throughout Armenia.

This famous account is undoubtedly a rendering in epic form of the Christianization of the northern Aršakuni kingdom by way of Caesarea of Cappadocia in the reign of Trdat the Great. It does not, however, relate the entire story of the Christianization of Armenia, and the date of this event has varied over an entire generation from 284 to 314, although the careful study of Ananian now points clearly to the later date. It would have been impossible for Trdat, the protégé of the Romans and of Diocletian in particular, to have set up in his realm at an earlier date a religion diametrically opposed to imperial policy, at the very time that Diocletian was unleashing the last and most violent Christian persecution. In fact, a passage from the Greek version of Agat'angełos carefully omitted from the Armenian one spells out Trdat's obedience to Diocletian in matters of religion:

> From a youthful age raised and educated by you [Diocletian] . . . hailing the gods who saved our power together with ourselves, I loathe the so-called Christians. What is more, I gave over to the bitterest death [after] tortures a certain Cappadocian [named] Gregory beloved by me, throwing [him] into a pit in which dwell snakes who devour [those] thrown therein. And now, Lord emperor, I will fulfill thy orders to me with all haste and willingness. (Garitte, 1946 #40, pp. 37, 293)

Moreover, on the basis of one of the historical passages in Agat'angełos, which notes that St. Gregory's consecration came at the time of an ecclesiastical council held at Caesarea (Agathangelos, #805, pp. 342/3-344/5), Ananian concluded that his consecration must have taken place in 314 (Ananian, 1961, pp. 43-73, 319-60), when we know that a council was indeed held in Caesarea under Bishop Leontios.

A second Armenian tradition, not found in Agat'angełos but clearly known to *The Epic Histories,* speaks of the coming of the apostle Thaddeus from Edessa, in the first century A.D., to bring Christianity to the Armenians, and of his martyrdom in the district of Artaz near Maku under King Sanatruk. Later this tradition, which gave an apostolic foundation to the Armenian Church, was linked to Agat'angełos' version of the Christianization of Armenia by having St. Gregory conceived at the site of St. Thaddeus's tomb in Artaz (Movses Khorenats'i, II, 74, 220-21). The connection of the account of St.

Thaddeus's missionary activity in Armenia to the Syriac *Acts of Addai* and the legendary Christianization of Edessa has long been demonstrated to be apocryphal (Adontz, 1970, pp. 269-70), but the early appearance of Christianity coming to Armenia from Palestine by way of Syria and Mesopotamia is equally beyond doubt. The second century African church father Tertullian already listed the Armenians among the people who had received Christianity, and the mid-third-century letter of Bishop Dionysios of Alexandria to an Armenian bishop named Meruzanes indicates a sizable community. The historian Adontz (Adontz, 1970, pp. 270-71) located this community in Sophēnē on the basis of the Armenian form of the bishop's name, Meružan, which was a dynastic name in the Arcruni house known to have ruled this district later (Adontz, 1970, p. 271). *The Epic Histories* insist on the Syrian origin of early Armenian missionaries such as Bishop Daniēl of Tarōn and on the importance of the role played by the great Mesopotamian bishop James of Nisibis. Even more significantly, he repeatedly identified Aštišat (Ashtishat) in Tarōn as the "first" and "mother church" of Armenia (P'awstos Buzand, III. x, xiv, pp. 77-80, 86). Consequently, it is now evident that two currents of Christianity reached Armenia successively. The first came to the southern portion of the country closest to the original center of Palestine by way of Mesopotamia at a very early date. The second was brought to the northern Aršakuni Kingdom of Greater Armenia in the second decade of the fourth century. Since, as we have seen, the southern Armenian Satrapies were fully sovereign states in the third century of the Christian era, and indeed Sophēnē had been a kingdom since Eruandid times, nothing impeded the identification of its Christianization as the first acceptance of the new faith by and Armenian realm.

With the Christianization of the entire country in the fourth century, Armenia received its ecclesiastical organization. At first dependent on Caesarea, where its patriarchs received their ordination until the death of St. Nersēs I in 373, the Armenian Church was endowed by the crown with the vast estates of the destroyed pagan shrines, especially in Daranałik' and at Aštišat of Tarōn. Two hereditary ecclesiastical families are known from the start: that of St. Gregory the Illuminator, in which the patriarchate was a hereditary office, and that of Ałbianos of Manazkert, bishop of the royal court, whose descendants repeatedly disputed the first place to the Gregorids. The few bishops known from the earliest period do not seem to have had fixed sees, but rather to have been representatives of the *naxarar tun*s, and even the patriarch apparently resided usually on his estates in Tarōn rather than at court. The bilingual training provided the descendants of the pagan priests, or *k'urm,* perpetuated the double Syrian and Greek traditions of early Armenian Christianity (Agathangelos, #840, pp. 374/5). Churches and especially martyria commemorating the saints were erected throughout the country, and isolated sites began to be peopled with hermits of the strictest, ascetic, Syrian type. Finally, the extensive missionary activities helped spread the faith northward to Iberia and Caucasian Albania (Koriwn, xv-xvii, pp. 37-42).

From its inception, the Armenian Church was part of the characteristic *naxarar* society of Aršakuni Armenia. Its leaders did not hesitate to play an independent political role, admonishing kings and nobles, or representing Armenia on various diplomatic missions, especially in the days of St. Gregory's great-great-grandson, St. Nersēs I "the Great" (355-73) and his son, St. Sahak I "the Great" (387-438) at the end of the Aršakuni dynasty. The other crucial contribution of the church under St. Sahak and his collaborator St. Maštoc' (St. Mashtots) was the composition of the Armenian alphabet through which the nation at long last found its own voice (Koriwn, i, iii, vi-ix, pp. 21, 27, 29-33). Thus from the start, the church helped to create a separate Armenian identity and provided a focus for the allegiance of the entire population that was independent of the political framework and consequently from the fate of the realm.

The Christian Aršakuni and the Partition of Armenia

The dominant event in the reign of Trdat the Great was unquestionably his amply documented collaboration with St. Gregory the Illuminator to root Christianity in Armenia. His reign is not otherwise well known, although he probably fought northern invaders and lived until ca. 330, late enough to send St. Gregory's younger son and successor Aristakēs to represent Armenia at the first Œcumenical Council of Nicaea in 325 (Agathangelos, #884-885, pp. 414/5-416/7), and thus to set the Armenian Church on a path of rigorous theological orthodoxy against the Arian doctrine condemned by the Council. The king's death seems to have been followed by considerable internal difficulties as well as a new barbarian invasion from the north. Xorenac'i even claims that the king was murdered by the nobles (Movses Khorenats'i, II. 92, p. 251), although *The Epic Histories* are silent on the subject. St. Gregory is said to have already withdrawn into solitude in the cave of Manē in his hereditary domain of Daranałik' (Agathangelos, #861, pp. 396/7; Movses Khorenats'i, II. 91, p. 248), and we do not know the precise date of his death, but his son and successor Aritstakēs was soon murdered in the southern district of Cop'k', again according to Xorenac'i (II. 91, p. 249) but not *The Epic Histories*. St. Gregory's elder son Vrt'anēs, who succeeded his brother in 327/8, nearly met the same fate at the hands of supporters of paganism while at the "mother church" of Aštišat in Tarōn (P'awstos Buzand III. iii, pp. 68-69). The emperor Constantine is known to have designated his nephew King of Kings of Armenia in 335, but the young man had not yet set foot in the country when he too was murdered in 337, and a classical source refers to the "return" of a king to Armenia by the Romans in 338/9.

Both the sequence and especially the chronology of the Christian Aršakuni reigning after Trdat the Great are open to question, largely because of the disagreements and confusion of the two main Armenian sources for the period: *The Epic Histories* and Movsēs Xorenac'i, supplemented for the last period by that of Łazar P'arpec'i (Ghazar Parbetsi), and the difficulty of reconciling them with the contemporary account of the Roman historian Ammianus Marcellinus, writing at the end of the fourth century. The sequence usually accepted by Armenian scholars—Xosrov III (330-338); Tiran (338/9-350), presumably the king "returned" by the emperor Constantius II; Aršak II (350-367); Pap (367-374); Varazdat (374-378); Pap's sons Aršak III (ca. 379-389) and Vałaršak, with a separate Aršakuni King Xosrov IV (384-389) in Eastern Armenia after the retirement of Aršak III in the West; the partition of Armenia between Rome and Iran ca. 387; Vramšapuh (389/401-417), replacing his brother Xosrov IV after a possible interregnum; a fleeting return of Xosrov IV in 417/8; Šapuh, son of the King of Kings Yazdgird I (Yazdagerd)(418-422); and finally Vramšapuh's son Artašēs/Ardašir (422-428)—presents a multitude of problems. Aršak II's reign is said to have lasted thirty years by Xorenac'i, but such a reign beginning in 350 is impossible, since Aršak is known to have lost his throne and eventually his life immediately after the surrender of Armenia to Persia in 364. The date of the partition of Armenia oscillates between 384 and 390. The incorporation of extraneous material into *The Epic Histories* leads them to confuse the emperors Constantius II (337-361) and Valens (364-378), as well as the Sasanian kings Narseh (293-302) and Šāhpur II (309-379). Tiran was the king blinded by the Persians (presumably in 350), according to the Armenian sources (P'awstos Buzand, III. xx, pp.

96-97), but Ammianus Marcellinus claims that this punishment was inflicted on Aršak II in 364 (Ammianus Marcellinus, XXVII, xii 3, vol. III, pp. 78/9). In short, it is all but impossible to reconcile these contradictions and to crowd the generations of the last Aršakuni into the 128 years separating the death of Trdat the Great in 330 from the end of the dynasty in 428. Consequently, historians have been driven to endless arithmetical calculations. Ingenious as many of these hypotheses have been, however, none has yet succeeded in providing an overall solution universally accepted by scholars.

Three main aspects dominated the turbulent history of late Aršakuni Armenia:

First among them was the Persian war constantly threatening under the King of Kings Šāhpur II, whose seventy-year reign in (309-379) loomed over most of the fourth century. Unsuccessful in his first three campaigns, which ravaged Armenia but failed to take Nisibis in 338, 346, and 350, Šāhpur made the most of the precarious state of the Roman army trapped in Mesopotamia to obtain the abandonment of Armenia by the Romans and the return of some of the eastern Satrapies in 364. Even this drastic step did not resolve the conflict over Armenia, and the war continued sporadically to the extinction of the Aršakuni dynasty and thereafter.

The second factor dominating the period was the tug of war between the church and the Aršakuni state that was the probable cause of the patent antagonism of the Armenian sources toward the Armenian kings, especially Aršak II and Pap, who are on the contrary praised by the Roman historian Ammianus Marcellinus. In their attempt to maintain a precarious equilibrium in the perpetual Roman-Iranian conflict, the Aršakuni kings usually sided with Rome against the Sasanian destroyers of their Parthian ancestors, but loyalty in the fourth century required not only political but absolute religious conformity. Consequently from 338 to 381 the Aršakuni kings sought to follow the pro-Arian policy of the Byzantine court, especially under Constantius II and Valens. This policy brought them into latent or open conflict with the rigorously orthodox and consequently anti-Arian patriarchs of the Gregorid house, whom the kings repeatedly replaced with more pliant primate from the rival house of Ałbianos of Manazkert. More violently, the conflict let to the murder at the king's order of St. Gregory's grandson, the patriarch Yusik/Husik (342-348) as well as of his successor the Syrian bishop Daniēl, and to the exile and eventual murder at the order of King Pap of Yusik's grandson St. Nersēs the Great, for whose murder the king soon paid with his life (P'awstos Buzand, III. xii, xiv;

IV, xv; V. xxiv, pp. 82-84, 86-91, 142-43, 145, 203-5). Peace between the crown and the church did not return until the acceptance of anti-Arian orthodoxy at Constantinople in 381.

The final thread running throughout this period is the turbulence of the *naxarars.* The pride of place unquestionably belonged to the Mamikonean *sparapets.* Their role has perhaps been overstressed by their panegyrist, the author of *The Epic Histories,* as against the silence of the Bagratuni historian Movsēs Xorenac'i, but they unquestionably came to overshadow and eventually dominate the crown, first as hereditary commanders-in-chief and protectors of both king and realm, but eventually as regents and kingmakers after the murder of Pap. In spite of the remonstrances of the patriarchs Nersēs and Sahak urging their loyalty and the attempt of the kings to keep them under surveillance at court, the centrifugal tendencies of the magnates manifested themselves again and again: Databey, *nahapet* of the Bznuni and the great *bdešx* of Aljnik', Bakur Siwni, connived with the Persians, and the treason of the *senekapet* or chamberlain, Pisak Siwni led to the capture and blinding of Tiran, according to *The Epic Histories* (P'awstos Buzand, III. viii-ix, xx, pp. 75-77, 94-97). The successive *mardpets* repeatedly proved untrustworthy, and the treason of Andovk Siwni helped to break the *modus vivendi* established between Armenia and the Sasanians and eventually led to the war that ended in the conquest of Armenia by the Persians in 364. Most threatening and extensive were the nefarious activities of Meružan Arcruni, whom the Armenian sources invariably portray as the arch traitor and apostate leading the Persian armies against his own country (P'awstos Buzand, IV. xxiii-xxiv, xxxi-xxxvii, xxxix-xliii, xlv-xlviii, lviii-lix; V. i-ii, iv, xxxviii, xliii, pp. 155-58, 161-67, 178-80, 186-87, 189, 222-28), but who, as lord of one of the autonomous Satrapies, may have been pursuing an independent policy and merely providing a focus for a pro-Persian party opposed to the generally pro-Roman Mamikoneans in Armenia. Whatever their purpose, these constant revolts unquestionably sapped the strength of the kingdom from within, and the kings retaliated brutally. The Armenian histories abound in tales of the great *naxarar* clans: the Bznuni, the Ṙštuni, the Arcruni, and the Kamsarakan among others, annihilated to the last child. But even these savage reprisals did not have the desired effect. The magnates were to have the last word, if we credit Xorenac'i's assertion that the end of the Aršakuni dynasty and of the Armenian kingdom at the hands of the Persians came at the request of the Armenian *naxarars* themselves (Movses Khorenats'i, III. 63-64, pp. 339-41).

The dominant reign of the fourth century unquestionably belongs to Aršak II, although he probably came to the throne in 350, rather than 338, and consequently ruled less than fifteen years. The reign opened peacefully with the ordering of the realm and the return of the magnates to their dignities, although the king does not seem to have resided in the new capital at Duin but preferred his "royal encampment" *(banak ark'uni)*. In the words of *The Epic Histories:*

> Profound peace reigned at that time. All those in the land of Armenia who had hidden, fled, or been lost reassembled and lived undisturbed in great peace under the protection of King Aršak. Then . . . the realm of Armenia became peaceful, organized, ordered and stable, and after this each one of the inhabitants peacefully enjoyed his own possessions . . . he reinstated the military contingents of the mightiest magnates according to each one's rank as had been done by former kings. And he brought the magnates into submission . . . And so the royal power of the Armenian land was renewed and invigorated as it had formerly been: every magnate on his *gah,* and every official *[gorcakal]* in his station. (P'awstos Buzand, IV. i-ii, pp. 107-8)

The ordering of the realm was paralleled by the reform of the church under the new patriarch, Nersēs I, restored to the seat of his ancestors in 353 after the abnormal period following the murder of Yusik when the patriarchate had temporarily passed from the Gregorid house. Consecrated like his ancestors at Caesarea, Nersēs probably called the first Armenia council at Aštišat of Tarōn early in his patriarchate to institute new regulations for the Armenian Church. Zoroastrian and pagan customs such as consanguineous marriages and lamentations for the dead accompanied by mourning dances and lacerations of arms and faces were forbidden. The eating of meat was severely restricted, the liturgy regulated, and a broad program of charitable foundations instituted by the church. Throughout the land, "in every district," hostelries, hospitals, leprosaria, orphanages, and poor houses with their own revenues ministered to the poor, the abandoned, the stranger, and the sick under the supervision of deacons or bishops. These benevolent institutions, which have commonly been attributed to an imitation by St. Nersēs of the activities of his contemporary St. Basil of Caesarea, actually appeared in Armenia earlier than in Cappadocia and did not have the monastic character of the Basilian foundations. They were directly supervised by the patriarch through his deputies, who like himself took no celibate vows, rather than entrusted to monastic communities. These do not seem to have existed in Aršakuni Armenia, where we find only individual hermits living without a rule and seeking their salvation in total seclusion.

The auspicious beginning of Aršak II's reign was not to last. St. Nersēs I, sent on a mission to the Byzantine Empire in 358 to fetch the king's bride Olympias, returned to face the renewed Arianism of the Roman and Armenian courts and was exiled for some nine years, together with other anti-Arian bishops, while a royal appointee, to whom *The Epic Histories* refer contemptuously as Č'unak (Chunak) "the man of nothing . . . the slave of the slaves of the King" (P'awstos Buzand, IV. xv, pp. 145-46), whom the Armenian bishops refused to consecrate, replaced him on the patriarchal throne. The attempt to find a new source of support for the royal authority through the foundation of the new city of Aršakawan (Arshakavan) in Kogovit ended in the destruction of the city whose nonnoble population was suspect to the magnates and the church alike. The restlessness of the *naxarar*s provoked the murder of the Mamikonean *tanutēr* Vardan and the annihilation of the Kamsarakan lords of Širak (Shirak) and Aršarunik' (Arsharunik) at the order of the king. Most serious of all was the execution of the king's nephews Gnel and Tirit' in 359. The romantic tale of love and jealousy related by the Armenian sources—in which Tirit''s passion for his cousin's wife P'aṙanjem (Parandzem) of Siwnik' (Siunik) led him to slander Gnel to the king, who had him executed, only to succumb in turn to P'aṙanjem's beauty and marry her, with the resultant murder of Tirit'—has obscured the implication, found in Movsēs Xorenac'i, that, as Aršakuni *sepuh*s entitled to wear the crown, both Gnel and Tirit' were possible foci of rebellion against the king. The complicated sequence of the marriage of Aršak II and P'aṙanjem and the murder of the king's Greek wife Olympias in 361 cannot yet be unraveled; it is entirely possible that in spite of his adherence to Christianity, Aršak II had more than one wife simultaneously, in Persian fashion. Be that as it may, the immediate result of Gnel's death was the total alienation of the church, and the patriarch Nersēs was not seen at court again in Aršak's lifetime.

The final disaster, however, was to come from without. Aršak had been greatly favored by Constantius II, who remitted all the Armenian taxes and gave Aršak an imperial bride in whose honor special medals were struck bearing the portrait of Alexander the Great's mother Olympias with the legend OLYMPIAS REGINA. Ammianus Marcellinus reiterated that Aršak was the "steadfast and faithful friend" of the Romans

(*Ammiani Marcellini,* XXV. vii, 9-13; vol. II, pp. 532/3-534/5). Less
enthusiastically, *The Epic Histories* show Aršak oscillating between the
two empires and at times favored by the Persians as well. After the break
with Persia caused by the maneuvers of Andovk Siwni and the revolt of
Meružan Arcruni, the *sparapet* Vasak Mamikonean won repeated victories against the Persians, although he could not capture Meružan, but
Aršak's participation in the emperor Julian's disastrous campaign
against Persia spelled the doom of Armenia. Under the terms of the treaty
dictated by Šāhpur II to the emperor Jovian in 364, which Ammianus
Marcellinus stigmatizes as ignoble, Aršak II and his kingdom were
abandoned to the Persians together with a portion of the autonomous
Satrapies "beyond the Tigris" and the city of Nisibis. Making the most
of the opportunity, Šāhpur II ravaged Armenia despite the desperate
resistance of Queen P'aṙanjem entrenched in the royal fortress of
Artagers in Aršarunik'. Decoyed to Persia, Aršak II was perhaps blinded
and imprisoned in the Persian "Castle of Oblivion," the name of whose
inmates might never be spoken, where he committed suicide after a few
years, according to the account of *The Epic Histories* (P'awstos Buzand,
V. vii, pp. 197-98). The Armenian *sparapet* Vasak Mamikonean was
flayed alive. Finally Artagers fell and Queen P'aṙanjem was hideously
put to death, though Aršak's heir Pap found refuge on Roman territory
at Neocaesarea in Pontus. In retaliation for Andovk's treachery, his
domain of Siwnik' was singled out for Šāhpur's vengeance. The earlier
Armenian cities: Artašat, Vałaršapat, Zarehawan, Zarišat, Van, and
Naxčawan (Nakhchavan) were destroyed and their inhabitants, Jews as
well as Armenians, deported to Persia. After "thirty years of war" the
Persians were victorious and Armenia depopulated and looted. The
*naxarar*s fled "hither and yon," Persian garrisons were placed in the
Armenian fortresses, fire temples erected at Christian shrines, even
including the one at Ējmiacin, and Meružan Arcruni together with his
brother-in-law Vahan Mamikonean, the renegade brother of the
sparapet, to whom Šāhpur had given his own sister in marriage, were
set as governors over the Armenian lands (P'awstos Buzand, IV, lv,
lviii-lix, pp. 173-76, 178-80).

The catastrophic effects of the Persian conquest of Armenia horrified and alarmed the Romans so that the new *sparapet,* Mušeł
(Mushegh) Mamikonean, now obtained from the emperor Valens the
return of Aršak's son Pap, who was reinstated ca. 367 with the support
of an imperial army. Like his father, Pap began by a reconciliation with
the church and the nobility. The patriarch Nersēs the Great returned from

exile, and in 371 the *sparapet* routed the Persians and the Albanians at the foot of Mt. Npat/Niphates near Bagawan (Bagavan), as well as King Šāhpur II himself in an epic battle on the eastern border of Armenia, which drove the Persians from the country. A series of victories restored the former borders of the kingdom. Unfortunately, Pap's acceptance of Valens's openly Arianizing policy brought him again into conflict with the church. Consequently, the Armenian ecclesiastical historians are particularly hostile to the young king whom they accuse of having been devoted to the *dews* (*devs*) from childhood (P'awstos Buzand, IV. xliv, V. xx, pp. 164-65, 202-3), whereas Ammianus Marcellinus praises his gallantry. Resorting to the violent methods of his predecessors, Pap had the patriarch murdered in 373, dispersed and destroyed his charitable foundations, and appointed a successor without recourse to the traditional approval of Caesarea which refused to consecrate the royal candidate or recognize the authority of the Armenian primate over his own bishops. The murder of the patriarch alienated the *sparapet* as well as the magnates; Ammianus Marcellinus speaks of plots instigated in Armenia by the very imperial generals who had helped restore Pap on the throne. The king was summoned in 374 to meet Valens at Tarsus, where he successfully escaped the machinations of his enemies, but he was murdered at the instigation of the Romans on his return to Armenia (Ammianus Marcellinus, XXX.i; vol. III, pp. 294/95-306/307).

The murder of Pap inaugurated the decline of his house. His successor and probably nephew, to whom *The Epic Histories* refer disdainfully as "a certain Varazdat from the same Aršakuni house (P'awstos Buzand, V. xxxiv, p. 215)," soon found himself at odds with the all-powerful *sparapet* Mušeł Mamikonean. The king's attempt to throw off the Mamikonean tutelage by having Mušeł murdered and replaced by a *sparapet* of his own choosing from another house resulted only in his own defeat and expulsion from Armenia ca. 378, as Manuēl Mamikonean returned from Persian captivity to avenge his kinsman Mušeł and claim his hereditary office (P'awstos Buzand, V. xxxv-xxxvii, pp. 215-20). With Varazdat's exile all effective Roman support in Armenia came to an end, as their disastrous defeat at Andrianople in 378 withdrew the last garrisons from Armenia and turned the attention of the empire westward. At home, the *sparapet* Manuēl Mamikonean dominated the situation. Benefiting from the internal instability of Persia after the death of Šāhpur II in 379, Manuēl finally hunted down Meružan Arcruni and enthroned the two young sons of Pap, Aršak III and Vałaršak, under the nominal regency of their mother Zarmanduxt.

The marriage of the two young kings respectively to the daughters of Manuēl and of the *aspet* Sahak Bagratuni provides a clear index of the power achieved by the magnates over the crown (P'awstos Buzand, V, xxxvii-xxxviii, xliii-xliv, pp. 221-22, 224-28). In the absence of any Roman protector, however, Manuēl was also compelled to recognize the authority of the Sasanians, to pay tribute to the King of Kings, and to accept the presence in Armenia of a Persian "governor," or *marzpan*. Even this compromise was short-lived. Manuēl died ca. 385, and Aršak III, unable to withstand the hostility of the pro-Persian party among the *naxarar*s, fled to Ekełeac' (Ekeghiats) in western Armenia while the Persian court at the request of the Armenian nobility, replaced Vałaršak (who had presumably died) with Χosrov IV, who ruled with a Persian tutor in the eastern portion of the country in 384/5. The partition of Armenia had been achieved de facto even though the date of its ratification by the so-called Peace of Ekełeac', between the Roman emperor Theodosius I and the Sasanian king Šāhpur III (probably in 387) is still debated. Under the terms of this agreement, Greater Armenia was divided unequally by a line running north to south from a point east of Karin, soon to be fortified and renamed Theodosioupolis by the Greeks (modern Erzerum), to Mesopotamia west of Nisibis, which remained Persian. The partition thus left approximately four-fifths of the Armenian territories on the Persian side. A belt of Armenian peripheral lands fell away to its neighbors: Gugark' in the north to Iberia, Utik' and Arcax (Artsakh) in the northeast to Caspian Albania, Paytakaran and Parskahayk' in the east to Atrpatakan (modern Azerbaijan), and Korček' and Ałjnik' in the south to Mesopotamia, thus leaving a considerably reduced territory. Aršak III resided in Ekełeac' in Roman territory, while Χosrov IV kept the Aršakuni capitals of Artašat and Duin.

The partition of Armenia marked the last stage of the Aršakuni dynasty in Armenia. On the Roman side, no king replaced Aršak III, who died after two and a half years, ca. 390, and many of the *naxarar*s who had accompanied him moved back to the Persian side. In Persarmenia, as the Greek sources began to call it, Χosrov IV, who had become suspect to the Sasanians—perhaps because of his nomination of St. Sahak I, the last patriarch of the Gregorid house, without consulting the Persian authorities—was recalled, either immediately (ca. 389) or, according to some scholars, after an interregnum that lasted until 401. The reign of Vramšapuh (401?-417) brought a last moment of glory to the Aršakuni as he presided together with St. Sahak, whom he had sent to Persia to conciliate the Sasanian court, over the creation of the Armenian alphabet. But the Armenian sources know little more about him. With his death a fleeting reappearance of Xosrov IV was followed by outright annexation as Yazdgird I set his own son Šapuh (Shapuh) on the Armenian throne. Xorenac'i sneeringly portrays the cowardice of the Sasanian prince (Movses Khorenats'i, III. 55-56, pp. 323-26), and a last Aršakuni, Vramšapuh's son Ardašēs or Ardašir (422-428), was sent to Armenia at the request of the Armenian magnates. The centrifugal tendencies of the nobles, however, were beyond control. Disregarding the appeals of St. Sahak, the Armenian *naxarars* themselves requested that the Persians recall the last Aršakuni king, which was followed by the deposition of the patriarch.

For the first time in centuries, Armenia found itself without a king. Far to the west, Armenia Minor, which had first become a single province under Diocletian, was divided by Theodosius I into two regular provinces: Armenia I, with its capital at Sebastia/Sivas, and Armenia II, with Melitēnē as its capital. They were administered by ordinary Roman governors, while the garrisons stationed there were commanded by a military duke *(Dux Armeniae)*, although these territories remained demographically Armenian for a long time to come. The former Aršakuni lands between the Euphrates and the line of demarcation, now known as Armenia Interior, enjoyed a special status under a civilian official known as the "Count of Armenia" *(Comes Armeniae)* residing at Karin/Theodosiopolis, whose prerogatives are not precisely known. Persarmenia was ruled by a viceroy, or *marzpan*, appointed by the Sasanians. The only semblance of Armenian autonomy lay in the still-sovereign Satrapies of the south.

FOR FURTHER INFORMATION

For the sources of, or more information on, the material in this chapter, please consult the following (full citations can be found in the Bibliography at the end of this volume).

Adontz, 1970.

Ananian, 1961.

Asdourian, 1911.

The Cambridge History of Iran

Der Nersessian, 1969.

Garsoïan, 1985.

Manandyan, 1965.

Russell, 1987.

Thierry and Donabedian, 1989.

Toumanoff, 1963, 1966, 1969, 1976.

THE ARŠAKUNI (ARSHAKUNI)/ARSACID DYNASTY

All dates are A.D. Some dates are approximate and still in doubt.
Names in brackets are not members of this dynasty.

Vonones, 12-c.15

Orodes, c.15/5-c.18

[Zeno/Artašēs (Artashes) of Pontus, c.18-34]

Aršak (Arshak) I, 34-c.35

[Mithridates of Iberia, c.35-37, 42-51]

[Rhadamistes of Iberia, 51-54?]

Trdat/Tiridates I, 53-c.60

[Tigran VI, c.60-c.61/62]

Trdat I, c.62/66-c.75

Sanatruk, 75-110?

Axidares, 110-113?

Parthamasiris, 113-115?

[Roman annexation, 115-117]

Vałarš (Vagharsh)/Vologeses I, 117-138/140

Aurelius Pacorus 161-163?

[Sohaemus, 164-185, with interuptions]

Vałarš (Vagharsh)/Vologases II, c.180-191

Xosrov (Khosrov) I, c.191-216/217?

Trdat II, c.216/217-252

[Hormizd-Ardašir (Ardashir), Sasanian, 252-c.272]

[Narseh, Sasanian, c.273-293]

Xosrov (Khosrov) II, 279/280-287 (K'aj in Western Armenia?)

Trdat III, 287-298 (in Western Armenia)

Trdat IV the Great, 298/299-c.330

Xosrov (Khosrov) III Kotak, c.330-338

Tiran, c.338-350

Aršak (Arshak) II, 350-c.364/367

Pap, 367-c.374

Varazdat, 374-378

Aršak (Arshak) III, c.378-c.389

Xosrov (Khosrov), IV, 384-389 (in Eastern Armenia)

Vramšapuh (Vramshapuh), 389/401-417

Xosrov (Khosrov) IV, 417-418

[Šapuh (Shapuh), Sasanian, 418-422]

Artašēs (Artashes)/Artašir (Artashir), 422-428

5

THE *MARZPANATE* (428–652)

Nina Garsoïan

Persarmenia

With the end of the Aršakuni dynasty, the divided lands of Greater Armenia were set on divergent paths. The newly acquired imperial lands of Armenia Interior east of the Euphrates gradually followed Armenia Minor toward de-Armenization, although their special status was maintained for more than a century and they generally preserved their demographic Armenian majority. The southern Satrapies kept their full sovereignty until the end of the fifth century and then survived with a reduced status until the great reform of Justinian in 536 altered the administration of all the Armenian lands under Roman control. Despite its clearly dependent status and periodic persecutions, Persarmenia under Sasanian *marzpans*, who gave their name to this period of Armenian history, ultimately succeeded in preserving nearly intact its native *naxarar* social structure and the increasingly autonomous church that were to characterize Armenia in the absence of a political focus. The Sasanian domination did not begin auspiciously for the Armenians, who revolted repeatedly. Consequently, Armenian literature born in the second half of the fifth century, at the very moment of the desperate struggle to preserve Armenian culture from Persian assimilation, naturally portrayed Iran as eternally alien and hostile to Armenia.

In doing so, however, the early Armenian historians obscured and simplified a far more complex situation.

The first contacts of the Sasanian authorities with the Christian, mostly Syrian, communities within their empire were relatively uneventful. The main threat to the official Zoroastrianism of the dynasty in the late third century was Manichaeanism, which was ruthlessly extirpated while other religious groups, only occasionally disturbed, were not actively persecuted. This relatively neutral situation changed radically with the official recognition of Christianity by the Roman emperor Constantine I early in the fourth century. According to the political theory prevailing in this period in both Constantinople and Iran, political loyalty was inseparable from religious conformity and the Christians in Iran, the "slaves of the Roman Caesar their coreligionist," were now perceived as a subversive element directed against the safety of the Sasanian state. Again and again the Persians accused the Christians of being "Roman spies in the land of Persia": "These men are traitors to your majesty . . . since their faith and rites agree with those of the Romans," and they portrayed the Persian kat'ołikos (catholicos) as "an emissary sent by the Armenians and Romans" to plot against the King of Kings. On their side, the Christians tried to counter these accusations by desperately reiterating their loyalty to the Sasanian state:

> All of us unanimously implore our merciful God that he add to the days of the victorious and illustrious King of King Yazdgird [I] and that his years be lengthened from generations to generations and centuries after centuries. (*Synodicon Orientale,* p. 258)

Under these circumstances, it is not surprising that the first great persecution was directed at the Christians by King Šāhpur II in 338, as war flared against the successors of Constantine in heavily Christian Mesopotamia. In general, the situation of Christians in the Persian empire automatically worsened in times of open conflict with the Romans.

The first Sasanian *marzpan* appointed for Armenia in 428 seems to have been a relatively tolerant and reasonable man, and the grant of the office of *hazarapet* to the native *naxarar* Vahan Amatuni left the civilian administration and consequently a considerable amount of authority in the hands of the Armenian magnates. Even so, the position of the Armenian Church immediately worsened. The Persian authorities deposed the hereditary Gregorid patriarch St. Sahak I in 428, seemingly

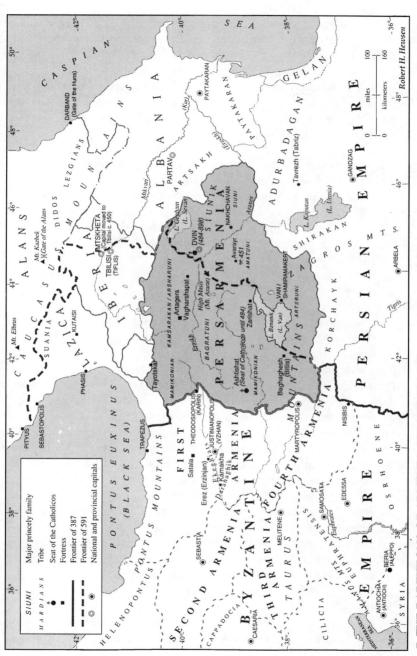

7. *THE PARTITIONS OF ARMENIA, 387 AND 591 A.D.*

with the adhesion of some of the *naxarars*, who repeatedly turned to the Persian court, stripped him of his domains, according to Xorenac'i, and replaced him at first with an Armenian Surmak, but immediately thereafter with two Syrians, Brk'išoy (Brkisho) (428-432) and Samuēl (432-437), who were presumably Christians from Persia, among whom the Syrians were a dominant majority. Armenian sources have left us unedifying portrayals of the morals of the two Syrian primates, but the authority of St. Sahak was severely curtailed:

> [The Persian King] . . . gave the archiepiscopal throne to another Syrian, Samuel by name, so that he might be a rival and antipatriarch to Sahak, and he set his duties: to assist the *marzban* and to oversee the assessment of the required taxes, the law courts, and other secular institutions. And Sahak the Great he set free; leaving him a few villages from the same [patriarchal] domain that he might reside only in his own see with the authority only to give the traditional religious instruction and to ordain those whom Samuel might accept. (Movses Khorenats'i, III. 65, p. 343)

Not only were the Syrian primates direct Sasanian appointees, their presence in Armenia was intended to break the increasingly close contacts of the Armenian and Greek Churches encouraged by the Gregorids and to link Armenian Christianity to the official church of Persia. The later Chalcedonian source known as the *Narratio de rebus Armeniae* even dates from Surmak's usurpation the "waywardness" of the Armenian bishops, the condemnation of the Armenian Church by its former patron, Caesarea of Cappadocia, and the prohibition to the Armenian patriarch to ordain his own bishops. The absence of the Armenians from the Œcumenical Council of Ephesus in 431 and the calling of a local synod at Šahapivan (Shahapivan) in 444 to legislate in ecclesiastical matters point to the growing isolation of Persarmenia from the West. The refusal of St. Sahak to return to the patriarchal throne after the death of Samuēl in 437 indicates the alienation of the Hellenizing party in the Armenian Church, which turned to Constantinople for dogmatic advice. The Sasanian court apparently refused to ratify the choice of Maštoc''s disciple Yovsēp' (Hovsep')/Joseph, who remained a priest, rather than a bishop, and merely the vicar of the patriarchal throne.

A sharp turn for the worse came with the accession of the new Persian king Yazdgird (Yazdagerd) II in 439 and the rule of his prime minister Mihr-Narseh, whose fervent devotion to Zoroastrianism is attested not only by the hostile Armenian historians, but also by the *Sasanian Lawbook.* Our two main sources for the ensuing events, Łazar P'arpec'i's *History of Armenia* and Ełišē's *History of Vardan and the Armenian War,* agree in the main, although they differ in details such as the origins of the Armenian revolt.

The first signs of trouble came with the summons to the Armenian cavalry to serve against the Huns on Persia's eastern border while a Sasanian official was sent to take a census that harshly increased and extended the obligations of Armenia:

> First: he cast the freedom of the church into slavery.
> Second: he included in the same census the Christian monks living in monasteries.
> Third: he increased the tax burden of the country.
> Fourth: by slander he pitted the nobility against each other, and caused dissension in every family.
> He did this in the hope of breaking their unity, scattering the clergy of the church . . . they taxed both bishops and priests, not merely of inhabited land but of desolated areas . . . They did not act in accordance with royal dignity, but raided like brigands, until they themselves were greatly amazed as to whence all this treasure came and how the country remained prosperous. (Ełišē, ii, pp. 76-77)

The Armenian *hazarapet* was replaced by a Persian official, and "he also brought a chief-magus as judge of the land."

At first no one opposed these harsh measures because "no one yet openly laid hand on the church" and the Armenian cavalry distinguished itself in the East, but the subsequent royal edict openly imposing Zoroastrianism on Armenia, as well as on Iberia and Caucasian Albania, provoked an immediate reaction. A council assembled at Artašat under the presidency of the *marzpan* Vasak Siwni, the *sparapet* Vardan Mamikonean (Mamikonian), the *bdešx* of the Iberian March, and the acting kat'ołikos Yovsēp', to reaffirm the loyalty of Armenia to both the Sasanian state and the Christian faith. Unable to accept this contradiction, King Yazdgird II summoned the Armenian magnates to his court, where all of them, Vardan as well as Vasak, were constrained under threat to accept Zoroastrianism, at least outwardly. An unexpected attack from the East forced the Persians to release the Armenian nobles, although the *bdešx* and the sons of the *marzpan* Vasak Siwni were kept as hostages, and the Magians were sent to spread Zoroastrianism through all the Caucasus.

The immediate background of the open Armenian rebellion is not always clear, but the first overt acts seem to have come not so much from the *naxarars*, humiliated and disgraced by their religious compromise, as from the common people incited against the magians by the implacable clergy. Vardan Mamikonean may even have intended to retire into exile, although Łazar P'arpec'i and Etišē disagree on this subject. The villain of the fifth century for the Armenian historians is Vasak Siwni, the traitor par excellence (as Meružan Arcruni had been in the fourth century), although his motives are not always clear and he was not alone in his stand. A sizable pro-Persian party, including the *aspet* Varaz-Tiroc' (Tirots) Bagratuni, some of the Arcruni, and a number of other nobles, listed by Łazar as well as Etišē, clearly existed in the country and opposed the policies of Vardan Mamikonean and his supporters.

In spite of this latent internal division, the armed rebellion of 450 began as a joint operation as the Armenian magnates bound themselves by a solemn covenant *(uxt)* and retook a number of fortresses and villages. Warned by Caucasian Albanians of the Persian advance, Vardan Mamikonean, who now emerged as the unquestionable leader of the rebellion, marched north to meet them at the same time as an unsuccessful embassy was sent to seek help from Constantinople. Vardan routed the Persians in the summer of 450 and concluded an alliance with the northern Huns. But the opposing policy of Vasak Siwni, who had remained behind in Armenia, compromised this initial success, and the absence of Greek support gave a free hand to the Persians. After an initial offer of amnesty and toleration, a large Persian army including an elite corps of the "immortals" and a contingent of elephants advanced from the east in the early summer of 451. On June 2 it was met by the Armenian magnates in the region of Artaz, at Awarayr (Avarayr) near Maku. Overwhelmed by the Persian host and abandoned by the supporters of Vasak, who fled from the field, the *sparapet* Vardan and the majority of the Armenian nobility perished in the battle whose memory was to be preserved by the Armenian tradition for more than fifteen centuries.

The aftermath of the battle is not altogether clear, as accounts differ. Apparently alarmed by the Persian losses and the continuing Armenian guerrillas, King Yazdgird II recalled his troops as well as the *marzpan* Vasak, whom he imprisoned. The principality of Siwnik' was bestowed on Vasak's rival Varazvałan (Varazvaghan) and many of the

surviving supporters of Vardan were deported southeast of the Caspian
Sea and imprisoned. The leaders of the clerical opposition, the acting
kat'ołikos Yovsēp' and the priest Łewond (Ghevond), were martyred in
Persia. Nevertheless, a new *marzpan* was sent in 451 to pacify Armenia
with a more tolerant policy and the prisoners were eventually released.
The *bdešx* of Iberia returned to Armenia in 455, bringing with him the
nephews of Vardan Mamikonean. The other *naxarar*s were released by
459-460. The great Armenian clans had unquestionably been profoundly shaken by the rebellion of 450-451 and the losses of Awarayr,
but they were in no sense destroyed.

The tension between Armenia and Persia continued in the next
generation, as the children of the magnates fallen at Awarayr grew to
manhood. The new Armenian kat'ołikos, Giwt (Giut) (461-478), accused
of secret negotiations with Byzantium, was ordered to leave his residence
at Duin, the seat of the *marzpan*s, summoned to Persia, and finally allowed
to settle in semiretirement in the northwestern Armenian district of
Vanand, although he was not deprived of his dignity. An internal quarrel
in Iberia between the new *bdešx* and Vaxtang (Vakhtang) Gorgasal, whom
Łazar P'arpec'i calls "King of Iberia," involved Armenia in a new
rebellion. Summoned by the Persians against Vaxtang, the new *sparapet,*
Vardan's nephew Vahan Mamikonean, hesitated then sided with the
Iberians at the urging of the kat'ołikos Yovhannēs (Hovhannes)/John I
Mandakuni (478-490). Early in 481 the Armenians occupied Duin, aban-
doned by the Persian *marzpan,* and named as governor the Armenian *aspet*
Sahak Bagratuni. The returning Persian *marzpan* was defeated and killed
by Vahan's brother on the north slope of Mt. Ararat, while Sahak
Bagratuni and Vahan held Duin. The following spring they in turn routed
the Persians near the battlefield of Awarayr, despite the continuing
presence of an opposition party in Armenia. These victories were, however, compromised by the disagreement between the Armenians and the
Iberians that led to a Persian victory in which both Sahak and Vasak
Mamikonean lost their lives. Vahan was then forced to take refuge in the
distant northwestern district of Tayk' whence he carried on guerrilla
warfare in 483. Fortunately for the rebels, the disastrous defeat and death
of the Persian King of Kings on the eastern frontier in 484 restored the
Armenian situation since neither of his successors found himself in a
position to reconquer Armenia. In return for his support, Vahan received
from the new Persian king the confirmation of his dignity as *sparapet,* the
return of his domains as well as those of his Kamsarakan supporters,
freedom of religion, and the right of appeal directly to the Persian court,

bypassing the authority of the *marzpan*. In 485 Vahan himself was appointed *marzpan* of Armenia, which he ruled until 505 or 510, and a modus vivendi between Iran and Armenia was finally achieved.

The *marzpan*ate of Vahan Mamikonean, who enjoyed almost total autonomy, marked a period of prosperity according to the Armenian historian Sebēos, followed by the later Armenian author Stephen of Tarōn, usually known as Asołik. Another of the periodic invasions was contained. Duin and Vałaršapat were rebuilt and the cathedral of Duin restored, while the kat'ołikos Yovhannēs Mandakuni, who settled at Duin, regularized the liturgy and reordered the church. The survival of a number of impressive stone basilicas from the fifth century provide material evidence of extensive architectural activity and consequently of the wealth and stability of Armenia throughout this period. A Byzantine edict of 408-409 preserved in the *Justinianic Code,* and reconfirmed by the peace treaty of 562 designated Artašat as one of the three frontier points where international trade with Persia was permitted. Customs posts were established there and supervised on the imperial side by financial officials known as "commercial counts" *(comites commercium).* The sixth-century Byzantine historian Procopius lavished praise on the favorable location and wealth of Duin in his time:

> Now Doubios [Duin] is a land excellent in every respect, and especially blessed with a healthy climate and abundance of good water; from Theodosiopolis [Erzerum] it is removed a journey of eight days. In that region there are plains suitable for riding, and many very populous villages are situated in very close proximity to one another, and numerous merchants conduct their business in them. For from India and the neighboring regions of Iberia and from practically all the nations of Persia and some of those under Roman sway they bring in merchandise and carry on their dealings with each other there. And the priest of the Christians is called "Catholicos" in the Greek tongue, because he presides over the whole region. (Procopius, "The Persian War," II, xxv, 1-3, vol I, pp. 478/9-480/1).

As far back as 450, Ełišē had also noted that the Persians themselves had been amazed at the wealth they found in Armenia. Most important of all, the traditional social structure of the country does not seem to have been disturbed.

These favorable conditions were temporarily disrupted after Vahan's death by the resumption of the Byzantine-Persian war in which

Roman Armenia suffered considerably. On the Sasanian side, this period was marked by the recall or death of Vahan's brother and successor *marzpan* known as Vard Patrik "the Patrician," followed for a decade by a series of Persian governors. At the same time, repeated invasions of Huns from the north of the Caucasus raided Armenia at the instigation of Byzantium, which was regaining a foothold along the southeastern shore of the Black Sea by 521. Nevertheless, under the twenty-year *marzpan*ate of the Armenian *naxarar* Mžež (Mzhezh) Gnuni (527-548), who successfully fought off the invaders, Persarmenia maintained the autonomy won by the Mamikoneans in the preceding century and even flourished under Persian rule, as we shall see.

Byzantine Armenia and the Reforms of Justinian I (527-565)

In contrast to the survival of national institutions in Persarmenia, the Roman territories were relatively peacefully but irreversibly transformed into ordinary Byzantine administrative units. This was already the status of the westernmost Armenian lands of Armenia Minor, divided, as we have seen, into Armenia I to the north and Armenia II farther south at the end of the fourth century and administered by Roman civilian governors subordinate to the *vicar* of the large imperial administrative district or diocese of Pontus, who answered in turn to the highest Byzantine civilian authority in the region, the Praetorian Prefect of the East. A parallel ecclesiastical administration culminated in two archdioceses or eparchies headed respectively by the metropolitans of Sebasteia/Sivas and Melitēnē/Malatia. We learn from the contemporary army list that two legions, plus cavalry and lesser detachments, were stationed primarily at Satala in Armenia I and Melitēnē in Armenia II. They were under the command of the *Dux Armeniae* residing at Melitēnē, whose authority extended over Pontus and Armenia Interior as well, and who answered directly to the commander-in-chief for the East.

Armenia Interior was ruled from the time of the partition of ca. 387 by a special civilian official known as the *Comes Armeniae* ("Count of Armenia"), whose position vis-à-vis the local *naxarar*s is not defined but probably resembled that of the *marzpan* on the Persian side. His status in the Byzantine hierarchy was probably that of a vicar; as such he presumably ranked higher than the governors of Armenia I and II. Legally, Armenia Interior was a *civitas stipendiaria,* that is to say it had some autonomous rights but was required to pay taxes and furnish military contingents to the *Dux Armeniae*. Unfortunately, we know very little concerning the local magnates. The royal Aršakuni maintained themselves in western Armenia, and some rose high in the imperial hierarchy at Constantinople long after the death of King Aršak III. Some of the Bagratuni also attempted to come over to Byzantium in Justinian's time but were murdered by mistake. Finally, a branch of the Mamikonean house inherited the patriarchal domains in Daranałik' (Daranaghik) and Ekełeac' (Ekeghiats), districts that lay in Byzantine Armenia as a result of the partition after the death of St. Sahak I in 439, but we do not know how these *naxarars* fulfilled their obligations.

The first group to suffer a loss of status were the Satrapies that had maintained their independence as *civitates foederatae*, "allies," even after the partition. Their hereditary rulers had full sovereign rights and merely sent military contingents and the occasional gift of a gold crown to the emperor. The participation of the satraps in the rebellion of 485 against the Byzantine emperor led to the abrogation of their sovereign rights and the loss of their hereditary rulers, thus reducing them with one exception to the level of taxable *civitates stipendiariae* governed by imperial officials.

Far more extensive reforms were introduced soon after the accession of Justinian I in 527. A first imperial decree sought to bring order into the conflicting jurisdiction of the *Dux* and the *Comes Armeniae* as well as of the local magnates. The offices of both the *Dux* and the *Comes* were abolished and a new extended military command, that of *Magister militum per Armeniam, Pontum Polemoniacum et gentes* was created. The authority of the new official and the extension of his jurisdiction over all the imperial Armenian territories were spelled out by the decree:

> We have found it necessary to create by the present law a special military commander for parts of Armenia, Pontus Polemoniacus and the Nations [Satrapies] . . . We entrust to thy care certain provinces, namely Greater Armenia, which is called Interior and the Nations (namely Anzetena [Hanjit], Ingilena [Angełtun (Angeghtun)], Asthianena [Hašteank'], Sophena [Cop'k' Šahuni (Dzopk Shahuni)], in which lies Martyropolis, Balabitena [Balahovit] as well as First and Second Armenias and Pontus Polemoniacus, together with their Dukes. And the Count of Armenia is to be abolished altogether. We entrust [to thee] certain legions, not only those which are now being constituted, but also those chosen from the ones in the capital, those

in the East, and certain other regiments. Furthermore, the number of soldiers in them shall not be diminished. . . . (Adontz, 1970, p. 107)

This new master of the army, under whose command were three dukes and an extensive staff, moved his residence eastward to Armenia Interior at Theodosiopolis/Karin, which was extensively refortified and became the anchor point of the imperial defense in the north. The same was done for Martyropolis in Mesopotamia and the new fortified city of Dara created a few years earlier in the same region, northwest of Nisibis. In general, the eastern border of the empire, which up to that time had been so open that, according to the contemporary historian Procopius,

> the inhabitants of this region whether subjects of the Romans or the Persians have no fear of each other . . . they even intermarry and hold a common market for their produce and together they share the labors of farming . . . (Procopius, *Buildings,* III, iii, 7-14, vol VII, pp. 192/3-194/5)

was closed by a continuous series of fortifications with permanent garrisons that intensified the isolation of the two portions of Armenia from each other.

Justinian's civilian reform promulgated by the imperial *Novella XXXI* of 18 March 536, "On the Establishment of Four Governors for Armenia," went much farther and completed the transformation of the imperial Armenian territories. With this new legislation the special status of Armenia Interior and the Satrapies was completely abolished. Moreover, since the lands affected by it included the former Armenia I and II and some adjacent Pontic lands as well, the division between Greater Armenia and Armenia Minor along the Euphrates River was partially obscured, as was the differentiation of Armenian lands from those of Pontus to the north. Under the terms of the *Novella,* four new imperial provinces all named Armenia (I,II,III, IV) were created to replace earlier administrative districts: (1) A new Armenia I was made up of most of Armenia Interior together with a portion of the former Armenia I and some Pontic territories. It included several cities, Theodosiopolis/Karin (east of the Euphrates), Satala (west of the river in old Armenia Minor), as well as several others and bordered on the Black Sea in the region of Pontus around Trapezus (modern Trebizond). (2) The new Armenia II consisted of the remaining, or western portion of the former Armenia I and additional Pontic territory. Its capital was

Sebasteia/Sivas, and four other cities were attributed to it. (3) Armenia III coincided with the former Armenia II, in the southern portion of what had once been Armenia Minor, with Melitēnē/Malatia as its capital. (4) Finally, Armenia IV was composed of the lands of the abolished Satrapies and had Martyropolis (modern Silvan) in Mesopotamia as its capital. Governors were appointed for the four new provinces, and special staffs of tax collectors saw to the revenue. The new legislation did not create total uniformity in the territories affected since their governors were not equals. Those of Armenia I and III, who had military as well as civilian authority, outranked their respective colleagues in II and IV. Nevertheless, all traces of native autonomy and privileges had been wiped out as well as the distinction between Armenian and Byzantine territories.

Complementing this profound administrative reorganization came other legal measures that were to reach even deeper into the intrinsic life of the Armenian society found in these regions, as the historian Nicholas Adontz long since observed (Adontz, 1970, pp. 141-56). Innocuous at first sight, these edicts extended the principles of Roman law to Armenian lands with far-reaching results. Inheritance henceforth was to be through formal testamentary dispositions, daughters were to inherit as well as sons and were to receive dowries at marriage. The mild and even benevolent tone of these regulations hid the total disruption of the fundamental structure of *naxarar* society in imperial Armenia. The inalienable possessions traditionally held in common by the entire *tun* now became the property of the *tanutēr,* who passed it to his immediate family, dispossessing the other *sepuhs.* Not only did this obviously create dissensions within the clan, but it made the possessions far more vulnerable since only a few persons, or even one man, rather than the united clan, stood in the way of confiscation. The provision that all children, females as well as males, should inherit, as well as the institution of the dowry, meant the rapid fragmentation of the great territorial units that had been the economic bases of the *naxarars*' power.

The Justinianic legislation and the traditional structure of Armenian society were clearly incompatible, and the magnates at first attempted to resist. In 538 the imperial proconsul appointed as governor of Armenia I was murdered, and the master of the army in Armenia was also killed by his brother-in-law who then turned to the Persians for support. Ten years later, a conspiracy of two members of the Aršakuni family (Arsaces/Aršak and Artabanes/Artawan), also failed, but the words used by Aršak to arouse his kinsman, cited by Procopius, show the bitterness of the *naxarar*s and the gradual de-Armenization of the land:

> He had . . . given proof of his nobility of spirit . . . But at the present juncture . . . he was utterly cowed, and he continued to sit there without a spark of manhood, though his fatherland was kept under strictest guard and exhausted with unwonted taxes, his father had been slain on the pretext of a covenant and his entire family had been enslaved and was scattered in every corner of the Roman empire. (Procopius, "The Gothic War," III. xxxii, 6-7, vol. IV, pp. 420/1-422/3)

The evidence of the *Letters* sent to the Byzantine emperor by the bishops of Armenia I and II in 458 explicitly shows that this region was still demographically and linguistically Armenian in the middle of the fifth century, but the effects of the Justinianic legislation, the systematic policy of deporting Armenians to the Balkans practiced by his successors, and the lure of imperial service, through which Armenians reached all the way to the throne, gradually drained the leadership from Byzantine Armenia. Transformed into imperial officials and gradually assimilated, the remaining local magnates vanished without trace, so that our knowledge of the *naxarar* families and of their prerogatives must perforce be drawn exclusively from Persarmenia, where they were able to survive and maintain their traditional institutions.

Byzantine Expansion
and the Armenian Partition of 591

Byzantine expansion toward the east, which marked the last century of the *Marzpan*ate, extended the scope of the Justinianic reforms with their implicit threat against the very core of Armenian social and cultural institutions. The imperial frontier moved radically forward under Justinian's successors, and they briefly controlled most of the Armenian highlands at the turn of the fifth to the seventh century, on the eve of the Arab invasions. The result of the heavy-handed Byzantine policy of assimilation was, however, to antagonize and embitter the *naxarar*s and especially the Armenian Church, fearful for their autonomy and their very survival, and so to push them toward an open break with the empire.

The first move came soon after Justinian's death, at a time when the stability of Persarmenia had already been shaken by a separatist

movement in the region of Siwnikʻ, whose ruler obtained the autonomy
of his principality from the Persian king. The religious zeal of the
Zoroastrian Persian *marzpan* (who apparently exceeded his instructions,
since the Armenian sources invariably praise the Persian king's benevolent attitude toward Christians) also aggravated the situation within the
country. In 571, the building of a fire temple in the capital of Duin
provoked the rebellion of Vardan Mamikonean (usually referred to as
Vardan II to distinguish him from his fifth-century namesake) supported
the katʻołikos Yovhannēs II Gabełean (Gabeghian) (557-576). The
marzpan was killed and Duin taken by the rebels. Making the most of
the opportunity, the emperor Justin II took the Persarmenians under his
protection, at first rejecting the Persian protests. But, despite repeated
victories in Armenia against the invading Persian armies and even the
rout of the Persians near Melitēnē, the Byzantines, more concerned with
the fate of Mesopotamia than of with that of Persarmenia, withdrew.
Under the terms of the armistice concluded in 575, Persarmenia was
returned to the Sasanians, and Vardan II (with his supporters and the
katʻołikos) was forced to take refuge in Byzantine territory, where he
settled in western Asia Minor. Greater Armenia had borne the brunt of
the Persian campaign, while the future Byzantine emperor Maurice went
on to pursue a scorched earth policy in the southern Armenian border
district of Ałjnikʻ/Arzanēnē, burning and ravaging the land and deporting some 10,000 of its Armenian population to Cyprus in 577.

The new crisis in Persia, where the young King Χusrō (Khosrov) II
was driven from the throne in 591 by an usurper, proved far more
advantageous for Byzantium. In return for the help given him by Maurice
to regain his throne, Χusrō II ceded to Byzantium a large portion of
Persarmenia as well as of Iberia, so that the new line of demarcation
between the two empires lay considerably east of the earlier partition of
ca. 387. In the north of the Armenian plateau the border now ran from
Gařni, along the Azat River just west of Duin, down to Arest at the
northeastern corner of Lake Van.

> He [Χusrō] gave him [Maurice] all of Arwastan to Nisibis and the
> Armenian lands which were under his power: the Tanutērakan *tun* all
> the way to the Hurazdan River with the district of Kotēkʻ up to the
> village of Gařni and to the sea of Bznunikʻ, and the town of Arest,
> and the district of Gogovit to Hacʻiwn [Hatsiun] and to Maku. While
> the region of the *gund* of Vaspurakan remained under the domination
> of the Persian king. (Sebēos, iii, p. 27)

The newly organized lands were apportioned into imperial provinces as before, although the precise divisions are still open to considerable disagreement, since no decree such as Justinian's *Novella* exists from this period. Insofar as can be deduced from the confusing sources, the new Armenia I of Maurice coincided with Justinian's Armenia III. Armenia II remained unchanged, and the term Armenia III disappeared altogether from the new administrative roster. A new southern province composed of territories now acquired from Persia received the name of Armenia IV or Upper Mesopotamia, while the former Armenia IV with some districts drawn from Armenia Interior was now called Justiniana, or the Other Armenia IV. Even though the exact form of the changes remain unclear, it is evident that such an administrative restructuring coming less than two generations after Justinian's reform left little of the original framework of the region.

The damage done to Armenia during the reign of Maurice was not merely structural. The antagonism of the emperor finds its expression in an apocryphal letter from Maurice to the Persian king quoted by Pseudo-Sebēos:

> They [the Armenians] are a disloyal and disobedient nation, they stand between us and create dissensions. Let us make an agreement, I will gather up mine and send them to Thrace, let you gather up yours and order them to the East. If they should perish there, then enemies will have perished and if they should kill others, it is our enemies that they will kill, and we shall live in peace, for, as long as they shall remain in their country we shall have no rest (Sebēos, vi, pp. 30-31).

This policy of depopulation was immediately put into effect. The Armenian *sparapet* Mušeł Mamikonean, who had helped restore Χusrō II on the throne, became suspect to the Persians because of his family's long pro-imperial policy. He was well received at the Byzantine court but was sent with a large contingent recruited in Byzantine Armenia to command the imperial army in Thrace, where he is said to have died in combat. Mušeł was not the only Armenian magnate sent to the Balkans. The Armenian *naxarar*s sought to be exempted from this service "so that they might not die in the regions of Thrace but might live and die in their own country." As a result, some rebelled and were executed, and many Armenians fled from imperial territory back to Persarmenia, according to Pseudo-Sebēos, and were warmly received. Even after Maurice's death in 602 his successor continued this policy proclaimed in his edict:

> I require the tribute of 30,000 cavalrymen from the land of Armenia.
> Therefore, let 30,000 household gather before me and settle in Thrace.
> (Sebēos, xx, p. 54)

The fate attributed by Sebēos to Smbat Bagratuni, thrown to the wild beasts in the hippodrome and heroically overwhelming them single-handed, smacks more of the ancient Armenian epic traditions of the *gusan*s than of history, but Smbat's deportation by Maurice to the army in Africa from which he subsequently escaped to Persia, where a brilliant career awaited him, is very much in keeping with the hostile Byzantine policy of the period.

The Evolution of the
Armenian Church During the Marzpanate

The growing alienation of the Armenians from Byzantium was not provoked exclusively by the imperial administrative policies. It was greatly intensified on both sides by dogmatic divergences that increasingly opposed the two churches and by the repeated imperial attempts to force Armenia into communion with the Byzantine Church. The jurisdictional break between the Armenian and the Greek churches had already taken place, as we have seen, by the fifth century, as Armenia severed its early ties with Caesarea of Cappadocia and gradually asserted its independence from the protectorate of the Greek ecclesiastical world.

The residence of the Armenian kat'olikos in Persian territory throughout this period also affected the position taken by the Armenian Church and turned its eyes away from the West. As early as 410, the Persian church recognized to the Zoroastrian King of Kings all the prerogatives enjoyed by the Christian emperor on Byzantine territory. The Sasanian ruler summoned ecclesiastical councils and promulgated their decrees; his ratification allowed bishops to take possession of their sees, whose importance followed that of the cities in which they were located. These practices seem to have been followed in Persarmenia whose church apparently accepted the secular jurisdiction of the Sasanians. Armenian ecclesiastical sources might criticize the personality of the Syrian primates sent by the Persian court in the fifth century, as we have seen, but they did not question its right to appoint them, nor did they express dismay at the *naxarar*s' repeated requests that the King of Kings send them a patriarch. According to the account of Łazar P'arpec'i

(III. 64, p. 167), the patriarch Giwt, accused before King Pērōz, quite rightly denied that he or anyone could take away his episcopal ordination, but he did not question the king's right to depose him and take away the secular prerogatives of his office. Yovsēp'(Hovsep), one of the martyrs after 451, chosen as primate by the Armenians without Persian ratification, does not seem to have had the full authority of a patriarch and is usually referred to as a vicar rather than as the kat'ołikos by the Armenian sources. Armenian church councils were customarily dated according to the regnal year of the Sasanian rulers (although a calendar based on the Armenian era beginning in 552 was also introduced), and the Armenian church councils of the early seventh century were convened with the permission of the Persian ruler.

The elaboration of the doctrinal position of the Armenian Church came relatively slowly. As early as the beginning of the fifth century, the church had already become preoccupied with the writings of the Byzantine patriarch Nestorius and of his teacher, who distinguished the divine from the human nature of Christ. This doctrine condemned by the Œcumenical Council of Ephesus in 431 was likewise rejected by the Armenian Church, which fully concurred with the decision taken at Ephesus that the two natures of Christ should not be distinguished after His Incarnation. The outright rejection of the christological definition adopted at the next Council of Chalcedon in 451, and regarded as tainted with Nestorianism by most of the eastern churches, had a slower evolution in Armenia. The next official text to reach the country from Byzantium in the second half of the fifth century was probably the *Henotikon* promulgated by the emperor Zeno in 482. It reaffirmed the authority of the Council of Ephesus with its condemnation of Nestorianism and was ambiguous about Chalcedon. Under the next emperor, Anastasius, at the beginning of the sixth century, this document was given a clearly anti-Chalcedonian interpretation, stressing the unity of Christ's nature. The praise of the Armenian sources for the pious emperors Zeno and Anastasius show the doctrinal direction taken by the Armenian Church. Nevertheless, neither the First Council of Duin in 506, which condemned the writings of Nestorius and reaffirmed the orthodoxy of the *Henotikon,* nor the Second Council of Duin in 555 under the kat'ołikos Nersēs II, which again condemned the Nestorians, explicitly mentioned Chalcedon. The open condemnation of Chalcedon came only in 607, when the Armenian bishops assembled at the urging of the Persian *marzpan,* Smbat Bagratuni, formally anathematized it and the *Tome* of Pope Leo I on which it was based. Even after this decision, a sizable pro-Chalcedonian party continued to exist in Armenia, as evidenced by the composition of a treatise such as the *Narratio de rebus Armeniae* ("Account of the Affairs of Armenia"), which championed this doctrine. The immediate result of the Armenian conciliar decision was to extend the dogmatic breach to the Iberian Church, whose kat'ołikos accepted union with the Byzantine Church in 608, perhaps in part to free himself from the protectorate that the Armenian Church had extended over Iberia and Caucasian Albania in the preceding centuries.

Even before taking the formal stand that marked its religious breach with Byzantium, however, the position of the Armenian Church was unmistakably clear and its rejection of the Chalcedonian doctrine had historical repercussions far beyond the purely ecclesiastical sphere. In the Byzantine Empire, the acceptance of the official imperial orthodoxy with its Chalcedonian Christology was part of the loyalty demanded of all subjects, and an oath of orthodoxy was a prerequisite for imperial service. Armenian *naxarars* seeking to rise in the imperial hierarchy thus found themselves cut off not only from their native language and culture but from religious ties with their compatriots in Persarmenia, and Armenian bishops on imperial territory no longer recognized the authority of the kat'ołikos. The price of imperial asylum and support was acceptance of Chalcedonian orthodoxy, as Vardan II Mamikonean and the kat'ołikos Yovhannēs II were to learn when they took refuge in Constantinople at the time of the Armenian rebellion of 571 to 574, although later Armenian sources attempted to disguise or deny this fact.

The situation became far more acrimonious with Maurice's policy to enforce religious unity over the greatly enlarged Armenian territories he ruled after 591. The first attempt to call a Council of Union of all the Armenians that same year failed, as the kat'ołikos Movsēs II (574-604), residing at Duin on Persian territory, returned a contemptuous answer to the emperor in which he rejected the Greek use of leavened bread for the host and the admixture of water (symbolic of Christ's separate earthly nature) to the chalice of communion, both of which were unacceptable to the Armenians:

> I shall not cross the Azat river—that is the Persian border—to eat the
> *p'urnid* [oven-baked bread] of the Greeks, nor will I drink their
> *t'ermon* [hot water]. (Garsoïan, 1983, p. 223)

In retaliation, Maurice installed an antipatriarch, Yovhannēs of Bagaran, at Awan (in the suburbs of modern Erevan) and for twenty-two years the two kat'ołikoi faced each other over the Persian border, adding religious schism to the political and administrative division of Armenia and embittering the antagonism of both parties.

No solution was found for the disagreement, although the open schism ended with the disappearance of Yovhannēs of Bagaran, deported to die in Persia at the time of Xusrō II's reconquest in 611 of the territories he had ceded to Byzantium. The bishops of the reconquered territories, who had supported Yovhannēs, were brought back into communion with the kat'ołikos Abraham I (607-615). The growing religious divergence with Constantinople continued to affect the position of Armenia in the seventh century. The repeated attempts of the Byzantine emperors to force Armenia into religious union with themselves both under Heraclius, who obtained in 632/3 the temporary adhesion of the kat'ołikos Ezr (630-641), and even under his successor in 652/3 (after the beginning of the Arab invasions of Armenia) only embittered the Armenian clergy and helped alienate much of the population.

The consequences of the religious schism were not all negative for Armenia, however, since the growing threat from Byzantium was balanced by the improving position of the Armenians living under Persian domination. As Armenia became "schismatic," and consequently unacceptable in the eyes of Byzantium, its status improved in the eyes of the Sasanian authorities who no longer feared an Armenian alliance with the empire. The last King of Kings favored the Armenian *naxarars* and posed as the protector of the Armenian Church. The best illustration of this favor is the brilliant career of Smbat Bagratuni, who fled from Byzantium after his disgrace under the emperor Maurice, as we noted earlier. Granted the exceptional title of *Xosrov šnum (Khosrov shnum* or "the joy of Xusrō), Smbat was appointed *marzpan* of Vrkan/Hyrkania south of the Caspian Sea and viceroy of the East under Xusrō II. Not only was Smbat allowed to call the Council of 607 that elected the kat'ołikos Abraham I, thus putting an end to a three years' interregnum in the Armenian patriarchate, and subsequently to act as co-president of the general church council held in the Persian capital of Ctesiphon in 610 to which Armenian bishops were also invited, but he was further permitted to rebuild the church of St. Gregory at Duin. The Persian governor complained to the king, says the historian Pseudo-Sebēos, that the church

> is too close to the fortress and may result in danger from the enemy,
> [but] the order came from the king, "let the fortress be destroyed and
> the church be built in that place." (Sebēos, xvii, p. 47).

Similarly, the increasingly favorable position of the Armenians in the Persian Empire once their dogmatic position had made them personae non gratae to the Byzantine court is reflected in the praise of the Armenian source for the Persian kings, both the tale of Χusrō I's apocryphal deathbed conversion to Christianity and Pseudo-Sebēos' assertion repeated by Asołik that

> the King [Χusrō II] ordered a search of the royal treasury, and they found written down the true faith of Nicaea which he found in accordance with the faith of the realm of Armenia [and] sealed with the seal of King Kavad and his son Χosrov [I]. Thereupon King Χosrov decreed 'Let all the Christians within my dominion hold to the faith of the Armenians.' And [also] those who were [already] united with the Armenians in the region of Asorestan [Mesopotamia], both the metropolitan Kamyešoy [Kamyesho Kamišō'] and the other bishops . . . And King Χosrov ordered a copy of the orthodox faith sealed with his seal and placed in the royal treasury. (Sebēos xxxiii, p. 116; Asołik II iii, p. 127)

Armenia During the *Marzpan*ate

The period of the *Marzpan*ate in Armenian history has received little attention from scholars and is usually passed over as a time of troubles. Indeed, it is not difficult to document the precarious position of the country, reduced in size by the loss of its border territories and serving too often as a battlefield in the continuous Byzantine-Sasanian wars that culminated in the reconquest of most of Armenia by Χusrō II (who crossed the entire country in 610/1 to sack Karin/Theodosiopolis in the west) and the retaliatory campaigns of the emperor Heraclius from 624 to 629, reaching the Persian capital of Ctesiphon, and briefly reestablishing the partition line of 591 in Armenia. The Persian efforts to impose Zoroastrianism on the land in the sixth century provoked the rebellions of the two Vardans and decimated the *naxarar*s. Subsequently, the religious schism of 591 to 611 split the country and alienated it from Byzantium. Deportations drained Armenia of many of its leaders, and the preeminence of the great Mamikonean house, generally favorable to Byzantium, was shaken after the sixth century. Nevertheless, the fifth, sixth, and early seventh centuries simultaneously nurtured the development of Armenian civilization. Despite periodic persecutions,

Persian favor, especially after the Armenian rejection of Chalcedon, permitted the creation of Armenian literature and the growing independence of the kat'oɫikate, both on Persian territory.

The prosperity of the country noted by the Armenian Eɫišē and the Byzantine Procopius manifests itself in the extensive buildings that covered Armenia in the seventh century, not only in the reconstruction of the cathedral of Duin and of the church of St. Hrip'simē at Vaɫaršapat by the kat'oɫikos Komitas in 616/7, but in a multitude of churches that prefigured the massive development of the next generation. The capacities of Armenian science find their illustration in the education and career of the seventh-century polymath Anania Širakac'i (Shirakatsi), mathematician, astronomer, cosmographer, and composer of treatises on arithmetic, the calendar, weights and measures, and lunar eclipses. Perhaps most significantly, although the anonymous the *Ašxarhac'oyc'* *(Ashkharhatsuyts)*, "Armenian Geography," composed in the early seventh century, noted the multiple divisions of the country and reflected an ideal rather than a realistic situation, it also recorded a concept of national consciousness and unity. All but destroyed in Byzantium as a result of the Justinianic legislation, the fundamental Armenian social and ecclesiastical institutions had simultaneously solidified in Persarmenia during the *Marzpan*ate to the point where they could maintain themselves without the support of a political structure and could sustain a national consciousness sufficiently deeply rooted to withstand the brunt of the Arab domination.

FOR FURTHER INFORMATION

For the sources of, or more information on, the material in this chapter, please consult the following (full citations can be found in the Bibliography at the end of this volume).

Adontz, 1970.

Ananian, 1961.

Asdourian, 1911.

The Cambridge History of Iran

Der Nersessian, 1969.

Garsoïan, 1984-85, 1985.

Manandyan, 1965.

Russell, 1987.

Sarkissian, 1965.

Thierry and Donabedian, 1989.

Toumanoff, 1963, 1966, 1969, 1976.

6

THE ARAB INVASIONS
AND THE RISE OF THE
BAGRATUNI (640–884)

Nina Garsoïan

The explosive expansion of the Arabs in the middle of the seventh century totally revolutionized the face of the Near East and modified radically the history of the Armenian plateau for centuries to come. Externally, the total conquest of the Sasanian Empire by the Arabs and the retreat of Byzantium to a defensive position far to the west had a twofold effect on Armenia. No counterbalancing power was left in the area to support and protect the Armenians against the new conquerors. The balance of powers maintained for so long between Rome and Iran was irremediably broken for some two centuries in favor of total Arab domination. Once this domination was established, however, Armenia found itself for the first time in almost a millennium outside the theater of international warfare which was now pursued either farther west in Asia Minor or to the south in Mesopotamia. Internally, almost all the Armenian territories found themselves reunited as the Arabs reached north of the plateau to Tiflis in Iberia and westward to the Euphrates and beyond. All the lines of demarcation bisecting the country, whether those of 387 or of 591, disappeared, and only the southernmost border of the districts of Ałjnikʻ (Aghdznik) and Korčekʻ (Korchek) were fused with Arab Mesopotamia. This overall unification, however, covered a gradual inner fragmentation as the overriding authority of the Mamikoneans (Mamikonians) uniting the military forces of the country as a function of their office of *sparapet,* or commander-in-chief, began to be challenged. There is no doubt that the Mamikoneans were still the dominant family of the sixth and perhaps even the seventh centuries with their extensive domains in northern Taykʻ, southern Tarōn and Sasun, the central Bagrewand (Bagrevand) and Aragacotn (Aragatsotn), and with their powerful supporters, the Kamsarakan lords of Širak (Shirak) and Aršarunikʻ (Arsharunik), as well as the Gnuni of Manazkert north of Lake Van. They generally continued to pursue the traditional pro-Byzantine policy of their house, but their power was not undisputed, as it had been before, and gradually declined. The Bagratuni had achieved authority as early as 481, when Sahak Bagratuni had briefly been chosen *marzpan* by the Armenian rebels, and the far more brilliant career of his descendant Smbat *Χosrov šnum* in the first decades of the seventh century had greatly enhanced the prestige of this house whose main base was in Sper, in the extreme northwest of the plateau, but who also held other domains in Kogovit with the stronghold of Daroynkʻ, east of Bagrewand, and in southern Tmorikʻ. Other houses were also powerful: the house of Siwnikʻ maintained its autonomy to the southeast of Lake Sevan, while the Ṙštuni (Rshtuni) controlled their own territories south of Lake Van as well as those of the Bznuni northwest of the lake, and the Kamsarakan held the north-central districts of Širak and Aršarunikʻ. When the emperor Heraclius, on the eve of the Arab invasion, created the new title of *išχan* (ishkhan) or "prince" of Armenia, challenging the authority of both the *sparapet* commanding the troops of Persarmenia and the almost-powerless Persian *marzpan,* and further joined to it the high imperial dignity of the *curopalates,* he bypassed the obvious great magnates to choose a minor *naχarar,* David Saharuni, who was then succeeded by the *sparapet* of Persarmenia, Theodore Ṙštuni, under whom the two halves of Armenia were reunited in 639. Thus the chaotic events of the mid-seventh century encouraged the jockeying for power among ambitious *naχarar*s.

The Arab Conquest of Armenia

As "all the Armenian nobles lost land through their disunity and only the God-loving and valiant *išχan* of the Ṙštuni put in order the troops of his region and watched day and night," (Sebēos, xxix, p. 94) the first

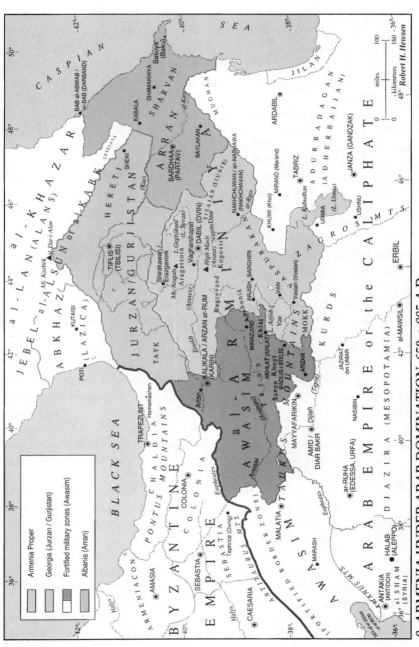

8. *ARMENIA UNDER ARAB DOMINATION, 650–c. 885 A.D.*

Robert H. Hewsen

Arab raid coming from the Mesopotamian border districts of Ałjnik' and
Korček' broke into Tarōn over the pass of Bałeš (Baghesh)/Bidlis and
swept northward through Χlat' (Khlat) on the north shore of Lake Van.
The Arab army then went on through the districts of Bznunik', Ałiovit
(Aghiovit), and Kogovit to the undefended capital of Duin, which it took
and sacked on October 6, 640, taking loot and captives. Theodore
Ṙštuni, who had now officially received from the Byzantine emperor
the titles of *išxan* and *curopalates,* attempted a counterattack into
Mesopotamia ca. 642, but a second raid coming this time from
Azerbaijan (Adherbaijan) in the east struck at the region of Gołt'n
(Goghtn) and Naxčawan (Nakhchavan) in the valley of the Araxes. The
Arabs conquered Artaz in Vaspurakan and met the joint forces of
Byzantium and Theodore Ṙštuni, whose disagreement led to the rout of
the imperial army in Mardastan in 643 or 644.

These early raids and others that may have occurred in 644-645
were merely plundering expeditions; their dating is highly controversial,
since the Arab sources composed at least two centuries later contradict
one another and Armenian sources are equally confused, while Greek
evidence is nonexistent for this period. The great campaign of 650, sent
by the governor of Syria and future Caliph Mu'āwiyah, was a far graver
matter, as Armenia was seriously divided internally by the high-handed
Byzantine policy. Denounced to the imperial authorities, Theodore
Ṙštuni was replaced by the former Persian *marzpan* Varaz Tiroc'
Bagratuni, son of Smbat Χosrov *šnum,* then reinstated once more in his
dignity at the death of Varaz Tiroc' "whether the Armenian princes liked
it or not." At the same time, a decree of the Byzantine emperor imposing
Chalcedonianism on Armenia provoked a council held at Duin in 648
or 649 under the presidency of Theodore Ṙštuni and the kat'ołikos
Nersēs III, which once again rejected the union, and consequently
removed any hope of help from the empire.

The Arab army, coming once more from Azerbaijan, divided into
three branches, one directed at Arran/Caucasian Albania, another at
Vaspurakan where it was defeated by Theodore, and the third, breaking diagonally through Ayrarat (the heartland of Armenia) all the way
to Tayk' and K'art'li or eastern Iberia, ultimately returned to join the
Arab forces besieging Naxčawan on the Araxes. Left without support
by Byzantium or the vanished Sasanians, and perhaps embittered by
the political and religious pressures to which he had been subjected,
Theodore Ṙštuni took the crucial step of breaking with the empire. He
concluded with Mu'āwiyah a treaty whose favorable terms have been

preserved in the *History* of Pseudo-Sebēos, although Armenian ecclesiastical historians understandably accuse their acquiescing magnates of "having made a covenant with death and an alliance with Hell":(Sebēos, xxxv, p. 132)

> Let this be the covenant of agreement between me [Muʿāwiyah] and you for as many years as you shall wish. And I shall not take tribute from you for 7 [3?] years, then in accordance with the oath, you will give as much as you wish. And you will keep 15,000 horsemen in your country and give [them] bread from the country, and I shall reckon it in the royal tribute. And I shall not summon the cavalry to Syria, but wherever else I shall order you, you should be ready for action. And I shall not send *emir*s into your fortresses, no Tačik [Tadjik] cavalry, not even a single horseman. No enemy shall enter into Armenia, and if the Roman [emperor] comes against you, I shall send troops to your assistance, as many as you shall wish. And I swear before the great God that I do not lie. (Sebēos, xxxv, p. 133)

Freedom of religion was also assured by a contemporary agreement between the Arab general and the city of Duin cited by the Arab ninth century historian al-Balādhurī:

> In the name of Allah, the compassionate, the merciful. This is a treaty of Ḥabîb ibn-Maslamah with the Christians, Magians and Jews of Dabîl [Duin], including those present and absent. I have granted you safety for your lives, possessions, churches, places of worship, and city wall. Thus ye are safe and we are bound to fulfil our covenant, so long as you fulfil yours and pay the poll-tax and *kharâj*. Thereunto Allah is witness; and it suffices to have him as witness. (al. Balādhurī, II, pp. 314-15)

At first, the counterattack of the Byzantine emperor in 652/3 was well received by a number of *naxarar*s and by the katʿołikos Nersēs III, who had taken refuge in the northwestern border district Taykʿ. "The emperor and all his troops cursed the lord of R̄štunikʿ and took away the dignity of his authority." Mušeł Mamikonean was named in his place "commander of the cavalry," and the emperor took up residence at Duin in the palace of the katʿołikos. But Theodore took refuge in his own strongholds, and neither the moun-

taineers of Siwnik' nor Caucasian Albania could be subdued by the
imperial army.

> The preaching of Sunday of the Council of Chalcedon in the church
> of St. Gregory [at Duin]. And the celebration of the liturgy in Roman
> [Greek] fashion by a Roman priest, and the communion of the
> emperor and the Kat'ołikos, and all the bishops, who willingly and
> who unwillingly . . . (Sebēos, xxxv, p. 136)

only increased the tension. The emperor returned home without having
accomplished anything, the kat'ołikos again took refuge in Tayk', and
Theodore Ṙštuni, still more embittered, returned, having been honored
by Mu'āwiyah at Damascus and given "authority over Virk' [Iberia],
Ałuank' (Aghvank) [Albania] and Siwnik' in exchange for his
allegiance.

The intensified war between Byzantium and the Arabs continued
to devastate Armenia for a time. The stronghold of Karin/The-
odosiopolis, renamed Ḳālīḳala by the Arabs, fell in 653, and 2,000
Arabs from Syria and Mesopotamia were brought there and given land.
Profiting from the death of Theodore Ṙštuni in 654, the emperor
briefly named as *išxan* Hamazasp Mamikonean, who reaffirmed the
ties of Armenia with Constantinople, while the Arabs were distracted
by the internal quarrels that followed the murder of the caliph 'Uth-
mān. The kat'ołikos Nersēs III returned to finish his church dedicated
to the Vigilant Heavenly Host at Zuart'noc' (Zvartnots). But with the
accession of the first Umayyad caliph Mu'āwiyah in 661, Arab domination over Armenia was reaffirmed once and for all. A council of
magnates presided over by the kat'ołikos Nersēs III accepted the
inevitable and agreed to send hostages to the Arab capital and pay a
yearly tribute of 500 gold *dahekan*s. In exchange, the caliph
Mu'āwiyah freed the hostages and installed Hamazasp's brother
Grigor Mamikonean "with great honor" as *išxan* of Armenia, a dignity
he held for more than twenty years until his death:

> During his reign, Grigor, Prince of Armenia, governed the land of the
> Armenians peacefully and kept it free from all marauding and attack.
> He feared God in perfect piety, was charitable, hospitable and cared
> for the poor. It was [Grigor] who built a house of worship in the town
> of Aruch [Aruč], in the district of Aragatsots [Aragacotn], an elegant

church to the glory of the name of the Lord, and adorned it in memory
of his [own] name. (Łewond, ch. 4, p. 54)

The claim is confirmed by the dedicatory inscription commemorating
Grigor and his wife Helinē/Helen on the great domed basilica of Aruč west
of Erevan.

Armenia in the Seventh Century

The description of Grigor's *išxan*ate by Łewond the Priest, just cited, is,
to be sure, idyllic and exaggerated. The country was not constantly at
peace, since Grigor himself ceased to pay tribute and revolted against the
Arabs in 680 at the death of the caliph Mu'āwiyah and is also said to have
died battling a northern Turkic Khazar invasion in 685. A few years after
his death, the emperor Justinian II overran Armenia in a last attempt to
reconquer the country and took away hostages, perhaps even the
kat'ołikos Sahak III (677-703). Even so, the first period of Arab domination immediately after the conquest was not seriously damaging for
Armenia, and there is no perceptible cultural break with the preceding
period of the *Marzpan*ate. As we have already noted, the unity of the
territory was re-created by the disappearance of internal political divisions. Far from being an annexed territory, Armenia through almost the
whole of the seventh century had the status of an autonomous, if tributary,
state whose sphere of influence, far from being reduced, was extended
northward, as we shall see, to the adjacent lands. No Arab troops were
stationed in Armenia, except in the Mesopotamian border districts, and
no foreign governors were sent to Armenia until the end of the century.

The relatively mild terms of Mu'āwiyah's treaty are readily ex-
plainable by the Arab need for the support of the famous Armenian
cavalry, especially at home as a barrier against the Khazars, whom their
Byzantine allies urged to attack the caliphate from the rear by raiding
southward through the Caucasian passes or by forcing the Arab fortified
position at Derbent on the Caspian. Since manpower was of primary
importance, taxes remained relatively light. According to Łewond, the
500 *dahekan*s of Mu'āwiyah's tribute were not increased by his son. In
the words of the later Armenian chronicler Samuel of Ani, the Arabs

> took from each house four [silver] *dirrhem*s, three *modii* [about 30
> kg.] of sifted wheat, one hempen rope and a gauntlet. But it was

ordered to levy no taxes from priests, as from the *azat* and from cavalrymen. (Manandyan, 1965, p. 130)

A Syrian chronicle observes that until the early eighth century,

This entire country was noted for its innumerable population, many vineyards, fields of grain, and all kinds of magnificent trees. (Manandyan, 1965, p. 130)

The excavations of the city of Duin show not only the reconstruction of the church and the extensive palace, but an active urban life as well. The sharp increase in the number of coins found there, from less than two dozen for the fifth and sixth centuries to more than 300 for the seventh, is an index of the rising trade. The great cathedral churches built by the Kamsarakan and the Mamikonean next to their palaces at T'alin and Aruč in Aragacotn, as well as those elsewhere at Vałaršapat, Ōjun (Odzun), and Sisian, the smaller foundations that proliferated throughout the country, and the numerous sculptured stelae that date from the seventh century, all testify to the continuity of the building activity begun during the *Marzpan*ate and serve as a concomitant index of economic stability and prosperity, while their dedicatory inscriptions indicate the survival and concern of the *naxarar tuns*.

There is, finally, no evidence of religious persecution during this period and even in the earlier part of the eighth century. Ecclesiastical sources record no forcible conversions, and the two martyrs, David of Duin and Vahan of Gołt'n, were Muslims converted to Christianity and consequently punishable as renegades under Islamic law. On the contrary, the activity of the kat'ołikate was not constrained. The kat'ołikos Anastas (662-667) sought a perpetual calendar from the great mathematician Anania Širakac'i, although the death of the patriarch precluded its adoption. The relics of St. Gregory the Illuminator were solemnly transferred from his burial place in northwestern Daranałik' to Vałaršapat, a portion granted to Albania (underscoring the close link between the two churches), and the Armenian patronage reiterated again by the kat'ołikos Elias (703-717). Once again, Łewond praises the successor of Grigor Mamikonean, the "patrician" Ašot (Ashot) Bagratuni, as an opulent, magnificent and charitable prince,

zealous in his love of learning; and he adorned the churches of God with the arts of spiritual *[vardapetakan]* teaching and with a multitude of ministers; and he honored them with distinguished services at his own expense. And he built a church in his domain of Dariwnkʻ. (Łewond, ch. 5)

As late as the first quarter of the eighth century, the great katʻołikos and theologian Yovhannēs Ōjnecʻi (Hovhannes Odznetsi) (717-728) could reform the church and give it a firm doctrinal base by completing the first collection of Armenian canons; repress the heresies of the native Paulicians (who were violent iconoclasts) and of the Phantasiasts (who denied that Christ had had a real body); and call two councils (at Duin in 719 against the heretics and at Manazkert in 725/6 to reaffirm the dogmatic position of the Armenian Church and its agreement with the Syrian Church) without any interference from the Arab authorities. On the contrary, Asołik affirms that upon Yovhannēs's probably apocryphal visit to Baghdad, the caliph "was struck with admiration, doubled his consideration and regard and sent him back to Armenia covered with honors and gifts."(Asołik, 1883, II, ii, p. 133)

The Creation of the Province of Armīniya and the Period of Arab Domination

Both Armenian and Arab sources agree that the situation in Armenia worsened perceptibly with the last decade of the seventh century. The ravages of the Khazar invasions continued throughout the eighth century. More fundamentally, not only did the invasions of Justinian II wreak havoc in Armenia, which the Greek troops treated as enemy territory, but they probably contributed to the decision of the caliphate to conquer the land outright and put an end to its semiautonomous status. At the same time, the general regularization of the vast Muslim empire, with its concurrent fiscal demands, and the increasing Muslim piety of the later Umayyad caliphs, and especially their Abbasid successors, could not fail to have a deleterious effect on Armenia at a time when Byzantium, embroiled at home in the Iconoclastic controversy of the eighth century, could provide neither support nor a counterbalancing force to the preponderance of the caliphate in the Near East.

In 693 the Umayyad caliph appointed his brother Muḥammad ibn Marwān governor of Armenia, Adherbaijan/Azerbaijan and Djazira or Upper Mesopotamia, reaching all the way to Melitēnē in the west. His authority was recognized in the same year by the new *isxan* of Armenia,

Smbat Bagratuni (693-726), but Byzantine troops remained in the south, and a new imperial campaign even attempted to retake the country in 698. The reconquering expedition of Muḥammad ibn Marwān took place in 701, according to both Armenian and Arabic sources. Moving northward from Mesopotamia, he entered the Armenia border district of Mokk', where he succeeded in obtaining by deceit the fortresses, which he dismantled, putting the men to the sword and sending the women and children into captivity. From there he moved northward into the central districts of Greater Armenia. The struggle for Duin was arduous and protracted, and the Armenian capital had to be taken twice, but Muḥammad ibn Marwān ultimately subdued the entire country as well as Iberia and Caucasian Albania. The formal annexation of Armenia must date from this period, although the confusion of Arab sources, which usually date it from the earlier expedition of 650, has obscured this fact. An Arab province called Arminiya, including not only most of the Armenian plateau except for the southern border annexed to the Djazira, but also Eastern Iberia and Caucasian Albania, was created, with Duin as its capital and as the residence of the Muslim governor, or *ostikan*. Arab garrisons were quartered at Duin as well as in a number of other cities, including Tiflis in the far north. Karin/Ḳālīḳalā and Meliténē/Malatia became the anchor points of the Arab military system in the west. Muḥammad ibn Marwān was installed as the first *ostikan* of Armīniya, although some authority was conceded to the native magnates, since the title of *išxan* of Armenia was maintained almost continually and the traditional office of *sparapet* reappeared in the eighth century, even though it was no longer hereditary in the Mamikonean house as it had been formerly.

The new *ostikan* inaugurated his rule by the removal of both the *išxan* of Armenia Smbat Bagratuni and the kat'oɫikos Sahak III, who were sent to Damascus. Islamic law was rigorously applied, the Persian martyr David of Duin was executed, and monasteries were brutally ravaged. The Armenian sources complain bitterly of the *ostikan*,

> a wicked, insolent and an impudent man, extremely malicious by nature; he implanted within himself the seeds of hypocrisy like the venom of a serpent and tortured the princes and the *azat*s of Armenia with bonds and plundered the property and the possessions of many people. Then he also put the great Sahak [III] in fetters and sent him to Damascus. Along with him he also sent the prince of Armenia, Smbat son of Smbat. He plundered the entire ornaments of the

churches of Christ and made the old and the young wail, mourn and grieve. (Yovhannēs Drasχanakertc'i, xx, p. 107)

Angered and alarmed by this policy, the *išχan* Smbat, who returned from the Umayyad capital of Damascus in 703, took counsel with the *naχarars*, among them his own brother Ašot and Vard, the son of Theodore Ṙštuni, and decided to turn for help to Byzantium. At first the Armenians were victorious at Vardanakert on the lower Araxes, and the rebellion spread from Vanand in the west to Vaspurakan in the southeast, but Smbat then retired to the north of Tayk' and Muḥammad ibn Marwān was sent again to subdue Armenia. The posthumous embassy of the kat'ołikos Sahak III, who had died on the way but whose body, bearing a letter imploring Muḥammad to spare the Armenians, was brought to Harran by his bishops, saved the church and even extended its authority. The new kat'ołikos Ełia (Eghia)/Elias (703-717) was authorized to hold a council in Partaw (Partav)/Bardha'a at which he deposed the Albanian kat'ołikos accused of Chalcedonianism, had him exiled together with his supporter, the widow of the prince of Albania, and consecrated a new kat'ołikos for Albania, whose dependence on the Armenian Church in this period is evident from these proceedings. The secular Armenian nobles, however, did not fare so well. Defeated by Muḥammad ibn Marwān in 705, the *išχan* Smbat Bagratuni, who had received from Byzantium the title of *curopalates,* fled for refuge to the imperial territory on the eastern shore of the Black Sea and Muḥammad ibn Marwān retook Duin, which had been captured by the rebels. At the order of the Muslim authorities, the governor of Naχčawan summoned the Armenian *naχarars* on the pretext of a census, which would include them in the cavalry register. According to Łewond, those of noble birth were separated from the others who were locked in the churches of Naχčawan and Gołt'n, farther down the Araxes, and set on fire. The nobles, stripped of their wealth under torture, were then executed in their turn. Only a few magnates are mentioned by name among the victims, but the sources assert that almost the entire Armenian nobility perished or was deported, and "our realm made heirless of its *naχarars*."

The massacre of Naχčawan did not destroy the Armenia clans, since only the adult *naχarars* had been exterminated, but it crippled them for a generation. However, the Arabs still needed Armenian collaboration against the Khazar threat, and the ferocious policy of Naχčawan was not continued. The new Arab *ostikan,* whom Łewond praises as a "prudent man full of worldly wisdom," pacified Armenia, urged the exiles to return, and Smbat Bagratuni resumed his office of *išxan* probably in 709 rather than 711. The city of Duin was rebuilt by the *ostikan*

> stronger and greater in size than it was before; he fortified it with gates and buttresses, surrounded the city wall with a moat and filled it with water for the protection of the fortress. (Łewond, ch. 10, p. 67)

This relatively benevolent policy was maintained for a time, the activity of the kat'ołikos Yovhannēs Ōjnec'i received no check from the Muslim authorities, and, as noted earlier, the execution of Prince Vahan of Gołt'n ca. 737 cannot be interpreted strictly as an act of persecution, since he had been taken prisoner as a child after the massacre of Naxčawan, raised as a Muslim, and abjured that faith upon his return to Armenia. On the secular side, the *išxan* Smbat is recorded for the last time as being present at the Council of Manazkert, but nothing is known of the later part of his rule. At first his successor as *išxan*, Ašot Bagratuni, the grandson of his earlier namesake praised by Łewond, does not seem to have been recognized officially by the Muslim authorities for some five years, although he held the office de facto. But in 732 the new *ostikan* came to Duin and conferred on him "the authority of patrician over the realm of Armenia by order of [the caliph] Hišam and honored him greatly." Thereafter Ašot collaborated effectively in the Muslim campaign against the Khazars and shared in the booty. The *ostikan* also authorized the payment to the Armenian cavalry of a yearly stipend of 100,000 *dirhem*s retroactive for the three years that it had been withheld. Hence, not only had the institution of the Armenian cavalry rapidly recovered from the bloodbath of Naxčawan, but the Muslim authorities still took the responsibility of its maintenance.

Three factors contributed to the reversal of this enlightened policy and provoked a new Armenian explosion in the middle of the eighth century. Even before the disappearance of the Arab dynasty of the Umayyads and the accession of the more strictly Muslim dynasty of the Abbasids in 750, the tax policy of the caliphate had undergone radical change. As a result of a general census of the Armenian lands taken in 724-725, all tax privileges were revoked and taxes were now levied not by household, as before, but by head, by size of property, and on cattle as well, thus greatly increasing the fiscal burden of the country. The disappearance of international trade resulting from the endemic Byzantine-Arab warfare added to the country's economic woes. Equally damaging for the stability of the country was the increasing rivalry of its two greatest houses. Long accustomed to a preponderant position in Armenia, the Mamikonean viewed as a direct threat to their prestige the rising power of the Bagratuni, who were favored by the Umayyad governors. The grant of the *išxan*ate to Ašot Bagratuni in 732, making this office all but hereditary in the Bagratuni house, outraged the Mamikonean brothers Grigor and David, but the immediate result of their protest was their own exile to Yemen at the order of the *ostikan*. At the death of the caliph Hišam in 743, however, the brothers returned to Armenia, began to oppress the magnates of Vaspurakan and raised a general rebellion in which they attacked the *išxan* Ašot, (Łewond, ch. 25, pp. 117-18) who barely escaped with his life. Reversing the previous situation, Ašot now fled to complain to the caliph at Damascus, while Grigor Mamikonean took over his office of *išxan* with the approval of the local *ostikan*. Unfortunately for the Mamikonean, the tide turned against them once again. The last Umayyad caliph, who had greatly benefited from the support of Ašot Bagratuni and his troops in his claim for the throne, refused to ratify the decision of his *ostikan*. Ašot consequently returned to Armenia with great honor at the order of the caliph, David Mamikonean was executed, and Grigor could only bide his time awaiting an opportunity to avenge his brother.

The overthrow of the Umayyad dynasty and the usurpation of the Abbasids a few years later provided an opportunity both for the vengeance of the Mamikonean and for the growing dissatisfaction in Armenia in general. The Armenian magnates met together in 748 and persuaded the *išxan* Ašot, now bereft of his patron, to join with them, albeit unwillingly. The rebels made contact with the Byzantine emperor Constantine V, whose successful campaigns against the Muslims had brought him to Asia Minor and who was operating in Pontus at the time. The Armenians also received the support of an anonymous group called by Łewond "sons of sinfulness who know neither the fear of God nor awe of princes nor respect of the elders," who were probably the Paulician heretics condemned earlier by Yovhannēs Ōjnecʿi (Garsoïan, 1967, pp. 136-37), and whose numbers and power were increasing on the Upper Euphrates at that time. Another revolt in Sasun to the south helped distract the Arabs, and the rebels succeeded in capturing the major Muslim stronghold of Karin. These initial successes failed, however, to abate the tension between the Mamikonean and the Bagratuni and to preserve a united front against the Arabs. Ašot Bagratuni sought to withdraw from the rebels and was seized and blinded at the order of

Grigor Mamikonean. The fragmentation of the rebellion spelled its doom. No help came from Byzantium. Grigor Mamikonean sickened and died at Karin in 749, and his brother Mušeł failed to obtain official recognition. Ašot "the Blind" nominally continued to rule the country despite his handicap, but by 750 the new Abbasid caliph had successfully reestablished the mastery of the Muslims over Armenia.

The collapse of the second rebellion within the century seriously sapped the strength of the Armenian nobility. The greatest sufferers were undoubtedly the Mamikonean, who lost all of their domains except for Bagrewand and Tayk'. The Bagratuni, suspect to the new dynasty because of their support of the Umayyads, went into temporary eclipse, were forced to abandon Kogovit, and withdrew from Vaspurakan, where the Arcruni seemingly began to entrench themselves, although the history of this family remains obscure until the middle of the next century. Karin was retaken, refortified, and garrisoned with Arab troops from the Djazira. The emperor Constantine V, who had given no help to the Armenians against the Arabs, now compounded the damage by transferring the Armenian population from the districts of Karin and Melitēnē to the Balkans in 755. The new Abbasid caliph sent his brother on a tour of all his dominions. According to Łewond,

> [he] first went to the land of Armenia and caused grave torment and endangered all, leaving them in extreme poverty, to the extent of claiming taxes on behalf of the dead . . . he cruelly tortured the inhabitants of our country by imposing a heavy poll tax, equivalent to many silver *zuzēs*, and branding everyone's neck with lead seal.
>
> [In response], the houses of the nobles, some willingly and others not, gave horses, precious clothing, and other provisions of gold and silver as gifts, just to fill the mouth of the dragon which had come to attack and corrupt the country. (Łewond, ch. 28, p. 123)

The Bagratuni regained their position in 753 as one of them, Sahak, was named *išxan* while his kinsman Smbat, the son of Ašot the Blind, appears at the same time in the revived office of *sparapet*. Nevertheless, the exactions increased still further under the new *ostikan*, who ruled Armenia on three occasions (752-754, 759-770, 775-780), even though his mother was said to have been an Armenian princess, the daughter of the "patrician" of Siwnik'. The support of the Armenian cavalry was now stopped. "A set number of horsemen was demanded from the princes and they were compelled to maintain this military contingent at [the expense] of their own house." Łewond (ch. 33, pp. 127-129) even insists that the supply of silver gave out, so that taxes had to be paid in kind, and that they fell alike on *naxarar* and *ṙamik* as well as on the clergy. The population hid or fled from this extortionate policy, and some of the magnates abandoned their homes and emigrated, as did Šapuh Amatuni who, according to Asołik, moved to the empire with 12,000 of his retainers.

The revolt brought on by these oppressive measures began in Vaspurakan, which was simultaneously threatened by the infiltration of Muslims from Azerbaijan. These were met by three brothers from the Arcruni house now ruling Vaspurakan after the district had been abandoned by the Bagratuni. By 762 all three brothers were dead and the *išxan* Sahak Bagratuni may also have been put to death. Still, the rebellion continued to smolder, and the leadership now passed for the last time to the Mamikonean.

According to Łewond, the first signal of the great rebellion of 774-775 was given by Artawazd Mamikonean, who killed a Muslim tax collector in the northwestern district of Širak and was consequently driven to flight into Byzantine territory by the *ostikan,* who compelled the Armenian *sparapet* Smbat to accompany him. Artawazd's example was then followed by his kinsman Mušeł Mamikonean, who massacred the tax collectors in his district and withdrew into the fortress of Artagers in Aršarunikʻ. He then went on to raid in Bagrewand, laid siege to the fortress of Kars, defeated an Arab contingent sent from Duin near Bagawan, and pursued them as far as the Mamikonean center in Aruč. Encouraged by these early successes and inspired by a messianic prophecy, interestingly branded as false by Łewond, perhaps wise after the event:

> Behold, the hour of your salvation has come, and now shortly the scepter of the kingdom shall soon be restored once again to the house of Tʻorgom. (Łewond, ch. 34, p. 131)

The Armenian *naxarar*s flocked to his support. They bound themselves to each other by an oath, despite the prudent advice of Ašot Bagratuni (the son of the former *išxan* Sahak), who is said to have attempted to dissuade them from this perilous enterprise at a time when the Abbasid caliphate was at the height of its power. The rebels even succeeded in persuading the *sparapet* Smbat to join them, albeit against his will, but the Bagratuni house was divided, as Ašot continued to oppose the rebellion, while the Arcruni and their supporters stayed in Vaspurakan, thus splitting the Armenian forces in two.

Mušeł Mamikonean and Smbat *sparapet* moved to besiege Karin while the Arcrunis retired to their fortresses at the opposite end of Armenia when a new Muslim army of 30,000 invaded Armenia in the spring of 775 from the Mesopotamian border region of the Diyār-Bakr. The Arabs first turned eastward to Χlat' on Lake Van, and on April 15, 775, destroyed the infantry of the Arcruni coalition at Arčēš (Archesh) on the north shore of the lake. The Muslims then moved northwestward through Apahunik', and on April 25, on the banks of the Euphrates/Arsanias (Murad Su) in the district of Bagrewand, they routed the second Armenian army which was hastening back from the siege of Karin. The disastrous battle of Bagrewand left most of the Armenians, nobles and *ramik* alike, as well as both their leaders, Mušeł Mamikonean and the *sparapet* Smbat Bagratuni, dead in the field.

The Appearance of the Muslim Emirates

There is little doubt that the aftermath of the battle of Bagrewand marked one of the darkest hours in Armenian history. Bled three times in as many generations, some of the *naxarar* houses failed to recover. The Bagratuni, perhaps the least hurt, paid for their loyalty to the vanished Umayyad dynasty by the loss of their domains of Tmorik', Kogovit, and whatever was left of their possessions in Vaspurakan and the south, with the exception of the small district of Mokk'. The *sparapet*'s son, Ašot, later known as *Msaker* (the meat or man-eater), was driven to take refuge in the fastness of his mountain domain in northwestern Sper, farthest removed from the Arab threat. His prudent cousin and namesake Ašot, son of the former *išxan* Sahak, may have been appointed *išxan* by the Muslims in 775 because of his refusal to join the rebellion, though even here, the quasi-monopoly of the Bagratuni on this office was temporarily broken in 781 by the appointment of a relatively minor *naxarar*, Tačat Anjewac'i (Tadjat Andzevatsi), driven back to the east from Byzantium by the antagonism of the empress Irene. The *sparapet* Bagrat Bagratuni was to die of exhaustion with the other magnates serving with the Armenian cavalry against the Khazars in the Caspian region of Arran through the unbearable heat of the summer of 784.

Other houses were still less fortunate. The Gnuni lords of Ałiovit, driven from their domain after the death of their *tanutēr* Vahan on the field of Bagrewand, implored the help of Ašot Bagratuni and were moved by him to northwestern Tayk', whence they may have passed altogether into Byzantine territory. The Amatuni lost most of their possessions, except Artaz in Vaspurakan, where they became a minor house. The last of the Kamsarakan, Nerseh, died in Arran together with the *sparapet* Bagrat Bagratuni and the *išxan* of Armenia, Tačat Anjewac'i. The house of Gołt'n had vanished even earlier with the martyrdom of its *tanutēr* Vahan in 737. Nor do we hear any more of the Řštuni and Saharuni. Perhaps worst hit of the great magnates were the Mamikonean leaders of the rebellion of 774-775, who had lost their *tanutēr* Samuēl as well as their leader Mušeł himself at Bagrewand. Both of Mušeł's sons, who had taken refuge in Vaspurakan, were put to death by Meružan Arcruni, who blamed their father's revolt for the woes it had brought on Armenia. Of Mušeł's four daughters, one, whose name has not even been preserved, sought safety in marriage with a newly come Arab freebooter named Djahhāf. Of the vast Mamikonean domains, nothing was left but minor branches surviving in a portion of Tarōn and for a time in Bagrewand. Even the Arcruni did not long enjoy the safety of their growing domains in Vaspurakan. The new *ostikan* appointed by the caliph Hārūn al-Rashīd at his accession in 786 was at first welcomed by them at Duin, but he soon threw all three Arcruni brothers into chains. Meružan saved himself through conversion to Islam, but his brothers, Hamazasp and Sahak, who refused to apostatize, suffered martyrs' deaths. The brilliant building activity of the earlier part of the century significantly came to an abrupt stop, not to be resun.ed for a full century.

The marriage of an heiress of the great Mamikonean house with an unknown Arab adventurer is an indication of the profound political and even demographic change in the life of Greater Armenia, which paralleled the migration or disappearance of many of its native *naxarar* houses. Up to the time of Hārūn al-Rashīd at the end of the eighth century, no appreciable Arab population had settled on the Armenian plateau, although the infiltration of the north Arabian tribe of Bakr into the border district of Ałjnik', with its main city of Amida, then part of the Djazīra, was so massive that the names of both the region and the city were transformed respectively into *Diyār* (house, land) of Bakr and Diyarbakir. Listing the governors sent by Hārūn al-Rashīd, the ninth-century Arab historian Ya'kūbī, who was familiar with Armenia since his grandfather had been *ostikan* in 775 at the time of the great rebellion and he had served there himself in his youth, now commented on the influx of Arabs into the country:

Rashīd appointed Yūsuf ibn Rashīd al-Sulami in place of Khuzayma ibn Khazim. He transplanted a mass of Nizārī to this land, and [until then] the Yemenites had formed a majority in Armīniya, but in the days of Yūsuf, the Nizārī increased in number. Then he [Hārūn] named Yazīd ibn Mazyad ibn Za'ida al-Shaybānī and he brought from every side so many of the Rab'īa that they now form a majority, and he controlled the land so strictly that no one dared move in it.

    After him came 'Abd-al-Kabīr ibn 'Abd-al-Hamid . . . whose home was Harrān. He came with a multitude of men from Diyār Mudār, stayed only four months and left. (Ter Ghewondyan, 1976, p. 31)

As the studies of the Armenian scholar Aram Ter Ghewondyan have now demonstrated, the *ostikans* of the Shaybānī house, who governed the Diyār-Bakr and Armīniya in almost hereditary succession in this period, infiltrated the plateau on the southwestern shore of Lake Van, although their main migration was in the Caspian district of Sharwān north of the Kura River. The *ostikan* sent to govern the province of Armīniya by the Abbasids between 752 and 780 was the first to shift his residence in 789 to Partaw/Bardha'a on the lower Kura, leaving a deputy in the capital of Duin in Armenia proper, and the Shāybanā created a hereditary principality for themselves in Azerbaijan. The foundation of the city of Ganjak (modern Ganja in the Azerbaijani republic) in 844 helped to accelerate the Islamization of the eastern districts bordering on Armenian proper. The main activity of the other great tribe, the Sulaym, who alternated with the Shaybānī in the hereditary governorship of Armīniya, was more damaging to Armenia itself.

    We do not know the exact path or date of the Arab settlements in Armenia, but they unquestionably benefited from the vacuum created by the weakening or disappearance of the *naxarar* houses after Bagrewand. The Kaysite/Kaysikk' subgroup of the Sulaym began to move into Atiovit, abandoned by the Gnuni, and spread around the northern shore of Lake Van at Xlat', Arčēš, and especially to the stronghold of Manazkert. Their kinsmen, the 'Uthmānids/Ut'manikk', installed themselves at Berkri, east of the lake. The Mamikonean son-in-law Djahhāf seems to have been a member of the same family, although it is possible that he was a Kurd rather than an Arab. We know very little of Djahhāf's background, nor does he seem to have settled in a specific place, but the later Armenian historian Vardan Arewelc'i (Areveltsi) explicitly states that he "was planning to gain control of the whole land through his wife." (ch. 41, p. 182) In pursuing this policy, Djahhāf fought both Ašot Bagratuni for the control of Aɫiovit and the representatives of the caliphate. He briefly seized Duin, but according to Vardan "the citizens fell on [his son] Abdl Melik', killed him, and closed the city gate" (Ibid). The Djahhāfids were routed, although they did not disappear at once, as Vardan claimed, since Djahhāf's grandson was married to a Bagratuni princess and raised a rebellion in the twenties of the ninth century, while another member of the family created troubled in Siwnik' until his defeat by the local prince, and at least one more member of the family is recorded. The Djahhāfids were probably little more than brigands looting wherever the opportunity presented itself and then disappearing in the face of resistance. Nevertheless, Djahhāf's son was sufficiently settled to have struck coins in his name, probably at Manazkert, since they carry the mint mark "Bahunays" from the district of Bahunis/Apahunik' to which the city belonged. The establishment of the Ḳaysites around Lake Van was far more extensive and permanent.

These Arab settlements were designed primarily for defensive purposes to bolster the Arab frontier defensive system, the *thughur*s in their war against Byzantium. Despite Ya'kūbī's claim, the Arabs never formed anything like a majority of the population on the Armenian plateau in this period. The new emirates soon fought against each other and against the representatives of the caliphate. Their rulers intermarried with the neighboring Armenian magnates, and some converted to Christianity, as did the emirs of Arzn in Aɫjnik' and Baɫēš/Bidlis on the borders of Tarōn, who married Bagratuni and Arcruni princesses in successive generations of the mid-ninth century and supported their Armenian kinsmen against the Muslims. Nevertheless, the emirates were no longer mere garrisons or governors who came and went in rapid succession. Their establishment in the heartland of Armenia, as well as on its borders, and as far north as Tiflis in Iberia, often provided an advance march for Muslim invasions, especially from Azerbaijan, which regularly used Goɫt'n and Naxčawan in the valley of the Araxes as stages in their advance on Duin. Even more fundamentally, they controlled the main urban centers of Armenia: the capital of Duin as well as Naxčawan on the main transit road of the valley of the Araxes; the military stronghold of Karin in the west; Xlat', Arčēš, and Berkri on the shore of Lake Van; Manazkert, where an Armenian mint was located, as well as in the capital. Thus their presence transformed and complicated the decentralized internal pattern of the country by the addition of

a new and alien element that increased the difficulty of achieving a
unified and stable political system.

The Rise of the Bagratuni

Tragic though they were, the troubled last years of the eighth century
also proved to be a turning point in the history of medieval Armenia.
On the international scene, Byzantium still generally remained militarily
on the defense first half of the ninth century, although tentative religious
overtures were unsuccessfully made to Ašot *Msaker* around 811-813.
The establishment of a Paulician republic on the Upper Euphrates
protected the northwestern region of Armenia from direct attack from
the west. The creation of the Arab military frontier zones or *thughur*s
based on Melitēnē and Karin removed the theater of war from the center
of Armenia, as did the residence of the *ostikan* of Armīniya at
Partaw/Berdha'a in Azerbaijan rather than at Duin in Armenia proper.
The brilliance of the Abbasid caliphate dimmed rapidly after the great
caliphs of the early ninth century, and the Arab emirs of Armenia
pursued with each generation a local policy of native dynasts, which
increasingly placed them at odds with the attempts at control of the
ostikan sent from the Abbasid capital of Baghdad.

Internally, the guerrilla activity carried on by Ašot *Msaker* from
Sper began to bear fruit. He took most of Tayk' and Tarōn from the
Mamikonean, and his struggle with the *Djahḥāfids* gave him control
of Aršarunik'. More important, his war against the Arab emir allowed Ašot to resume the traditional Bagratid stance of loyalty
toward the caliphate against local rebels, and so to pursue his expansionist policies undisturbed by the Muslim authorities. The discovery
of silver mines in Sper not only helped to relieve the tax burden of
the country in general, but helped Ašot *Msaker* acquire the domains
of the now-ruined Kamsarakan: Aršarunik' and Širak, with the
fortress of Ani. De facto, if not de jure, Ašot was *išxan* of Armenia
before the end of the eighth century, a title that was conceded to him
officially by the caliphate in 804, according to the Armenian chronicler Samuel of Ani, while his brother Šapuh assumed the dignity of
sparapet. Farther north, the establishment of another branch of the
family headed by Vasak, the uncle of Ašot *Msaker,* in the decade
following the battle marked the beginning of the future royal house
of the Bagratuni of Iberia.

The development of the two other great houses of medieval Armenia, the Arcruni of Vaspurakan and the princes of Siwnik', cannot be traced with equal clarity. There is no doubt that the Arcruni were consolidating themselves in Vaspurakan through the first half of the ninth century, as is evident from later reports and from their domination of the other great houses of the area, who either disappeared altogether or reemerged as Arcruni vassals in the course of this period. The growing concern of the caliphate, and perhaps its policy of support to the Bagratids so as to create a counterbalancing power in Armenia, all likewise suggest the growing power of the Arcruni and their gradual control of the entire area of Vaspurakan, but the confusion of their family historian T'ovma Arcruni does not permit any more precise account until the second half of the ninth century. The history of Siwnik' is likewise difficult to trace through this period. The region had always shown signs of autonomy and separatism in earlier times and had even succeeded in having its autonomy recognized by the Sasanians in the sixth century. Almost nothing is known concerning its history for more than a century, but at the beginning of the great rebellion of Bābak against the caliphate in Azerbaijan (817-836), Vasak prince of Siwnik' sought to benefit from this challenge to the authority of the Abbasids and gave his daughter in marriage to the rebel. The alliance with Bābak was not always advantageous for Siwnik', as we shall see, and after Vasak's death in 821 his lands were divided between his two sons: Sahak, prince of western Siwnik' or Gełakunik' (Geghakunik), with the famous religious and intellectual center of Makenoc' (Makenots) Vank', and P'ilippos, prince of eastern Siwnik' or Vayoc' Jor (Vayots Dzor) (modern Eghegnadzor), southeast of Lake Sevan, where the local dynasts were to erect the still more distinguished monastic center of Tat'ew (Tatev). The internal quarrels of the princes delayed the development of Siwnik', but here too, the seeds of a major non-Bagratid principality had been sown early in the ninth century.

The revival of Armenia did not, however, proceed smoothly or unchecked. In the west, the caliphate, alarmed by the accumulation of power in the hands of Ašot *Msaker,* made the most of his death in 826 to divide the Bagratuni dignities and lands between two of his sons. The eldest, Bagarat, held the southern territories of Tarōn and Sasun with the new prestigious title of *išxanac' išxan* "Prince of Princes" (ca. 826-851). His youngest brother Smbat, usually known as Χostovanoł *(Khostovanogh),* "the Confessor," who had been a hostage at the Abbasid court, received his uncle Šapuh's office of *sparapet* and kept the northern Bagratuni domains of Sper and Tayk'. The quarrels of the two brothers intensified this division. To the east, the great revolt of Babak in Azerbaijan during the first part of the ninth century distracted most of the attention and forces of the caliph for two decades and allowed considerable freedom of action to the Armenian *naxarars*. In the acid words of the Arab historian al-Balādhuri:

> [Harun al-Rashid's *ostikan*] . . . introduced the system by which Dabil [Duin] and an-Nashawa [Naxčawan] paid land tax according to the area, not the produce. The Armenian patricians did not cease to hold their lands as usual, each trying to protect his own region; and whenever an *'âmil* [tax collector] would come to the frontier they would coax him; and if they found in him purity and severity, as well as force and equipment, they would give the *kharâj* and render submission, otherwise they would deem him weak and look down upon him. (al-Balādhurī, II, p. 330)

But this freedom increased neither their unity nor the peace of Armenia. In Siwnik', Bābak's marriage to the daughter of Vasak had allowed him to establish himself in the districts of Arcax (Artsakh) and Balasakan in 824, which he controlled for twelve years, until the end of his career. But the rebellion of the local dynasts against the overlordship of Bābak led only to his devastation of Gełakunik' and Balasakan. In the central provinces, the continuing success of Bābak against the caliphate encouraged a challenge to the authority of the contemporary Shaybāni *ostikan*. Joining together in one of the local alliances between the Christian *naxarars* and Muslim emirs that was to characterize the history of medieval Armenia, Sahak, prince of western Siwnik', the Djaḥḥāfid emir and the usually cautious *sparapet* Smbat, abandoning on this occasion the loyalist tradition of the Bagratuni house toward the caliphate, disregarded the conciliatory intervention of the kat'ołikos Dawit' II and defied the *ostikan* in 831/2, according to the Armenian historian Yovhannēs "the Kat'ołikos." (Yovhannēs Drasxanakertc'i, xxv, p. 117). Unfortunately for the rebels, the Prince of Princes Bagarat held aloof with the forces of the south, and the *ostikan*, taking the initiative of the attack, routed them in a bloody battle on the Hrazdan River north of Duin. Sahak of Siwnik' was killed, and his domain passed to his son Grigor Sup'an I. The Djaḥḥāfid emir fled to Siwnik' to bring more trouble on the region, and Smbat *sparapet* took refuge in his northern domains. The disturbances related to the insurrection of Bābak continued until 836, when the major campaign mounted by Afshin, appointed by the caliph, finally succeeded in detaching the princes of Albania, Siwnik', and Arcax from Bābak by promises of autonomy and tax remission, and thus obtained the betrayal and capture of the rebel in 837.

Religious quarrels added to the internal dissensions and opposed Bagarat Bagratuni to his brother Smbat *sparapet,* thus dividing Armenia between northern and southern parties. The election of the new kat'olikos Yovhannēs of Ovayk', in 833 provoked denunciations against him to the Prince of Princes Bagarat Bagratuni, who after some years had him deposed and relegated to the monastery of Ayrivank'. He simultaneously informed the Armenian bishops of the necessity to elect a new primate. Fortunately for Yovhannēs of Ovayk', he found a champion in the *sparapet* Smbat and the northern magnates, who called together a synod that restored the kat'olikos to his throne, which he occupied until 855 in spite of the opposition to Bagarat Bagratuni and his southern supporters, among whom we find his nephew Ašot Arcruni. The patriarchate of Yovhannēs of Ovayk' was also marked by a resurgence of heresy in the district of T'ondrak, south of Manazkert, which gave the heretics their name. The historian Asołik mistakenly attributed the appearance of the first T'ondrakec'i (Tondraketsi)leader to the time of the later kat'olikos Yovhannēs the Historian, but his near contemporary, the learned prince Grigor Magistros, correctly observed that

> This accursed one appeared in the days of the Lord John and of Smbat
> Bagratuni. (Garsoïan, 1967, p. 140)

which must be a reference to the alliance of the kat'olikos Yovhannēs of Ovayk' and Smbat *sparapet.* This doctrine of the heretics has been hotly disputed, although it bore manifest resemblances to that of the earlier Paulicians condemned by the kat'olikos Yovhannēs Ōjnec'i. Consequently, the appearance of the T'ondrakec'i in this period in Armenia may well have been caused by the eastward flight of Byzantine Paulicians, whose rigid iconoclasm subjected them to persecution within the empire after the victory of the opposed iconodule doctrine at the Council of Orthodoxy held in 843. It has also been suggested that the T'ondrakec'i had been influenced by the social theories of the followers of Bābak, although this thesis of social unrest among the lower classes of society cannot be demonstrated, since the heretical doctrine eventually reached into the ruling class of the magnates as well as the hierarchy of the church, whose peace the heretics were to disturb for centuries to come.

A last attempt to reestablish full control over Armenia was made by the Abbasids after their final crushing of Bābak's revolt, and the attention given by all Arab historians to the Armenian rebellion of 850 to 855 reflects the alarm of the caliphate. The new caliph, al-Mutawakkil (847-861), sent a new *ostikan* to collect the Armenian tribute in 850. The Prince of Princes Bagarat sent an embassy bearing gifts and the tribute to meet him at the border, but would not allow him or the tax collectors to cross into Armenia or move freely within the country. The *ostikan* withdrew, though he left two deputies to put down the southern alliance of Bagarat and Ašot Arcruni of Vaspurakan, who had risen with their supporters and scattered the Muslim forces. The *ostikan*'s son and successor was only partially successful. He attacked Ašot Arcruni from the direction of Azerbaijan but failed to capture him. However, he succeeded in seizing Bagarat Bagratuni through treachery and sent him off in 851 to the new Abbasid capital of Sāmarrā before falling himself in the struggle to overcome the Armenian mountaineers in the southern districts of Χoyt' (Khoyt) and Sasun.

Deciding to crush the rebellion once and for all, the caliph al-Mutawakkil then sent a formidable army, to whose leaders he had promised hereditary holdings in Armenia, under the command of the Turkish general Bughā al-Kabir "the Elder." Bughā began his advance by moving from the borderland of the Diyār-Bakr against the southern magnates and began the conquest of the country piecemeal. The division of Armenia into the southern and northern groups of magnates, the absence of its two leaders with the captivity of Bagarat and the refusal of Smbat *sparapet* to join the rebels, facilitated his task. According to the historian T'ovma Arcruni, the

> Tačiks [Muslims] of Armenia who dwelt in various regions of the land and guided Bugha on his way in and out of the country. (Thomas Artsruni, III. ii, p. 198)

Coming to Χlat' on Lake Van, Bughā divided his army in two. Half went to devastate the districts south of the lake. He himself, accompanied by the *sparapet* Smbat, the official native ruler of Armenia during his brother's absence, moved to Vaspurakan, where he forced the capitulation of Ašot Arcruni and sent him, with his son Grigor-Derenik, as well as other *naxarar*s from Vaspurakan to join Bagarat in captivity at

Sāmarrā. Ašot's brother Gurgēn continued the guerrilla war in Vaspurakan, and even defeated the Arabs with the help of the local nobles at the "Bloody Lake" (Arean lič/Arian lij). But he too was soon captured and sent to Sāmarrā, while Vaspurakan was ravaged and a multitude of prisoners sold into slavery. Having completed the conquest of the south, Bughā now moved to Duin and attacked the northern magnates, who were faced with the choice of apostasy or annihilation. In the spring of 853 Bughā attacked Siwnik', penetrated into western Iberia, where he defeated and killed the local Muslim emir and burned the city of Tiflis, and overran Caucasian Albania. The entire province of Armīniya was now overcome and ravaged until Bughā's triumphant return to Sāmarrā, bringing a multitude of captive *naxarars,* among them the *sparapet* Smbat whose neutrality or continuous loyalty to the Muslim authorities had not saved him from sharing the fate of the other Armenian magnates.

The condition of Armenia after the devastating expeditions of Bughā was once more tragic. The Arab emirs profited from the captivity of the Armenian princes to expand their own possessions. The captives at Sāmarrā, who included almost all the Armenian magnates—the Prince of Princes Bagarat Bagratuni with his two sons; Smbat *sparapet*; Ašot Arcruni with his brother Gurgēn and his son Grigor-Derenik; the princes of eastern and western Siwnik'; Grigor Mamikonean, prince of Bagrewand, as well as the lords of numerous minor houses—given once again the choice between conversion to Islam or death, agreed to at least a nominal apostasy and eventually made their way home in disgrace after the death of al-Mutawakkil in 861. Only Smbat *sparapet* "the Confessor" refused to compromise his faith, despite his ambiguous political stance, and died in captivity at Sāmarrā after 862.

Outwardly, then, the situation of 855 seemingly resembled the one that had followed the earlier Armenian defeat at Bagrewand, but neither the international nor the internal conditions were the same. The resurgence of Byzantium under the warlike reign of the Armenian emperor Basil I "the Macedonian" (867-886) threatened the rapidly decaying Abbasids in the second half of the ninth century. Al-Mutawakkil's brutal repression had been a last effort. The return to an international balance of power created a favorable climate for the return of Armenian independence, which now developed unchecked. In Vaspurakan, another Arcruni, Gurgēn, prince of Mardastan, continued the guerrilla war against the Arabs and maintained himself in the Arcruni's domain in a series of actions now clearly recorded by the Arcruni house historian T'ovma but that also formed the core of the national epic of *Dawit' of*

Sasun. Similarly, in the north Ašot Bagratuni, the son of the captive Smbat "the Confessor," returned to the policy of his grandfather Ašot *Msaker* and harried the Arabs with increasing success from his refuge in Tayk'. The reconstitution of the principalities of the Arcruni and Bagratuni was already on the way, and another crucial, if intangible, element had been added to the growing fortune of the Bagratuni. Through the martyr's death of the earlier Smbat *sparapet* on the field of Bagrewand and the steadfastness of his grandson and namesake the *sparapet,* Smbat "the Confessor" at Sāmarrā, in the face of Muslim pressure and the concessions of the other magnates, the Bagratuni now finally achieved the spiritual prestige that the death of St. Vardan at Awarayr had so long conferred on the Mamikonean.

FOR FURTHER INFORMATION

For the sources of, or more information on, the material in this chapter, please consult the following (full citations can be found in the Bibliography at the end of this volume).

"Arminiya," *The Encyclopaedia*   Laurent, 1919.
          of Islam.   Ter Ghewondian, 1976.
Der Nersessian, 1945, 1978.

7

THE INDEPENDENT KINGDOMS OF MEDIEVAL ARMENIA

Nina Garsoïan

The Altered International
Situation in the Late Ninth Century

A s noted at the end of the preceding chapter, external conditions in the second half of the ninth century were propitious for the reestablishment of political autonomy on the Armenian plateau. In the east, the power of the Abbasid caliphate declined rapidly after the murder of the caliph al-Mutawakkil in 861, and its influence over Armenian affairs became correspondingly weaker. The main Muslim threat to the Armenian princes at the end of the ninth and all of the tenth centuries came not so much from the Abbasid caliphs at Baghdad as from neighboring emirs, such as the Hamdanids based on Mosul and Aleppo, who reached their zenith in the mid-tenth century, and the rulers of Azerbaijan (Adherbaijan). Particularly in the case of the latter, their attacks could and did do great harm to Armenia, especially in the reign of Smbat the Martyr (890-913/4), but they were not sustained and might be offset by various alliances or occasionally by appeals to the authority of the distant caliph. On the western border of Armenia, the Byzantine emperors returned to an offensive military policy against Islam after more than two centuries on the defensive. By 863 the great imperial victory of Poson on the Euphrates destroyed the powerful Muslim emirate of Melitēnē/Malatia, and in the 870s the emperor Basil I crushed the Paulician republic. These victories brought the imperial armies once again to the upper and middle Euphrates and consequently into direct contact with the Armenian lands. Nevertheless, the main concerns of Byzantium through much of the tenth century were, first, to secure the main points of communication toward the east: the Euphrates crossing near Melitēnē and the pass of the Cilician gates in southeastern Anatolia leading from central Asia Minor to the Cilician plain and the eastern Mediterranean coast; then to reconquer the former imperial territories of Mesopotamia, Cilicia, and Syria. Consequently, Armenia was increasingly involved with the Byzantine Empire during this period, but it was not yet the primary target of the imperial policy. This relative weakness or unconcern of the great powers on either side of Armenia created and equilibrium between them that provided a particularly favorable climate for the development of the major local dynasties. Left largely to their own devices, these dynasties hastened to exploit these conditions to further their autonomy and eventually to achieve independence with the coronation of Ašot I in 884.

According to the historian T'ovma Arcruni (Thomas Acruni, III, xiv-xv, pp. 264-74), the surviving captive princes began to return home from Sāmarrā around 857-858. As was observed earlier, many *naxarar* families had not survived the tragic years of the preceding century so that power had gradually accumulated in a few dominant houses. Even there, progress did not manifest itself simultaneously. The dynasty of the Siwnik' still remained divided between the prince of Gełakunik' in the western portion and the prince of Vayoc' Jor in the east, who was considered the "senior" *(gaherec'/gaherets)* prince of Siwnik'. In Vaspurakan, the situation remained confused until the beginning of the tenth century. The returning prince, Grigor-Derenik Arcruni (857-886/7), found himself opposed by his kinsman, Gurgēn, prince of Mardastan (855/58-ca. 896), who had led the guerrillas against the Muslims at home and annexed most of the Arcruni domains during their exile at Sāmarrā. Driven back by Grigor-Derenik, Gurgēn continued to battle his kinsman as well as the local emirs and the heirs of Bagarat Bagratuni in eastern Tarōn, to carve himself a principality centered around the principality of Anjewac'ik' (Andzevatsik) south of Lake Van into which he had married. Even where dissensions did not arise, the prestige of the returning Armenian magnates was greatly impaired by their apostasy.

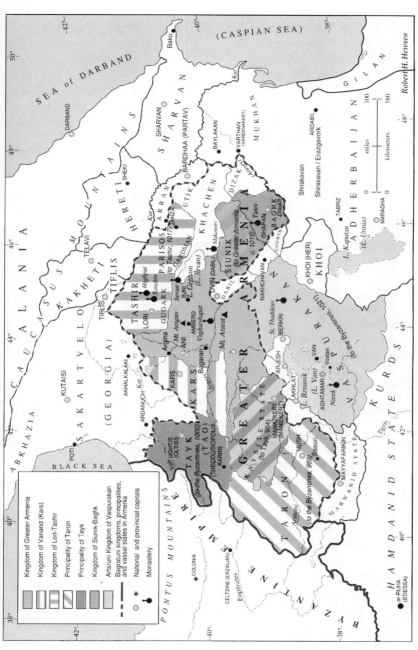

9. ARMENIA IN THE BAGRATUNI / BAGRATID PERIOD, c. 885-1064 A.D.

Under these circumstances, the advantage unquestionably belonged to the Bagratuni.

Ašot I "the Great" (855-884, 884-890)

Immediately after the deportation to Sāmarrā of Smbat *sparapet* "the Confessor" in 855, his son Ašot Bagratuni assumed his father's title and the leadership of the Armenian opposition in the north. Imitating from his distant refuge in the Bagratuni lands bordering on Tayk' the policy that had already proved successful under his grandfather Ašot *Msaker* at the beginning of the century, Ašot systematically reconquered the territories of Širak and Aršarunik' which became the core of his domain. The death of Grigor Mamikonean (Mamikonian) in 862 gave him further opportunity of expanding this domain by annexing the district of Bagrewand south of the Araxes. The increasingly dominant position of Ašot was simultaneously supported by a whole nexus of marriage alliances that linked him with the ruling families of Armenia: two of his daughters, Mariam and Sop'i (Sophia) married Vasak Gabur, prince of Gełarkunik', and Grigor-Derenik Arcruni of Vaspurakan; Ašot's sister was the wife of Bagarat I Bagratuni, prince of Iberia, while in the next generation one of his granddaughters wed Ašot II of the Bagratuni branch in Tarōn and another, the powerful Arcruni prince, Gagik Apumruan, regent of Vaspurakan for Grigor-Derenik's minor sons. Not only did these family relationships give Ašot ample opportunity to intrude into, and on occasion play arbiter in, the affairs of these principalities, especially in the continuing quarrels of Grigor-Derenik Arcruni and his kinsmen, but his seniority within the family made of him the unquestionable *tanutēr* of all the branches of the Bagratuni house with precedence over his kinsmen in Iberia as well as Tarōn. His transfer of the office of *sparapet* to his own brother Abas insured that power would not be divided between different branches of the family, as it had been in the preceding generation under Bagarat and Smbat "the Confessor."

On the international scene, Ašot consolidated his position in the west by assuring Byzantium that he had never wavered in his allegiance to the empire. Yet, when the Greeks reiterated their constant policy of implementing this allegiance by a religious union, Ašot backed the Armenian kat'ołikos Zak'aria. A council met at Širakawan (Shirakavan), one of the Bagratuni residences, to consider the Byzantine position presented in a presumed letter from Photius, patriarch of Constantinople, and returned an answer, which though ambiguous seemed to provide a *modus vivendi* for Chalcedonians and anti-Chalcedonians throughout Transcaucasia. Armenia's relations with Byzantium were consequently not impaired by this action, which renewed the collaboration of the Bagratuni and the kat'olikos begun by Smbat "the Confessor" and Yovhannēs of Ovayk' in the preceding generation, and it won for Ašot the all-important support of the church. This mutually beneficent collaboration was to continue with the election as kat'olikos of Ašot's candidate, Gēorg Gēvorg II of Garni (877-897), whom he supported against the secessionist tendencies of the Albanian Church, whose kat'olikos elected without the ratification of Armenia, was forced once again to seek his consecration from Gēorg II at Duin.

Alarmed by the growing menace of Byzantium on the Euphrates, the caliphate also sought to ensure Ašot's loyalty as early as 862, and the *ostikan* of Armīniya was ordered to confer on him the title of "Prince of Princes" formerly held by his uncle Bagarat Bagratuni, Prince of Tarōn. The historian Yovhannēs "the Kat'olikos" may have exaggerated when he claimed that the *ostikan*,

> investing him [Ašot] with many robes as well as royal insignia, [and] entrusted him with the taxes [*sak*] of Armenia and all the royal [tribute] *bekar*.(Yovhannēs Drasxanakertc'i, xxvii, p. 125)

Asolik even claimed that Ašot had been appointed Prince of Princes not only of Armenia but of Iberia as well. There is no doubt that the Abbasid *ostikan*s ruling the larger administrative unit of Armīniya from their residence at Partaw/Bardha'a occasionally still sought to enforce their direct authority over Armenia proper during the 870s of the ninth century with the help of the warlike Kaysite emirs of Manazkert. Nevertheless, Ašot's investiture in the name of the caliph officially acknowledged his authority over the local Muslim emirs as well as over the Christian *naxarars*. Ašot consequently used his position as representative of the caliph to consolidate his hold over Aršarunik' by repelling the attacks of the Djahhāfid emir, whom the *sparapet* Abas routed and drove from Armenia, and to extend a degree of control over the capital city of Duin during the 880s without serious interference from the Muslim authorities, even though he still preferred to remain in the Bagratuni residence in Bagaran in Širak.

Yovhannēs the Kat'olikos was probably correct in viewing Ašot as already de facto King of Armenia from the time of his investiture as

Prince of Princes in 862; inscriptions refer to him as king from the middle of the next decade. Consequently, a number of scholars have argued that Ašot's formal coronation at Bagaran by the kat'oⱡikos Gēorg II with a crown brought by the *ostikan* in the name of the caliph on August 26, 884 (Yovhannēs Drasxanakertc'i, xxix, p. 128) should not be overstressed, since it added no substantial powers to those he already possessed. In their view, the sending of crowns was a customary courtesy of the period and need not have had a crucial importance. This argument is further bolstered by the fact that both Arab and Greek sources continue to refer to Ašot as merely "Prince of Princes" and not king, while his recently discovered official Arabic seal styles him even more modestly, Ashut ibn Sinbat (Ašot son of Smbat), without any title whatsoever. Moreover, Ašot never achieved full sovereignty, since he struck no coinage of his own and remained tributary to the caliphate.

Nevertheless, even though Ašot's coronation apparently brought him no tangible additional prerogatives, and he remained to some degree subordinate to the *ostikan* in Partaw, the significance of the brilliant coronation ceremony at Bagaran in the eyes of a society for which visible symbols were of paramount importance should not be underestimated. Ašot I's prestige had unquestionably been enhanced both at home and abroad. The tenth-century Muslim geographer Ibn Ḥawḵal probably rendered Ašot's new status more accurately than other Arab sources when he referred to him as "King of Armenia." Not to be outdone by his rival the caliph, the Byzantine emperor Basil I hastened in his turn to offer "terms of peace, harmony and friendship to our King Ašot," whom he addressed as "beloved son" (Yovhannēs Drasxanakertc'i, xxix, p. 129). According to Yovhannēs the Kat'oⱡikos, the Armenian *naxarar*s and princes had "unanimously" requested Ašot's elevation from the caliph, and the later historian from Siwnik' Stephen Ōrbelean's (Orbelian) identification of these "princes" as the two rulers of Siwnik' as well as Grigor-Derenik Arcruni of Vaspurakan supports Yovhannēs's claim that recognition of Ašot's preeminence united all Armenia from north to south.

Ašot I maintained this dominant position in the few remaining years until his death ca. 890. His own domain, which stretched eastward across the central district of Ayrarat to Lake Sevan and the border of Vaspurakan, according to Stephen Ōrbelean, was increased by portions of the northern districts of Gardman and Utik', which Ašot conquered from the local mountaineers with the help of his faithful cousin, Baɢarat I of Iberia, as well as by the border Armeno-Iberian district of

Gugark' pacified by the crown prince Smbat in the last years of the reign. Presiding over the welfare of his family far and wide, Ašot also supported the Iberian Bagratid heir, Atrnerseh II, and confirmed him as *curopalate* of Iberia (888-923). At the opposite end of the Armenian plateau, Ašot first sought to mediate in the attack of his son-in-law Grigor-Derenik Arcruni in an expedition against the Muslim emirs west of Lake Urmiah. Ašot appointed another of his kinsmen, Gagik Apumruan Arcruni (the husband of his granddaughter), as regent for Grigor-Derenik's minor sons Sargis-Ašot, Χač'ik-Gagik (Khachik-Gagik), and Gurgēn, and as support for their widowed mother, Ašot's own daughter Sop'i. Thus, a new autonomous state based on the northwestern portion of the plateau, such as Armenia had not known for centuries, was re-created by Ašot "the Great" and recognized as such by the contemporary world.

The Bagratid Crisis
Under Smbat I "the Martyr" (890/91-914)

The powerful personality and achievements of Ašot I had overwhelmed his contemporaries and united the loyalties of the Armenian princes, but it also masked a number of latent flaws in the newly created state. The domain of the Bagratuni based on northwestern Širak, where Ašot normally resided at Bagaran, was an excellent refuge in times of trouble (as the events of the ninth century had amply demonstrated), but it was neither sufficiently extensive and powerful nor sufficiently central to serve as a base for the control of the entire Armenian plateau. Ašot I's decision not to move to the Aršakuni and subsequently Sasanian administrative capital of Duin in the valley of the Araxes, and his successors' usual inability to wrest it from Muslim governors, compounded the problem. The eastern valley of the Araxes with the Muslim emirates of Gołt'n and Naxčawan consequently remained a threatening wedge leading from Azerbaijan to Duin in the heartland of Armenia and separating the northwestern Bagratuni possessions from the Arcruni territories of Vaspurakan in the south and the lands of Siwnik' in the east. In general, the presence of the various Muslim centers at Tiflis, Karin, Duin, Manazkert, Χlat', Arčēš, Berkri, Naxčawan, Gołt'n, Ałjnik' and Azerbaijan aggravated the geographical fragmentation of the Armenian highlands and perpetually impeded any policy of political, religious, or demographic unification and of centralization, even though the local emirs also pursued self-serving policies, neither presenting a unified Muslim front nor supporting the representatives of the distant caliphate.

More fundamentally, no constitutional framework held the various principalities together or linked them into a single state. The old *naxarar* structure that had flourished in the days of the Aršakuni and the *Marzpan*ate was beginning to break down as the common lands of the *tun* split into apanages for its leading members and consequently opposed different branches of the same family to each other. This tendency already manifested itself in the days of Ašot I as Grigor-Derenik Arcruni and his father struggled with Gurgēn, prince of Mardastan, over Anjewac'ik'. The Iberian Bagratids increasingly went their own way and battled among themselves; the Bagratids of Tarōn, descended from the Prince of Princes Bagarat, drew apart from their northern kinsmen. This divisive tendency reached the royal house itself at the king's death as the *sparapet* Abas, based on the fortress of Kars, abandoned his long loyalty to his brother Ašot to turn against his nephew Smbat I. Still more crucially, the Bagratid claim to a dominant position within the land rested ultimately on the personal authority of the ruler rather than on any traditional or legal foundation that might have curbed the centrifugal tendencies of the magnates. According to the Aršakuni system of hereditary offices, the Bagratuni "coronants" had placed the crown on the head of their Aršakuni lords but had never been entitled to wear it. Consequently, they had not even been the first among their equals in a society where every clan jealously guarded its own prerogatives, and both the vanished Mamikonean and the belligerent Arcruni rightly or wrongly claimed royal descent. More immediately, the new legitimacy bestowed on Ašot by his coronation at the hands of kat'ołikos rested upon the continuing goodwill and collaboration of the Armenian Church, thus raising potential questions of mutual relations of church and state and limiting the king's freedom of action in various areas such as Armenian religious concessions to Byzantium. The additional sanctification of the royal house rested only on its apocryphal descent from the biblical house of David first reported in the mid-tenth century . These elements of weakness were to manifest themselves all too soon after Ašot I's death.

The first years of Smbat I's reign continued the successful pattern of his father's days, even though his uncle Abas, entrenched in the fortress of Kars, made the most of the young king's absence in Gugark' to dispute the succession. Two years were needed before Smbat could assert his authority, despite the intervention of the kat'oɫikos Gēorg II and the support of the *curopalates* Atrnerseh II of Iberia. This inauspicious beginning ended, however, in Smbat's coronation by the kat'oɫikos at his residence of Širakawan or Erazgawork' (Erazgavork) with the same pomp as his father:

> Smbat was presented with a royal diadem on the order of the caliph, by Afšīn (Apshin) the Ismaelite prince of Atrpatakan [*ostikan* of Azerbaijan] ... and along with it he was given robes wrought with gold, and swift steeds bedecked with ornaments and shining armor forged with gold. They came forth to meet him at the place of assembly, and returned to the holy church with the patriarch Gēorg, who pronounced the solemn blessings on him, and investing him with the gold embroidered robes ...., he placed on his head the royal crown. Smbat emerged from the spiritual nuptials to rule over all of Armenia. (Yovhannēs Drasxanakertc'i, xxx, p. 132)

Abas' attempt to vent his resentment by having the kat'oɫikos deposed proved unsuccessful. Like his father, Smbat also secured his position on the Byzantine side:

> Placing his kingdom on a firm foundation, Smbat tried to establish peaceful relations with everyone . . . First, in compliance with the alliance of his father, he did not withdraw from the friendly affection for Leo [VI] Emperor of the Romans. He honored the latter with many gifts and worthy presents in accordance with his gentle temper. In return the Emperor gave to him an exceedingly great many number of gifts, namely, beautiful weapons, ornaments, robes wrought with gold, goblets, and cups, and girdles of pure gold studded with gems. But a greater honor than these was, that the Emperor addressed Smbat as his 'beloved son' by means of a treaty of friendship. (Yovhannēs Drasxanakertc'i, xxxi, pp. 137-38)

The king even succeeded in allaying the *ostikan* Afshin's understandable alarm at this friendship with Byzantium by arguing that his policy would prove economically beneficial to the caliphate as well:

> Why are you coming upon us in anger for no reason? If it is because of the alliance I have made with the Emperor, this was for your benefit also. [I thought that] I might obtain with ease those items that you

yourself and the caliph needed from the land of the Greeks, and present you with noteworthy garments, ornaments and vessels for your own use. Likewise, I wished to clear the way for merchants of your faith, so that they might have access to their land, and enrich your treasury with the riches of the Greeks. (Yovhannēs Drasxanakertc'i, xxxi, p. 138)

Consequently, the *ostikan* who had advanced to Armenia with an army returned to Azerbaijan after exchanging gifts with the king.

Smbat's early policy proved equally successful at home. On Good Friday, April 21, 892, he recaptured the city of Duin, which had closed its gates against him, sent its Muslim commanders in chains to the Byzantine emperor Leo VI, and reestablished his full control over the city. Yovhhannēs "the Kat'oïikos," who always praises the Bagratuni, gives a considerable expanded description of Smbat's realm:

. . . setting about to annex many lands, he watched over all of them, and brought them into obedience, some by means of gentle words, others by force. Accordingly the great Curopalate of Georgia [Atrnerseh II] and his adherents persuaded by the righteousness of his wonderful order all submitted to him. But whoever lifted their hands against him, he repressed with daring force, and subdued them beneath his feet. Thus, he extended the boundaries of his domain as far as the city of Karin in the northeast, and to the farther side of Kłarǰk' [Kghardjk], as far as the shore of the great sea [Black Sea] and the borders of Egrisi [Abkhazia], as well as to the foot of the Caucasus Mountains, that is to say, Gugark', and Canark' [Dzanark] as far as the Gate of the Alans, where he also seized the fortress guarding the pass [Darial]. From there the boundary [ran] southward to the city of Tiflis (Tp'xis) along the course of the Kur River, and [continued] on to the district of Uti, as far as the city of Hunarakert, to Tus and to Šamk'or [Shamkor]. Thus he enlarged the limits of his domain and brought these beneath the yoke of the royal tributes, *bekar*s and taxes, and dedicated the weapon he used valiantly in battle as a sign of victory.(Yovhannēs Drasxanakertc'i, xxxi, p. 139)

This picture, which includes a large portion of western Iberian lands and reached all the way to the Darial Pass in the main Caucasus chain, probably reflects Smbat's sphere of influence rather than his actual domain, as Yovhannēs himself implies when he speaks of

Atrnerseh II's recognition of Smbat's suzerainty. Nevertheless, Asołik also furnishes a more than glowing picture of the prosperity of Armenia in this period:

> During his reign Smbat ruled over all his domains, on Armenia and on Iberia and acquired the cities of his opponents. In his reign, as under the rule of his father, there was prosperity and peace in the realm of Armenia according to [the words of] the prophet: 'Everyman rested under his vine and under his fig tree' [I Kings 4:25]. The farms became towns and the towns cities through the increase in the population and wealth until the very shepherds and cowherds themselves were clad in silken garments. And he [Smbat] built the church of the All-Savior in Širakawan with a cupola of great height and walls of dressed stone. (Asołik, III. iii, pp. 12-13)

The report is at least partially confirmed by the reappearance of architectural monuments in Armenia after the long hiatus of the eighth century. Ašot I was praised by Yovhannēs the Kat'ołikos for his endowment of churches and the twin foundations of Smbat's aunt, Mariam, princess of Siwnik', (the churches dedicated to the Mother of God and to the Holy Apostles) still standing on the former island in Lake Sevan. The main blow to this flourishing situation was the frightful earthquake that destroyed the city of Duin in 893/4 and struck the imagination of both Armenian and Arab writers who have left descriptions of the catastrophe. The cathedral and the residence of the kat'ołikos collapsed, forcing Gēorg II to take refuge in Vałaršapat, the city walls and most of the houses were leveled, and the loss of life horrendous, though the figures of 70,000 and 150,000 respectively given by T'ovma Arcruni and the Arab historian Ibn al-Athir are unquestionably inflated.

The auspicious beginning of the reign began to wane, however, even before the end of the ninth century under external and internal pressures. Most ominous was the outbreak of war with the Turkish Sādjids ruling in (Persian) Azerbaijan, which began immediately after the destruction of Duin and continued intermittently to the end of the reign. The *ostikan* Afshīn belonging to this family had been granted by the caliph authority over Armīniya as well as Azerbaijan, where he was carving a principality for himself. As such, Smbat's independent policy could not be tolerated by him. The first Sadjid attack took Naxčawan, and recaptured Duin. Afshin seized the kat'ołikos Gēorg II, but his defeat by Smbat at the foot of Mt. Aragac (Aragats) forced him to come to terms and retreat to Azerbaijan. The kat'ołikos was ransomed through the intervention of the prince of Šakē, who had assumed the title of King of Caucasian Albania in 893, and he returned to settle at Vałaršapat instead of his residence at Duin, destroyed by the earthquake.

Smbat's authority likewise faced a whole series of internal challenges. Despite his new status, the ruler of Albania seems to have remained loyal to the Bagratuni, but the prince of eastern Siwnik'/Vayoc' Jor temporarily wavered in his allegiance, according to Yovhannēs "the Kat'ołikos." The young prince of Vaspurakan, Sargis-Ašot, actually went to pay court to Afshīn, though he obtained nothing and was imprisoned with his brothers on his return by Grigor Apumruan, to whom Smbat I may even have granted Vaspurakan jointly with Gurgēn, prince of Anjewac'ik'. Far to the south, the Shaybani emir of Ałjnik' seized the Bagratid domain of Tarōn in 895. Led astray by Grigor Apumruan, who had remained loyal until then, Smbat I was routed by the Shaybanids and barely escaped northward to Bagrewand. Apumruan's treason was soon avenged, as the ablest of the Arcruni heirs, Χač'ik-Gagik, whom he had unwisely released, killed him with the help of the local magnates and reestablished his elder brother Sargis-Ašot as senior prince of Vaspurakan. Nevertheless, the growing suspicion and hostility between the Bagratuni and the Arcruni would soon have serious consequences for the king. Encouraged by Smbat I's difficulties in the south, Afshīn attacked a second time in the north. Crossing through Utik' and Gugark', he struck directly at the heart of the Bagratuni domain, seized the queen with a number of the royal household and the royal treasure in the fortress of Kars, which surrendered, and retired with his booty to Duin while Smbat took refuge in Tayk'. This time the Sadjid terms were harsher. To obtain the release of his wife, Smbat was compelled to send his eldest son and heir, Ašot, and his nephew as hostages; to give one of his nieces in marriage to Afshīn; and to pay a tribute to the ostikan's son, who was left behind to govern Duin, while Afshī now turned to Vaspurakan, capturing the fortresses of Van and Ostan and forcing the Arcruni princes to flee to the mountains.

The position of Smbat I was seriously compromised at this point especially since he was also faced with the rebellion of the Ḳaysite emirs of Manazkert, who took the opportunity to refuse the tribute they owed to the king, but it was not yet critical. The newly elected kat'ołikos, Yovhannēs "the Historian" (897-924/5), from whom we derive much of our knowledge of contemporary events, continued the collaboration of the church with the crown. In the north, the *curopalate* Atrnerseh II, who had remained loyal, was rewarded by Smbat with the crown of Iberia in 899. The prince of Siwnikʿ returned to his allegiance. In the south, the Bagratuni heir of Tarōn regained his domain in 898 after the death of the Shaybānid conqueror. The Ḳaysites were crushed by 902 with the help of Sargis-Ašot Arcruni and returned to their former status of tributaries of the Bagratid crown, although their base of Manazkert was not captured. The Bagratid crown prince Ašot was finally released from captivity, and Smbat even obtained from the caliph al-Muḳtafī the separation of Armenia from Azerbaijan with the right of forwarding the Armenian tribute directly to Baghdad, thus bypassing the *ostikan.* Finally, the governor left at Duin fled on hearing of Afshīn's death in 901, after having ruled the city for only one year. Unfortunately, the new *ostikan,* Afshīn's brother Yūsuf (901-919, 922-929), was to pursue the war against Armenia even more relentlessly with catastrophic results for the king. The situation in the country, where the separatist tendencies of the princes soon continued, rapidly grew chaotic.

The beginning of Yūsuf's rule was as circumspect as that of his brother, since Smbat had the support of the caliph, who rightly suspected the *ostikan* of rebellious plans. Even so, Yūsuf immediately sought to reassert his authority over Armenia. The first campaign, again following the northern path through Utikʿ to Duin, was met by the king near Aruč to the west of the city with a large force, which overawed the invaders, and it consequently ended in mutual gifts. Yūsuf showered Smbat with a new crown and diadem and precious garments, designated the crown prince Ašot as "Prince of Princes," honored the katʿolikos as well, and withdrew into Azerbaijan. In this period Yovhannēs "the Historian" could still praise the prosperity of Armenia, where "each one lived on his own patrimony" and the "chief *naxarar*s, being secure and at ease from the onslaught of the enemy, built in monasteries, towns, and *agarak*s churches of thick walls of stone and mortar" (Yovhannēs Drasxanakertcʿi, xl, pp. 157-58), and favorable relations were maintained with the Byzantine empire.

The first signs of trouble came from the north, where the prince of the coastal Iberian district of Abkhazia revolted against his father-in-law, King Atrnerseh II. Smbat I at first supported Atrnerseh, defeating and capturing the prince of Abkhazia, but then conceded to him the crown to which he aspired, winning his alliance but alienating the more powerful king of Iberia, who now broke his long loyalty to his Armenian kinsmen and turned against Smbat. The king's reward of

Sargis-Ašot Arcruni for his help against the Ḳaysites by the grant of
the city of Naxčawan north of the Araxes River antagonized the new
prince of eastern Siwnik', also named Smbat (whom the king had
confirmed as "senior prince of Siwnik' and lord over the entire realm
of Sisakan"). Smbat of Siwnik', who considered Naxčawan part of his
domain, consequently refused to pay the royal tribute and turned to
the emir of Azerbaijan in 903. The king's attempt to remedy the
situation by returning Naxčawan to Siwnik' merely aggravated matters
by alienating Xač'ik-Gagik Arcruni, who had replaced his brother
Sargis-Ašot as senior prince of Vaspurakan in 905, and pushing him
likewise toward Yūsuf.

The turbulence of the magnates was increased by Yūsuf, who had
made peace with the caliph against whom he had rebelled. As a result
of this reconciliation, Armenia in 907-908 found itself faced with the
necessity of paying a double tribute: to the caliph in Baghdad and to the
emir of Azerbaijan as well. Outraged by the king's order to provide one
fifth of their possessions, the *naxarar*s grew restive. The magnates of
Vanand plotted with Atrnerseh of Iberia to murder Smbat I, and the
keeper of the royal domains surrendered the fortress of Ani in Širak to
Atrnerseh II. The plot failed, and the King of Iberia was forced to sue
for peace, but a far more damaging situation was already developing in
Vaspurakan under the leadership of the warlike and ambitious prince
Xač'ik-Gagik Arcruni, supported by his younger brother Gurgēn and the
local princes. Seeking revenge against both his uncle King Smbat I and
Siwnik' for the loss of Naxčawan, but mostly concerned with his own
aggrandizement, Gagik set out for Azerbaijan, where he received a
crown from Yūsuf in 908 as King Gagik I of Vaspurakan, thus creating
in the south an autonomous Arcruni kingdom opposed to that of the
Bagratuni in the north. The embassy of Yovhannēs "the Historian"
attempting to mediate the troubles ended only in the captivity of the
kat'ołikos, who remained prisoner for a considerable time, was ransomed with difficulty, and retired to Gugark'. Gagik I Arcruni is
understandably the hero of his kinsman T'ovma's *History of the Arcruni
House,* which praises at length the new king's bravery, generosity, and
benevolence, as well as the conspicuous prosperity of his realm. The
elegant palatine church of the Holy Cross on the island of Ałt'amar
(Aghtamar) still stands as testimony to Gagik's extensive and splendid
building program. His ability was beyond question, but his defections
struck a mortal blow at Smbat I. The split of Armenia brought about by
the creation of the Kingdom of Vaspurakan was never to be repaired and

added yet another element to the complicated pattern of Christian and Muslim principalities developing on the Armenian highlands. Immediately after Gagik I's coronation, Yūsuf made use of his new ally, to march on Armenia, and in 909 the war between Smbat I and the Sadjids entered into its final phase. Advancing from Azerbaijan up the valley of the Araxes by way of Naxčawan, Yūsuf met with Gagik I and his brother Gurgēn Arcruni to overrun most of Siwnik', which bore the first brunt of the attack. The senior prince, Smbat of Eastern Siwnik', succeeded in escaping to Vaspurakan, but his kinsman Grigor Sup'an II, prince of Western Siwnik' was forced to make his submission to the *ostikan* at Duin, where the latter had established his winter quarters and which became his base of operations, while the king, who had fled northward, made his way back to Širak. In this moment of crisis, the hold of Smbat (whose gentleness is repeatedly stressed by Yovhannēs the Kat'ołikos) on the loyalty of his vassals proved insufficient. Even the *sparapet* Ašot Bagratuni abandoned his uncle and rallied to the support of Yūsuf, as did the leading princes, according to Asołik:

> To him [Yūsuf] came Atrnerseh King of Iberia and Gagik prince of Vaspurakan, who was the son of Smbat's sister, and Ašot the son of Smbat's brother Šapuh, together with all their forces, abandoning King Smbat and betraying him out of envy and for the prosperity of the Armenian realm. (Asołik, 1917,III, iv, p. 17)

The last stand of the royal army commanded by the crown prince Ašot and his youngest brother Mušeł was crushed the following spring by Yūsuf and Gagik I Arcruni north of Duin. Prince Mušeł was captured, while the king sought refuge in the impregnable stronghold of Kapoyt Berd "Blue Fortress" in Aršarunik', and the northern districts were overrun. Yūsuf treated the captive Armenian princes with unwonted ferocity: Mušeł, the king's son, Smbat Bagratuni, the king's nephew, and Grigor Sup'an II of Western Siwnik' were poisoned and Yūsuf's armies devastated northern Armenia, while the other princes of Siwnik' fled to the distant districts of Gardman and Arcax in the north. Smbat I sought help to no avail from the caliph, distracted by a rebellion in Egypt, and from Byzantium, while the Armenian princes turned away.

> Those [who survived], whether they were related to him or not, remained aloof from him in deed and in thought, some very much

against their will, and the others for no reason at all. They preferred
to recognize [the domain of] the foreigners rather than his. Those
whom he loved with friendship dissociated themselves from him and
joined the enemy. Certain others, who were annoyed at him, even rose
and disgracefully attacked him intending to kill him in compliance
with the intrigues of the Hagarite . . . (Yovhannēs Drasxanakertc'i,
xlviii, p. 174)

The fortress of Kapoyt Berd could not be taken by the Muslims,
but Smbat I finally surrendered to put an end to the slaughter. Yūsuf first
received him honorably, but soon returned to his former cruelty.
Dragged to the siege of the stronghold of Ernjak (Erndjak) where the
princesses of Siwnik' were still holding out, the king was savagely
tortured to death at the order of the *ostikan* in the hope of forcing the
defenders to surrender, and his headless corpse was exposed on a cross
in the capital of Duin.

The Revival of Armenia Under Ašot II *Erkat'* (914-928/29) and Gagik Ārcruni (908-943?)

The kat'ołikos Yovhannēs "the Historian" follows his grim account of
Smbat I's "martyrdom" with descriptions of the tragic state of Armenia
after his death: attempts at forcible conversions to Islam accompanied
by intensified persecution and executions; the scorched earth policy and
attacks of the northerners, Abkhazia, Gugark', and Utik', resulting in
widespread famine; and the internal quarrels of the magnates increasing
the fragmentation of the land:

Our kings, lords and princes tried to break up and take away the homes
of each one of the original *naxarar*doms, and in accord with their
whims, created new *payazat*s and *spasalar*s of their own. Brother rose
against brother, and kinsman against kinsman, because jealousy,
malevolence, agitation and absolute hatred turned them against one
another. Thus falling on one another *en masse,* they fought as enemies, and . . . shed more of their own blood than that of the enemy.
They tore down with their own hands all their cities, villages, towns,
*awan*s, *agarak*s and houses.(Yovhannēs Drasxanakertc'i, lii, p. 186)

Nevertheless, the savagery of the king's death brutally awakened the senior Armenian princes. Gagik I Arcruni, whose support of Yūsuf had become increasingly unwilling, took over the leadership of the Armenian resistance. Vaspurakan bore the brunt of Yūsuf's attacks, giving a breathing space to Smbat I's son Ašot II, usually known as *Erkat'*, "the Iron King." Following yet one more time the traditional policy of his house in times of trouble, Ašot *Erkat'* entrenched himself in the Bagratuni domains in the northwest from which he systematically drove out the Muslim invaders, whom he also defeated in Bagrewand with the help of his brother Abas. He then advanced northward through Gugark' as far as Tiflis, where he again defeated the Muslims before returning home.

Ašot *Erkat'*'s success bore immediate fruit. Gurgēn, prince of Iberia, and, more important, the old King Atrnerseh II, turned back to the support of their Bagratid kinsman. Atrnerseh had Ašot II crowned King of Armenia. Meanwhile, Gagik I of Vaspurakan, supported by Smbat, prince of Eastern Siwnik', and the southern Bagratuni princes, continued to hold off Yūsuf from a stronghold in the southern mountains. The remaining princes of Siwnik' held out in the mountains of their domains, and the kat'ołikos Yovhannēs made his way south to Tarōn. Yūsuf sought to counter Ašot II's new prestige by installing his cousin and namesake, the *sparapet* Ašot, at Duin, but the critical situation in Armenia had already aroused the attention of Byzantium, where the patriarch Nicholas Mystikos wrote in 914 to the Armenian kat'ołikos urging a union of all Christians against the Muslims. The correspondence led to an invitation from the Byzantine court, and in 914 Ašot II traveled to Constantinople, where he was received with royal honors, treated again as a "beloved son," and presumably granted the title of Prince of Princes attributed to him in contemporary Byzantine sources. The earlier political alliance of the Bagratuni with Byzantium seemed fully renewed, and Ašot's journey to Constantinople is noted by the Greek sources as well, but the kat'ołikos, "thinking that there might be people who might look askance at my going there, and assume that I sought communion with the Chalcedonians" (Yovhannēs Drasxanakertc'i, lv, p. 198), preferred to remain at home.

The situation in Armenia was still murky when Ašot II returned home in 915 with a Byzantine army to face the opposition of his namesake whom Yūsuf had crowned as anti-king and whom he was unable to drive out of the capital of Duin where he was residing under the *ostikan*'s protection. The "war of the two Ašots" dragged on for two years (918-920) despite the mediations of the kat'oɫikos and the support given to Ašot II *Erkat'* by both princes of Siwnik'. Even so, Ašot II steadily consolidated his position in the face of this rivalry and continuous rebellions, especially in the north. He wrested the powerful northern fortress of Šamšuildē (Shamshuilde) from its governor, who had appealed for help to the emir of Tiflis; quelled the revolt of Utik'; escaped the conspiracy of his own brother Abas plotting with Prince Gurgēn of Iberia; and seized Gardman from his own father-in-law, who had also attacked him. Gradually he annexed the lands of Western Siwnik' as well, so that Siwnik', reduced to its eastern portion, weakened by interior quarrels and isolated from the Bagratuni holdings by the emirate of Goɫt'n, no longer presented a serious threat.

The other crucial factor in the Armenian recovery was the reversal of Yūsuf's policy, as he now recognized King Ašot II, to whom he sent a crown. Ašot's position was further improved by Yūsuf's recall and imprisonment for rebellion against the caliph in 919 and the arrival of a new *ostikan,* who maintained a benevolent policy toward Bagratid Armenia. He not only recognized the legitimacy of Ašot *Erkat'* but granted him the title of *Šahanšah (Shahanshah),* "King of Kings," which raised him above all the rulers of the area, effectively ending de jure as well as de facto the career of the anti-king Ašot who, bereft of his Muslim support, could not maintain himself at Duin and was forced to make his peace with his cousin and retire to his own domain at Bagaran in Širak ca. 920. The submission of the anti-king and Ašot II's renewed control of the capital marked the effective recovery of the Bagratuni kingdom despite continuing difficulties in the northern borderland of Utik'. The same stabilization manifested itself in the south where the *ostikan* first attacked and looted, but soon concluded an agreement with Gagik I Arcruni, who maintained and extended his hold over Vaspurakan as far north as the central district of Kogovit, supported by the remarkable loyalty of his kinsmen and vassals.

The consolidation of the country, especially in the north, was strained to some degree by the renewal of external pressures at the end of Ašot II's reign, but its autonomy was not seriously compromised. The earlier help given to the king by Constantinople came at a price, since the Byzantine emperor saw himself as the image of Christ on earth and consequently as the suzerain as well as the protector of all Christian rulers, with the right to intrude into their internal affairs and their lands. The imperial view on the terms of the relationship with Armenia was clearly spelled out by the emperor himself in his treatise *On the Administration of the Empire*:

> since the prince of princes is the servant of the emperor of the Romans, being appointed by him and receiving his dignity from him, it is obvious that the cities and townships and territories of which he is lord also belong to the emperor of the Romans.(Porphyrogenitus, *De admin.* ch. 43, p. 201)

Undoubtedly alarmed by Ašot II's negotiations with the *ostikan* and his official recognition by the Muslims as *Šahanšah,* the Byzantine armies under the leadership of the empire's ablest general, the Armenian Yovhannēs Kurkuas (Hovhannes Gurgen), interfered both in the north, where they supported the rebels, and in the south, where they brought increasing pressure on the Ḳaysites emirate and the principality of Tarōn. In 922 Kurkuas even seems to have made a first attempt to seize Duin, jointly defended by the *ostikan* who was in residence and Ašot II, who had been summoned to his support, according to Asołik:

> In the second year of his reign he [the emperor Romanos I Lekapenos] raised a great host and sent the *Demeslikos* [Grand Domestic] to the city of Duin held by the emir Spukʿ who called Ašot *Šahanšah* to his assistance. And the Greeks came, they besieged Duin but could not take it, and returned from there. (Asołik, 1917, III, vi, pp. 24-25)

The contemporary Yovhannēs the katʿołikos is curiously silent about this expedition.

The release of Yūsuf by the caliph in 923 added to the difficulties. On his return to Armenia, Yūsuf first turned against Vaspurakan, from which he extorted "two to three times the amount of tribute" before returning to Persia. His new deputy seized the princes of Siwnikʿ, whom he held at Naxčawan, and he brought back in chains to the capital forty of the "foremost *gaherecʿ* (princes) and glorious *nahapet*s of the noble families of the city of Duin, who had come to meet him. Abandoning once and for all the traditional seat of the katʿołikate, Yovhannēs "the Historian" fled from Duin, with the Muslim troops in pursuit, first to the "Monastery of the Caves" (Ayri Vankʿ/Gełard [Geghard]) and then to his own "small fortress of Biwrakan," where he had built an impressive basilica, then to the former anti-king Ašot Bagratuni at Bagaran, and finally to the relative quiet of Vaspurakan, where he died some two years later, ca. 924/5, at Gagik I's royal residence on the island of Ałt'amar. The damage done by the Muslim armies was considerable, but Ašot II, who had fled to the island in Lake Sevan, defeated their commander, who retreated toward Duin only to be routed again north of the city. An almost simultaneous Greek attack on Duin failed again in 927/8, beaten off by the population as well as the garrison, according to the Arab historian Ibn al-Athir.

The withdrawal of the Greeks as well as of the *ostikan* left Ašot II master of his own house at the end of his reign. The Sādjids, for all the harm they had done, were mere soldiers of fortune whose power had collapsed even before Yūsuf's death in 929. The resultant confused situation in Azerbaijan—where various Kurdish and Daylamite chieftains battled for power (in what the historian Minorsky has termed "the Iranian interlude" (Minorsky, 1958, pp. 14, 19-20) of the tenth century, during which Iranians generally replaced Arabs in the Muslim emirates)—lessened to some degree its threat to Armenia. The attention of Byzantium was increasingly diverted southward by the war against the great Hamdanid emirs of Aleppo and Mosul, and Bagratid Armenia was again left in peace, though the empire continued to manifest its displeasure by failing to grant the title of prince of princes to Ašot's brother and successor Abas. Seemingly less battered than the north as a result of the diplomatic skills of its ruler, the Arcruni kingdom of Vaspurakan continued to flourish under the aging Gagik I, whose prestige was greatly enhanced by the favor shown him by Byzantium, since he seems to be the prince of princes addressed in a letter of the patriarch Nicholas Mysticos rather than the northern Bagratuni king, and by the asylum provided for the kat'ołikos in the last years of Yovhannēs "the Historian."

The Apex of the Bagratuni Dynasty (929-1020)

Our information concerning the affairs of Bagratuni Armenia, and of the country in general, declines sharply with the end of the *History* of Yovhannēs the Kat'ołikos, whose last recorded events date from 923-924. The history of the capital of Duin is particularly obscure and chaotic in the tenth century. The main dangers for the autonomy of the Armenian states, in addition to the ever-present threat of Byzantium's claim to suzerainty over the land, and the internal tendency to ever-greater fragmentation, came from the neighboring Muslim powers. In the north, the Kurdish S̲h̲addādid emirs and Daylamite Sallārids (also called Musāfirids) struggling to dominate Azerbaijan alternatively seized control of Duin by way of the valley of the lower Araxes, which was still controlled by the local Arab dynasty of the emirs of Gołtʿn. In the south, the Hamdanids holding Aleppo and Mosul between 941 and ca. 967 exerted increasing pressure on the Ḳaysite emirate which they eventually destroyed, as well as on the Christian principalities of Tarōn and Anjewacʿikʿ. Northern Armenia had obviously been seriously drained by the long Sādjid wars, since Ašot II's successor, King Abas (928/9-952/3), apparently made no effort to extend his dominion or reconquer Duin and in general, left much of the initiative to Gagik I Arcruni, who was still ruling over Vaspurakan until 937 or even 942/3. Nevertheless, the work of Ašot II had obviously not been in vain. The Armenian kingdoms were now sufficiently rooted to survive well into the eleventh century. As the Bagratuni reaffirmed their autonomy from external domination and gradually retook their earlier precedence over Vaspurakan after the death of Gagik I, their prestige and Armenian culture reached their zenith under Abas's descendants: Ašot III *Ołormacʿ (Voghormadz)* ("the Merciful") (952/3-977), Smbat II *Tiezerakal* ("the Master of the Universe") (977-989/90), and Gagik I "the Great" (989/90-1017/20).

Asołik praises the return of peace and prosperity to Armenia under the reign of Abas, who remained the sole Armenian Bagratuni ruler after the death of his cousin, the antiking Ašot of Bagaran in 936, though much of his energy was spent in adorning his capital of Kars, where he erected a new cathedral, and in protecting it from the raid of Prince Bēr of Abkhazia, who sought to force the consecration of the church according to the Greek Orthodox and not the Armenian rite, rather than in expanding of consolidating his realm. Numerous religious foundations, among them the great monasteries of Hoŕomos Vankʿ (934) and Narek (935), also date from his reign in which religious questions again became acute. The katʿołikos Anania Mokacʿi would have to fight through most of his pontificate (943?-967) against the secessionist tendencies of the bishop of Siwnikʿ, supported by the katʿołikos of Caucasian Albania and the local princes who resisted the centralizing policy of the Bagratuni king and the Armenian katʿołikos. In this, as in military matters, the leadership still came at first from Gagik I of Vaspurakan, who continued to extend his protectorate over the katʿołikate by having three successive primates elected from the southern house of the Ŕštuni after the death of Yovhannēs "the Historian" and keeping them in residence at his court, until Anania Mokacʻi finally made his way back north after the death of the powerful Arcruni king.

Duin remained in Muslim hands (since a coin struck there in A.H. 319 [=A.D. 931] still commemorates the Sādjids and a silver *dirrhem* dated ten years later bears the name of the Kurdish emir of Azerbaijan), but a number of victories are recorded in southern Armenia. In the same year (931) the Arab historian Ibn al-Athir recorded the collaboration of the Greeks with King Gagik I Arcruni against the Ḳaysite emirate and the Continuator of Tʻovma Arcruni also noted a victory of his kinsman against a nameless Muslim general, "a certain man, Arab by race; versed in warfare and military deeds" (Thomas Artsruni, Cont. IV, ix, p. 362), who had defeated King Abas but was routed by Gagik near Duin. Finally, the prince of Anjewacʻikʻ in Vaspurakan is also said to have defeated and killed another raider from Azerbaijan. The only indication of strain in Vaspurakan and among the southern rulers in general comes from two minor Muslim historians, who report that during the Hamdanid campaign of 940, the emir Sayf al-Dawla had received at Χlatʻ and Datuan on Lake Van the submission of the Ḳaysite emirs, as well as of Gagik I, of his son and of the prince of Tarōn, whom he stripped of some of their possessions before going on to loot the revered shrine of Surb Karapet (St. John the Precursor) at Muš (Mush). Sayf al-Dawla's attention was primarily focused on the Ḳaysites, whose emirate was destroyed by 964, but it was partly diverted northward by the Byzantine capture of the key fortress of Karin in 949. His hastily assembled principality fell apart soon after his death in 967, before he had done lasting damage to Armenia outside the regions already held by the Ḳaysites.

The accession of Abas's son Ašot III (952/3-977), who pursued a more energetic policy than his predecessor (despite the surname of *Ołormacʻ* "the Merciful," derived from his support of the church and of monastic foundations), marked the return of the full prestige of the Bagratuni house. The king failed in his attempt to retake Duin the very year of his accession, and the capital remained in Muslim hands, but he may have been more successful in the south, where the Armenian historian Matthew of Edessa (Mattʻeos Uṙhayecʻi/Matteos Urhayetsi) records an Armenian victory against the Hamdanids. One of the main indications of Armenia's autonomy was its final achievement of fiscal independence. According to a tax list of 955 preserved by the Arab geographer Ibn Ḥawḳal, the following tribute was due to the Sallārid emirs of Azerbaijan from the Armenian lands:

al-Wayzūrī lord of Wayzur [Vayoc' Jor], fifty thousand dirrhems and gifts . . . the Banu-Dayrani [Sons of Derenik] were compelled to abide by the obligations of the agreement by which they were to pay one hundred thousand dirrhems per year, but were dispensed for four years . . . An agreement was made with the Banu Sunbat [Sons of Smbat I] for their districts of Armenia Interior stipulating two million dirrhems. They subsequently received a reduction of two hundred thousand dirrhems—Sinharib lord of K̲h̲adjin [Senek'erim of Χač'ēn] was taxed one hundred thousand dirrhems and horses to a value of fifty thousand dirrhems (Ibn Ḥawḳal II, pp. 347-48).

Hence, it is evident that a considerable tribute had been paid by the Arcruni "sons of Derenik" in Vaspurakan, as well as by the lords of Eastern Siwnik' or Vayoc' Jor and Χač'ēn (Khachen). Something had even been paid by the Bagratuni "sons of Smbat," Ašot II and Abas for the region of Armenian Interior, corresponding to northwestern Armenia from Naxčawan to Karin, but no tax was recorded for the contemporary reign of Ašot III.

The return of the kat'ołikos Anania Mokac'i from Vaspurakan to the north and his coronation of Ašot III in 961 in his new capital of Ani in Širak also contributed to the king's growing stature, as did his supervision of ecclesiastical affairs. The schism of the bishop of Siwnik' supported by the kat'ołikos of Albania had already come to an end in 958 at the Council of Kap'an, where the kat'ołikos reasserted his authority over Siwnik' by consecrating its new metropolitan. The successive councils of Širakawan and Ani summoned by the king to elect new primates and settle dogmatic disputes testified further to his authority and concern, as did his continuation of the great Bagratuni monastic foundations at Hałbat (Haghbat) and Sanahin. This growing prestige conferred on the king an authority that reached beyond the Bagratuni domains and extended over all the other Armenian princes, as it had in the days of Ašot I, and even Duin may have returned to Bagratid overlordship between 957 and 966. The Byzantine advance annexed Tarōn in 967/8 and razed the former Ḳaysite stronghold of Manazkert in 968/70, but when the Byzantine emperor John Tzimiskes, who was also of Armenian descent, appeared on the Armenian border in 974 with a considerable army, the princes closed ranks around the Bagratuni king:

Then all of the kings of Armenia, the *azat*s and the greatest *išxan*s of the realms of the houses of the East came together to the Armenian

king Ašot Bagratuni: P'ilippē king of Kap'an and Gurgēn king of
Albania, Abas lord of Kars and Senek'erim lord of Vaspurakan and
Gurgēn lord of Anjewac'ik' and the whole of the house of Sasun and
they camped in the district of Hark', up to eighty thousand men.
(Matthieu d'Edesse, I. xv, p. 14)

Faced with their combinded forces, the emperor preferred to move
southeastward into Mesopotamia and to acknowledge the authority of
his "beloved son," the *Šahanšah* Ašot III.

The one major source of weakness that would manifest itself in the
later Bagratuni kingdom was brought about by the king himself. Faced
with the constant restlessness among the various members of the ruling
house that had already manifested itself in the opposition of the *sparapet*
Abas to his new nephew Smbat I and the war of the two Ašots, the king
sought to obviate this danger by creating apanages for his kinsmen. When
Ašot III moved the capital from Kars to Ani in 961, he granted the former
city with its district of Vanand and eight more districts surrounding it to
his brother Mušeł, who assumed the royal title two years later. Ašot III
likewise granted the northern district of Tašir (Tashir) with the great
fortress of Šamšuildē and the royal monasteries of Hałbat and Sanahin to
his youngest son, Gurgēn or Kiwrikē, probably as early as 972. He is titled
king of Albania at the assembly of Hark' of 974 and is likewise called
king on the inscription above the relief of the donors on the church of the
Savior at Sanahin built between 966 and 972, although later Armenian
sources date the creation of this secondary Bagratid kingdom, usually
called Tašir-Joraget (Tashir-Dzoraget) or Loṙi, as late as 980. Both
Vanand and Tašir-Joraget were unquestionably subordinate to the main
kingdom of Ani, but they formed autonomous units within the larger
Bagratid sphere. The same pattern of fragmentation repeated itself in
Vaspurakan, where the grandsons of King Gagik I—Ašot-Sahak, senior
prince of Vaspurakan proper, Gurgēn-Χač'ik, lord of Anjewac'ik' and
Senek'erim-Yovhannēs, lord of Ṙštunik'—divided their father's kingdom
among themselves. The two elders successively assumed the dominant
position until 1003 when Senek'erim-Yovhannēs drove out his nephews,
the legitimate heirs, and reunited the Arcruni kingdom for the last time.
Finally, the remains of the principality of Siwnik', now reduced to the
district of Bałk' (Baghk) with the fortress of Kap'an and the great
monastery of Tat'ew, which was the seat of the metropolitan of Siwnik',
also became a kingdom probably in the 970s. We have already seen from

the tax list of 955 preserved by Ibn Ḥawḳal that the princes of Vayoc' Jor and Χač'en paid their taxes directly to the Sallārid emirs of Azerbaijan rather than to the Armenia king. Hence, by the end of the century, the Armenian plateau was subdivided into a series of kingdoms that satisfied the ambitions of their rulers but fostered their centrifugal aspirations and sapped the cohesiveness of the Bagratuni and Arcruni realms, which once again were held together only by the authority and personal qualities of their rulers.

Smbat II was proclaimed king on the very day of his father's death, perhaps to prevent the intervention of his uncle, Mušeł of Kars, who then sought to arouse the Sallarid emir of Duin against Smbat in revenge for the king's seizure of a fortress in Širak which Mušeł considered his own. However, the Sallārid attack of Ayrarat was halted in 982 by the emir of Gołt'n, who took from them "Duin and all his cities," while the two Bagratids were reconciled through the mediation of their kinsman, the curopalate David of Tayk' (Georgian Tao), a junior member of the Iberian branch of the family. The emir of Gołt'n then turned against Ašot Arcruni of Vaspurakan, whom he defeated with the help of a contingent Muslim *ghazi,* or fighters for Islam. In 989 he also retook the city of Duin from the new Kurdish house of Rawwādid emirs of Azerbaijan, who had seized it from him two years earlier. The struggle of Gołt'n with the Rawwādids also served the interests of Smbat II, who had been compelled to pay tribute to them at the time of their capture of Duin in 987. The king even "concluded with him [the emir of Gołt'n] a treaty sealed with an oath through the mediation of [kat'ołikos] Lord Χač'ik, that they would live in peace with each other." Subsequently, however, Smbat violated the agreement and sought the help of the Sallārids to regain Duin, much to the indignation of Asołik:

> And [Smbat's] second evil deed was the violation of the covenant that
> he had concluded with the emir of Gołt'n, whereas that one [the emir]
> kept his oath according to his heathen religion, this one [the king]
> even though a Christian did not keep his word and being forsworn,
> gave Armenian troops to help make Salar emir, a thing repulsive to
> God, had he not been stopped by fear of betrayal by his brother Gagik
> (Asholik, 1917, III. xxix, pp. 136-37).

The main achievement of Smbat II's reign was his extension and embellishment of the new Bagratuni capital of Ani:

He filled the moats of Ani and built above it a circular fortification
from the Axurian river to the valley of Colkoc'ac' (Dzoghkotsats).
He built it from stones bound with a lime mortar, with bastions and
tall towers; it was far higher than the old wall, enclosed the full extent
of the city, and [had] cedar doors reinforced with iron fixtures and
large solidly embedded nails. He also laid the foundation of a magnificent church in this same city of Ani under the direction of the
architect Trdat, who had also built the church of the Kat'olikos at
Argina (Asholik, 1917, III. xi, pp. 49-50).

Smbat II maintained the autonomy of his kingdom unimpaired and had
the wisdom to support—together with his cousin, King Abas of Kars
(984-1024), and their contemporary David of Tayk'/Tao—their young
kinsman, King Bagrat of Eastern Iberia, in his claim to the coastal region
of Abkhazia; an action for which Smbat II received the Abkhazian
border fortress of Sakurēt'i.
　　The *curopalate* David of Tayk' (966-1000), great-grandson of
King Atrnerseh II of Iberia, was unquestionably the most distinguished
man of his period, although his principality never became a kingdom.
Asolik praises him enthusiastically:

For he was a gentle and merciful man, more than all the kings of our
time. And he was a source of peace and prosperity for all of the East
and especially for Armenia and Iberia; for he halted the tumult of war
everywhere through his victories over all the surrounding nations. All
the kings submitted to him of their own will (Asolik, 1917, III. xliii,
p. 162).

His bicultural Armeno-Iberian court in the northwestern border
district of Tayk'/Tao was one of the great cultural centers of the time.
Yet his brilliant career ultimately turned against his kinsmen and to the
advantage of Byzantium. The help given by David to the Byzantine
emperor Basil II (976-1025) at the time of the great revolt of Bardas
Skleros (976-979) earned him a vastly expanded domain that stretched
southward from Tayk' along the entire western border of Bagratid
Armenia. It included the military district *(Kleisura)* of Χaldoyaṙič
(Khaldoharidz), the fortress of Karin with its district, and the provinces
of Basean, Hark', and Apahunik' with the city of Manazkert which had
been retaken by Byzantium a decade earlier but which David could not
recapture from the Kurdish Marwānid emirs, who had succeeded the

Ḳaysites in this area, until 992-993. He then removed the Muslim population of the city, filled it with Armenians and Iberians, and twice put to flight the armies sent against him from Azerbaijan, with the help of the Bagratid kings of Ani, Kars, and Iberia. In the north, David's patronage of his young relative Bagrat of Eastern Iberia, whom he adopted and who was able to reunite Iberia and Abkhazia into a single kingdom in 978, gave him a form of protectorate over most of Christian Transcaucasia that he was to enjoy until his death. Unfortunately, however, David's backing of a second revolt against Basil II in 989/90 undid much of his achievements. After his defeat of the rebels, Basil II compelled David to will all his lands to the Byzantine Empire, although he was allowed to keep them for his lifetime. No sooner had the *curopalate* died (March 31, 1000), perhaps at the instigation of the pro-Byzantine party among his nobles, than Basil II claimed the fulfillment of the agreement of 990. As we shall see, the emperor's successive campaigns, culminating in the annexation of all the lands of David of Tayk', were to mark the establishment of Byzantium on the Armenian plateau and the crucial break in the international equilibrium that protected the autonomy of the Armenian kingdoms.

The last of the great kings of Ani, Gagik I (898/90-1017), also came to the throne on the day of his predecessor's death, as Asołik had noted in his condemnation of Smbat II's disloyalty toward his ally, the emir of Gołt'n and Naxčawan. However, a royal governor was set over Duin, which seems to have remained part of the Bagratuni kingdom through most of Gagik's reign. The king also acquired considerable lands at the expense of Siwnik', according to Asołik, who claimed that

> he ruled over a larger number of fortresses and districts from the borders of Vayoc' Jor, Χač'ēn, and P'aṙisos than his brother, and no one was able to inspire fear in Armenia [in his time] (Asołik, 1917, III. xxx, p. 138).

His support of David of Tayk' against the incursions of the Kurdish Rawwādid emir halted the first attack from Azerbaijan. A second Ibero-Armenian coalition routed him again near Arčēš in 998 and prevented the Rawwādids from reconquering the lands of the Ḳaysites and Marwānid emirates. Similarly, an alliance with Bagrat of Iberia helped to drive back the advance of the other Kurdish Shaddādid emir holding Ganǰa since 970.

The senior position of the king of Ani vis-à-vis the other Bagratid kings of his generation was fully maintained by Gagik I, especially after the death of David of Tayk'. The southern kingdom, subdivided by the grandsons of Gagik I Arcruni and weakened by the usurpation of the youngest, Senek'erim-Yovhannēs, who drove out his nephews in 1003, could offer no challenge to the Bagratuni despite the protectorate extended over Vaspurakan by the emperor Basil II after his campaign of 1001. The southern kingdom would soon be distracted by the attacks by the attacks of Daylamite and Turkmen raiders. Gagik's cousin Abas of Kars seems to have accepted his subordinate position willingly. The king's more turbulent nephews were more sharply brought to heel. Abusahl, lord of Kogovit, who had slandered Gagik to Basil II, saw his domain devastated by an Armenian army commanded by the king's son Yovhannēs. David *Anholin (Anhoghin)* "the Landless," king of Tašir-Joraget (989-1948?), who had subjected the emirate of Tiflis and claimed to be an "independent king" *(ink'nakal ark'ay)* on an inscription of 996 at Sanahin, saw himself attacked by a royal army and forced to make his submission:

> Through the mediation of the patriarch, Lord Sargis, he submitted to the King [Gagik] and came to meet him at Širakawan. And Lord Sargis made a covenant of peace [between them]. David agreed to submit like a son to his father, and Gagik to love him with fatherly concern (Asołik, 1917, III. xlv, p. 167).

The more benevolent attitude of Gagik I toward Siwnik', to which he returned some of its ecclesiastical privileges lost in 958, was probably a result of the intercession of Queen Katramidē, the daughter of the king of Siwnik'. The same haughty demeanor marked the relations of Armenia to Byzantium. When the emperor Basil II came to the Armenian border 1000/1 to claim the inheritance of David of Tayk', all the Armenian and Iberian rulers—Bagrat of Abkhazia and his father Gurgēn of Iberia, Abas of Kars, and Senek'erim-Yovhannēs of Vaspurakan—hastened to meet him and make their submission. Basil II then

> came to the district of Hark' to the city of Manazkert and thence into Bagrewand, where he camped in the plain near the city of Vałaršakert [Vagharshakert], [and] there waited for the coming of Gagik King of Armenia. But he [Gagik] considered it demeaning to come to him (Asołik, 1917, III. xliii, p. 165).

Gagik remained defiantly behind the walls of Ani. Like his predecessor John Tzimiskes in 974, Basil II did not insist. He refortified the stronghold of Karin in 1018, but made no further attempts against Armenia as long as Gagik I lived.

The Armenian Church in the Bagratuni Period

The crucial role of the Armenian Church during the periods of the *Marzpan*ate and the Arab domination (when it substituted itself for the crown as the focus of national allegiance) continued during the revival of the medieval kingdoms.

To be sure, royal influence and occasional control over the church manifested itself in all the medieval Armenian kingdoms. The dogmatic councils of Širakawan under Ašot I and later, again at Širakawan and at Ani, under Ašot III were held under royal sponsorship at the royal residence, although the kat'ołikos normally preferred to live away from court, first at Duin or Vałaršapat until the forced departure of Yovhannēs "the Historian" in 923 then at Argina near Ani after the return of Anania Mokac'i from Vaspurakan to the north. He moved to Ani itself only in 992. The contemporaries found this royal patronage entirely acceptable, and Asołik related without the slightest misgivings that the Council of Ani elected Step'annos III Sewanec'i (Stepannos III Sevanetsi) ''in accordance with the will of Ašot Šahanšah" (Asołik, 1917, III, viii, p. 41), or that "Gagik King of Armenia installed as Kat'ołikos the lord Sargis" after the king had "called together a council of bishops from the realm of Armenia and the Greek regions" (Asołik, 1917, III. xxxii, pp. 143-44). In 1036 king Yovhannēs-Smbat Bagratuni briefly forced the deposition of Petros I Getadarj (Getadardz) (1019-1036, 1038-1058) and the election of a new patriarch. The protectorate of Gagik I Arcruni over the church in the latter part of his reign manifested itself equally clearly in his offer of asylum to the fleeing Yovhannēs V "the Historian," and even more so in the successive election of three subsequent Řštuni kat'ołikoi, who remained in residence at the court of Vaspurakan. Later in the tenth century, the kat'ołikos Vahan of Siwnik' also found refuge in Vaspurakan, after his deposition by the Council of Ani in 969/70, and Gagik I's son would not hesitate to imprison his rival, the kat'ołikos Step'annos III. The earlier election of the future kat'ołikos Vahan as bishop of Siwnik' in 958 may well have been influenced by the fact that he was the son of Prince Juanšēr of Bałk' (Jvansher of Baghk). Even

Gagik-Abas, the last king of Kars/Vanand would see to the election of
the kat'oḷikos Grigor II Vkayasēr in 1065/6. Still later, according to the
Armenian chronicler Matthew of Edessa:

> In the year 530 of the Armenian Era (1081-1082) the archbishop of
> Širak, who resided in the city of Ani and whose name was Lord Barseḷ
> (Barsegh) [Basil], went to the realm of Armenia to the city of Loṙē in
> the district of Aḷuank' [Albania] to the King of Armenia Korikē
> [Kiwrikē I], son of Dawit' Anhoḷin, son of Gagik [Gurgēn]; and
> Barseḷ asked for consecration as Kat'oḷikos of Armenia. Then King
> Korikē gathered together the bishops of the land of Aḷuank' and,
> taking along the Kat'oḷikos of Aḷuank' Lord Step'annos to the mon-
> astery called Haḷbat, they consecrated Lord Barseḷ onto the throne of
> St. Gregory as Kat'oḷikos over the entire realm of Armenia at the
> order of King Korikē and of Lord Step'annos who held the see of the
> holy apostle Thaddeus (Matthieu d'Edesse II. cxx, p. 185 corrected),

As late as 1140, the last Bagratuni rulers of Loṙi/Tašir met in the
fortress of Tawuš for the consecration of the kat'oḷikos of Caucasian
Albania. In the same troubled times, the Armenian kat'oḷikos Petros
Getadarj sought refuge at the court of Senek'erim-Yovhannēs Arcruni
at Sebastē/Sivas ca. 1047 after the surrender of Ani to Byzantium. A
decade later the kat'oḷikos Χač'ik II would likewise flee to the last
Arcruni heir residing in Cappadocia. Finally, most of the great monasteries of this period were all royal foundations: the churches of Lake
Sevan dedicated by Ašot I's daughter Mariam of Siwnik' (which marks
the beginning of the great architectural revival under the Bagratids), as
well as the famous centers of Tašir—Haḷbat and Sanahin, founded or
restored by Ašot III's queen; the Arcrunid monastic foundations at
Hadamakert, Aparak', and Varag in Vaspurakan; Kot', Makenoc'
(Makenots), Gndevank', and especially the great monastery of Tat'ew
in Siwnik'. Similarly, the cathedrals of Bagaran, Širakawan, Kars, Ani,
and the church of the Holy Cross of Aḷt'amar, all of which are directly
linked to the reigning dynasty, also serve to underscore the royal concern
and protectorate over the church.

At the same time, however, the great ecclesiastical figures of the
period—Gēorg II Gaṙnec'i (877-897), Yovhannēs "the Historian" (898-
924/5), Anania Mokac'i (943?-967), Χač'ik I (972-992), and finally the
enigmatic figure of Petros I Getadarj—easily dominated the scene both
in their new position of coronant presiding over the royal consecration

and in their more secular role of ambassadors and peacemakers. The Armenian tradition of patriarchal families going back to the descendants of Gregory the Illuminator continued with Yovhannēs "the Historian," a kinsman of his predecessor Maštoc', with the three successive Ṙštuni patriarchs, with the transmission of the kat'oɫikate from Anania Mokac'i to his nephew Χač'ik I, with the latter's brother Petros Getadarj and Petros's nephew Χač'ik II, and finally through the long line of Pahlawuni kat'oɫikoi who would occupy the patriarchal throne from Grigor II Vkayasēr (1065-1105) through the entire twelfth century. This continuity helped perpetuate a definite ecclesiastical policy. The status of the kat'oɫikos is perhaps best illustrated by the Byzantine ambassadors coming in 914 to invite Ašot *Erkat'* to Constantinople. Past masters in matters of protocol, the official imperial envoys paid their first visit to the kat'oɫikos Yovhannēs "the Historian" and only then sought out the young ruler in his domain. The move of Yovhannēs from the north to Vaspurakan helped shift the balance of prestige to Gagik I Arcruni in the last years of the reign of King Ašot II, while the return of kat'oɫikos Anania Mokac'i to Argina and his coronation of Ašot III reestablished the authority of the Bagratids. By the end of the period of Armenian independence, the position of the kat'oɫikos was so firmly entrenched that not even the equivocal policy of Petros Getadarj could undermine it, and the bishops assembled at Ani in 1038 forced his return against the claims of the royal candidate imposed by Yovhannēs-Smbat. The jurisdiction of the Armenian kat'oɫikos in this period was not limited to the Bagratuni Kingdom or even to the Armenian lands. The Council of Kap'an in 958 reaffirmed his authority not only over the dissident bishopric of Siwnik', but also over the kat'oɫikos of Caucasian Albania, who had supported the schism. The religious concessions made to Siwnik' by Gagik I Bagratuni in 1005/6 were more ceremonial than substantive in character. Even more interesting is the greeting in the letter of the Byzantine Patriarch Nicholas Mystikos to Yovhannēs "the Historian" in which he refers to "the Armenians, the Iberians and the Albanians who collectively comprise your faithful flock," thus implying that the jurisdiction of the Armenian kat'oɫikos extended over the whole of Transcaucasia and that the long-standing schism between the Armenian and Iberian churches had found some kind of solution in the later ninth century.

The growing power of the Armenian Church may in part have fostered the great expansion of the heretical movement of the T'ondrakec'i (Tondraketsi), which is also recorded in the tenth century in a number of regions far from its home district of Apahunik' north of Lake Van. The heretics may have supported the insurrection of the peasantry of Siwnik' against the great monastic center of Tat'ew in this period, but the main references to them now record their penetration into the upper classes of society. The Armenian historian Aristakēs Lastivertc'i (Lastiverttsi) speaks of aristocratic ladies, mistresses of villages, a bishop, Jacob of Hark', and Prince Vrver of Širi (Shiri) in the northwestern district of Mananaɫi (Mananaghi). The regular clergy was apparently also infected in this period, since the great mystic poet Grigor Narekac'i (Narekatsi) wrote at the direction of the Council of Ani a letter of reproof and admonition to the abbot of the monastery of Kčaw (Kchav) in the southern district of Mokk'. The survival of the T'ondrakec'i into the mid-eleventh century when they were actively persecuted by the learned duke of Tarōn and Vaspurakan Grigor Magistros Pahlawuni reveals the depth to which Bagratid society had been penetrated and disturbed by the heresy.

Other religious groups, such as the Nestorians surviving in the southern border districts and Syrian communities in communion with the Armenian Church, were also found in Armenia, but the most crucial as well as the most obscure and controversial problem is that of the relationship between the Armenian Church and official Byzantine Chalcedonian Orthodoxy. The continuing presence of Chalcedonian Armenians under the Bagratuni is beyond doubt, even though their presence has long been obscured by the common reference to them as "Iberians." The pro-Greek tendencies of the monastery of Narek, founded in 935 by monks reputedly fleeing from Cappadocia, were well known, and both Grigor Narekac'i and his father incurred blame because of them. Siwnik' must have contained a number of Chalcedonian sympathizers, since its bishop, Vahan, elected kat'oɫikos in 967/8, was deposed for such tendencies by the Council of Ani in the following year. Similarly, the asylum granted to Vahan after his deposition by Gagik I Arcruni and the king's surviving letter about a possible ecclesiastical union with Byzantium point to the presence of the same inclinations in Vaspurakan. Finally, the refusal of Yovhannēs "the Historian" to accompany Ašot *Erkat'* on his journey to Constantinople in 914 lest he be suspected of Chalcedonianism suggests that the position of the kat'oɫikos himself was not beyond question. As late as 974, the assembled Armenian bishops were willing to compromise so far as to present Vahan of Siwnik''s suspect confession of faith as "orthodox" to the Byzantine emperor John Tzimiskes.

A cultural rapprochement, perhaps helped by the kinship between the Armenian and Iberian Bagratids, seemed to be in the making and to explain the spiritual protectorate over Transcaucasia attributed by the Byzantine patriarch to the Armenian kat'oɫikos at the beginning of the tenth century. The best example of this hybrid world was undoubtedly to be found in the border region of Tayk'/Tao with its splendid churches, such as Oški (Oshki) and Išxan (Ishkhan) uniting Iberian and Armenian features, and most of all the bilingual and bicultural court of the *curopalate* David. Unfortunately, this seeming trend toward reconciliation rapidly provoked a violent reaction, perhaps linked once more to the expansionist policy of Byzantium in the East. Asoɫik reports both the brutal punishment of Prince Bēr of Abkhazia, blinded ca. 943 by King Abas for his attempt to have the cathedral of Kars consecrated according to the Orthodox rite, and the conversion of

> the *marzpan* Demetr who was the *išxan* of the fortress of Gag . . . abandoned the Armenian faith of his fathers, and obtaining the help of the Iberians bathed in their twice mortal [baptismal] water (Asholik, 1917, III. xxx, p. 140).

The kat'oɫikos Anania Mokac'i was also said to have imposed a second baptism on those who had already received Orthodox baptism in violation of the canons which forbid the repetition of this sacrament. The election of his successor, Vahan of Siwnik', by the Council of Širakawan in 967, immediately brought dissensions among the bishops because of "the love and agreement with the Chalcedonians expressed in his letters." Vahan was deposed and fled to the king of Vaspurakan, who also imprisoned Ašot III's candidate, elected by the Council of Ani in the following year. The schism ended with the death of both rivals, but the tension with the Greeks increase under the newly elected kat'oɫikos Χač'ik I (972/3-992/3), most of all among the Armenians on imperial territory in the region of Sebastē/Sivas, whose metropolitan bishop showed particular antagonism toward them. For the first time Χač'ik consecrated bishops for external sees. The learned Armenian *vardapet* Yovhannēs was killed by the Iberians, who remained in communion with the Greeks, and the polemic on both sides reached such a level of bitterness that the Armenian chronicler Matthew of Edessa denounced the eleventh-century Duke of Antioch Philaretos (Armenian P'ilardos Varažnuni [Varazhnuni]) as

the eldest son of Satan . . . [and], an enemy of the Christian faith . . .
[because] he held to the Roman [Chalcedonian] customs and religion
although he was an Armenian on [both] his father's and mother's side
(Matthieu d'Edesse, II. cvi, p. 173).

The Social and Economic
Development of Armenia and the Bagratuni

The evidence for the prosperity of Armenia during almost the entire
period of the medieval kingdoms, some of which has already been cited
earlier in this chapter, provides an important corrective to its complex
and often unstable political history. This evidence is based not only on
the written sources, many of which are, interestingly, in Arabic rather
than Armenian, but on an increasingly large archaeological documentation. The enormous artistic and cultural flowering of the period, attested
by a multiplicity of visual and literary monuments, provides an index
not only to the taste and refinement of the ruling class and the skill of
contemporary artists, but to the powerful economic base that made such
a development possible. Nevertheless, an important series of questions
on the internal life of Armenia in the period of the Bagratuni and Arcruni
kings still requires investigation and some of the answers will have to
be provided by further archaeological material.

From the point of view of its social structure, Bagratuni Armenia
does not seem to have produced a radical change from the earlier pattern.
As we have seen, no constitutional framework was introduced to rein-
force the hold of the king over his vassals. The titles of "Prince of
Princes" and subsequently *Šahanšah* acknowledged the ruler's authority
de jure over both the Christian and Muslim princes of the region, but
this authority continued to rest de facto on the personal qualities and
prestige of powerful figures, such as Ašot I Bagratuni or the two Gagiks
of Vaspurakan and Ani. To be sure, the cohesion of the collective *tun*
had been seriously impaired by the growing system of apanages given
to junior members of a family, but the noble classes of the *naxarar*s or
*išxan*s, the lower nobility of the *azat*s, the hierarchy of the clergy, and
the great majority of the taxable *ṙamik*s and *šinakan*s are still clearly
identifiable throughout the period and also show no appreciable geographical variations within the country. The powerful cavalry continued
to provide the military force of the state, and it rested as before on the
azat contingents serving under the local princes, their immediate lords.

As such, the medieval period seems to have been one of evolution and refinement in institutions, but not of innovation in the basic structure of society.

One of the main elements of transformations was demographic rather than social. The majority of the population unquestionably remained Armenian until the mid-eleventh century at least throughout the region, with the exception of the southern border region of Ałjnik', administratively linked to Mesopotamia at an early date and heavily Arabized. The tenth-century Arab sources themselves attest that the cities of the Araxes Valley remained Armenian despite Muslim overlordship. According to them, the Christians formed the majority of the cities' population. The contemporary geographer Ibn Ḥawḳal specified that Armenian continued to be spoken at Duin and Naxčawan, whereas Arabic was the language of Partaw/Bardha'a in Azerbaijan (Ibn Ḥawḳal II, p. 342). Nevertheless, considerable Muslim settlements resulted from the creation of the emirates in the ninth and tenth centuries. The cities of the emirates on the north shore of Lake Van were heavily Muslim, and we learn from Asołik that the Armenian quarter at Xlat' must have lain outside the city walls, since the churches and the bishop's residence were to be found there late in the tenth century. These Muslim settlements were primarily Arab in the early period and appear to have remained so at Karin, which was primarily a garrison city with surrounding villages, and in the emirate of Gołt'n, which preserved its local dynasty. In the southern districts, however—where the Kurdish Marwānids replaced the Arab Ḳaysites after the brief Hamdanid interlude, and especially in Azerbaijan, where the Daylamite Sallārids, the Kurdish Rawwādids, and the increasingly powerful Shaddhdids jockeyed for power—the Iranian ethnic element began to dominate in the late tenth century. Ibn Ḥawḳal again specifies:

> the language of Azerbaijan and of the majority of the inhabitants of Armīniya is Persian which they use as a common language, but among themselves they use Arabic . . . a language which the merchants and lords of domains use with elegance (Ibn Ḥawḳal, II, p. 342).

Similarly, the presence of Muslim groups, first Arabs and subsequently Daylamites and Kurds coming from Azerbaijan, were attested at Duin. At times this demographic transformation could be reversed temporarily, as was the case at Manazkert, where David of Tayk' expelled the Muslim population in 992/3 and replaced it with Armenians and Iberians, the latter of whom may have been ethnic Iberians or Chalcedonian Armenians, to whom this term was also applied. Even so, the ethnic unity of the plateau had been breached and was not to be reconstituted.

One of the most interesting problems of the period, that of the medieval Armenian cities, still requires considerable investigation. The great revival of international trade between Byzantium and the caliphate as well as the Far East and the northern Russian lands and the creation of a network of routes, attested by the contemporary Arab geographers and minutely studied by Manandyan (1965, pp. 155-72), clearly fostered an urban development. The main trade route through Armenia ran from the Caliphate to Trebizond on the Black Sea by way of Ani, Kars, and Arcn near Karin. At Kars it linked to secondary routes leading northward through Artanuč (Artanuch) to the eastern Black Sea ports or through Ardahan to Abkhazia and Eastern Iberia. In the south, the route from Ardabil and Maragha in Iran led to Her/Xoy (Khoi) and from there either along the north shore of Lake Van through Berkri, Arčēš and Xlat‘ to Bidlis and Diarbekir, or westward by way of Manazkert to Arcn, Erzincan, and Sivas, or yet again northward through Naxčawan to Duin, which was linked through Siwnik‘ with Bardha’a, from which other routes led farther north to Tiflis. The main road from the caliphate to Russia was called the "Great Armenian Highway."

There is no doubt that Armenian cities flourished in the tenth century as a result of this revival of international trade as well as from a considerable amount of local manufacture, and contemporary sources speak with some exaggeration of forty-five cities and twenty-three additional settlements. Strategically placed at the junction point of a number of the trade routes, Duin was unquestionably the main urban center of Armenia even after the destructive earthquake of 893, and it was not overtaken by Ani until the very end of the tenth or even the eleventh century. Like Procopius in earlier days, Arab writers praise the beauty and wealth of the city. According to *The Book of Roads and Kingdoms* of al-Istakhri.

> Dabil [Duin] is greater than Ardabil. This city serves as the capital of
> Armenia and in it is the palace of the governor just as the palace of
> the governor of Arran is in Bardha’a . . . There is a wall around Dabil.
> Here there are many Christians and the main mosque is next to the
> church . . . Dabil is the capital of Armenia and there stays Sanbat ibn

Ašhut [King Smbat I]. The city is always in the hands of the Christian nobility, and the Christians form the greater part of the population of Armenia also known as "the Kingdom of the Armenians" (Manandyan, 1965, pp. 143-44).

The importance of the city was equally great in the second half of the tenth century, although a warning note was sounded by the Arab geographer al-Mukadasi:

> Dabil is an important city, in it are an inaccessible citadel and great riches. Its name is ancient, its cloth is famous, its river is abundant, it is surrounded by gardens. The city has suburbs, its fortress is reliable, its squares are cross-shaped, its fields are wonderful. The main mosque is on a hill and next to the mosque is the church. The Kurds watch over the town. By the city is a citadel. The buildings of the inhabitants are made of clay or stone. The city has many gates such as Bab ['gate']-Keydar, Bab-Tiflis and Bab-Ani. Despite all of its advantages the Christians are a majority there. Now its population has already diminished and its citadel is in ruins (Manandyan, 1965, p. 144).

Recent archaeological excavations that have uncovered a considerable portion of the city have borne out much of the information of the Arab geographers by identifying both a citadel and the central portion of the city, which contains the cathedral and the adjacent ruins of the palace of the kat'ołikos, probably converted into a mosque during the eleventh century.

The rapid growth of the new capital of Ani described as "the city of one thousand and one churches" by Matthew of Edessa is likewise attested by archaeological evidence. The first walls erected under Ašot III had to be supplemented within a generation by new ones that trebled its area in the days of Smbat II, who expended much of his energy on the adornment of the city. By the eleventh century, the capital was apparently composed of a citadel as well as upper and lower cities enclosed by the two lines of fortifications, and Matthew of Edessa claimed that its population was reaching 100,000. This figure is probably inflated, but the evidence of considerable settlements beyond the walls as well as a cemetery covering a square kilometer point to an urban center considerably larger than contemporary ones in the West. Armenian historians such as Asołik concentrated primarily on the description of royal ecclesiastical foundations, such as the cathedral of Ani, begun by Smbat II and completed by Gagik I's wife, Katramidē of Siwnik':

> The pious queen . . . completed the building of the church founded by Smbat, a magnificent edifice with lofty vaults and a sanctuary surmounted by a heavenlike cupola. And she adorned it with tapestries embroidered with purple flowers woven with gold and painted in various colors, and with vessels of silver and gold through whose resplendent brilliance the holy cathedral in the city of Ani shone forth like the heavenly vault (Asołik, 1917, III, xxx, p. 139).

The archaeological excavations directed by N. Marr at the beginning of the twentieth century revealed primarily the elaborate urban development of the city with its paved streets, water system for drinking water as well as sewage, baths, caravansarais, and bazaars.

Similarly, Kars had grown by the mid-eleventh century from a fortress to a city "enriched by the goods bestowed upon it by sea and land," according to the contemporary historian Aristakēs Lastivertc'i (Aristakès de Lastivert, xv, p. 74). Most remarkable of all was the unfortified commercial city of Arcn founded near Karin/Theodosiopolis and described by the twelfth-century Byzantine Kedrenos:

> Arcn is an open and very rich city with a very large population. There lived local merchants and a large number of Syrians, Armenians and other peoples. Taking strength from their numbers, they did not find it necessary to live within walls despite the proximity of Theodosiopolis, a large and strong city with inaccessible fortifications (Manandyan, 1965, p. 145).

And goods from all over the East were exchanged in its markets.

Despite this clear evidence for the prosperity of the great commercial cities of Armenia, a puzzling series of problems concerning their integration into contemporary society remain to be solved before general conclusions can be reached. Part of these difficulties derive from the fact that the excavations of Duin are still incomplete and the evidence for the period of Muslim domination in the city is far less satisfactory than that for the earlier period of the *Marzpan*ate, which had relied on stone rather than clay for its buildings material. At Ani, where no systematic work has been possible since the beginning of the twentieth century, earlier results remain unverified. Consequently, the chronology of the sites is difficult to establish with precision, and the portion of the evidence belonging to the Bagratid period rather than to later ones is still uncertain.

One of the puzzling aspects of this urban development is that with the exception of Kars, Ani, and Arcn, whose rise comes late and belongs to the eleventh rather than the tenth century, all the main cities of this period are to be found in the Muslim emirates rather than in the Christian principalities. Even Duin, as we have seen, was more commonly ruled by various Muslim governors in the tenth century than under the control of the Bagratuni kings. The previously cited comment of Ibn Ḥawḳal that the native language of the merchants in Armīniya was Arabic; the observation in Kedrenos's account that the "local merchants" of Arcn were distinct from the Armenians and Syrians also found in the city; and the total absence of Armenian coinage throughout the Bagratid period, which depended on either Byzantine or Muslim currency, all suggest that much of the international commerce and the centers enriched by it were not primarily in Armenian hands.

This hypothesis finds support in the picture of the purely Armenian society provided by the contemporary native sources. As in earlier times, the magnates normally lived in their fortified strongholds rather than in urban centers, and we hear of no Muslim peasant communities in the countryside. Like their nobles, the ruling houses of the period showed a distinct preference for isolated sites and fortresses. Such were the Bagratuni residences of Bagaran and Širakawan and even Kars and Ani through most of the tenth century, as well as the fortresses of Šamšuildē, Loṙē and eventually Macnaberd (Madznaberd) and Tawuš favored by the junior royal line of Tašir-Joraget. The princes of Siwnik' clung to their strongholds of Ernǰak and Kap'an, while the Arcruni preferred the fortress of Nkan or the protected island of Ałt'amar in Lake Van. To be sure, such preferences were often dictated by considerations of safety, but the Christian princes showed a curious aversion to urban centers even when they held the upper hand. Neither Ašot the Great, nor Ašot III, nor yet Gagik I cared to hold directly and reside in the central capital of Duin, and the Bagratuni in general showed no sense of geographical loyalty, moving from generation to generation from Bagaran to Širakawan/Erazgawork' and eventually to Kars and Ani. The constant picture derived from the account of Yovhannēs Kat'ołikos, in which the Muslim *ostikan* remains firmly based on his residence at Duin while the Armenian king withdraws to his stronghold of Erazgawork' or even more commonly to camps in the countryside, is particularly telling in this context, and it clearly recalls the preferences of the earlier Aršakuni. Obviously, no clear-cut divisions existed in this society, and the Armenian and Muslim worlds necessarily coexisted, yet the impression of polarization between a mercantile and urban Muslim group with practically no roots in the countryside and a para-feudal Christian aristocracy surrounded by its traditional peasantry seems inescapable.

A chronological problem compounds the difficulty of estimating the importance of the cities within the fabric of Bagratuni society. As was already observed, the architectural evidence from Duin is disappointing for this period. Ani continued to flourish in the twelfth and thirteenth centuries, and the other major sites have not yet been studied. Consequently the internal organization of the Armenian cities and the participation of the urban population in their administration, let alone the history of the period, still requires considerable study. Both the Arab historian al-Balādhurī and the Armenian Continuator of T'ovma Arcruni speaks of the "elders" of Duin, and Yovhannēs Kat'ołikos alludes to the "senior nobles . . . of the noble families of the city of Duin" imprisoned by Yūsuf's deputy in 923 (Yovhannēs Drasxanakertc'i, lxv, p. 221). Some sort of aristocracy was consequently present in the city, and Ibn Ḥawḳal's reference to the "Christian nobility" supports the conclusion that it was Armenian. We have, however, no evidence whatever for the relationship between these "elders" and the ruling feudal nobility, and except for their unlucky overtures to the Muslims in 923, we do not hear of the participation of such "elders" in political events until the very end of the period under consideration, when their deliberation concerning a suitable protector at the moment of the surrender of Ani in 1045 was recorded by Aristakēs Lastivertc'i (Aristakès de Lastivert, ix, p. 52). Similarly, archaeological evidence demonstrates the presence of considerable workshops at both Duin and Ani, while the marginal decorations of manuscripts depict a varied collection of craftsmen. Much of this evidence is, however, of later date, so that the existence of an elaborate system of artisans' guilds unquestionably attested for the post-Bagratid period of the thirteenth century is far less clear for the period of the medieval kingdoms to which it has sometimes been attributed. All of these considerations and complexities suggest that the structure and the role of the cities in medieval Armenian society still require considerable study.

In contrast with the lack of precision in our knowledge of the status and configuration of urban centers, no such problems plague an estimate of the economic strength of the country repeatedly praised by Armenian and even more precisely by Arabic sources. Part of the prosperity of the period was unquestionably derived from the exchange of foreign goods

carried along the transit routes, which enriched the cities. Early in the
ninth century, King Smbat I had called the attention of the *ostikan* Afshin
to the advantage for the caliphate derived from the role of Armenia as
an intermediary between caliphate and Byzantium. Even so, much of
Armenia's economic importance derived from the country itself.

The natural resources of the land were thoroughly familiar to the
Muslim world. The silver mines of Sper, the iron of Vaspurakan, and
the copper of Gugark' supplied local industries as well as the mints
located at Duin, Manazkert, and Bardha'a. Lead, borax, arsenic, mer-
cury, copper sulfate, and salt from the mines of Kulp' were exported to
the caliphate, as were natural dyes of which the most famous was the
scarlet *kirmiz*. The extensive forests covering the slopes of Mt. Ararat
supplied large quantities of timber as well as walnuts, filberts, and
almonds. The fertile valleys of the Araxes and of Vaspurakan were
particularly suited to the cultivation of cereals and fruit trees such as
peaches, apricots, and pomegranates. Wheat was exported from Armenia to Baghdad, according to the Arab historian al-Tabari. The vineyards
and wine industry of Duin were noted in the account of the unsuccessful
Byzantine siege of the city in 1049. The saltpeter (natron) of Lake Van
supplied the bakers of Iraq. The salted herrings of the lake called *tarrex*
in Armenian and *tirrikh* in Arabic as well as the *surmahi* of the Araxes
and Kura rivers, were in great demand on Muslim markets (Manandyan,
1965, pp. 150-51), as were the horses and mules of Anjewac'ik',
"reputed for their physical strength, their endurance, their swiftness and
their tenacity," according to Ibn Hawkal (II. p. 340). A tax list preserved
by the historian Ibn Khaldun specifies the following goods in addition
to monetary payments: 20 rugs, 580 pounds of *rakm* (?), 10,000 pounds
of *surmahi,* 10,000 pounds of *tirrikh,* 200 mules, and 30 falcons.

Even more prized than these natural products were the manufactured
goods produced in Armenia. Armenian sources praised the work of the local
goldsmiths, and the excavation of the workshops of Duin have found the
metalwork, glazed ceramics, and glassware for which the city was famous.
But the greatest demand was for "goods of Armenian type" *[asnaf al-
Armeni],* textiles dyed with the local *kirmiz* (primarily produced at the
dyeworks of Artašat, known as the *kirmiz* village to Arab sources), flowered
silks called *bosjun,* and gold embroidered garments. A detailed description
of these prized textiles is provided by Ibn Hawkal:

> From Dabil are exported goat-hair [cashmere] textiles and [ordinary]
> woolens such as, for example, rugs, pillows, cushions, saddle blan-

kets, laces for trousers and other textiles of the same type which are
of Armenian manufacture and dyed with *kirmiz*. This is a red dye for
goat-hair textiles and for wool. It is obtained from a worm which
weaves around itself as the silkworm encloses himself in a cocoon of
raw silk. They also produce there patterned silks of which many
similar are found in the Byzantine empire, although they are imported
from Armenia. And among the goods called Armenian are found
women's cloaks, cushions, rugs, tapestries, narrow rugs, round cushions, sofa pillows and saddle blankets. These tapestries are not
equaled in any part of the universe in any fashion or in any technique
(Ibn Ḥawḳal, II, pp. 335-36).

These must be the splendid garments repeatedly mentioned as
royal presents in the *History* of Yovhannēs Kat'ołikos and the tapestries
adorned with purple flowers and gold embroidery that decorated the
cathedrals of Argina and Ani, according to Asołik. Their splendor can
still be glimpsed in the caftans of figured brocade worn by the Arcruni
princes on the reliefs of the church at Ałt'amar, and especially in the
embroidered caftan of the king, as well as the red and gold dress and
veil interwoven with gold of the queen in the portrait of the royal family
of Kars preserved in the Gospel of Gagik-Abas of Kars in Jerusalem.
This flourishing civilization, documented by Muslim geographers,
goes far to rectify the image of relative instability suggested by a purely
political consideration of this period. Far from presenting the battered
aspect of the eighth century, royal Armenia emerged in the tenth century
not only as thriving at home but as one of the prosperous regions of the
East with a reputation acknowledged from afar. Its position between the
Byzantine and Muslim worlds provided wide contacts with the entire
range of Mediterranean and Oriental culture, and these in turn fostered
the amplitude and magnificence of its own artistic development that
soon came to be admired by outsiders. "Frankish" painters may have
been invited to decorate the church of the great monastery of Tat'ew in
Siwnik', but it soon counted more than 500 monks renowned for their
erudition and skill as painters, according to the local historian
Step'annos Ōrbelean (Stepanos Orbelian). Before the end of the
Bagratuni period, the Byzantine court itself, searching for an outstanding specialist capable of repairing the dome of the Church of Hagia
Sophia in Constantinople, which had been seriously damaged by the
earthquake of 989, would find it necessary to seek him beyond the
borders of the empire and invite the Armenian architect Trdat of Ani.

FOR FURTHER INFORMATION

For the sources of, or more information on, the material in this chapter, please consult the following (full citations can be found in the Bibliography at the end of this volume).

"Arminiya," *The Encyclopaedia of Islam.*

Der Nersessian, 1945.

Laurent, 1919.

Maksoudian, 1988-1989.

Ter Ghewondian, 1976.

Yuzbashian, 1988.

8

THE BYZANTINE ANNEXATION OF THE ARMENIAN KINGDOMS IN THE ELEVENTH CENTURY

Nina Garsoïan

Two factors emerge from the course of events described in the preceding chapters as the major causes hindering all efforts to create a stable and centralized state on the Armenian plateau. The first was the perpetual centrifugal tendency of the *naxarar*s, whose loyalty to their own house rather than to any common ruler was reinforced by the fragmented character of Armenia's mountainous setting, which isolated the various regions from each other. This absence of unifying elements goes far to explain the difficulties of the early Christian Aršakuni rulers who were unable to control the autonomous hereditary prerogatives of their magnates. It unquestionably underlay to a great degree the fragmentation of the medieval Bagratuni, Arcruni, and Siwni kingdoms, except for the sole occasion of the "Assembly of Hark'" in 974, when all the junior rulers supported the senior Bagratuni king, Ašot III, faced with the threatening Byzantine army of the emperor John Tzimiskes. The second factor was any break in the precarious international balance that prevented either of the formidable powers to the east and west of the plateau from overwhelming Armenia and annexing it outright. Such a break at the time of the rise of Islam paralleled by the retreat of Byzantium had led to the Muslim conquest and subsequent oppression of Armenia in the seventh and especially the eighth centuries, as we have seen earlier. External conditions had gradually returned to their previous equilibrium as the Byzantine armies turned again to the offensive in the second half of the ninth century, challenging success- fully the power of the declining Abbasid caliphate and especially the various Muslim principalities on its eastern border, and thus assisting indirectly in the contemporary development of autonomous and even- tually independent entities in Armenia after a hiatus of several centuries. Unfortunately for these principalities, however, the balance was to shift catastrophically, now to the Byzantine side, with the opening years of the eleventh century. The threat to the Armenian kingdoms was all the greater since the political theory of Constantinople revived under the Macedonian dynasty and inaugurated by the emperor Basil I (867-1056) recognized no Christian ruler as equal to or independent of the Byzantine emperor, and Byzantium's ultimate goal, even when it was masked for a time by diplomatic compromises, remained the total incorporation of the Armenian realms within the empire. No such common purpose united the Armenian kingdoms facing the long-range and carefully planned imperialistic policy of Byzantium, which consequently was able to carry out its piecemeal annexation of most of the Armenian lands on the eve of the advance of the Seljuk Turks from the east.

The First Phase of the Byzantine Advance:
The Themes of Tarōn, Iberia, and Vaspurakan (968–1021)

The first harbingers of danger from the west appeared in the tenth century at the time that the Bagratuni kingdom was reaching its zenith. The creation of the Byzantine "theme" or province of Mesopotamia, probably as early as A.D. 900, east of the Euphrates River on territory that had once been part of Justinian I's Armenia IV, brought the imperial administration within reach of the southwestern Armenian principality of Tarōn, ruled at that time by the descendants of the Prince of Princes Bagarat Bagratuni (ca. 826-851). Soon after this move, the campaigns of the Byzantine-Armenian general Yovhannēs Kurkuas failed to take Duin in 922 and again in 927/8, as we saw in the preceding chapter, but in 949 the future emperor John Tzimiskes stormed the great fortress of Karin/Theodosiopolis, the anchor point of the Muslim military defense against the empire in the northwest. Although Karin would temporarily be conceded by the emperor Basil II to the curopalate David of Tayk' in 979, the Byzantine Empire by the middle of the tenth century lay along the full length of the western border of Armenia.

The first intrusion came in the south. The Byzantine emperors had already viewed the Bagratuni princes of Tarōn as their vassals in a certain sense since the beginning of the tenth century, for they had accepted imperial titles, especially that of *strategos,* or "governor," and stipends from Constantinople, although Tarōn kept a degree of autonomy and its rulers sought to maintain uneasy relations with their Muslim neighbors as well. With the death of Ašot Bagratuni, prince of Tarōn, in 967/8, however, his sons were no longer able to withstand the pressure exerted upon them by the empire, which annexed their principality outright. The Tarōnite princes went on to pursue brilliant careers in Constantinople for generations to come, but the first portion of intrinsically Armenian territory had been lost to Byzantium and reduced to the level of an ordinary theme within the imperial administrative system.

The main thrust of the imperial expansion followed with the opening years of the eleventh century, as the emperor Basil II set out to reclaim the inheritance of the *curopalate* David of Tayk'. In three campaigns—1001, 1014 (in which he also took advantage of the death of King Bagrat of Iberia and Abkhazia) and 1021/2—the emperor retook all of the territories he had left to David of Tayk' in 979, including the crucial fortress of Karin—which the Byzantines refortified in 1018—and the city of Manazkert, conquered from the Muslims by the *curopalate* himself, as well as David's own hereditary principality of Tayk'/Tao. These imperial victories brought to Byzantium not only a considerable portion of territory taken from the Iberian Bagratids, but also a wide arc of lands comprising the western border districts of Armenia and curving eastward deep into the central plateau to reach as far as Manazkert north of Lake Van. By 1021, if not before, this vast territory was also absorbed into the empire to become the Theme of Iberia governed by an imperial *strategos* as was Tarōn and with Karin/Theodosiopolis as its capital.

Simultaneously with the imperial acquisition of the lands of David of Tayk' came the turn of one of the main realms of medieval Armenia, the Arcruni kingdom of Vaspurakan. In 1003 the last ruler, Senek'erim-Yovhannēs, the youngest grandson of the first king Gagik I Arcruni and the son-in-law of the Bagratuni king, Gagik I of Ani, had shouldered aside his nephews in the Arcruni senior line to become the sole king of Vaspurakan. As a result of this usurpation, his rule had always been precarious. It became all the more so in the second decade of the eleventh century as the plundering raids of various Turkmen groups, some of whom were probably in the service of the Iranian Daylamites of Azerbaijan, struck at Vaspurakan. Alarmed and weakened by these incursions, Senek'erim-Yovhannēs, together with his nephew the Arcruni prince of Anjewac'ik', went in 1016 to offer to Basil II the lands of Vaspurakan (including some 72 fortresses and 3000 to 4000 villages, according to the contemporary sources) in exchange for a vast domain farther west on Byzantine territory centered on the city of Sebasteia/Sivas to which the former Arcruni king moved in 1021, together with his entire family and some 14,000 retainers. Immediately after his departure, Basil II, who had sent imperial troops from the Balkans to Vaspurakan even before Senek'erim-Yovhannēs's offer, reduced the Arcruni kingdom to the Theme of Vaspurakan (also called Basprakania, Asprakania, or Media) of which Van probably became the administrative center. It was governed by a non-Armenian *strategos* and occasionally divided into Upper Media, which probably was formed of Senek'erim-Yovhannēs's own domain, and Lower Media, which may have corresponded to the Arcruni principality of Anjewac'ik' southeast of Lake Van, but also included Manazkert north of the lake. With the creation of this third imperial theme, Byzantine power was firmly established on the Armenian plateau of which it controlled the greater part with the exception of the Bagratuni kingdoms in the northwest and the surviving portion of Eastern Siwnik' or Bałk'.

The Annexation of the Bagratuni Kingdoms (1045–1065)

The Bagratuni kings likewise did not have to wait long for their turn. As we saw earlier, Basil II did not take any decisive action against the senior kingdom of Ani until the death of King Gagik I, despite his victorious campaigns against Iberia and Tayk'. With the Armenian king's death (probably in 1017 rather than 1020, as was formerly believed), however, the situation began to deteriorate in the kingdom of Ani now split between Gagik I's two sons, Yovhannēs-Smbat and Ašot IV *K'aǰ* (the Brave) (1017-1040/1). The elder brother kept the capital of Ani with most of the surrounding district of Širak, while Ašot IV received lands that should have included the city of Duin, but which he could not occupy since the city had already been captured by the Kurdish Shaddadid emirs coming from Ganǰa. In spite of the attempted arbitration of the new king of Iberia and the Armenian kat'ołikos, the two brothers fought throughout their lives, obviously sapping the stability of the realm, especially since Ašot IV sought support from all sides, including the court of Constantinople, which he visited. The early relations of King Yovhannēs-Smbat with Byzantium remain unknown, but the Armenian king, distracted by his brother's attacks, embroiled in territorial quarrels with his kinsman, the junior Bagratid king of Kars, and fearful of Basil II's wrath for the support given by Armenia to the Iberian king in his opposition to the imperial reconquest of the domains of David of Tayk', was soon left without room in which to maneuver. In this critical position, he seems to have had little choice other than to resort to a diplomatic move aimed at decreasing the immediate danger to his kingdom, but one that would ultimately lead to disastrous consequences. In 1022 the Armenian kat'ołikos Petros I Getadarj went to the winter quarters of the emperor Basil II at Trebizond and brought to him a will in which the childless king of Ani sought to win a partial respite by leaving his kingdom to Byzantium after his death. We do not know the immediate results of this action beyond the fact that Yovhannēs-Smbat was granted the imperial title of *Archon*, or "Ruler" of Ani and Basil II did not live to see the outcome of his Armenian policy. On the almost simultaneous death of Yovhannēs-Smbat and Ašot IV in 1040/1, however, the new Byzantine emperor claimed the kingdom of Ani under the terms of the king's earlier will, and the annexation of Bagratid Armenia entered into its final phase.

The scarce references and contradictory information of the Greek and Armenian sources do not allow us to reconstruct the murky details or the exact chronology of the fall of the senior Bagratuni kingdom with the desired precision. The motives of the personages dominating the scene at Ani, including those of the kat'ołikos Petros Getadarj, remain enigmatic for the same reasons, as do the policy and indistinct personality of the last young Bagratuni king, Gagik II, the son of Ašot IV, whose reign was to last only two years. At Ani, after the death of the two kings in 1041, the interests of the regent, the *vestis,* "overseer or steward" Sargis Haykazn, who had received many honors from the Byzantine Empire, clashed with those of the powerful Armenian *sparapet,* Vahram Pahlawuni, and his supporters. The Pahlawuni party succeeded in bringing the young Gagik II to Ani and in having him crowned, but they could not evict Sargis's forces from the citadel of the city. Gagik II maintained himself in the Bagratuni capital until 1042/3 and even fought off a Turkmen attack with the support of the Pahlawuni, but then, possibly persuaded by Sargis, or perhaps fearing the attacks of his ambitious kinsman David *Anhołin* (the Landless) of Loṙi-Tašir or of the S̲h̲addadid emir of Duin instigated by Byzantium, he accepted the invitation of the emperor Constantine IX to come to Constantinople. Once at the Byzantine court, Gagik II was kept in honorable confinement and eventually pressured into relinquishing his rights in Armenia in exchange for a domain in Cappadocia, as had been done earlier by the Arcruni king of Vaspurakan. In 1044 an imperial army twice failed to take Ani, which was protected by its great fortifications. In view of the critical situation the kat'ołikos, whom the king had left behind as governor of the city in his absence, decided, rightly or wrongly, to surrender it to Byzantium in 1045, although the "senior citizens" of Ani seem to have sought in vain to offer it to the king of Iberia, to King David of Loṙi-Tašir, and perhaps even the Kurdish emir of Duin, who may have been Gagik II's brother-in-law.

With the surrender of Ani on the eve of the Seljuk conquest, the Byzantine annexation of the Armenian plateau was all but complete, although the imperial army failed to take Duin from the S̲h̲addadids in the following year. Ani received a Greek governor, the former *strategos* of the Theme of Iberia, though he was soon to be replaced by an Armenian general in the service of Byzantium, Katakalon Kekaumenos. The territories of Gagik II's kingdom were joined to those of the Iberian theme, whose capital was moved from Karin to Ani and which now bore the name of "Iberia and Armenia" or "Iberia and Ani." The kat'ołikos Petros Getadarj was soon interned by the Byzantine governor, despite his surrender of the capital to the empire. He was summoned to Constantinople, where he was also honorably received but detained for a time like the former king, before being allowed to retire to the court of the Arcruni princes at Sebastē (Sivas), where he died in 1058. The Bagratid king of Kars, Gagik-Abas, still clung to his realm successfully for twenty more years, but even he was constrained to cede his city and lands to Byzantium after the Seljuk capture of Ani in 1064, before retiring in his turn to a domain in Cappadocia, where he died in 1069. The lands of the kingdom of Kars were added to those of the Theme of Iberia and Armenia, but this annexation brought little profit to the empire as the Seljuks captured Kars in 1065. By the time of the defeat of the Byzantine emperor by the Seljuk sultan Alp-Arslan at Manazkert in 1071, all that remained of the medieval Armenian kingdoms were a few fortresses north of Lake Sevan held by the descendants of the Bagratuni junior line of Loṙi-Tašir and the remains of the kingdom of Bałk' in

Eastern Siwnikʿ shielded by the rugged mountains south of the great monastery of Tatʿew. The imperial themes of Tarōn, Vaspurakan, and Iberia-Armenia carved out of the plateau earlier in the century likewise did not outlive the imperial defeat and were destroyed by the Seljuk invaders. Within a decade after Manazkert, the surviving lines of the Bagratuni and Arcruni dynasties settled in Cappadocia had also disappeared. All the heirs had been murdered under circumstances that still remain unclear, as does the chronology of their deaths.

The Administrative and Cultural Transformation of Armenia in the First Half of the Eleventh Century

The transformation of the independent Armenian realms into ordinary Byzantine provinces should probably not be viewed as exclusively destructive despite its obviously negative aspects. Imperial governors, whether Armenian or not, were enjoined to "care" for their province. Thus, the *strategos* of Ani in the mid-eleventh century, who was the son of the last king of Bulgaria, saw to the repair and heightening of the city walls and the improvement of the urban water system. He even remitted a number of taxes at the express order of the ruling empress, as we learn from an inscription on the south wall of the cathedral. Some Armenians, such as Katakalon Kekaumenos, were appointed governors of the newly created Armeno-Byzantine themes alongside Greeks or other "foreigners." Even lesser local authorities, such as the "senior citizens" of Ani, glimpsed in the sources at the time of the surrender of the city in 1045, seem to have kept a measure of power, although we known nothing concerning them beyond their existence. The dismissal of the local Armenian forces in 1055 by the emperor Constantine IX, which is often blamed for the collapse of the Byzantine defense of Armenia in the face of the Seljuk advance, may indeed have been unwise, but it was part of the general transformation of the imperial military system from one of local recruitment to one increasingly based on the use of mercenary contingents. As such, it was part of the reorganization of the army rather than a measure directed against the welfare of the Armenians. A number of magnates served willingly in the Byzantine administration in both civilian and military capacities, as was the case of the Armenian general Kekaumenos, named governor of Ani. Even the *sparapet* Vahram Pahlawuni, who had backed King Gagik II to the very end, accepted the command of the Armenian forces that accompanied the imperial army in its unsuccessful attack on Duin the very year after the annexation of Ani. His learned son, Grigor (Gregory) Magistros, first chose to follow the example of the Armenian rulers, surrendering his ancestral domain in Armenia to Byzantium and retiring to Constantinople and an estate on imperial territory, but by 1051 he had returned home, now as the governor of the themes united for his benefit. These Armenian officials of the Byzantine Empire were granted a multitude of exalted titles by the court of Constantinople in recognition of their dignity and services: among others to the *vestis* Sargis Haykazn; to the princes of Tarōn, both before and after the acquisition of their principality by the empire; and especially to Grigor Pahlawuni, *magistros,* duke and patrician. Even the conversion to Byzantine Orthodoxy normally mandatory for all forms of imperial service could be waived on occasion, as was done for Gregory Magistros.

Despite the Byzantine taxation and even the subsequent devastation of the Seljuk and other Turkmen invasions in the second half of the eleventh century, the culture and even the economic development of Armenia were not altogether destroyed. The works of the contemporary historians, such as Aristakēs Lastivertc'i, and the survival of the great monastic foundations at Hałbat, Sanahin, Tat'ew, and elsewhere, which served simultaneously as centers of learning, testify to the continuation of intellectual vitality in Armenia. The evidence for the existence of numerous scriptoria and the survival of illuminated manuscripts from the eleventh century, some relatively crude but others displaying the skill and richness of the Gospel of Gagik-Abas of Kars, preserved in Jerusalem, provide similar support for the enduring artistic tradition of Armenian masters. Ani, sold to the Shaddadids by the Seljuks in 1072 and disputed between its new Muslim masters and the increasingly powerful Iberian branch of the Bagratuni to the very end of the twelfth century, continued to flourish through these multiple vicissitudes well into the thirteenth century, and its building and commercial activities did not stop. The former capital, along with other Armenian cities, even produced a new class of powerful urban merchants, the *mecatun (metsatun),* distinct from the earlier *naxarar* aristocracy, such as Tigran Honenc' (Honents) whose inscription of 1215 on the splendid church he had built and decorated in honor of St. Gregory at Ani still testifies to his enormous wealth through the almost endless list of properties left for its maintenance.

Finally, it is worth noting that almost all the leaders who sought to re-create Armenian principalities on the middle Euphrates and in Cilicia at the end of the eleventh century and the early years of the twelfth, after the disappearance of Armenian independence and the collapse of imperial rule in the East, had begun their careers in the imperial service and usually continued to base their claim to authority and legitimacy on their Byzantine official position and titles, even when Constantinople could no longer provide them with any support and although all were ethnic Armenians. This pattern holds, with only a few exceptions, for the greatest of them: Philaretos Varažnuni (Varazhnuni), duke of Antioch late in the eleventh century; and his predecessors as dukes of Antioch; Χač'atur (Khachatur), whose name testifies sufficiently to his Armenian origin in 1068; and probably Vasak Pahlawuni, the son of Grigor Magistros in 1078-1079. The same was true for such lesser local rulers as those holding Melitēnē, Tarsus, and Maraš (Marash), as well as for the ancestors of the future Rubenid and Lambronac'i (Lambronatsi) dynasties of Cilicia. Armenian sources might claim a highly dubious Armenia royal descent from King Gagik II for the Rubenid prince T'oros I once his family was established in Cilicia, but even he and his successors well into the twelfth century still accepted and wore the exalted title of *sebaste* granted to them by the court of Constantinople.

Despite these various redeeming features, however, the Byzantine annexation of the Armenian medieval kingdoms had an undeniably deleterious effect on the country. Not only did it put an end to its independence and sovereignty and leave it weakened by the turmoil and resentment attendant on the imperial conquest, but it altered the administrative and demographic structure of the plateau. Administratively, the annexed Armenian kingdoms and principalities seem to have been treated as ordinary themes, as we hear of little if any concessions made to local customs, although the *strategoi* bore a variety of titles and separate governors were apparently appointed in some of the cities. We do not even know the location of the administrative center of the Theme of Tarōn, and whatever may have been the duties of the "senior citizens" of Ani, there is no indication that they were in any way important. The duties of the *strategos* were military as well as civilian and we find troops were sent from the newly created Armenian themes to serve when needed in the imperial Balkan campaigns, thus weakening the local defenses even before the dismissal of the Armenian forces in 1055. In addition to the governors, the contemporary Armenian historian Aristakēs Lastivertc'i also mentions "judges" (Armenian *datawor*) and inspectors. These officials, who do not seem to have been under the jurisdiction of the local governor, had fiscal as well as judicial responsibilities. Despite the occasional remissions, such as the one granted by the empress to the inhabitants of Ani in 1055/6, the collection of taxes was one of the main purposes of the imperial provincial administration. These fiscal policies necessarily increased the economic burden of the general population even where occasional privileged members of the upper classes continued to prosper.

The transformation of the Armenian lands under Byzantine domination reached deeper than their outward administrative alteration. To be sure, the new themes of Tarōn and Vaspurakan corresponded to the earlier Armenian principalities of the same name they had replaced. This was also true in a certain sense of the Theme of Iberia, though to a lesser degree after the lands belonging to the kingdom of Ani, and ultimately those of the kingdom of Kars, were included in it. Even where the boundaries of the successive administrative units were identical, the territories of the former Armenian principalities could subsequently be altered at will by the imperial authorities. Such were the already noted division of the Theme of Vaspurakan into Upper and Lower Media and the reunion of the themes of Tarōn and Vaspurakan jointly entrusted to Grigor Magistros in 1051. Lands not belonging to an original principality could also be added to it, as was the case in the fusion of Lower Media south of Lake Van with Manazkert and other centers north of the same lake that had not been part of Vaspurakan before its annexation. Even when temporary, these transfers and arbitrary divisions or fusions prevented the new administrative units from taking root in the region before they were called upon to face Seljuk attacks. They helped to blur the divisions between the earlier principalities and their sense of identity as well. The vast shift of native Armenian population westward from the plateau, as they followed their various lords from their homeland to new estates in imperial Cappadocia even before the arrival of the Seljuks, undoubtedly increased the Armenian component of the lands that had once formed part of Armenia Minor. Yet it necessarily altered damagingly the demographic balance of Greater Armenia, whose transformation had begun earlier with the implantation of the Muslim emirates throughout the plateau. This gradual transformation was all the more far-reaching in that the imperial authorities continued their earlier policy of enforcing conformity with the official church of Constantinople in the regions under their control. Consequently religious quarrels flared once again and the hierarchy of the Armenian Church was perturbed at all levels. Its patriarchs were detained or exiled, as were Petros Getadarj and his nephew and successor Xač'ik II (1058-1065), or they preferred to seek distant asylums and refuge outside the imperial territory altogether, as did the kat'ołikos Grigor Vkayasēr (1065-1105), elected in Cappadocia thanks to the protection of Gagik-Abas of Kars and under whose pontificate the Armenian kat'ołikate set out on the protracted wanderings that would keep it from its seat on the Armenian plateau for several centuries. On the secular side, an exception might be made for the kat'ołikos's powerful and distinguished father Grigor Magistros, but such exceptions were rare. Most of the Armenian nobles who rose in the imperial service had willy-nilly to accept the Chalcedonian doctrine of the Byzantine Church and found themselves consequently alienated from the religious, if not at first from the intellectual, traditions of their compatriots. Such policies understandably antagonized the great part of the native population as well as the hierarchy of the Armenian Church, and the echo of this resentment finds its clear expression in the hostile tone of the *Chronicle* of Matthew of Edessa.

Hence, even before the effects of the subsequent Turkmen and later Mongol invasions could manifest themselves, a profound transformation, which their coming would prolong and intensify, had already been initiated in the history of the Armenian people. The destruction of the native medieval kingdoms helped to create a vacuum of power at a particularly perilous moment. More seriously even than the demographic change gradually brought about by the growing migration of Armenians from the plateau, war, constraint, and the lure of careers to be made at the imperial court drained from Armenia the crucial leadership around which resistance or reconstruction might have clustered. In the north, the precedence now passed to the Iberian branch of the Bagratuni house, which was entering its most brilliant period in the twelfth and thirteenth centuries with the reunion of all Georgian lands under one rule, but increasingly, linguistic and religious differences had been drawing it away from its Armenian kinsmen even before their disappearance. In the imperial domains granted to them in exchange for their realms, all the heirs of the Armenian royal houses were dead before the end of the eleventh century. The tentative successor states to the south headed by men of relatively obscure origin, despite the inflated claims subsequently made for them, at first had neither the strength nor the legitimacy needed to marshal the loyalty of their compatriots and of the local population in general except in the distant mountains of Cilicia. All had vanished at the end of the first quarter of the twelfth century, replaced by Muslims or Latin crusader conquerors.

In the century following the disappearance of the medieval kingdoms, as in earlier times of troubles and foreign invasions, the fundamental religious, social, and cultural institutions of Armenia survived the collapse of the political system. The church provided a focus for loyalties; the main element of continuity even far from home was through the remarkable succession of the patriarchs from the Pahlawuni house, who held the kat'oɫikate, albeit with co-adjutors and faced with antipatriarchs, from 1065 to 1203. Their long tenure in such troubled times demonstrated that the Armenian tradition of the hereditary patriarchate going back to the house of St. Gregory himself still survived. The social structure of *naxarar* Armenia, even where modified by external influences, resurfaced in Cilicia. The Armenian language, and literature, and the Armenians' consciousness of their identity were not lost. Nevertheless, the centers of power shifted radically, and native sovereignty vanished from the Armenian plateau for centuries to come.

FOR FURTHER INFORMATION

For the sources of, or more information on, the material in this chapter, please consult the following (full citations can be found in the Bibliography at the end of this volume).

Adontz, 1970.

"Arminiya," *The Encyclopaedia
        of Islam,* 1960.

Arutjunova-Fidanjan, 1986-1987.

Dédéyan, 1996

Der Nersessian, 1945, 1969, 1978.

Manandyan, 1965.

Minorsky, 1953.

Ter Ghewondian, 1976.

Thierry and Donabedian, 1989.

Yuzbashian, 1975-1976, 1988.

9

ARMENIAN LITERARY CULTURE THROUGH THE ELEVENTH CENTURY

Robert Thomson

If by "literature" we understand the writing and scholarship of Armenians expressed in the Armenian language, then this development occurred quite late in the history of the Armenian nation. The political and social individuality of Armenia and the Armenians goes back to the days of the Old Persian Empire, but their literature was a product of Christian times, which went hand in hand with the cultural revolution wrought by the conversion of Armenia. In fact, the development of Armenian literature was both the result of an established Christian presence and at the same time a major factor in the final conversion of the populace at large to the new faith.

But to concentrate only on literature written in the Armenian language obscures two points. Long before the fifth century of the Christian era, Armenians had been familiar with classical culture. Latin and Greek sources inform us about the influence of Greek literature and thought, notably in court circles. In the first century B.C. King Artavazd, son of the more famous Tigran, gained a reputation as a writer of plays and histories. Inscriptions were set up in Armenia, and coins minted. Armenians became known in the universities of the Greek-speaking world as teachers and scholars. But all this literary activity was conducted in languages other than Armenian. The language of cultural aspiration was Greek—as it was for many peoples who bordered on the Eastern Roman Empire. On the other hand, Aramaic, the international lingua franca of the Iranian world, was used for official inscriptions; and Syriac was known in church circles.

The second point is that the Armenians possessed a rich heritage of oral tales and stories dealing with the gods, heroes, and noteworthy figures—real or imaginary—of the past. These tales were recited by bards *(gusan)* and accompanied on the lyre or other instrument. Such musical entertainments were popular in princely circles long after the collapse of independent kingdoms. Indeed, the tradition of wandering minstrels survived until modern times. But in pre-Christian Armenia the *gusans* did not put their songs into writing. Singers of tales, like dancing girls, were frowned upon by the clergy, who dominated Armenian written literature, and also by the compiler of the first secular law code in the twelfth century. So apart from a few fragments preserved by historians or antiquarian scholars, nothing survives of a long prewritten culture that reflected the real interests and enthusiasms of early Armenia. The written literature that developed with remarkable rapidity in the fifth century was the perquisite of a small group that deliberately set itself apart from pagan traditions. The books of classical and medieval times do not therefore give us a full picture of Armenian cultural life.

Invention of the Armenian Script

One of the most noteworthy features of Armenian literature is that it has a very precise beginning. Armenians, who were familiar with the pagan and early Christian literatures of the world around them, could only transpose that familiarity into their own tongue when a script for Armenian was invented. That momentous step was due to the efforts of Mashtots, also called Mesrop by writers after his own time, and was accomplished around the year A.D. 400.

Most of our knowledge of these events comes from a short biography of Mashtots written by one of his pupils, Koriun, after the master's death (Koriun, 1964). Although it is rather short on precise details and rather long on rhetorical description, this *Life of Mashtots* is important both as a historical source and as the first example of biographical writing in Armenian. Koriun says little about the early life of Mashtots. He was born in the province of Taron in western Armenia and received an education in Greek literature. We are not told where; but many of Mashtots's contemporaries went to the schools of Antioch and other centers of Greek learning. He entered the royal chancellery and advanced to an important position. However, he had a vocation for the religious life; abandoning the secular world, he became an ascetic hermit. After some time he began to attract disciples, and embarked on the career that would transform Armenia.

Mashtots's efforts were directed to preaching the gospel in remoter parts of the country. Although King Trdat (Tiridates in Greek) had been converted to Christianity at the beginning of the century, and St. Gregory the Illuminator had established the first organized Armenian bishoprics—the main episcopal see being at Ashtishat in Taron, Mashtots's native province—the whole country was by no means converted overnight. The pious exaggerations of Agathangelos (1976), whose *History* describes these events, are misleading. Another early historian, Pavstos (P'awstos) Buzand, describes in some detail the struggle of the church in fourth-century Armenia; there was much opposition from the old noble families with their pagan traditions and basically Iranian-oriented outlook (P'awstos Buzand, 1989). And from Koriun we learn that many areas were still entirely untouched by the Christian message. Mashtots set to work to eradicate "ancestral habits and the diabolical worship of demons."

It was in the course of his missionary activity that Mashtots realized the potential value of having the appropriate religious texts written in the Armenian language. Although the educated clergy used Greek or Syriac for the liturgy and could read biblical and theological books in those languages, that was of little help to the mass of the Armenian people. In concert with Catholicos (supreme patriarch) Sahak, Mashtots turned his attention to the development of a native script so that Armenians could have the requisite Christian books in their own language. The original impetus, therefore, in the development of Armenian written culture came from church authorities. And ecclesiastical concerns remained predominant in the literature of later generations.

There are some minor discrepancies in the accounts of Koriun and of other early writers concerning the precise details of the invention of the Armenian script. However, it is clear that Mashtots was the driving force, that the patriarch Sahak lent his full support and was later active as a translator himself, and that the king Vramshapuh was directly involved. Koriun says that the king, when informed of Mashtots's zeal, told him about a Syrian bishop Daniel who had put together a script for Armenian. That a Syrian should have taken the initiative is a good indication of the importance of Syrian missionary work in southern Armenia. The influence of Syriac vocabulary on Armenian ecclesiastical usage, and of Syrian writers on developing Armenian literature, also point to the strong ties that existed between these two Christian lands.

Naturally enough Daniel's alphabet was based on a Semitic script. The latter, as used for Hebrew and Syriac, had twenty-two letters, which rendered the consonants, but the vowels were not clearly indicated. The structure of the Semitic languages does not make this too grave a disadvantage. But Daniel's system—no trace of which has survived— was inadequate to cope with the richer consonantal structure of Armenian; nor could it render vowels, whose patterns in an Indo-European tongue are less predictable than in Semitic. So that attempt came to naught, and Mashtots went himself to Syria "in the fifth year of Vramshapuh," according to Koriun (1964). But since the beginning of Vramshapuh's reign has been variously dated, from 389 to 401, the precise date is uncertain.

Particularly important was Mashtots's visit to Edessa, for this was the center of Syriac-speaking Christianity on the Roman side of the border with Iran. He had taken a group of young pupils with him. These he divided into two groups and set to learning Syriac and Greek. Mashtots himself with his closest associates went on to Samosata on the Euphrates. There, in concert with a scribe competent in Greek literature, he worked out a script for Armenian that rendered all the nuances. This time it was based on a Greek model, with a separate sign for each vowel as well as for each consonant. The only exception was the vowel /u/; in this case Mashtots retained the diphthong of the Greek *ou*. The script invented by Mashtots has remained in use down to the present day; modern uppercase letters have hardly changed from the form given them more than 1,500 years ago, while the lowercase letters are based on medieval scribal hands. There is, however, one interesting anomaly. The most common vowel in Armenian is the short /ĕ/ [ը]. But this is practically never written except at the beginning of words. So one finds in *written* Armenian clusters of consonants, perhaps as many as five or six, which in *pronunciation* must be grouped into appropriate syllables containing the vowel /ĕ/. It is difficult not to suppose that here the influence of Syriac was at work, for even when vowel signs were later introduced, the short /ĕ/ was not rendered.

The First Translations

Once the script had been fashioned, Mashtots immediately set to work to translate texts into Armenian. The first such effort was a rendering of the Proverbs of Solomon. Armenians enjoyed fables, proverbs, and pithy sayings; many such texts of a secular nature were translated in later centuries, and in medieval literature the genre of the fable was popular. But Mashtots was concerned with books appropriate for the church and its missionary efforts, so he began with a biblical text. Koriun adds the personal comment that he himself used that first translated text when teaching writing to pupils.

The patriarch Sahak and Mashtots now directed a massive effort to render into Armenian as much Christian literature as possible in as short a time as possible. Groups of young men were gathered—since this was an ecclesiastical operation, we must suppose that these were the "seminarians" of the time. First they were instructed in the script, then they were sent abroad to the main centers of Christian culture in order to learn Greek or Syriac, or both. Koriun gives us some details. He mentions the names of several pupils in the entourage of Mashtots and indicates that some were sent to Edessa to learn Syriac, others to Melitene, or as far as Constantinople, to learn Greek. But he does not name precisely the texts that were translated. Only in vague terms does he refer to the Armenians now having in their own tongue "Moses who taught the law, with the prophets, Paul and the band of the apostles, and the gospel of Christ" (Koriun, 1964).

Most of Mashtots's own energies were devoted to missionary activity in the provinces to the east and north. But he did make one extended visit to the Armenians on the Roman side of the border, proceeding as far as Constantinople. There he greeted the emperor Theodosius II (408-440) and the patriarch Atticus (405-425) and received official permission *(sacra)* to carry on his educational work among Armenians in the eastern provinces of the empire. At this point Koriun refers to Mashtots collecting "many books of the church fathers" (1964). After 431 some of his pupils brought back from Constantinople other texts, including copies of the canons of the ecumenical councils held at Nicaea (325) and Ephesus (431). This new influx of texts prompted the patriarch Sahak to revise some of the earlier translations of "ecclesiastical books" and also to translate numerous commentaries on the scriptures. Koriun adds that Mashtots began himself to compose homilies with material taken from the prophets and gospels in order to wake people up to the truth of the Christian message. Though several collections of homilies survive from the early period, none of them can be securely identified as Mashtots's own work. But if he put into writing examples of his lifelong preaching, he was the first original writer in Armenian.

Before turning to the question of original compositions by the pupils of Mashtots—men such as Koriun or Eznik, who were the real founders of Armenian literature—we should first cast an eye over the translated material. The texts with which the first generation of native Armenian writers were most familiar, since they had had a hand in rendering them from Greek or Syriac, were naturally of great influence on their own outlook and literary methods.

It must not be imagined that theology in a narrow sense was the sole concern of Mashtots's pupils. The Bible formed the staple of reading and study, while those in church circles would naturally be familiar with the liturgy and cycles of readings from the church fathers. The homiletic works of John Chrysostom, Gregory Nazianzenus, Severian of Gabala, Eusebius of Emesa, Evagrius, or of the Syrians Afrahat and Ephrem figured prominently, as did the biblical commentaries of Chrysostom and Cyril of Alexandria. These provided a solid basis for instruction and a wide range of parallels, imagery, and interpretation that were assimilated by Armenian writers. The *Catecheses* of Cyril of Jerusalem formed a basis for exposition of the faith—such as the *Teaching of Saint Gregory,* which forms part of the story of Armenia's conversion as described by Agathangelos. Numerous lives of saints and martyrs provided models for the descriptions of persecutions in Armenia that were only too frequent. The lives and sayings of the Egyptian Fathers, popular throughout the Christian world, were a source of enjoyment and gave a pattern for the idiosyncracies of Armenian holy men and hermits. On a more sophisticated level the *Hexaemeron* by Basil of Caesarea (translated from the Syriac version) gave scholars information about the physical world and natural phenomena. It is curious, however, that Koriun and other writers describe the importance of Edessa and Constantinople but never refer to Jerusalem. Yet the liturgical practice of the holy city had great influence on the early Armenian Church; the Jerusalem *Lectionary* was among the first works translated into Armenian, and numerous Armenians went as pilgrims to the holy sites.

Special emphasis must be given to two works by Eusebius of Caesarea. His *Ecclesiastical History,* also translated from a Syriac version, not only provided a fund of historical information, widely quoted and adapted by Armenian writers, but offered a model for the writing of history in a Christian context—that is, a model for the description of the working of God's providence in the present world. Several Armenian historians, though not all, regarded the writing of history as a demonstration of the ultimate triumph of piety and truth over the forces of evil and death. Even more elaborate was Eusebius's *Chronicle*. This was an attempt to correlate the history of the world as known from Greek and other sources with the Bible. It was the main source for later Armenian knowledge of the empires of the ancient world; but equally important, it showed how the histories of the various nations meshed with each other. Beginning with Movses Khorenatsi (Moses of Khoren), Armenian historians relied on Eusebius's *Chronicle* not merely for information about the non-Armenian world but as a schema in which the history of Armenia had its rightful place. It thus became possible to set the ancient oral traditions about the origins of the Armenian people into the patterns of world history and to demonstrate the antiquity of Armenia as a distinct and individual nation.

The First Original Writers: Koriun and Eznik

The amazing efflorescence of written literature in Armenian following the invention of the script can be explained by a combination of two factors. In the first place, Armenians—or at least, those of the elite in both church and state—had long been familiar with the culture of late antiquity. Many, such as Mashtots himself, had received a good classical education; while the regular clergy were versed in Christian texts of various kinds written in Greek or Syriac. Second, the highest authorities in the land, the king and patriarch, gave their backing to an intensive effort to make this accumulated wisdom available in the Armenian language. There was, therefore, no long gap of several generations while a newly acquired learning filtered through to a newly educated group. On the contrary, the first translators were already men of learning; their horizons were widened by the long periods of study they had spent abroad; and they were writing for a small but sophisticated audience now able to read and write in Armenian as well as foreign tongues. Those first pupils of Mashtots composed original works, drawing on the traditions with which they were familiar—some now rendered into Armenian, but some still available only in Greek or Syriac. As time went on, Armenian writers naturally

had an ever-expanding body of literature in Armenian on which to
draw, as more and more texts were translated and as original works
began to set specifically Armenian patterns.

Armenian literature deals with Armenian themes, and over the
years it developed its own traditions in matters of style, imagery, and
form. But the earliest compositions do not differ in any startling way
from the type of work that was being produced in the fourth or fifth
century outside Armenia. So when Koriun composed a biography of his
master Mashtots, he already had in his mind some idea of how a
biography should be arranged. It is not surprising that there are parallels
between Koriun's biography and the *Life of Basil of Caesarea* by
Gregory Nazianzenus. And in its turn that Greek *Life* was part of a
long-standing literary tradition that had elaborated certain rules and
procedures. These were written down in textbooks of rhetoric, some of
which were later translated into Armenian. But anyone who had studied
at a regular school or university would have been familiar with the
standard practice. The particular importance of the biography of
Mashtots by Koriun is that these old traditions, more recently shaped by
Christian influences, were now applied for the first time to an Armenian
subject. Being the first, it set a pattern. So when Agathangelos set about
writing the life of St. Gregory the Illuminator, for his description of the
travels of Gregory as a Christian missionary he naturally took his model
from Koriun.

Much more complex was the work of Koriun's contemporary,
Eznik. Another student of Mashtots's, Eznik had traveled to Edessa and
Constantinople in order to learn Syriac and Greek, and had brought back
texts. Koriun gives us a few details of these journeys but says nothing
of Eznik's later career.

Although numerous homilies are attributed, rightly or wrongly,
to Eznik, his fame in modern times depends on an elaborate treatise
dealing with the problem of the origin of evil. Eznik expounded his
theme by attacking four groups who had the wrong understanding of
God as responsible for evil, and who did not interpret correctly the
Christian doctrine of man's free will. These four groups were: the
ancient pagan Greeks; the Persians—more precisely, the worshippers
of Zurvan as the supreme god; the Greek philosophers; and the
heretical sect of Marcion. Eznik refutes one by one their false interpretations and demonstrates that there is no created thing which is evil
by nature. Evil results from man's perversion of the free will given
him by God. Because of the method of argument, the work is often

known as the "Refutation of Sects." But that title does not bring out
Eznik's prime concern. One should bear in mind that the most important of his many sources was the Christian philosopher Methodius's (d.
311) "On the Freedom of the Will," which attacked dualism and
determinism as found in the gnostic system of Valentinus.

Ironically, however, Eznik's treatise—which has received attention from modern scholars for its information about Zurvanism—did
not have much influence on Armenian writers after his own time. The
themes of paganism, Marcionite heresy, or Persian mythology were
too closely related to the generation of Eznik and the times before him
to be adaptable to the needs of later centuries. By then paganism was
irrelevant; gnostic theories had been more or less forgotten, though
not entirely because the writings attributed to Hermes Trismegistus
still circulated in Armenia; and the Persian Zurvanites had gone the
way of all flesh. Eznik's work was not so relevant to the burning
concerns that vexed Armenia after the sixth century: to defend Christian Armenian traditions against the claims of the church of the
Byzantine Empire and against the temptations of conversion to Islam
for social and economic advantage. In matters of style too, Eznik's
work was untypical of Armenian writing. It is exact, sparse, extremely
particular in its analysis and progression. But most Armenian authors
were wordy, fond of elaborate imagery; and especially with some of
the *Histories* one sometimes has the feeling that they would sound to
best advantage if declaimed. Of course, most Armenians of the time
could not read and were therefore read to.

Koriun and Eznik cannot be left without two further comments,
which are of relevance to many other Armenian literary productions.
The earliest surviving manuscript with the full text of the *Life of
Mashtots*—as opposed to fragments or quotations—was written in
1672. And not only is there a gap of over a thousand years in the textual
transmission, giving plenty of time for scribal errors, confusions, or
misunderstandings to corrupt the text; by the tenth century an abbre-
viated version of the book was in circulation, which incorporated
traditions from sources later than Koriun himself. Other texts too, such
as the *History* of Ghazar Parpetsi (P'arpec'i) (Lazar of Parp), were
reedited long after they were composed (1991). So a good deal of
Armenian literature has not come down to us in the precise form in
which it was originally written.

The transmission of Eznik's treatise illustrates the second point.
Only one manuscript is known. This was written in the thirteenth century,

but the work remained unknown to the world at large until it was printed in Smyrna in 1762. Other works also have survived in only one manuscript, such as the *History* of Tovma Artsruni, which was not published until 1852. So the survival of the classics of Armenian literature was precarious. Indeed, if one remembers the many physical disasters that have befallen Armenia over the centuries—the destruction caused by invasions, burning, and looting, or the ravages of earthquakes—it is surprising that so much did survive. A few texts are known to be lost, such as the *History* by Shapuh Bagratuni of the ninth century (Thomson, 1988-1989); and some have survived in incomplete versions, such as the *Histories* of Ukhtanes and of Mekhitar of Ani. In some cases there is doubt whether a surviving text has been correctly identified when no title is found in the manuscript, such as the *History of Heraclius* attributed to Sebeos. But by good fortune we do seem to have most of the important authors.

The Early Historians

The most creative originality of the Armenians—at least in early and medieval times—lies in their art, more particularly their building and painting. As regards their literary culture, Armenians were more cautious in breaking new ground. This may be partly explained, perhaps, by the determined effort of the first sponsors of Armenian writing to eradicate the non-Christian past. Although songs about the ancient pagan heroes did circulate by word of mouth, sung by bards *(gusan)* at the courts of princes and on social occasions, such as weddings, these were not incorporated into the creative energy of ecclesiastical writers and scholars. The circle around Mashtots and their immediate successors were more concerned with assimilating the Christian culture of the world around them, rendering this—with appropriate adaptations—into Armenian, and using known prose forms to express their reaction to the specifically Armenian problems of the time. Eznik's originality in this sense is clear. But more typical of later Armenian interests, and more formative for later times, was the work of the historians.

Sahak and Mashtots had been more than "sponsors" of literary activity. They had created it, participated in it, and trained their pupils. But they were sponsors in the sense that they dictated the subjects of study and the texts to be translated. A different kind of sponsorship or patronage played a role in the writing of history. The interests of the great noble families required official spokesmen. Their endemic rivalry played out in the political and social spheres had its echo in the war of words and propaganda. Not all of the Armenian histories were written at the behest of a prince whose ancestry needed flattering or whose present preeminence needed justification in terms of the past. But most historians had a case to argue; and despite rhetorical disclaimers of objectivity, few were entirely dispassionate. Tendentiousness, however, does not detract from liveliness. The classic Armenian histories not only have many a good tale to relate; they make frequent use of letters and speeches that break up the narrative, attract the reader's attention, and subtly expound the writer's own interpretations.

The first Armenian historians are extremely shadowy figures. Agathangelos, the "good messenger," who describes the conversion of Armenia to Christianity; Pavstos Buzand, who chronicles the conflict of church and state in the fourth century; Eghishe, who describes the revolt of 450-451 against the Persian shah; Movses Khorenatsi, who gives the first comprehensive history of Armenia from its origins down to the time of Mashtots—who were they? Later traditions provide elaborate details. But we have no reliable information from their contemporaries; and their claims to have been eyewitnesses of the events they describe cannot necessarily be taken at face value. In any event, there was no writing in Armenian before Mashtots; and no compositions by Armenians in Greek or Syriac are attested. So the works of Agathangelos and Pavstos are not later translations into Armenian of books written earlier, as was once thought, but works written in the fifth century. They may well be based on remembered tradition, but they reflect the outlook of a date later than the period described.

Agathangelos

Of all works in Armenian literature the work of Agathangelos has the most complicated textual history. It is not surprising that the life of St. Gregory the Illuminator and the dramatic conversion of King Trdat (Tiridates) should have been of interest to Christians generally, and therefore known outside Armenia. But no other work of Armenian origin was translated in whole or in part into so many different languages, including Greek, Arabic, Syriac, Georgian, Latin, and Ethiopic. What is more, there were two different recensions of the *History,* so there are different Greek and Arabic versions; and since the state of the story was in flux, the Syriac version included events of later dates not found in the Armenian. We need not investigate here this very complicated picture.

But it is worth noting that the first version of Agathangelos has disappeared in Armenian. The text as known from Armenian manuscripts and as quoted by Armenian writers is that of a second recension, for which a date of the late fifth century is not implausible.

This *History,* which gives the received and accepted story of the conversion of Armenia, is a patchwork of several different sources. It begins with a rhetorical preface, in which Agathangelos likens the writing of history to a voyage over the billowing sea and introduces himself as a "Roman, not unskilled in literary composition," who was commissioned to write the book by King Trdat himself. He then sketches the political history of Armenia following the Sasanian revolution in A.D. 224, the Persian occupation of the country, and the eventual recovery of the throne by Trdat. He describes the tortures inflicted on Gregory—who is no less than the son of the man who murdered Trdat's father—the martyrdoms of nuns who had fled to Armenia from Rome, the divine punishments that befell the court, and the emergence of Gregory from the pit in order to cure the demon-possessed king, when everyone had assumed that he had died fifteen years previously. At this point Agathangelos introduces a sixty-day sermon, the *Teaching of Saint Gregory,* which is based on the standard instruction before baptism as found in such works as the *Catecheses* by Cyril of Jerusalem. The third section of Agathangelos's *History* describes the destruction of pagan temples, the consecration of Gregory in Caesarea in Cappadocia as the first bishop of Armenia, the building of churches, and the organization of a regular clergy. The *History* ends before Gregory's death, though later versions of the story discuss in some detail his final days and the later discovery of his relics.

As a literary composition, the *History* of Agathangelos is a fascinating mixture of fact and fiction, in which historical events of a hundred years are telescoped into a lifetime. The emphasis on the importance of Echmiadzin betrays the viewpoint of a fifth-century writer; for until the late fourth century the Armenian patriarchal see was at Ashtishat, an old pagan cult-site in western Armenia. But if the historian uses the book at his peril, for the literary critic it is a mine of information, since it demonstrates the wide learning of an author typical of his time. "Agathangelos," if one can so name the several authors who had a hand in this progressively more elaborate composition, was thoroughly conversant with the Bible; he drew on a wide range of hagiographical sources for his descriptions of tortures and martyrdoms, and on an impressive reading in the works of the church fathers for the *Teaching*. The *History* is not very cohesive, the last part being especially disjointed and evincing the influence of Koriun for the description of Gregory's missionary journeys. But by bringing together so many literary sources to bear on a topic that was Armenian, Agathangelos was blazing a trail. In comparison with Eghishe, for example, he is naive. But he tells his story with panache and must be reckoned as the first of a small group of writers who formed the Armenian literary tradition and set an indelible print on the way in which later generations viewed their Christian origins.

Pavstos Buzand

"Agathangelos," the good messenger, or bearer of good news, was certainly an appropriate pseudonym for the unknown redactors of earlier tradition concerning the conversion of Armenia. But the name borne by Pavstos Buzand has been misinterpreted. Writing about A.D. 500, the historian Ghazar Parpetsi assumed that it was the same as *"Biwzandatsi"* and meant "from Byzantium." Being a cleric of opinionated views, Ghazar upbraided his predecessor for writing a book unworthy of a man educated in that metropolis of learning. But *u* and *iw* are not interchangeable in Armenian. The clue to "Buzand" lies in the title given to the collection of books that included the four books of the historian Pavstos. This title, *Buzandaran,* means a collection of epic tales. Books three to six constitute the work of Pavstos. While the identity of the first two books is unclear, the context makes it plausible to see in them the Armenian version of the *Acts of Thaddaeus*—the story of the apostle Addai of the apostolic age and the first redaction of the life of St. Gregory the Illuminator.

In the nineteenth century the work of Pavstos appealed to popular writers because of its apparent emphasis on secular events: the precarious position of the Armenian kingdom between the Roman and Sasanian empires, the intricate politics of kings and princes who aimed at escaping the control of those powers on either side; the rivalries and deceits of the great noble families; the elaborate descriptions of battles, hunting scenes, and worldly concerns. It is certainly true that Pavstos gives a stirring picture of the life, social and political, of the fifty-year period from the death of King Trdat to the partition of Armenia into Roman and Iranian spheres circa 387. The ways in which Armenians of the time thought and behaved come out clearly.

Yet Pavstos was not a secular writer. He does not approve of those traditional, pre-Christian mores. He is horrified at the persistence of pagan ways, at the adoption of Zoroastrianism for political advantage, at the cruelty and immorality of many of the characters, especially royal ones, that he vividly portrays. Pavstos's heroes are the great Patriarch Nerses and the humbler holy men of the desert. Nerses strove to bring a Christian outlook to the court and was a staunch advocate of orthodoxy, opposing the Arian tendencies that influenced several Roman emperors of the time. On a more modest level, the hermits and saints in the wilderness strove to eradicate the paganism of the people. Of these ascetics and missionaries, the most noteworthy example was Mashtots, not yet mentioned in Pavstos. The *History* of Pavstos thus reminds us that the conversion of Armenia was a long, slow process, not accomplished in Gregory's time as Agathangelos would have us believe.

Pavstos has blended three major strands of oral tradition into his written account. The "Epic Tales" reflect the secular strands of royal history, covering the reigns of Trdat's successors down to the division of the kingdom and the deeds of the leading noble family, the house of the Mamikonians, in which the office of commander in chief was hereditary. Into those two main themes, which themselves contain numerous interpolations as they progress, Pavstos has integrated the ecclesiastical history of Gregory's successors as patriarch, with attendant digressions. Numerous repetitions and doublets indicate that Pavstos has not fully integrated his sources. But as a witness to the cultural life of a nation at a time of transition, these "Epic Tales," the *Buzandaran Patmutiunk,* are incomparable.

In particular, Pavstos emphasizes the legitimacy of family descent. In the secular realm, the Arsacids forfeited their claim through immoral conduct; in the ecclesiastical realm too, Gregory's successors often proved unworthy of their ancestor. But this theme of family legitimacy kept a firm hold on the Armenian tradition. Over a thousand years later historians and poets would still hope for the restoration of Armenian freedoms under the aegis of direct descendants of Trdat and of Gregory.

Eghishe and Ghazar

But despite the value of Pavstos Buzand as an historical source, his *History* did not have nearly as great an influence on Armenians through the ages as the work of Eghishe (Elishe, 1982). The *History of Vardan and the Armenian War* gave epic status to the leaders, lay and cleric, of the revolt against the Sasanian shah in 450-51. Curiously enough, we have two Armenian versions of these events, which are not mentioned by outside sources: that by Ghazar Parpetsi and that by Eghishe. Ghazar's *History* (Łazar P'arp'etc'i, 1991), written circa A.D. 500, is primarily devoted to the career of his patron, Vardan Mamikonian, the nephew of Vardan. But about a third of the book describes the rebellion prompted by the suppression of traditional Armenian liberties during the reign of Yazdagerd II, the final defeat of the Armenians on the battlefield at Avarayr in 451, the martyrdom of the leading clerics in Persia, and the final release from captivity of the Armenian nobles who had survived the war.

The main themes of the story are common to both Ghazar and Eghishe. It is not the difference in details that has given the latter's version its preeminence as a literary document, but rather his interpretation of the specific events in more general terms so that later generations could adapt them to their own times and altered circumstances. Eghishe interprets the war of 450-51 as a struggle between vice and virtue in which the Armenians are fighting for their ancestral customs. Death in that cause is more honorable than life with ignominy; the true patriot is the defender of Armenian Christianity against Zoroastrianism; apostasy not only leads to personal damnation, it brings about the ruin of the nation.

Eghishe's *History* is a tightly knit book in which his basic themes—the covenant of loyalty to church and country, and the valor of the virtuous as contrasted with the cowardice and baseness of those who abandoned that covenant—continually reappear. Through the effective use of speeches, letters, prayers, and exhortations, he elucidates the motives of his characters, Persian as well as Armenian, and the underlying aims that explain their actions. Herein lies the uniqueness of Eghishe, for no other Armenian historian clarifies so well the forces that affect men's actions. Eghishe's task as a writer is not just to describe the past, to leave a memorial of glorious deeds for the emulation of succeeding generations. It is his duty to point out the evil that men have done, so that his readers will not lust after the false glory of this world but devote themselves to truth and godliness. Impiety is not merely a personal failing, it has abiding consequences for the nation as well.

Eghishe, like most early Armenian writers, drew on a wide range of literary sources. Given his theme and approach, it is not surprising that biblical and hagiographical allusions abound. He is also indebted to the works that circulated under the name of "Hermes Trismegistus"; and he is the first Armenian to use the Jewish philosopher Philo, relying on Armenian versions of several of the latter's works for elaborate similes.

But one source had a particular influence, not merely providing him with picturesque vocabulary but with a general philosophy or outlook. That source is the books of Maccabees. Agathangelos had already used those texts in describing Armenian paganism; Pavstos borrowed various passages for his battle scenes and was the first to make an explicit comparison between the Armenians killed in war and the Maccabees. But Eghishe more than any other Armenian historian makes the theme of the Maccabees, who fought and died for religious freedom, applicable to the Armenians. The Persians take the place of the Seleucids, Shah Yazdagerd is depicted in the same terms as King Antiochus, while the idea of death for ancestral traditions is modeled, at least verbally, on a basic theme of the books of Maccabees. This parallel between the history of the Armenians and the Jews is made by other Armenian historians. Some of them tried to find physical links between the two peoples by means of fictitious genealogies. In fact, the Armenian nobles had no Jewish blood in their veins. But Armenian writers were able to draw on powerful symbols of constancy to an ideal both religious and national that struck a responsive chord in their readers' hearts.

Ghazar has no reference to Eghishe, whose *History of Vardan* may well be viewed as a later rewriting of this dramatic period. Ghazar begins his *History* by describing it as the "third" history of Armenia, following the books of Agathangelos and of Pavstos. He depicts the last years of the royal Arsacid dynasty, the struggle for religious freedom against Sasanian oppression, the setback after Avarayr in 451, and the final success thirty years later when Vardan Mamikonian was recognized as governor *(marzpan)* of Armenia by the shah in 485. Ghazar's approach to the writing of history is less episodic than that of Pavstos; he does not break the flow of the narrative to introduce stories not directly relevant to his main theme. And like other Armenian historians he uses speeches and letters to enhance the literary effect of his work. His book is also the first to contain a vision of the distant future, as opposed to a divine revelation for immediate purposes. This particular episode of Sahak's vision of the restoration of the Arsacid monarchy and of the patriarchate in the line of Gregory after 350 years is no doubt the addition of a later interpolator. But the theme of wishful predictions in the context of lamentation at present woes came to have a long history in Armenian literature.

Another significant feature of Ghazar's *History* is the role of his patron. Agathangelos claims to have been commissioned by King Trdat (who died over a century before the *History* was written), and Eghishe addresses an otherwise unknown David Mamikon. But Vahan

Mamikonian is a well attested historical figure of Ghazar's own time, whose appointment as *marzpan* forms the climax of Ghazar's book. Appended to the *History* is a letter addressed to Vahan. Ghazar had been attached to the monastery of the patriarchate at Echmiadzin, but was expelled because of slander. He defends himself, giving a brief account of his early life. After studying in Constantinople, he was brought up in the household of the Kamsarakan family. There followed two years of ascetic prayer in the wilderness, after which he was attached to the court of the Mamikonian family. He had thus known Vahan since the latter was young, and it was Vahan who had secured for him the position at Echmiadzin. So Ghazar had a friend to whom he could turn in adversity. Even if his defense is self-serving, it does provide a rare glimpse of social life at a more personal level than the grand themes of his *History*.

Movses Khorenatsi

A fifth writer belongs to the group of early classic historians—"classic" in the sense that their histories not only became models to be emulated, but also gave a view of the Armenian past that was adopted as the received, standard interpretation. The *History of Armenia* by Movses Khorenatsi (Moses of Khoren) is the most comprehensive work in early Armenian historiography, but also the most controversial. Movses claims to have been a pupil of Mashtots's, and he ends his work with a long lament on the evil days that befell Armenia following the deaths of Mashtots and of the patriarch Sahak and the abolition of the Arsacid monarchy (which had occurred earlier, in 428). On the other hand, there are indications in the book itself that it was written after the fifth century. Not only does Movses use sources not available in Armenian at that time, he refers to persons and places attested only in the sixth or seventh centuries. Furthermore, he alters many of his Armenian sources in a tendentious manner in order to extol his patrons, the Bagratuni family, who gained preeminence in the eighth century. But despite the fact that Movses Khorenatsi is not known or quoted by sources before the tenth century, he became revered in tradition as the "father of history, *patmahayr,*" and elaborate legends about his life, his other writings, and his association with Mashtots's other pupils gained credence after the year 1000.

The prime significance of Movses's *History of Armenia* is that as a literary composition, it was the most complex and sophisticated yet produced, and of all such works it had the greatest influence on later generations. Movses Khorenatsi is the first Armenian historian to discuss in detail the purpose and methods of historical writing. In elaborate rhetorical terms Agathangelos had referred to the great story he was about to tell; and Eghishe had spoken about the moral duty of a historian. But Movses is clear and dispassionate. For him the writing of history is not the exposition of divine providence or the preaching of right conduct. Rather, its basic purpose is to bequeath to posterity a reliable record of the deeds of great men—not only heroic and martial exploits, but also notable acts of good governance and accomplishments of learning and piety. There is no place for obscure men or unseemly deeds. Not that Movses refrains from describing moral turpitude when that is relevant, but such behavior is not the model that historians should hand down. The historian has other responsibilities: veracity, reliability, and chronological accuracy. These are assured when the historian compares his sources with each other, takes into consideration the oral tales passed down by the bards, and rationalizes tales that have a symbolic rather than literal meaning.

These explicit considerations point to several important features of Movses's social world. In the first place, his patrons belonged to the great noble house of the Bagratid dynasty, whose landed interests dominated the economic and political life of the time. The great deeds referred to by Movses are those that bring credit to members of such an aristocracy, martial valor and wise acts being the most prominent. Then the importance of such noble houses is enhanced by a glorious ancestry. Hence Movses's emphasis on genealogies, for the virtues of the fathers shed luster on their sons. In the second place, Movses has borrowed from the rhetoricians of classical antiquity for his themes of reliability, conciseness, and chronology. This is one aspect of Movses's use and adaptation of a wide range of Greek sources, secular and ecclesiastical, to Armenian material.

Furthermore, Movses refers to rationalizing or interpreting the old oral culture of Armenia; he thus recognizes its importance and its popular hold. But as a writer in Christian times, he cannot accept it. Living earlier, Pavstos had railed against pagan customs. Movses can afford a calmer attitude because paganism was no longer a positive threat. He deliberately quotes several snatches from oral tales still sung in remoter parts, and refers to Iranian fables that his readers would have recognized. So he gives us a glimpse of the bard of traditional Armenian society, but his Christian orientation prevents him from re-creating that vital aspect of past times.

The scope of Movses's *History* is greater than that of his predecessors in another more obvious way. Using the *Chronicle* of Eusebius as a pattern, he starts with the beginning of the world as described in the book of Genesis. Since all mankind descends from Noah, Movses elaborately sets forth the genealogies of Ham, Sem, and Japheth. Traditions in Greek literature already existed concerning the origin of the various nations. The Armenians supposedly descended from Japheth through Torgom. The Armenians themselves had a heroic ancestor Hayk—in whom they saw their own name for themselves, *Hayk,* the plural of *Hay.* This eponymous ancestor had settled in Armenia at the time of the giants. Movses makes Hayk the son of Torgom, and so Hayk's descendants can be set out in a column parallel to the lines from Sem to Abraham, and from Ham to the Assyrian monarchs. In accordance with his passion for chronology, Movses can now expound in order the legendary antiquity of Armenia, its attested role between Parthia and the Greco-Roman world after Alexander the Great, and the more recent history of Christian Armenia. These form the main themes of the three books of Movses's *History.*

It was a grand conception. Not surprisingly, it formed the basis of all later Armenian writing on the ancient past. And if there were divergences between Movses and other early Armenian historians, these were later glossed over. The authority of Movses Khorenatsi was not impugned until modern times.

This is not the place to describe in detail the contents of Movses's *History* or to identify his many sources. But one of the foreign sources had a special influence on his basic design, in addition to Eusebius; that was Josephus. The *Jewish Wars* had provided Movses with much information about the Roman-Parthian wars in which Armenia had played a significant role. But Movses often calls himself an "antiquarian." It was thus Josephus's *Antiquities of the Jews* that provided the underlying model. Josephus had expounded the glorious traditions of a nation whose significance could not be measured by its small numbers. Likewise Movses explains his purpose: "Although we are a small country and very restricted in number, weak in power and often subject to another's rule, yet many manly deeds have been performed in our land worthy of being recorded in writing" (book 1, ch. 3).

If the works of these Armenian historians have been described at length, it is because they are important for two main reasons. In the first place, they are our prime source for the history of early Armenia. Foreign sources refer to the politics of that country when, in times of war or international crisis, Armenian affairs impinged on other nations. But for the internal social, political, religious, and intellectual life of the country, we have little information save from Armenian sources.

These histories also tell us a good deal about their authors—not personal details of their lives, but rather the general outlook and preconceptions of their class. We must remember that Armenian writers belonged to a small group, the educated clergy and a very few laymen with comparable backgrounds, whose interests were often at variance with the culture of their patrons and whose Christian philosophy was opposed to the lingering pre-Christian traditions of the mass of the people. Steeped in Greek and Syriac learning, they brought their own interpretations to bear on the history of their land. And if pagan or Iranian motifs appear in the earliest texts, their significance was often unknown to later generations. Indeed, not until our own times have the complexity of early Armenian culture and the persistence of traditions with deep roots in Armenia's Iranian background been fully brought to light.

Rhetoric and Philosophy

The conscious activity of early Armenian writers and scholars was devoted to the assimilation of Christian and classical learning and their adaptation to specifically Armenian needs. It should be remembered that Armenians knew of classical culture through the schools and universities of the fourth and fifth centuries A.D. They did not translate into Armenian many of the old literary classics such as Homer, the Greek tragedians and poets, Herodotus, Thucydides, or the orators—though they were interested in the philosophers Plato and Aristotle and their later commentators. It was rather the works of later antiquity that Armenians read and studied, works that drew on a thousand-year tradition but were themselves often somewhat unoriginal schoolbooks. To this category belongs, for example, the standard text on grammar, Dionysius Thrax's *Ars Grammatica.* This was not merely translated; the terminology and examples were adapted to fit the characteristics of the Armenian language. The study of grammar remained of importance in Armenian scholarship; commentaries on Dionysius were written in later centuries, and there was a spate of original works in the thirteenth and fourteenth centuries.

Greek works on rhetoric were also influential in Armenia. Theon's manual, the *Progymnasmata,* was translated; while the influence of

Aphthonius is discernable in the earliest original Armenian composition of this kind, the *Girk Pitoyits,* Book of Chreiai, a technical term for maxims. This was falsely ascribed to Movses Khorenatsi, no doubt because of the latter's reputation for learning as a *kertogh,* grammarian, or poet. The great interest of this long treatise, of uncertain date, is that Christian examples are introduced alongside the examples from pagan mythology that were standard in the Greek models.

Grammar and rhetoric led to the study of logic. Here the translations of commentaries on Aristotle's *Categories* and *Analytics* formed a basis for later original Armenian commentaries. Porphyry's *Eisagoge,* Introduction [to Philosophy], was translated. But more significant for the development of a native Armenian philosophical tradition was the *Prolegomena,* Introduction, by David, a pupil of Olympiodorus's in Alexandria in the sixth century. This work, known in Armenian as *Definitions and Divisions of Philosophy,* was a basic textbook, an introduction to more elaborate commentaries on individual books of Aristotle or Plato. It set out the basic purposes of philosophical inquiry and expressed in succinct form the views of earlier thinkers. This type of work was also influential in the transmission of Greek learning to the Muslims.

The Armenian version of David's *Definitions* is interesting in that passages were adapted for an Armenian readership; it is also important in that it remained a standard textbook for Armenians as late as the seventeenth century, and because many commentaries were written on it. But most significant of all, the nebulous figure of David was developed into a member of the Armenian establishment; he became an actual pupil of Mashtots. There is nothing at all implausible in an Armenian studying and teaching in Alexandria. Many Armenians played important roles in the Greco-Roman world, as they later did in the Byzantine world, and some became professors of philosophy—Prohaeresius in Athens, for example, in the fourth century. What is to be rejected is not the possibility of David being of Armenian extraction, but his being a member of the circle of students around Sahak and Mashtots. This tradition, first attested only after A.D. 1000, was part of an effort to push many influential Armenian writers and scholars back in time to the "golden age." Elaborate tales were invented describing the careers of David, now called the "Invincible" philosopher, Movses Khorenatsi, Eghishe, and others less well known. By an understandable, if unhistorical, enthusiasm—and in recognition of their significance as founders of a specifically Armenian culture—these men came to be regarded as disciples of Mashtots in the flesh, rather than as formative figures of later generations who brought his work to full fruition.

There is one feature of these translations of technical works that deserves further attention. They are written in a style quite different from the elegant lucidity of earlier translations. They evince a striving for literalness at the expense of normal Armenian usage. The word order of the originals is strictly observed, and a new technical vocabulary developed. The remarkable feature of this vocabulary is that Greek terms were broken into their respective parts, the parts translated, and these then reassembled to make new Armenian words. They were direct "calques." The style, since it is patterned on Greek, is known as Hellenizing, and texts written in that style are ascribed to the Hellenizing, or Hellenistic, school. But the term "school" does not mean that they were produced in one place or by followers of a particular master.

The reasons for the development of such a literal style of translation are not clear. A similar, though not identical, tendency can also be seen in Syriac translations from Greek, which also became more literal with the passage of time. The main consideration seems to have been the desire for strict accuracy in the rendering of technical terms, both those of secular learning and of theology. Armenians soon became embroiled in the great controversies of the Christian world and had to defend their viewpoint when attacked, especially after their rejection of the definitions of the Council of Chalcedon. (This met in 451, but the Armenian split from communion with the Greek imperial church was not complete until over a century later.) But why the search for exact renderings of technical terms led to such slavish copying of Greek syntax is obscure. These translations are often classified according to the degree of literalness they exhibit. But the Hellenizing tendency did not follow a strict chronological development. Therefore the most literal are not necessarily the latest, or vice versa.

Technical Subjects:
Anania of Shirak (Anania Shirakatsi)

The question of Armenians studying abroad, and the development of secular studies such as grammar and logic, bring us to a unique figure in early Armenian scholarship and to an unusual document. Anania of Shirak, who lived in the seventh century, is the first Armenian to have devoted his attention primarily to mathematics and scientific subjects.

His books on mathematics were used as Armenian textbooks, while his ability in astronomy led to his being asked by Catholicos Anastas (662-667) to establish a fixed calendar. This was not in the end adopted; the old Armenian year moved back one day for every four years of the Julian calendar. Anania also wrote a *Chronicle*—the first of an increasingly popular genre in which significant events were listed in order under the year of their occurrence—and composed some theological works. These last are primarily concerned with Christian festivals, reflecting his interest in dates and the calendar, which in turn hinged on astronomy. Anania was a rarity in early Armenia, a lay scholar. But the great works of patristic writers were as familiar to him as to the clerical authors of his time. The *Hexaemeron* by Basil of Caesarea, for example, was a significant source for his work *On Clouds.*

In recent times, however, Anania has attracted attention because he left a few pages of autobiography (Anania Širakac'i, 1964). This is a rare personal statement, even if somewhat self-congratulatory like Ghazar's *Letter.* According to the *Autobiography,* Anania could find no teacher of mathematics in Armenia, so he made his way toward Constantinople. But he heard of a teacher in Trebizond, Tychikos, with whom he then studied for eight years before returning to Armenia. Anania complains of the lack of interest in mathematics shown by his compatriots. His own travels are unusual only in that the object of his search was a teacher of scientific subjects. Armenians in the past had gone as far as the Byzantine capital in search of theological texts; and that pattern was to be followed in future centuries.

Even more interesting are the details given by Anania concerning the career of Tychikos. The latter had been born in Trebizond and had served in the Roman army in Armenia, where he had learned Armenian. On leaving the army he had traveled for study to Alexandria, Rome, and Constantinople. This "grand tour" has parallels in the claim of Movses Khorenatsi to have studied in Alexandria, Rome, Athens, and Constantinople; and later historians credit the eighth century Stephen of Siunik with visits to Rome and Athens as well as Constantinople. That Armenians, who traveled all over the eastern Mediterranean, may have visited Italy is not unlikely. But there was no clearly demonstrable direct influence of Latin traditions on early Armenian literary culture.

Anania cannot be left without reference to another text, unique in early Armenian literature, which some modern scholars have attributed to him. This is the *Ashkharhatsuyts,* Geography (Ananias of Širak, 1992), which earlier Armenian tradition ascribed to Movses Khorenatsi but is now often ascribed to Anania. No other geographical treatise in Armenian is known before the thirteenth century. The author of this work based himself on earlier Greek sources, notably Pappus of Alexandria, whose original Geography has been lost. But to that general framework he added a very detailed description of Armenia, the Caucasus, and Iran, not found in Greek sources but based on contemporary information. Its importance as a historical document of the early seventh century is immense. But from the point of view of literary culture, it has a different kind of significance. The emphasis in this Geography is given to the political divisions of Armenia, the provinces and their subdivisions, rather than to the geology or natural geographical features of the land and its flora and fauna. It is a product of a social milieu based on landholding and bears witness to the interests of the great noble houses to which the historians had given expression in different terms.

Homilies

Not all Armenian writers were concerned with the grand themes of history or the scholarly activity that developed from the secular interests of late antiquity. The Christian message had taken root in Armenia long since; the church had developed its hierarchical organization and ritual practices. But the mass of the people were never so securely converted that vigilance could be suspended, while the development of an individual Armenian Church had brought conflict with other branches of Christendom.

Internally there had always been dissidents. Koriun refers to Borborites, Eznik to Marcionites. Later on the Paulicians and Tondrakians attracted the ire of ecclesiastical leaders. So it is hardly surprising that the genre of homilies is well represented in Armenian literature. Several collections are extant, the earliest anachronistically attributed to St. Gregory the Illuminator. This collection, the *Hachakhapatum,* deals with the nature of the Christian faith in its practical application: the requirements of a holy life, the consequence of sin, the importance of repentance. Although there is some discussion of dogmatic matters—the Trinity and the Incarnation—the *Hachakhapatum* is not a systematic treatise in any way comparable to the *Teaching of Saint Gregory* in the *History* of Agathangelos.

To Catholicos Hovhannes Mandakuni (John Mandakuni) are attributed thirty homilies dealing with repentance, prayer, and sin. These are more elaborate than the *Hachakhaptatum.* They stress the contrast between rich and poor, and the iniquity of usury. Their author refers particularly to sins such as envy, revenge, or drunkenness, to sexual perversions, magical practices, and excessive mourning for the dead. This last is a common theme in Armenian writers from Pavstos on, echoed in numerous conciliar decisions; it was a feature of pagan practice that lingered long. But although these homilies by Mandakuni (or by the later John Mayragometsi, according to some critics) deal with concrete situations, they also contain many themes that had become literary *topoi.* The warnings against Jews and Gentiles, the evils of usury, the moral dangers of theatrical performances, known in earlier pagan Armenia but not attested in Christian times, are themes introduced into Armenian written texts from patristic homilies rather than the spontaneous expression of dangers to fifth-century Armenian congregations. Important as such texts are as evidence for social conditions, traditional themes tended to be repeated beyond the times to which they were originally applicable.

These and similar works were designed for internal consumption, in the sense of strengthening Christian life among Armenians. Also aimed at Armenians were the attacks on Paulicians and other groups who rejected the authority of the established order. The most elaborate of these were composed in the eighth century by Catholicos John of Odzun. Earlier refutations of heretics are numerous, but they generally associate errors inside Armenia with heretics abroad. Such documents attest to the need of Armenian clerics to expound the Armenian doctrinal position and to defend it against Greek or Syrian church authorities.

Theological and Polemical Writings

The development of theological controversies in the church at large is not our concern; and the evolution of an autonomous Armenian Church, which no longer accepted communion with the Greek imperial church of Byzantium or the officially recognized church in Sasanian Iran, is treated elsewhere. Here we should merely draw attention to the offshoot of those events in so far as they called forth new genres of literary activity.

The many letters preserved in historians or in the collection known as the *Book of Letters* (an official compilation of documents from the fifth to the twelfth centuries) give a vivid picture of the debates between Armenians, Greeks, Syrians, and Georgians (Tallon, 1955). But they hardly qualify as "literature." The first treatise devoted to a technical dogmatic question is the work attributed to Catholicos John Mandakuni entitled: "Demonstration that one must say that the Lord is One Nature from two natures" (Tallon, 1955). Unlike many later works that hammer away at the errors of the Council of Chalcedon and the "heretical" views there expounded, this treatise does not identify John's opponents by name or attack them with opprobrious epithets. From a scholarly point of view, it is important as the first example of the adaptation of vocabulary associated with the Hellenizing school of translators to an original work.

In the area of theological dispute, translations continued to serve as models for Armenian writers. Of particular interest is the *Refutation of the Council of Chalcedon* by Timothy Aelurus, patriarch of Alexandria from 457 to 477. The Greek original is lost; so, as with works of numerous other patristic authors or by Philo, the Armenian version is a valuable historical source. Furthermore, the format of this work was influential in the development of a genre of writing with a long history in Armenia. Timothy had set out his arguments as a series of refutations, in which each section is primarily composed of extracts from earlier theologians. It is a "florilegium," a collection of "proof texts" from writers whose authority was respected by all sides. This *Refutation* was probably translated in connection with the second council of Dvin in 555, after which the break with the Greek church became irrevocable. It became an important weapon in the Armenian theological arsenal, frequently quoted in later centuries.

In the early seventh century the first original Armenian compilation of this kind was put together—the *Seal of Faith,* traditionally ascribed to the catholicos Komitas (615-628), but in its present form perhaps of a somewhat later date. It contained passages from Armenian, Greek, and Syrian authors that bolstered the Armenian doctrinal position. In later centuries other similar collections were compiled dealing with various matters of dispute; and in the historians long defenses of the Armenian position became common. Whether in the format of a speech or letter, their basic form was a connected string of quotations from acceptable authorities.

Less polemical in intent were commentaries on the Bible. From the earliest period commentaries by the great theologians, such as John Chrysostom, Cyril of Alexandria, Gregory of Nyssa, and Ephrem the Syrian, had circulated in Armenian versions. From such works, and many others, Armenians made commentaries in the form of extracts from different authors on the same verses of the biblical books. Original

Armenian commentaries begin with Stephen of Siunik in the early eighth century.

The predominant influence of ecclesiastical concerns on early Armenian writing and scholarship is clearly evident at that period. In 701 Salomon, then steward and later abbot of the monastery of Makenots in Siunik, composed the first calendar of feasts for martyrs *(tonakan)*. A much more grandiose compilation was that of Armenian canon law made by Catholicos John of Odzun (717-728). It included translations from Greek of the canons of early councils of the church and the original texts of Armenian councils and of collections attributed to individual prelates. It was another four hundred years before the secular laws of Armenia were codified and set in writing.

John of Odzun was one of the great administrative patriarchs. His attacks on Paulicians were noted earlier. He was also responsible for summoning two important councils. One at Dvin in 717 was directed primarily at internal problems. A second at Manazkert in 726 was aimed at a reconciliation of differences between the Armenian and Syrian churches. Representatives from the Syrian Jacobite Church attended, and agreement was reached in a decision to establish a joint monastery on the border between the two lands where both languages would be taught and translations made. But this agreement broke down, and harmony between the two churches was never fully established. An important consideration in this regard was the divergence of ritual practices between the two groups. Although surviving documents emphasize doctrinal differences between the various branches of eastern Christendom, occasional telling remarks point to the significance of divergent ritual as the visible symbol of incompatibility.

Noteworthy in this regard is a short document of the early eighth century that describes the process whereby the Armenian Church became independent of the Greek Church, the so-called *Narratio de Rebus Armeniae,* which has survived in a Greek translation but not in the original Armenian. The text is significant in that it was written from the pro-Chalcedonian point of view—an indication that not all Armenians supported the doctrinal position of the Armenian patriarchs. The *Narratio* describes the schisms caused in Armenia when at different times the Byzantine government was able to impose a forced union; some Armenians would accept, others would reject it. In 591 Catholicos Movses II (574-604) refused to cross the border between Iranian and Byzantine territory when summoned to Constantinople. According to the *Narratio,* he declared: "I shall not cross the Azat; I shall not eat oven-baked bread; I shall not drink hot water." The Azat was the river marking the border, but its meaning in Armenian ("free") is here used as a pun. Baked and leavened bread and the mixing of warm water with the wine were characteristics of Greek usage in the liturgy to which Armenians objected.

The codification of canon law, the compilation of liturgical books of ritual, and the writing of texts like the *Narratio* (and, according to some critics, the composition of the *History* of Movses Khorenatsi) indicate that in the eighth century Armenians were conscious of a long and specifically Armenian tradition behind them. The break with the Greek imperial church was over a century old, and the Armenian Church had now developed as a distinctly separate branch of Christendom with its own literary and religious traditions. On the other hand, the Armenians were not cutting themselves off from what they had always regarded as the prime source of learning—Constantinople. In the second decade of the eighth century Stephen, later bishop of the province of Siunik, spent several years in the capital translating works not yet available in Armenian. The most important of his translations was that of the corpus of writings ascribed to Dionysius the Areopagite. These mystical works, with a strong Neoplatonic tint, had had a profound impact on Christian thought in the East and were to have an even greater influence on the Latin West. In Armenia Stephen's rendering had a wide circulation, and commentaries were written on the corpus, beginning in the tenth century.

Historians: Seventh to Tenth Centuries

Important as such works of theology or philosophy were for Armenian scholarship, they do not reflect the broader concerns of political and social life that dominate the histories. The writing of history was the field of literary activity—at least in prose—in which the Armenians particularly excelled. And although later writers did not attain the classic status of a Eghishe or a Movses Khorenatsi, their works are significant not merely as sources for the events they describe, but as expressions of a specifically Armenian cultural ethos.

The last century of Sasanian Persian rule and the beginning of the Muslim era are described by the historian known as Sebeos. As with some other Armenian writings, notably Eznik's treatise discussed earlier, the surviving text has no heading and was identified by modern authors. So the correctness of the ascription of this history to the author mentioned in later sources as "Sebeos" has been challenged. This problem, however, is not very significant from our present point of view. The book, mistakenly called the *History of Heraclius,* is a late seventh century work of particular importance as the main source for Armenia in a period of transition. Its author paints a vivid picture of the lot of the Armenians caught between Byzantium and Iran in the long wars that preceded the defeat of the Sasanian dynasty by the emperor Heraclius and its final collapse before the Muslims. The Armenian situation is well caught in a letter supposedly sent by the emperor Maurice to Shah Khosrov, in which he suggests that they act in concert to rid themselves of the troublesome Armenians who lay between them.

Sebeos is the first writer to draw attention to another problem that in future centuries would loom ever larger: the fate of colonies of Armenians outside the homeland. The emperor Maurice had deliberately moved Armenian soldiers, with their families, away from Armenia to other regions of the empire. In part it was an attempt to weaken resistance to Byzantine control over western Armenia, in part an attempt to buttress the empire's defenses with proven troops. To the east a similar policy had been long standing. Armenians had always been obliged to provide military service in the campaigns of the shahs; this is clearly described by Eghishe and Ghazar. Usually the soldiers had returned home after their spell of duty. But Sebeos describes a colony of Armenians in Hyrcania, to the southeast of the Caspian Sea, who had been so long guarding that distant border that they had forgotten their language and were deprived of the services of a priest. The Armenian noble Smbat Bagratuni was then serving the shah as governor of that region. He remedied the situation by having a priest sent, who would not only strengthen their religious faith but also teach the soldiers their native tongue. One of Sebeos's themes was the unsuccessful efforts of Byzantine emperors to impose forced union on the Armenian Church. The role of that church and of the native tongue as instruments of national individuality thus comes out very clearly in this episode.

Sebeos was describing a time of difficulty. The even more oppressive days of Muslim domination are depicted by Ghevond (Levond) at the end of the eighth century. Important as his work is for military and political events, it is narrower in scope than that of Sebeos and cannot be counted as one of the major literary achievements of Armenian historiography. By the late ninth century the immediate danger of physical annihilation had passed. For 150 years, until the final collapse of Armenia and the ensuing Turkish domination of eastern Anatolia, there was renewed prosperity; and the development of economic life brought many visible changes—notably the growth of cities. Yet these economic changes did not greatly alter the structure of Armenian society. Two works written at the beginning of the tenth century are typical of Armenian historiography and informative about social concerns: the *History* of Catholicos Hovhannes Draskhanakerttsi (John of Draskhanakert) describes the growth of Bagratid power in northern Armenia, which was always economically more significant than the south; while Tovma (Thomas) Artsruni traces the fortunes of the Artsruni house in the area of Lake Van.

Following the tradition set by Movses Khorenatsi, John begins his *History* with a recapitulation of Armenian history from its origins, integrating Armenian tradition into the biblical account of Noah's descendants. As he comes closer to his own time, his narrative becomes more detailed. Movses had ended in the fifth century, so John used Sebeos for the ensuing two hundred years. In the more recent period the now-lost *History* by Shapuh Bagratuni served as the major source for the rise of the Bagratid family. But the main part of John's work is devoted to the thirty years (890-920) of which he had personal knowledge. As Catholicos of Armenia, John naturally played a prominent role in the politics of his time. His *History* is thus unique as a personal document, for no other Armenian historian was so involved in national and international affairs. The reader gains a rare glimpse of an Armenian who had firsthand experience of the problems he describes. Not the least of these problems was the pacification of the endemic rivalry and feuding of the noble families. The social instability—in the sense of turbulence among the barons, not revolutionary dangers from below—that so marks the pages of Pavstos Buzand was still the main disruptive force in Armenian life.

The ebb and flow of personal and dynastic rivalry comes out equally clearly in the *History of the Artsruni House* by Thomas, written at the beginning of the tenth century. This work is perhaps best known for the elaborate description of Gagik's palace and church on the island of Aghtamar. But that section forms part of a later addition; Thomas's own *History* ends before Gagik became king. Like John, Thomas begins his story with the origins of the Armenian nation, but he places his emphasis on the role of the Artsruni house. They were of old stock, claiming descent from the sons of the Assyrian king Sennacherib: as is related in II Kings, chapter 19, his sons killed their father and escaped to the land of Armenia. By the end of the ninth century the Artsrunis had attained a prominence second only to that of the Bagratid dynasty. Thomas's *History* is an elaborate attempt to rewrite the past, as known primarily from Movses Khorenatsi, Eghishe, and Sebeos, in order to show that his patron's ancestors had enjoyed as glorious an antiquity as their rivals. The details are not as important as the general attitude: the emphasis on genealogy, on the great deeds of the past—real or imagined—as giving justification for present claims, on heroic exploits in war and valiant resistance, even to martyrdom for the faith. Such were the virtues of the noble class whose interests Thomas and other Armenian historians defended.

Over half of Thomas's *History* deals with the events of fifty years: from the murderous invasion of the caliph's general Bugha, which began in 851, to the lifting of direct Muslim control, the establishment of a Bagratid kingdom in the north, and the prosperity of Artsruni lands under Gagik. This part is interesting on several counts. It is our main source, even if tendentious, for events in southern Armenia, written by a contemporary. As an interpretation of Muslim domination, it reflects the influence of Eghishe; Thomas depicts the caliphs and their minions in terms deliberately evocative of Eghishe's description of Shah Yazdagerd II and his attempt to crush Armenian liberties. And by extensive use of letters and speeches, Thomas portrays in vivid fashion the underlying social attitudes of the Armenian nobility. Eghishe's speeches had dealt with themes of perennial significance: cultural survival, the role of the church, the preservation of traditional values. Thomas's speeches deal with more specific issues: a noble's social responsibilities in caring for his land and punishing rebels, the ways of attaining that goal—largesse and liberal entertainments—the delights of hunting, and all the trappings of a nobleman's life in the country. Thomas's *History* did not have the relevance for later generations enjoyed by Eghishe's *Vardan and the Armenian War*. Yet as a social document it gives us a clearer insight into the personal concerns of the nobility of the time.

Thomas's *History* had little influence on later writers because the Bagratid house dominated the political scene, and it was their spokesman, Movses Khorenatsi, who fixed the standard version of early Armenian history. Thomas's rewriting of Armenian origins did not gain acceptance, while his picture of ninth-century Vaspurakan was too provincial to attract much attention. It is perhaps no accident that the only surviving complete text of the *History of the Artsruni House* was copied on the island of Aghtamar (in 1309). On the other hand, in more popular, less formal writings the exploits of the Artsruni heroes lived on. Reference was made earlier to the lost *History* by Shapuh Bagratuni. Ironically, a text discovered and published, wrongly, under his name in the twentieth century deals not with the Bagratid dynasty but with the Artsruni princes who appear in the pages of Thomas. The more recent editor of the full text wisely removed the ascription of this curious medley of popular tales from "Pseudo-Shapuh" to an "Anonymous Storyteller" (Thomson, 1988-1989).

Several other historical works deal with regions peripheral to the centers of political and economic life. West of Lake Van is the province of Taron, where St. Gregory the Illuminator had established the first church in Ashtishat. This province produced several historians, some with dubious credentials. Zenob, supposedly a Syrian and colleague of St. Gregory, describes the activities of the Illuminator and King Trdat; John, bishop of the Mamikonian, chronicles the exploits of nobles of that family at the turn of the sixth and seventh centuries. Both works are later compositions, of the tenth or eleventh century, designed to bring greater prestige to the area of Taron. (The most important historian from Taron, Stephen, known as "Asoghik," will be discussed later.)

On the opposite side of Armenia, across the Kura River, lay the country of Caucasian Albania. The Aghvank were not Armenian and spoke their own Caucasian tongue. Koriun claims that Mashtots invented a script for them; and indeed an alphabet and a few inscriptions have been discovered. But for literary purposes the Aghvank wrote in Armenian. Their history was set down by Movses Daskhurantsi (Moses of Daskhuran), of whose life nothing is known. His *History of the Aghvank* was probably composed in the second half of the tenth century, though there are a few later additions. This too is a tendentious work; it attempts to prove the independence and antiquity of the local Albanian Church. But it has great significance as a rare witness in Armenian to the history of a non-Armenian people. Although Armenians on occasion wrote about foreign nations, such as the Mongols, and adapted the chronicles of the Syrian patriarch Michael and of the Georgians, only the Aghvank adopted Armenian as their vehicle of literary expression.

The focus on ecclesiastical affairs, so important to Movses Daskhurantsi, is apparent in many Armenian authors—which is hardly surprising, given the predominant role of the church from the beginnings of Armenian literacy. So questions of doctrine, of governance, of opposition to heretics, all find their place in works generally regarded as "historical." Resistance to Greek attempts at enforced union figures prominently in the seventh and eighth centuries. But Armenians were not monolithic in their support of the national church. There were many who supported the doctrinal position of the imperial church of Byzantium and accepted the Council of Chalcedon. In such circles the Armenian original of the *Narratio* was composed; and against such "heretics" the later historian Ukhtanes inveighed.

Of Ukhtanes little is known. He was probably bishop of Sebaste at the end of the tenth century—a time when Armenian colonies were expanding westward beyond the Euphrates. His work has three sections: a summary of Armenian history down to Trdat, a description of the Armeno-Georgian schism at the beginning of the seventh century, and a section, now lost, on the Armenian Chalcedonians. The great interest of the middle section is that many of the documents used by Ukhtanes are also preserved in a separate collection, the *Book of Letters* mentioned earlier. Ukhtanes's *History* does not rank high as a literary composition, but it is a salutary reminder that Armenians were not unanimous in supporting their national church.

Religious Poetry: Gregory of Narek

The emphasis placed thus far on the role of the clergy—on bishops who played their part in worldly affairs, or scholarly monks writing in their monasteries, translating and commenting on learned treatises—should not obscure another aspect of literary activity. Armenia has produced many fine poets. At first such talents found their expression in religious hymns and prayers. By medieval times secular themes are introduced, though seemingly profane verse may disguise a mystical fervor in which the beloved is not of this world. Here we should turn to the greatest religious poet in Armenian history, the best loved of all Armenian literary figures in later ages, Grigor Narekatsi (Gregory of Narek).

Gregory was born in the middle of the tenth century and died probably in 1010. He spent all his life from childhood in the monastery of Narek, by the southern shore of Lake Van. Narek was an important center of learning, and Gregory's father, Khosrov, had been noted for his knowledge of Greek. An edifying story in the *Haysmavurk* (the *Synaxarion,* or collection of saints' lives arranged by days of the liturgical year) indicates that Gregory too was suspected of being a *tzayt,* a pro-Greek Chalcedonian. Messengers came to summon him to a tribunal where the charge was to be examined. Before setting out Gregory offered them a meal: roast pigeons. But it was a Friday, and the messengers were scandalized. Gregory excused his ignorance and said to the pigeons: "Fly away to your fellows because today is a fast-day." The roast pigeons came back to life and flew away. Thus were his critics silenced.

Gregory's reputation, however, depends on the more solid basis of a large number of hymns for feast days, panegyrics on holy figures, and most especially a collection of mystical prayers known as the *Book of Lamentations*. So famous did this become that it is commonly known simply as "Narek." The *Book of Lamentations* contains ninety-five poems, each of which is entitled "Conversation with God from the depths of the heart." These prayers deal with separation and reunion with God, dwelling in particular on the mystic's anguish at the separation caused by sin and his yearning for union. The language is often obscure, but vivid and innovative. Not least interesting is Gregory's use of rhythmical rhyming cadences, reminiscent of Arabic prosody, the *sadj*. The influence of Arabic, especially in southern Armenia in the tenth century or later, is hardly surprising given the political and economic ties between Armenia and the Muslim world. The large number of Arabic names in use among the Armenian nobility is but a small token of the social impact of Islam.

The Eleventh Century

Gregory of Narek, at the end of his *Book of Lamentations,* celebrated the advance of the "victorious and great emperor of the Romans, Basil," into northwestern Armenia in A.D. 1000. This eastward expansion of the Byzantine Empire had begun in the previous century. By 1045 Armenia had been incorporated into the empire, only to lose to the Seljuks within another generation what security had been temporarily gained. The demise of the independent Bagratid and Artsruni kingdoms and the establishment of large Armenian colonies to the west of the Euphrates River brought Armenians into much closer contact with Greek ecclesiastical and administrative authorities than had been the case for several hundred years. But Armenian solidarity was not totally compromised. The establishment of Armenian bishoprics outside the old homeland at the end of the tenth century, and the exile of the patriarch to Cappadocia after 1045, gave a focus for national feeling that survived until the

development of a new, smaller Armenian state in Cilicia at the time of
the Crusades.

Gregory (Grigor) Magistros

Armenian authors of the eleventh century are surprisingly ambiguous
in their attitude to these momentous changes. For some it was an
opportunity to imbibe more deeply of the Greek learning that for a
thousand years had attracted Armenians. Gregory Pahlavuni, known as
Magistros from his title in the Byzantine administration, illustrates the
most extreme limit of philhellenism; his son Vahram, who took the name
of Gregory as catholicos and earned the nickname of *Vkayaser*, "lover
of martyrs," was more typical in that his attention was devoted to
Christian rather than pagan learning. But others, notably the historian
Aristakes of Lastivert (Aristakes Lastiverttsi), were full of pessimism
and lamentation. It was the Armenians' sinfulness, supposed Aristakes,
that had brought such misfortunes upon their heads. The later Matthew
of Edessa stresses the terror and sense of helplessness that the sudden
appearance of the Turks caused in Armenia.

Over the centuries many Armenians had taken service in the
Byzantine government or army. Many had risen to positions of emi-
nence, and some had attained the imperial throne after a generation or
two of acculturation. Such Armenians were integrated into the ethnically
diverse population of the empire; they accepted the authority of the
Greek Church, and were more or less lost to Armenia in the sense that
their future careers had little direct influence on the cultural life of their
native land. Gregory Magistros is thus unusual; although he was a
familiar figure in Constantinople and served as duke of southwestern
Armenia for the imperial government after 1048, his literary activity was
pursued in Armenian. His interests were wide: He translated works of
Plato and Euclid, wrote a commentary on the *Grammar* of Dionysius
Thrax (which had been translated in the Hellenizing style, as noted
earlier), wrote poetry, and composed a series of letters on scholarly and
administrative matters. These last are quite unique in Armenian, being
not only personal letters, as opposed to official documents such as those
preserved in the *Book of Letters,* but also original in style. Gregory was
deeply imbued with the contemporary Greek enthusiasm for classical
learning. His letters abound in recondite allusions to the literature of
pagan antiquity; and their tortuous language, rich in neologisms, reflects
the rhetorical obscurity of Byzantine style. Important as they are as a

historical source, written by a man who played a major role in the politics and scholarship of his day, they are so daunting that no modern translator has yet tackled the whole collection.

Gregory's activity was not confined to scholarship of a recondite kind. He was noted for poems on religious topics, of which the most famous is a work of 1,000 lines summarizing the contents of the Bible for the benefit of a Muslim. During his period of service for the Byzantine Empire, he energetically opposed the Tondrakian sect in Armenia. Yet Gregory Magistros's literary work lies outside the mainstream of Armenian cultural activity. Later generations did not follow his enthusiasm for Byzantine patterns. Nonetheless, he remains a remarkable figure who illustrates, albeit in a rather extreme fashion, one of the courses open to Armenians at a time of political and cultural change.

Gregory Vkayaser

Gregory Magistros's son, Vahram, was more typical of Armenian scholarship in that he devoted himself to theological concerns. For forty years (from 1065 until his death in 1105) he held the patriarchal throne as Grigor (Gregory) II. But he did not inherit his father's administrative interests. Leaving all official duties to others, he directed his energy to seeking out and having translated hagiographical texts not yet available in Armenian. In that search he traveled widely in the Near East, from Constantinople to Egypt and Jerusalem.

Those forty years were a period of transformation in Armenian life: A new home was being forged in Cilicia, and contact with the Crusaders introduced the Armenians directly to the culture of Western Christendom. Grigor Vkayaser's activity draws attention to the scattering of Armenian communities, already well under way before his time. His concern for Greek literature was nothing new. For more than six centuries Armenians had been ever anxious to make available in their own language religious and other texts written in Greek, despite the strained relationship between the two churches. However, this translation activity was not directed to the rendering of contemporary Byzantine authors, but rather of earlier patristic writers, the common heritage of all Christendom.

Although the eleventh century marks a turning point in Armenia's political fortunes, there was no sudden break in traditional literary activity. The mass of Armenians continued to live in Armenia; indeed, the economic prosperity of Armenian cities was probably greater after the loss of political autonomy than before. New artistic ideas were introduced in the realm of miniature painting by Armenians established in Asia Minor. But although the transformations under way in Armenian life are echoed by the historians, their works are not dramatically different from those of their predecessors. Armenian scholarship did not follow the path of Gregory Magistros. In fact, the newer trends, such as interest in medicine or the development of lyrical poetry, ambiguously religious and erotic, owe more to the influence of Arabic and Persian than to Greek.

Asoghik

The two significant historians of the eleventh century, Stepanos Asoghik (Taronetsi), nicknamed *Asoghik,* "teller" of tales, and Aristakes of Lastivert, do not evince any sharp break with earlier traditions of historiography, although their works are quite different from each other in approach. Stephen begins with a brief résumé of the early history of the world based on earlier authors: the Bible, Eusebius of Caesarea, and for Armenia, Movses Khorenatsi. He lists the various Armenian historians and repeats some of the tales that had arisen concerning obscure figures such as Movses Khorenatsi. Such traditions as those attested to by Thomas Artsruni and Stephen were not all accepted in later times. But the desire to associate great figures of the past with Mashtots himself was strong. Stephen was the first to include David the "Invincible" philosopher in that circle, and later Eghishe swelled their ranks.

The second half (Book III) of Stephen's work deals with the history of the hundred or so years before his own time. He discusses events outside Armenia as well as local history—hence the title of his book, "World History." But there is no coherent thread, for the narrative reads as a series of disconnected episodes. A new feature is his division of material into three sections. Each chapter gives first a summary of the major political events, then commentary on the religious history of the time, and finally information about literary and scholarly figures. Although this schematic approach has parallels in some later chronicles—the Syrian patriarch Michael, for example, actually divided his pages into three separate columns—it did not set a precedent for Armenian historians.

Aristakes of Lastivert

The *History* of Aristakes is quite different. It deals with only two generations, from 1000 to 1071, rather than with the entire span of the history of the world; and it is a very personal document, expressing at length the author's sentiments at the disasters that befell Armenia. So although it has greater coherence than Stephen's work as a progressive exposition, the narrative is frequently interrupted for lamentations and disquisitions on Armenian sinfulness, which brought upon them the various misfortunes. Laments were not uncommon features of Armenian historical works; but they had previously been confined to set pieces at appropriate occasions. And poetic laments *(voghb)* were a significant feature of later Armenian literature. But Aristakes's *History* is unique in its integration of narrative and lachrymose comment.

Schools and Scholarship

Although some Armenian historians were well-known persons of their time, most of the famous early authors remain vague figures. We know little or nothing about their background and upbringing, save that the great majority were churchmen or monks. Our ignorance of their formal education obscures the importance of the monastic schools. What hints about courses of study do survive, as for example in the letters of Gregory Magistros, are more pertinent to advanced learning. Nonetheless, some general characteristics of Armenian learning and scholarship, and hence of formal literary activity, do emerge from the role of the *vardapet* in Armenia.

The position of *vardapet,* "master of instruction," a celibate cleric, was a unique office in Eastern Christendom, with no exact parallel in Greek or Syrian tradition. The closest parallel for the early period is the role of the *herbads* in Zoroastrianism. These were priest-teachers whose function was to teach orally. Their role as missionaries in the greater Iranian Empire is reminiscent of the itinerant nature of the first Armenian *vardapets.* The most outstanding example of the latter is Mashtots with his circle of students.

As time went on, the need for such missionary activity in Armenia diminished. The *vardapets* became settled in monasteries, even if they moved from one to another, and they acquired a specific status in the ecclesiastical hierarchy. In the later compilations of canon law their duties are clearly spelled out. But the most important result of the development of this office was the continuing hold of the church over education and learning. There were no secular schools in early or medieval Armenia. The wealthy may have had private tutors, and in the fourth and fifth centuries a few, (again wealthy), Armenians studied in the secular schools of the Greek world. But the autobiography of Anania of Shirak makes it clear that after Armenia had become firmly Christian, there were very few laymen teaching secular subjects in Armenia. For those who progressed beyond the elementary level, the Bible and various theological texts provided the basic educational diet. Grammar and rhetoric, logic and philosophy were not neglected; here the basic texts translated in the Hellenizing style were put to good purpose. But even technical subjects were pursued with a view to their ecclesiastical use. In this regard the career of John the Deacon (Hovhannes Sorkavag or Imastaser) or Philosopher, who died in 1129, may serve as a fitting conclusion to this sketch of Armenian literary culture.

Brought up in the monastery of Haghbat in northeastern Armenia, John first devoted himself to the study of music. As he grew older he studied "at the feet of *vardapets.*" But his biographer places more emphasis on John's spiritual development and ascetic virtues than on details of the texts and authors he studied. However, these did include historical writings, commentaries, and biblical texts. He later moved to Ani, where he began to teach grammar, "the key of knowledge." Medieval Armenians regarded grammar as more than the study of a shifting language; it offered insights into eternal verities. John also pursued mathematics and became familiar with works of Aristotle and Plato. Among his works are a chronicle, poems, and theological writings. But his scholarly fame depends on his interest in astronomy. This he put to practical use by composing a perpetual calendar as well as several tables dealing with phases of the moon and similar topics. In this regard his only predecessor was Anania of Shirak; but the latter held no official position in the church.

The difference in emphasis between the scholarly activity of John the Philosopher and the concerns of his biographer raises an interesting question. To what extent did the populace at large appreciate the written classics of Armenian literature? Were they indeed even aware of the existence of most of them? John's biographer probably had a sound sense of his contemporaries' interests. His emphasis lies on John as a holy man, noted for his ascetic achievements and his ability to work miracles. These were more tangible measures of fame than scholarly treatises. He had in mind the edification of the Armenian people, the needs of the church, and the greater glory of God.

Oral Tales and the *Sasnadzrer*

But even those who could read on the simpler level, without compre-
hending the profundities of John's original works, were a minority in
Armenia. The mass of the people was illiterate. The old pagan epics had
perhaps not been suppressed entirely, but they had been driven out of
the acceptable canon. And since the medieval writers do not describe
the lives and interests of the majority of their fellow countrymen, except
to castigate reprehensible practices, we cannot know for sure what oral
tales delighted the leisure moments of humbler folk. A vast wealth of
popular stories, fables, and poems has been recorded in recent times;
much of it undoubtedly goes back many centuries. But by far the most
elaborate product of oral composition is the fourfold cycle of tales
concerning the wild heroes of Sasun, the *Sasnadzrer.*

This oral collection was not recorded in writing until the 1870s.
There are many versions in different dialects; for it was not the deliberate
composition of a single individual, but was created by the stylized
retelling of traditional tales by generations of bards. There is therefore
no "original" text to be reconstructed from the "variants." The legendary
heroes form four generations: Sanasar and Balthasar; Mher the Great;
David of Sasun, after whom the whole cycle is often named; and Little
Mher. Their successive exploits are narrated in rhythmic prose to form
four sections of a whole. The unifying theme, around which are woven
numerous extravagant adventures, is the defense of the homeland
against foreigners: the caliph of Baghdad appears at the beginning, while
David does battle with the king of Egypt. The basic situations thus reflect
the periods of Muslim domination in the eighth to ninth centuries and
again in later Mamluk times when the kingdom of Cilicia collapsed. But
there are reminiscences of earlier and later periods, while the whole is
a timeless tale of the exploits of heroes greater than ordinary mortals.

It is well to end with these oral tales—rather misleadingly often
called an "epic"—for the written literature of early and medieval Armenia reflects the ethos of only one segment of Armenian society. Prose
writing is rather formal, and belles lettres are hardly represented until
modern times. Poetry gave an opportunity for more spontaneous expression, but was mostly confined to religious themes. Yet there was a
vivacious side to Armenian life. It will not be found in learned treatises,
but it does emerge in the *Sasnadzrer,* in tales such as the "Pseudo-
Shapuh," and in miniature painting.

FOR FURTHER INFORMATION

For the sources of, or more information on, the material in this chapter, please consult the following (full citations can be found in the Bibliography at the end of this volume).

Aristakes de Lastivert, 1973.
Asoghik, 1883, 1917.
David, 1983.
Garitte, 1952.
Garsoïan, Mathews, and
    Thomson, 1982.
Ghewond, 1982.
Grégoire de Narek, 1961.
Hachakhapatum, 1927.
Hairapetian, 1995.
Hewsen, 1992.
Inglisian, 1963.

Johannes Mandakuni, 1927.
Johannis Ozniensis, 1834.
Lebon, 1929.
Movses Dasxuranc'i, 1961.
Movses Khorenats'i, 1978.
Renoux, 1993.
Shalian, 1964.
Tallon, 1955.
Thomson, 1995.
Yovhannes Drasxanakertc'i, 1987.
Yovhannes Mamikonean, 1993.

10

ARMENIA DURING THE SELJUK AND MONGOL PERIODS

Robert Bedrosian

During the eleventh to fourteenth centuries, Armenia was subjected to a number of attacks and invasions by Turco-Mongol peoples. The most important of these were the invasions of the Seljuks in the second half of the eleventh century, of the Khwarazmians (1225-1230), and of the Mongols (1223-1247). At the end of the fourteenth century, an already exhausted Armenia was devastated again by the Turco-Mongol armies of Timur-Leng. During the four centuries examined in this chapter, important changes took place in the demographic, economic, and sociopolitical history of the Armenian highlands. If at the beginning of the eleventh century Armenians constituted the majority of the population in many areas, at the end of the fourteenth century there were few areas where Armenians were still the majority. If in the twelfth to thirteenth centuries Armenia's economy and trading situation was to be envied, at the end of the fourteenth century, the Armenian highlands were so unsafe that caravan traffic practically ceased. If at the beginning of the eleventh century the *nakharar* (lordly) system prevailed across large areas of the highlands, at the end of the fourteenth century *nakharar* practices were confined to inaccessible mountain regions.

Although the invasions differed from each other in participants, severity, and consequences, they had certain similarities. Each successive wave pushed before it, brought along with it, or dragged in its wake thousands of virtually uncontrollable nomadic warriors. Their interest lay solely in plunder and in securing pasturage for their enormous herds of sheep. When totally unchecked, such nomads devastated the cities searching for loot. They destroyed the countryside and the complex irrigation systems, turning cultivated fields into pasturage; and they reduced the possibilities for internal and international trade by infesting the trade routes between cities and attacking caravans. In scholarly literature, this unrestrainable element is referred to as Turkmen, and it is contrasted with those forces among the nomads interested in the establishment of stable forms of government and a sedentary or semisedentary existence. Centralizing forces within the various Turco-Mongol states to arise in the eleventh to fourteenth centuries were obliged to support a very delicate balance. On the one hand, the warlike Turkmens were the best, most determined fighters, and therefore necessary for victorious expeditions. On the other hand, their impulse to destroy and move on had to be fought—often literally—by those wishing to maintain authority. The Turkmens were the bane not only of the sedentary Christian Armenians and Muslims of the Middle East, but also of many rulers of stable Seljuk and Mongol states. In the end, this balance proved insupportable. The Turkmens brought down each of the Turco-Mongol states their vigor had given birth to.

Armenian sources for the history of Armenia in the eleventh to fourteenth centuries include literary histories such as those by Aristakes Lastiverttsi (Aristakes of Lastivert) (d. ca. 1073), Vardan Areveltsi, Kirakos Gandzaketsi (Kirakos of Gandzak) (both d. ca. 1271), Stepanos Orbelian (d. 1304), and Tovma Metzopetsi (Thomas of Metzop) (d. 1446); chronicles by authors such as Matthew of Edessa (d. ca. 1140), Samvel Anetsi (Samuel of Ani) (d. ca. 1180), and Mkhitar of Ayrivan (d. ca. 1290); as well as inscriptions and colophons. Among important foreign sources are the thirteenth-century works of Ibn al-Athir, William of Rubruck, Juvaini, Ibn Bibi, Bar Hebraeus, and the fourteenth-century Rashid al-Din, Abu'l Fida, Qazvini, the *Georgian Chronicle*, Ibn Battuta, Johann Schiltberger, and Ruy Gonzalez de Clavijo.

Armenia on the Eve of the Seljuk Invasions

The Seljuk invasions of Armenia began in the early 1040s. For some twenty years before that date, however, Turkic bands had been raiding parts of eastern, northeastern, and southern Armenia. From 1020 to 1040 these incursions were made by Turkic elements serving in the army of the Persian Dailamites of Azerbaijan and by nomadic Turkmens themselves often displaced by the Seljuks of Iran. Driven by a desire for booty and captives, relatively small bands of Turkmens (sometimes fewer than 5,000) were able to wreak havoc on many unfortified places in Armenia. In addition to superior military effectiveness, several political and demographic factors explain the ease with which the invaders gained control of the Armenian highlands. Among these were the shortsighted policies of the Byzantine Empire toward the Armenian princes and their lands, divisions among the Armenian lords, and the demographic expansion of Turkic peoples.

From the late tenth century on the Byzantine Empire had followed a policy of removing prominent *nakharars* from their native lands, absorbing those lands in the structure of the empire, and giving the *nakharars* in exchange lands and titles elsewhere. The decision of many lords to leave was frequently the result of coercion, though throughout the tenth to eleventh centuries there were also pro-Byzantine factions within the Armenian kingdoms, supporting Byzantium's aims. Already in 968 the southwestern district of Taron was annexed. In 1000, a large area embracing Tayk, Karin, and Manzikert (to the north of Lake Van) was annexed to the Byzantine Empire. In 1021 King Senekerim Artsruni of Vaspurakan ceded his kingdom to the empire and moved to Cappadocia. He was followed in 1045 by King Gagik II of Ani and King Gagik-Abas of Kars (1064). The Byzantine policy of removing important lords from their Armenian lands and settling them elsewhere (principally on imperial territory, in Cappadocia and northern Mesopotamia) proved shortsighted in two respects. First, it left eastern Asia Minor devoid of its native defenders. Second, it exacerbated Armeno-Greek ethnic tensions by the introduction of thousands of Armenian newcomers into Cappadocia. The empire compounded its error by disbanding a 50,000-man local Armenian army, ostensibly to save money. As a result, the land was left defenseless as well as leaderless. This imprudent military decision subsequently was to have an impact on the Byzantine Empire itself, since with the Armenian lands vulnerable, Byzantine holdings in central and western Asia Minor were open to invasion.

The demographic expansion and westward movement of Turkic peoples in the tenth to eleventh centuries was another important factor in the invasions of Asia Minor. In the tenth century Armenia's eastern neighbor, Azerbaijan, was becoming increasingly populated with Turkmens of the Oghuz tribe, coming there across Central Asia and northern Iran. The Oghuz and other Turkic people also were invading and migrating across southern Russia to areas north of the Caucasus. In the eleventh century, as the Oghuz and others invaded Asia Minor, so to the north the Kipchak Turks were occupying the central steppe regions, from the Carpathian to the Altai Mountains.

In about 1018, at the very time Byzantium was trying to induce King Senekerim Artsruni of Vaspurakan to exchange his lands, Vaspurakan was under attack from Turkic peoples serving the Muslim emirs of Azerbaijan. Around 1021 the area from Nakhichevan to Dvin was raided by Turkmen Oghuz serving in the Persian Dailamite armies. From 1029 onward, Turkmen groups began raiding various parts of Armenia from the direction of Azerbaijan to the east as well as from northern Mesopotamia. These initial attacks in the period from 1016-1018 to 1040 bore the nature of plundering expeditions and were carried out by nomads not under direct control of the Seljuks. This situation changed, however, after 1040. In that year two Oghuz brothers, Tughril-Bey Muhammed and Chagri-Bey Daud of the family of Seljuk conquered the Ghaznavid kingdom of Iran and established the Seljuk Empire.

The Seljuk Invasions of Armenia

After the Seljuk conquest of Iran in 1040, Armenia became a conscious target of Turkish invasion, for several reasons. First, as a result of Turkmen successes in the preceding period and from espionage, the Seljuks knew that the Armenian lands were undefended. Second, Tughril-Bey, head of the Seljuks, was facing a dilemma with the Turkmens, which he solved temporarily by deflecting them to Armenia. After capturing the Iranian cities of Rey (1042) and Hamadan (1043), he closed them to the Turkmens to prevent them from laying waste the central provinces of Iran. Thousands of disgruntled nomads therefore headed for Azerbaijan, whence they entered Armenia. Armenia, a Byzantine possession, became a magnet for the newly Muslim nomadic Turkmens who could satisfy their lust for booty and gain religious merit by attacking Christian infidels. This was the effective military strategy of the Seljuk leadership: first to encourage or compel the Turkmens into an area to pillage and terrorize, then to send in troops more loyal to themselves, to take control. In 1042 some 15,000 Turkmens from the Urmia area attacked and looted Vaspurakan and defeated Byzantine forces near the city of Arjesh on the northeastern shore of Lake Van, while yet another group was raiding around Bjni in the northern district of Ayrarat.

Once again, in 1047, Tughril had difficulties with the Turkmens. In that year he formed an army of 100,000 Turkmens from Khorasan, entrusting it to his brother, Ibrahim Innal. The intention was for Innal to unite with the Turkmens already in Azerbaijan and to invade Armenia. At the same time, Tughril was able to rid the center of the Seljuk Empire of the Turkmens, whose presence in Iran was a steady drain on its resources. Thus from the mid-1040s to about 1063, detachments of Turks, more or less controlled by Seljuk sultans and their generals, penetrated deeper into Armenia, destroying numerous cities and devastating entire districts: Ani (attacked, 1045), Vagharshavan in the western district of Basen (1047), the Mananaghi district of western Armenia (1048), Ardzin in the northwest (1048-1049), Baiburt (1054), Melitene/Malatia in the southwest, Colonea in the northwest (1057), Sebastia/Sivas (sacked, 1059), Ani (captured, 1064), Kars (1065), and Caesarea (1067), to mention only the better-known sites.

The Seljuks did encounter some resistance from Armenians as well as from the Byzantine Empire. For example, in 1042, Khul Khachik Artsruni of Tornavan attempted a heroic but futile resistance against 15,000 Turkmens in Vaspurakan. In 1042-1043, an unspecified number of Turkmens raiding Bjni in northeastern Armenia were defeated by King Gagik II Bagratuni and Grigor (Magistros) Pahlavuni. In 1053 the Armenians of Surmari destroyed an army of 60,000 Turks. It is important to note that during this very period, 1040 to 1070, the Armenian kingdoms and principalities simultaneously were under attack from Byzantium, which seemed oblivious to the danger facing it. Thus in 1044, when Turkmens were raiding and pillaging the Armenian countryside, Byzantium disbanded a local defense force of 50,000. In 1064-1065, the Byzantine Empire succeeded in bullying King Gagik-Abas of Kars to cede to it his kingdom; however, before the empire could claim it, the Seljuks under Alp-Arslan (Tughril's nephew) had snatched it away. Armenia's enmity toward the Byzantine Greeks was further aroused by Byzantine attempts to force the Chalcedonian issue again. This led to bloody race riots and assassinations on both sides. Consequently, all segments of the Armenian population did not respond in a uniform way to the Seljuk invasions. Indeed, some few Armenians saw the anti-Byzantine Turks not as the agents of God sent to punish Armenians for their sins, but as an excellent vehicle opportunely available to themselves for vengeance against the Greeks. The contemporary

non-Armenian sources in particular accuse the Armenians of siding with
the Turks, deserting from the Byzantine armies sent to defend Armenia,
and even joining the enemy.

The Seljuks also encountered resistance from ambitious individual
commanders of the Turkmens, unwilling to subordinate themselves to
Seljuk authority. For example, in 1049, 1052 to 1053, and later in the
mid-1080s, the Seljuk "regular army" was warring against Turkmen
rebels in Asia Minor, a situation that exacerbated the chaos. In 1070-
1071, in what is regarded as a battle of major significance in world
military history, the forces of the Byzantine army were defeated by the
Seljuks under Alp-Arslan at Manzikert on the northern shore of Lake
Van. With that defeat, the Byzantine Empire ceased playing a role of
importance in the affairs of central and eastern Asia Minor. While it
appears that most of historical Armenia had been subjected to sack by
1070-1071, in several remote mountain areas small Armenian principalities continued to exist throughout the eleventh and twelfth centuries,
although encircled by inimical forces and under perpetual attack. These
areas comprised districts in northern and northeastern Armenia (Gugark,
Siunik, and Artsakh), plus southern and southwestern Armenia (parts of
Vaspurakan and Mokk and Sasun). Consequently, it would be incorrect
to speak of the Seljuk conquest as being fully consummated in the
eleventh century. Some few parts of Armenia never succumbed.

The Seljuk invasions acted as a catalyst on Armenian emigration.
In the eleventh century, the Byzantine government had followed a policy
of removing powerful Armenian lords and their dependents from their
native Armenian habitats and settling them to the west and southwest.
Thus, Cappadocia and Armenia Minor *(Pokr Hayk),* areas that centuries
earlier had hosted sizable Armenian populations, suddenly became
re-Armenized on the eve of the Turkish invasions. The invasions themselves quickened the tempo of Armenian emigration and extended its
range in a southwesterly direction (into Cilicia) and northward (in
Georgia). The *nakharars,* relocating as they did with sometimes large
forces, occasionally were powers to be reckoned with. Several such
powerful and ambitious *nakharars* carved out for themselves principalities over an extensive area stretching from Cilicia on the Mediterranean,
southward to Antioch, eastward to Edessa, northward to Samosata, to
Melitene/Malatia and elsewhere.

Armenian historical sources describe the period of the Seljuk
invasions as one of chaos, accompanied by widespread destruction of
human life and property. Some few areas were able to spare themselves

by making agreements with the Seljuks, but the generalized fate of Armenia's cities was sack (sometimes more than once), frequently accompanied by the massacre and/or enslavement of part of the population. Survivors of the invasions in some areas faced starvation, since the Turkmens often destroyed crops and cut down fruit-bearing trees in the surrounding villages. The situation of shock and confusion that many cavalrymen or *azats* (the "gentry") found themselves in, dispossessed from their lands, was described by the late-eleventh-century author Aristakes Lastiverttsi (Aristakes Lastivertc'i): "The cavalry wanders about lordlessly, some in Persia, some in Greece [Byzantium], some in Georgia. The *sepuh* brigade of *azats* has left its patrimony and fallen from wealth; they growl wherever they happen to be, like lion cubs in their lairs" (1985). Members of the *azatagundk hayots,* the cavalry of Armenia, clustered around successful bandits such as Gogh Vasil or Philaretus Varazhnuni, in lands southwest of Armenia. Others found a warm reception in Georgia. Many remained in their own neighborhoods, living in caves and making sorties against the Turkmens whenever possible. During the fifty-odd years of the invasions (ca. 1020s-1070s), according to Lastiverttsi, the Armenian chroniclers, and the later Turkish epics (the *Book of Dede Korkut* and the *Danishmend-name*), Armenian churches were looted and some were converted to mosques. The period of the invasions also had a devastating effect on international trade crossing the Armenian highlands. Not only had the majority of Armenia's cities been sacked, but the unsettled conditions rendered caravan traffic unpredictable and dangerous.

Armenia and the Seljuk Domination

The death of Alp-Arslan in 1072 brought welcome changes for the Armenians. Alp-Arslan's son, Malik-Shah (1072-1092) unlike his father and great-uncle Tughril, was less a nomadic warlord than a cultured, benevolent governor. Under the tutelage of a farsighted and prudent vizier, Nizam al-Mulk (1063-1092), Malik-Shah moved to restrain Turkmen depredations against his Christian and Muslim subjects. Iran was the center of the empire of the Great Seljuks, and it was Iranian rather than Turkic culture that the young sultan and his successors promoted. The Seljuk Empire of Iran, proclaimed in 1040, lasted little more than one hundred years. It, in turn, was destroyed by another wave of Turkic nomads, the Kara Khitai. In Asia Minor a variety of states arose during the late eleventh and twelfth centuries, virtually independent of Iran and often inimical toward each other. The most important of these were the Danishmendid state centered at Sebastia/Sivas, the Seljuk Sultanate of Rum (or Iconium) centered at Iconia/Konia and the state of the Shah-Armens centered at Khlat.

Policies of the rulers of these states were conditioned by military, demographic, and economic factors. In 1070-1071, the same year as the Byzantine disaster at Manzikert, the Seljuk general Atsiz captured Jerusalem. This event became the impetus for the First Crusade, which was to halt Turkish penetration westward. By 1099 Europeans had established principalities in Edessa, Antioch, and elsewhere in the Levant, strengthening the hands of both Byzantium and Cilician Armenians. Throughout much of the twelfth century, the Turkic states of Asia Minor were dangerously encircled by Christian powers: Georgia to the north, Byzantium to the west, and the Crusader states and Cilician Armenia to the south and southwest. Thus the activities of the new overlords of eastern Asia Minor were conditioned by the military might of their neighbors. Another conditioning factor was the centrifugalism that quickly manifested itself among the different Turkic overlords. Indeed, prior to the establishment of Seljuk control over much of the Armenian highlands by the late eleventh century, the proliferation of small, sometimes mutually hostile, Muslim emirates had begun. In the east, embracing parts of eastern Armenia, Caucasian Albania, and Azerbaijan was the emirate of Gandzak (ruled independently from 1148 to 1225). In the south, in the areas of Diarbekir and Khlat, the holdings of the Muslim Marwanid emirs quickly were confiscated by the Artukids of Aghdznik (1101-1231) and the Seljuk Shah-Armens of Khlat (1100-1207). In the west, the Danishmendids (1097-1165) ruled a large area including Sebastia/Sivas, Caesarea, and Melitene/Malatia. In the northwest were the emirates of Karin/Erzerum (ruled by the Saltukids, 1080-late twelfth century) and Kars (ca. 1080-1200). From 1118 Erzinjan and Tephrice/Divrigi belonged to Mangujek, founder of yet another dynasty. The ruling dynasties of these states sometimes were joined together by marriage ties or sometimes united to fight a common enemy (usually Georgia to the north). But more often they were at war with each other. Throughout the twelfth century, the Seljuk Sultanate of Rum, centered at Konia in the west, was trying to gain control over the above-mentioned states. This did not happen until late in the century.

Another factor conditioning the behavior of the new overlords was their own status as a numerical minority. During and after the conquest,

Turkic rulers and Muslim state-supported institutions expropriated the lands and properties of scores of lords and churches. They also became the new legislators or promulgators of law. Nonetheless, they had to contend with the reality of an overwhelmingly Armenian Christian population in eastern Asia Minor and a Greek population in western Asia Minor. In the twelfth century especially, a modus vivendi of sorts had developed between the rulers and the ruled. Matthew of Edessa, for example, describing the situation in the time of Malik Ismael ibn Yaqut (1085-1093), wrote that "everyone ruled his patrimony in his time." According to Vardan Areveltsi, when the Shaddadid Manuchihr ruled Ani-Shirak, he recalled from exile Grigor Pahlavuni and restored his holdings. Furthermore, Armenians, Greeks, and Georgians serving in the armies of the Shah-Armens and the sultans of Rum also received *iqtas,* originally conditional landholds that quickly became hereditary. The intermingling of cultures and institutions between the conquerors and the conquered was paralleled by intermarriage between the two peoples. It was through the gradual merging of newcomer and settled, the conversion to Islam of the previously Christian population, and the supplemental influx of invading Turkmens in the thirteen to fifteenth centuries that Asia Minor metamorphosed from being Greek, Armenian, and Christian to being Turkish and Muslim.

The establishment of Muslim political overlordship over an Armenian Christian population in eastern Asia Minor did not immediately lead to widespread conversions to Islam. This was to occur in the twelfth and succeeding centuries. But during the time of the Seljuk invasions, Armenian Islamization seems to have been limited to those obliged to convert to save their lives and to the tens of thousands of Armenian women and children forcibly removed from their homes and sold on the slave markets of the Middle East. In this early period too, several influential Armenian *nakharar* women were sought after as brides by Seljuk rulers. Presumably many of them converted. Subsequently, after the establishment of Seljuk political control, other Armenians converted, be they young Armenian boys, *gulams,* absorbed into the Seljuk military schools, or the skilled Armenian bureaucrats and artisans who dominated many important positions within the various Turkish states and who figure prominently in Turkish epic literature. Martyrologies of the twelfth century also point to considerable voluntary conversion, prompted by the elevated status in the newly developing society converts could enjoy and especially by financial inducements. The result of this conversion, forcible or voluntary, was the creation with time of a distinct group— almost excluded from the Armenian sources as "renegades" but apparently not yet fully accepted by their new Muslim coreligionists either, who in their writings usually style them as "Armenians." Despite conversion by some, most Armenians remained true to their own distinctive form of Christianity. This fact, coupled with the reality of an Armenian majority in eastern Asia Minor, led to a certain "Armenization" of the Seljuks. Not only did Armenians of different faiths—Apostolic, Orthodox, Muslim—constitute the bulk of the population in eastern Asia Minor during the Seljuk domination, but fairly quickly an Armeno-Turkish community came into existence through intermarriage. Intermarriage occurred not only between the families of Armenian civil servants and Turkish lords but at the very pinnacle of the state. By the thirteenth century few Seljuk sultans of eastern Asia Minor lacked an Armenian, Georgian, or Greek parent or grandparent. Evidence even suggests that the great warlord and founder of the Danishmendid emirate, hero of the Turkish epic (the *Danishmendname*), emir Malik Danishmend himself, was a Muslim Armenian. Judging from the many clearly Armenian names of his comrades-in-arms who waged holy war against the Byzantine Christian "infidels," the same was true of his inner circle. Danishmendid coinage usually was stamped with the sign of the Cross and/or a bust of Christ. The hereditary rulers of the powerful emirate of Khlat in southern Armenia styled themselves *Shah-i-Armen* (Persian for "king of the Armenians") and married Armenians. Armenization was not solely an ethnic process, but a cultural one as well. Seljuk architecture took some of its inspiration from Armenian architecture. In the eleventh to thirteenth centuries, many of the structures themselves were designed and built by Christian and Muslim Armenians.

The late twelfth century was a period of great brilliance in the history of central and eastern Asia Minor. In 1207 the Seljuks captured the port of Atalia on the Mediterranean; in 1214 they acquired Sinope on the Black Sea, thereby opening their state to world trade. As a result, revenues available to the Seljuk Sultanate of Rum increased dramatically, leading to a quickening of cultural and architectural development throughout Asia Minor. With the aid of the Georgian Bagratid dynasty, a small Byzantino-Georgian "empire" of Trebizond was established in 1204, becoming another important center for international exchange. Historians regard the early thirteenth century as the time when four societies—the Sultanate of Rum, Georgia, Trebizond, and Cilicia—achieved the pinnacles of their development. This was a period of economic and cultural interaction and dynamism.

The Emergence of Georgia

The emergence of Georgia as a great military power in the late eleventh to twelfth centuries temporarily shifted the scales in favor of Caucasian cultural as well as political supremacy in eastern Asia Minor. Because of Georgia's military might, much of northern historical Armenia once again came under the political control of Armenians, though briefly. Those parts that were not were either tributary to Georgia or had made peace with that state. Georgia's successes in this period may be attributed to a number of factors, internal and external. Internally, the royal Bagratid dynasty of Georgia had succeeded in restraining the rebellious and separatist Georgian lords. Externally, Seljuk preoccupation with other neighbors and the Crusades left eastern Asia Minor an easy object of Georgian military ambitions.

During the reign of David (called "the Restorer" and "the Builder," 1089-1125), Georgia had become a haven for Armenian lords and lordless *azats* displaced by the Seljuk invasions. The historian Matthew of Edessa wrote that David "received and loved the Armenian people; the remnants of the Armenian forces assembled by him." He also built a special city, Gori, for the refugees. According to the medieval Armenian translation of the Georgian *History of Kartli,* David knew the Armenian language and had as his father-confessor the monophysite *vardapet* Sarkavag from Haghbat monastery in northeastern Armenia. During the reign of this king, the armies of Georgia commenced clearing southern and southeastern Georgia of nomadic Turkmens, capturing from them Shamshulde and many strongholds in the Armeno-Georgian districts of Somkhiti (1110), Lori, Agarak, and the Kiurikian holdings (1118), Shamakhi, eastern Gugark, western Utik, Gag, Kavazin, Kayian, Kaytson, Terunakan, Norberd, Tavush, Mahkanaberd, Manasgom, and Khalinchkar (1123). The same year Ani was taken, though that city passed back and forth between the Georgian and Muslim emirs many times throughout the twelfth century. During the reigns of David's successors, Demetre I (1125-1155) and Georgi III (1156-1184), the conquests continued though at a slower pace. Throughout this period, the Georgian army was swelling with Armenian volunteers, enthusiastically participating in the liberation of their country. Furthermore, the Georgian Bagratid dynasty, themselves of Armenian descent, very definitely favored certain Armenian nobles long since established within Georgia and within that country's ruling structure. Such lords as the Zakarian/Mkhargrtselis, Orbelian/Orbelis, and Artsruni/Mankaberdelis not only commanded the victorious armies, but were left in charge of the newly established administrations.

The Georgian Bagratid dynasty reached the apogee of their power under Queen Tamar (1184-1213). Under Tamar's generals, the energetic brothers Zakare and Ivane Zakarian, the Armeno-Georgian armies surged ahead reclaiming one after another fortress, city, and district: Anberd in the Aragatsotn district (1196), Shamkor, Gandzak, Artsakh, Siunik, Shirak, the Ayrarat plain and Ani (ca. 1199), Bjni (1201), and Dvin (1203). They now turned upon the southern and western emirates, defeating the renowned sultan of Rum, Rukn al-Din, in the district of Basen (1204). In 1204 or 1205, they reached as far south as Manzikert and Arjesh on the northern shore of Lake Van, although this area was not taken until ca. 1209. Ivane's daughter, Tamta, was married to the Shah-Armen of Khlat in 1210. In a great final burst, General Zakare marched through Nakhichevan and Jugha (Julfa), through (Persian) Azerbaijan to Maran, Tabriz, and Qazvin, looting and sacking Muslim settlements. By the time of Zakare's death in 1213, Georgia was the most powerful state in the region, while the status of the Armenians, be they inhabitants of historical Armenia, of Georgia, or of the numerous small communities stretching in a belt to the southwest to the independent Cilician kingdom had been changed in a very positive way.

The personalities of the dynamic individuals who shaped Armenian affairs in this period may be examined through unique perspectives. Because such people as the Zakarids, Artsrunids, and Orbelians functioned both in Georgian and Armenian milieux, both Georgian and Armenian historians wrote about them. The reader is treated to two sides of their personalities. Thus the information available in the Armenian historians Kirakos Gandzaketsi, Vardan Areveltsi, and Stepanos Orbelian is amplified in the *Georgian Chronicle*. Furthermore, the lives of Queen Tamar and her Armenian commander-in-chief Zakare are symbolically alluded to in the great Georgian epic of the thirteenth century, the *Man in the Panther's Skin*. This exquisite creation of the troubadour Shota Rustaveli reveals, among many other things, the chivalrous ideals of the period and the wealth and exoticism of the court which enjoyed war booty, tribute, and the fruits of trade with far-flung states.

The Zakarid Period

The first decades of the thirteenth century in northeastern Armenia are known as the Zakarid period, after its most influential family. In the late twelfth century the Armenian Zakarids were used by the Georgian Bagratid dynasty to counter the native Georgian lords. Zakare and Ivane Zakarian, both notable generals, also held official positions within the Georgian court. Zakare was the commander-in-chief of the army *(amirspasalar)* as of 1191 and the "grand marshal" *(mandaturt-ukhutses)* from 1203 on; while his brother, first appointed foremost vizier at court *(msakhurt-ukhutses)* became *atabeg* in 1212, an office that was instituted within the Georgian court at Ivane's own request. To reward their military prowess, the Georgian crown entrusted adminis-tration of the many liberated districts of northeastern Armenia to Zakare and Ivane. The nature of the Zakarid brothers' service to the Georgian crown seems to have been primarily of a military sort. Armenian lands recaptured from the Turks paid taxes to the Zakarids, who probably paid some taxes to the Georgian Bagratid dynasty. During the Zakarid period, which lasted until about 1260, Armenian economic and cultural life reached a new plateau.

The properties under the overall jurisdiction of *amirspasalar* Zakare and later of his son Shahnshah were located in the northwestern parts of the reconquered lands: Lori, Ani, Aragatsotn, Bagrevand, Tsaghkotn, Kogovit, Surmari lands from the Virahayots Mountains to the southern border of Tsaghkotn, from Bolorpahakits to Erevan. Ani was the center of this realm. Subject to Zakare's house were both newly created families (such as the Vachutians) and branches of old *nakharar* families (such as the Pahlavunis, Artsrunis, Mamikonians, and others).

Under the jurisdiction of *atabeg* Ivane Zakarian and later of his son Avag were the eastern areas: Bjni, Gegharkunik, Vayots Dzor, most of Artsakh, Siunik, Nakhichevan, Dvin, and Erevan. The center of this realm was first Dvin and later Bjni. Subject to Ivane's house were the Orbelians, Khaghbakians, Dopians, and others. The Orbelians, who originally had been the Zakarids' overlords in Georgia, were, in the changed situation of the late twelfth and thirteenth centuries, their subordinates in Armenia. Another of Ivane's subordinates was Vasak Khaghbakian, originally from the Khachen area, who had helped in the reconquest of Vayots Dzor, Bjni, and Dvin. This family came to be known as Proshian after Vasak's energetic son Prosh (1223-1284). A number of new and old *nakharar* families became associated with the Zakarids through marriage alliances with three of Zakare's and Ivane's sisters. Their sister Vaneni was married to Abas II Kiurikian of Matsnaberd. Dopi married Hasan, prince of the old *nakharar*dom of Artsakh in eastern Armenia, receiving as dowry a large area on the southern shore of Lake Sevan and the Sotk district in Siunik. Her descendants are known as the Dopiank. Khorishah Zakarian, another sister, was married to Vakhtang, lord of Khachen district. The family was named after Hasan Jalal, the issue of this union. The Hasan-Jalalians ruled southern Khachen. Within the vast territories under their jurisdiction, the two Zakarid brothers apparently established many of the same offices as existed in the Georgian court. The men chosen by them to fill these offices were those same individuals who had been instrumental as warriors in the reconquest of Armenian lands. The service tendered to the Zakarids by their appointees consisted of military aid and the payment of taxes. Thus, in return for his service, Zakare titled Vache Vachutian his "prince of princes." Members of the Khachen aristocracy served as Zakarid *hejubs,* chamberlains, court directors, and guardians of Zakarid children. Prince Bubak, Ivane's subordinate, is styled "prince of princes" and "the great *sparapet*" in the sources. Bubak also was known by the Georgian title of *msakhurt-ukhutses*—the same title originally held by Ivane in the Georgian court. This lends credence to the view that the Zakarids created a partial microcosm of the Georgian court hierarchy on their own lands.

The nobility of Armenia in the early thirteenth century consisted of different elements. One substantial group included men of ambition and military talents from newly arisen families, who were rewarded by their Zakarid overlords with grants of land and/or rights of administration. Before and after receiving lands and villages, this category of thirteenth-century lord derived much wealth from booty taken during military campaigns. Another element is referred to in the sources from the twelfth century on as *metsatun,* which means literally "of a great house." In fact, these were men of great financial wealth who formed the upper class in the many Armenian cities that had recuperated from the Seljuk dislocations. These men, too, lacked antique pedigrees and did not belong to the old *nakharar* families. Their wealth had been gained through trading and money-lending, and a substantial part of the *metsatuns'* assets were in cash. However, these merchants reinvested their capital in land, buying not only entire estates but also shares of establishments, such as mills. An inscription of one *metsatun,* Tigran, from the historically unknown family Honents, on the wall of the church of St. Gregory in Ani (ca. 1215) indicates the far-flung and multifaceted nature of *metsatun* wealth. From the inscription of another *metsatun,* one learns that about 1242, a certain Umek purchased the church of Getik for "40,000 red [gold] ducats," a currency that clearly indicates that such merchants as Umek were participating in the lucrative international trade with Italian city-states. A third element of the nobility was the high clergy of the church, including bishops and the directors of numerous monasteries founded in this period.

Non-noble elements of Armenian society in the eleventh to thirteenth centuries, as in earlier centuries, are essentially omitted from the sources. Certain economic historians suggest that the Seljuk invasions of the mid-eleventh century may have had a temporary "liberating" effect on the peasantry, since the economy of the nomads did not require attachment to the soil. As martyrologies of the eleventh to twelfth centuries suggest, conversion to Islam, the religion of the new conquerors, became a means of socioeconomic elevation for many Armenians of different economic classes in Muslim-ruled areas. However, for the bulk of the peasantry that remained Christian, the twelfth to thirteenth centuries brought increasing attachment to the soil. Georgian documents from this period indicate that peasants attached to a particular plot also could be sold with the land they worked. Urban artisans—metalworkers, builders, weavers, and the like—were a group that grew in size during the twelfth to thirteenth centuries. Their status as non-noble is clear, though they seem to have acquired certain special rights in this period as well as their own guild organizations.

As in Georgia proper, Rum, and Cilicia, the culture of northeastern Armenia blossomed at the end of the twelfth and the beginning of the thirteenth century. The material wealth deriving from international trade was the basis for this. Among the major intellectuals of the period belong the poet-catholicos Mkhitar Heratsi (Mekhitar of Her), the author of a medical textbook; grammarians; theologians; and translators such as Shnorhali's nephew Grigor Tgha; Nerses Lambronatsi (Nerses of Lambron); Mkhitar Gosh, the codifier of Armenian law; Davit Kobayretsi; Grigor Skevratsi; Vardan Aygektsi; Aristakes the Rhetorician; Hovhannes Garnetsi; and Vanakan Vardapet.

The Turco-Mongol Invasions of 1220 to 1230

Beginning in the 1220s, the Caucasus and eastern Asia Minor were subjected to a new round of Turco-Mongol invasions. The first of the thirteenth-century incursions was made in 1220-1221 by a detachment of some 20,000 Mongols who had been sent across Central Asia by Genghis-Khan in pursuit of the shah of Khwarazm. The latter succeeded in evading his pursuers and had, in fact, died in obscurity on an island in the Caspian Sea the same time the Mongols were entering the Caucasus. The Mongol's route into Armenia was from the southeast, from western Nakhichevan north to the Aghstev region. The outcome of this first clash with Caucasian forces was that some 10,000 Armenians and Georgians commanded by King Georgi IV Lasha and his *atabeg* Ivane Zakarian were defeated in the Kotman area of northeastern Armenia. Northern Armenia and southeastern Georgia were looted before the invaders returned to their base in Utik. Despite its success, this army had not been sent for conquest but to pursue the Khwarazm-Shah and to conduct reconnaissance for future operations. Thus, considering their mission accomplished, the Mongols departed via the Caucasus Mountains to the north, destroying the city of Shamkor en route.

The second invasion of the Caucasus took place immediately after the Mongol departure in 1222, and was caused by it. This time the participants were nomadic Kipchak Turks from the plains to the north. In their turn defeated by the Mongols, one sizable body of Kipchaks fled from them in a southward direction. These nomads pillaged and looted from Darband south to Gandzak in Azerbaijan. *Atabeg* Ivane mustered troops and went against them, but he was defeated, having underestimated their strength. What was worse, many *nakharars* were captured, then killed or ransomed for huge sums of money. The Kipchaks continued looting and raiding different parts of the Caucasus until 1223, when Ivane, in alliance with other Caucasian peoples, finally defeated them, killing or selling them into slavery. The Kipchak raids, though less serious than the invasions that preceded and succeeded them, nonetheless contributed to the continued unsettled state of affairs initiated by the Mongols, depleted the Armeno-Georgian military of some capable leaders, and undoubtedly weakened the army's morale.

The third devastation of Armenia took place from 1225 to about 1230, during which time various parts of the country were subjected to raids and invasions by the ethnically diverse armies of the new Khwarazm-Shah, Jalal al-Din Mangubirdi. Like his father, he offered stubborn and occasionally successful resistance to his Mongol pursuers. This was, however, at the expense of other peoples, notably the Armenians and Georgians. At the head of an army of some 60,000 Turkmens and Kipchak mercenaries, Jalal al-Din invaded northeastern Armenia following the age-old route of invasion, through Nakhichevan and northward. He took and devastated Dvin, and at Garni defeated the 70,000-man-strong Armeno-Georgian army commanded by Ivane. This was followed by the capture of Gandzak, Lori, and Tiflis, where a frightful massacre of Christians ensued with the active participation of resident Muslims, who viewed Jalal as a liberator. The northern cities of Ani and Kars and the southern cities of Khlat and Manzikert were besieged unsuccessfully in 1226. Certain areas, such as Tiflis and Dvin, soon were retaken by the Caucasians, but Jalal al-Din continued devastating one or another section of Armenia until 1230, when he was decisively beaten near Erzinjan by a united force composed of troops of Malik Ashraf of Khlat, the Seljuk sultan of Rum, Cilician Armenian, and Crusader detachments. Jalal was murdered the next year by a Kurdish peasant. His raids and devastations had lasted seven years. Not only did he bring mass destruction of human life and property, but also famine and pestilence, since as contemporary historians noted, Jalal al-Din and his unruly troops frequently cut down fruit-bearing trees and vineyards and burned the crops. Furthermore, remnants of his mercenaries continued to practice banditry well into the 1230s in different parts of central Asia Minor. Following the deaths of King Georgi IV Lasha (1223) and Ivane Zakarian (1227), Christian Caucasia, already seriously weakened, was no longer able to offer united resistance against attackers, at the very moment when it was needed most.

The Mongol Conquest of Armenia

The fourth thirteenth-century invasion of Armenia occurred in 1236. It was short and merciless, and confined to the northeastern and northern regions. In that year, the Mongol general Chormaghun, now established at the Mongol summer camp *(yayla)* in the Mughan plain of Azerbaijan, sent out detachments under various commanders to capture all the key fortresses in northeastern Armenia. Unlike the first appearance of the Mongols in the Caucasus, which had been for the pursuit of a fugitive, their reappearance now was for the purpose of conquest and occupation. On this occasion, the Mongols traveled with their families, carts, and

herds—their "portable economy." They also brought along sophisticated Chinese siege machinery, rock-hurling and wall-battering devices.
Upon receiving news of the return of the Mongols, the ruler of Georgia,
Queen Rusudan (1223-1247) with many of the lords fled to the security
of western Georgia, while others holed up in their fortresses. But no one
was secure. The Mongols, having divided up the districts in advance,
proceeded to take them one by one. Molar-noyin took the territories of
Ivane's nephew Vahram of Gag. The Kiurikian fortresses of Matsnaberd
and Nor Berd fell, and about the same time the clerical historians
Vanakan and Kirakos Gandzaketsi were captured. Ghatagha-noyin took
Gardman, Charek, Getabek, and Vardanashat. The Zakarid holdings of
Lori fell, followed by Dmanis, Shamshulde, and Tiflis. *Atabeg* Avag
Zakarian was among the first of the Caucasian notables to submit to the
Mongols. He was rewarded and gifted by them, while he and his troops
were used in the conquest of recalcitrant areas. Seeing that submission
to the Mongols did not mean sudden death, the remaining princes went
to them and were reinstated in their lands. The historian Vardan
Areveltsi wrote that everything was surrendered to them in a short
period, without toil or labor. Although the Mongols frequently spared
cities that surrendered without a fight, surrender did not always elicit
their sympathy. Fearing the harsh fate suffered by Ani, Kars surrendered
but was devastated nonetheless. During the course of 1236, the Mongols
subjugated by sword or treaty all of northeastern and northern Armenia.
They met with no serious resistance anywhere.

The Mongol conquest of western and southern historical Armenia
took place between 1242 and 1245. These lands, though inhabited by
Armenians, were under the political domination of the Seljuks, or in the
case of Khlat, of the Ayyubids. In 1242 the Mongol general Baiju-noyin
took Karin/Erzerum after a siege of two months. Part of the population
was massacred and part was led away into slavery. Participating in the
Mongol campaigns in western Armenia were the lords of newly conquered eastern Armenia, who in a number of cases were able to amelio-
rate the lot of Armenians in some western cities. The Mongols spent the
winter of 1243 at their base in Azerbaijan, but returned in springtime to
crush the forces of the Seljuk sultan of Rum, Ghiyath al-Din Kai
Khusrau, at Kose Dagh, near Erzinjan. The defeat of the Seljuks at Kose
Dagh was an event of the greatest significance for the Armenians both
locally and abroad in the independent state of Cilicia. Like dominoes,
the remaining key cities of central Asia Minor fell: Erzinjan, Caesarea,
Sebastia/Sivas, Melitene/Malatia, and Divrigi. In 1245 Baiju-noyin

captured Khlat, Amida, Edessa, and Nisibis. By that year the Armenian populations, be they in Caucasian Armenia, western Armenia, southern Armenia, or even Cilicia, were to a greater or lesser degree all formally under the overlordship of the Mongols.

The Mongol Domination

During the more than one hundred years of Mongol domination, the Armenians experienced periods of benevolent, even enlightened rule and of capricious benighted misrule. The years from 1236 to 1250, though not without conflict, did not witness radical changes in Armenia's governing structure. Apparently, prior to 1243 no permanent formal taxes had been imposed on Armenia, the conquerors contenting themselves instead with the rich booty and plunder to be had from the many areas taken by military force. But in 1243 by command of the Great Khan Guyuk himself, taxes amounting to between one-thirtieth and one-tenth of value were imposed on virtually everything movable and immovable, and a heavy head tax of 60 silver *drams* was collected from males. The severity of the taxes and the brutal manner of their collection triggered an abortive uprising of the lords in 1248-1249. This rebellion, which was discovered by the Mongols while still in the planning stages, was crushed at the expense of human and animal lives and crops in numerous districts of northeastern Armenia and southern Georgia. Some of the arrested Armenian and Georgian conspirators, unable to raise the huge ransoms demanded for their release, were tortured or killed.

After the accession of the Great Khan Mongke (1251-1259), a thorough census was made of all parts of the empire from 1252 to 1257. The Iranian emir Arghun personally conducted the census of Caucasia in 1254, which significantly increased the tax burden. An administrative change regarding Armenia occurred in the mid-thirteenth century. This was the establishment of the Il-Khanid Mongol substate over the territory of Iran and the inclusion of Caucasia into it, beginning in 1256. Prior to that time the Caucasus had formed a single administrative unit composed of five *vilayets*. Following the granting of Iran as a hereditary appanage to Hulegu Khan in 1256, Armenia experienced another shock caused by nomads on the move. First, Hulegu chose as his residence Mughan in Azerbaijan, which until then had been the camping grounds of Baiju-noyin. Hulegu ordered the latter and all the nomadic Mongol and Turkmen warriors subordinate to him to evacuate the Caucasus, in order to create room for his own entourage. With considerable grumbling the displaced Baiju and his hosts moved westward, sacking the cities of Karin/Erzerum, Erzinga/Erzinjan, Sebastia/Sivas, Caesarea, and Konia as they went. Almost simultaneously some of Genghis-Khan's grandchildren descended on the Caucasus through the Caspian Gates in order to settle near their relation Hulegu. This unruly group also caused much damage as it traveled and extorted whatever it could from the sedentary population. The proximity of new powerful masters in 1256 in addition to the information obtained by them from the census of 1254 had yet another immediate ramification for the Caucasus. Now the *nakharars* were obliged to participate in all military ventures of the Il-Khanids on a regular basis, providing a specified number of troops yearly. Armenian and Georgian warriors fought in all the major Mongol campaigns in the Middle East from 1256 onward, which resulted in the deaths or enslavement of large numbers of Christian Caucasians abroad. Heavy taxation coupled with the onerous burden of military service in distant lands led to rebellion. The second Armeno-Georgian rebellion occurred between 1259 and 1261. Though of longer duration than the rebellion of 1248-1249, this one too eventually was brutally crushed.

In the 1260s the Caucasus became an occasional theater of warfare between the Il-Khanids and yet another Mongol state, that of the Golden Horde, centered in the lower Volga with its capital at Sarai. The organizer of this state, Berke-Khan (1257-1266), a devout Muslim, was outraged by the anti-Muslim policies of the shamanist Hulegu and especially by his massacre of the Muslim population of Baghdad in 1258. Not only did Berke and his successors attempt to infringe on the uncertain boundary between his realm and Hulegu's (i.e., the Caucasus), but they also entered into an alliance with the increasingly powerful Mamluk state in Egypt. The latter were the most ferocious enemies of the Il-Khanids in the Near East and the only power to have dealt the Mongols a severe military defeat there in 1260. During the decade of the 1260s, the Caucasus was invaded by forces of the Golden Horde in 1261 and 1265-1266. The Il-Khans were also faced with rebellions of Mongol chiefs resident in the Caucasus. For example, in 1268 one of Genghis-Khan's great-grandsons, Teguder, rebelled in the Caucasus. Teguder's holdings included parts of southern Georgia and the area around Lake Sevan in Armenia. Armeno-Georgian troops aided in the suppression of this rebellion, just as they had fought for the Il-Khans against Berke.

The Mongols had a number of bases of support within Armenian society. Among these were the church hierarchy, the merchants, and certain of the lords who received special status and were Mongol favorites. Many of the Mongol generals and their wives were Nestorian Christians at the time of the invasion and sympathized with the Armenian Christians. In 1242, for example, they facilitated the return of Nerses (the Catholicos of Caucasian Albania) to his seat since "for a long while neither Nerses nor his predecessors had dared to circulate throughout the dioceses because of the bloodthirsty nation of Tajiks" (Kirakos Gandzaketsi, 1986). In 1248, when Catholicos Kostandin of Cilicia sent to Greater Armenia gifts and money for the monastery of St. Tadeos, the work was expedited by the Mongols. In the early 1250s Smbat Orbelian received a decree "freeing all the churches of Armenia and the priests" (Orbelian, 1859), and with encouragement from General Baiju's Christian wife, Smbat renovated Siunik's religious seat, Tatev. According to Arghun's census of 1255, neither church nor clergy was to be taxed, though the sources report numerous instances of illegal exactions from both throughout the remainder of the century. Mongol religious policy was quite complex and underwent numerous shifts. For example, at the time of the census conducted by Arghun and Buqa (1243), Muslims were used to terrorize Christians. Yet in 1258, during the siege of Baghdad, the Mongols encouraged the Christians in their army brutally to exterminate the city's Muslim population. But in retaliation for the Caucasian rebellion of 1259 to 1261, Mongols destroyed churches and the Georgian catholicosate itself, and the emir Arghun (himself a Muslim) had the Christian prince Hasan Jalal tortured to death for failure to apostatize. Clearly, Mongols adroitly used the Christians in Muslim areas and the Muslims in Christian areas for espionage and maintenance of terror.

Armenian merchants (the *metsatuns*) were another base of support for Mongol rule during the thirteenth century. During the period of the invasions, the Mongols took some pains to prevent caravans from being attacked. At the time of the destruction of Karin/Erzerum (1242), special consideration was shown to wealthy Armenians there. The support of the merchants derived from such special treatment and from the huge profits they earned by participating in international trade. Merchants in the Mongol Empire, which united the Far and Near East, carried on a brisk and lucrative trade with the West. During the Mongol period, maritime trade expanded as the Italian states of Genoa and Venice founded trading centers along the north shore of the Black Sea. The cities of Tabriz and Sultanie in Azerbaijan were also major trading centers where Genoese and Venetian merchants had their offices. The main caravan route through Asia Minor ran from Ayas (in Cilician Armenia) through Sebastia/Sivas, Erzinga/Erzinjan, and Karin/Erzerum, to Tabriz. Another important route went from Tabriz through Khoi, Arjesh, Manazkert, Karin/Erzerum to Trebizond on the Black Sea. Exported were spices, silks, gems, drugs, and other Oriental luxuries; imported were woolen cloths, linen, furs, and other manufactured goods from the West. Armenian merchants were to be found at all points along the trade routes. Ayas, the point of departure for the Far East, was a city of Cilician Armenia; there were also concentrations of Armenian merchants at Trebizond, Tabriz, Sultanie, in Central Asia, and the Far East, and in the cities of southern Russia, the north shore of the Black Sea, and throughout Italy. Because of their far-flung connections, Armenian merchants sometimes were used by Mongol officials as couriers. It is interesting that there also seems to have been a large number of Armenian clerics present at the courts of the khans and along many of the major stops across Asia to the Far East. The majority of these were engaged in translational activity and/or serving the needs of the families of Armenian merchants. The favorable economic situation for the merchants finds reflection in the inscriptions carved on the walls of churches and other structures erected by their wealth. These inscriptions mention tens of thousands of "red [gold] ducats" lavished on the construction and maintenance of new and existing structures. References to Italian ducats in inscriptions from the mid and late thirteenth century confirm the continuing ties of these merchants with the Italian city-states.

Another group that served as a base of support for the Mongol regime consisted of certain prominent lords whose allegiance was directly to the Mongols. Such favorites, in Armenia as well as in other parts of the Mongol Empire, were given *inju* status, which meant that they paid taxes and fulfilled other obligations directly to their Mongol patrons. The effect of this practice was the same in the Caucasus as elsewhere, namely, the detachment of certain powerful lords from the preexisting political arrangements. If before the Mongol domination the lords of northeastern Armenia were subject to the Zakarids, who were subject to the Georgian crown, the Mongols now altered this arrangement by attaching these lords directly to themselves. The best known example of this involved the Armenian Orbelians of Siunik. Smbat Orbelian was granted *inju* status by Mongke-Khan in 1252 on a trip to the Far East. Another prince who apparently received *inju* status from

Mongke was Hasan Jalal (ca. 1257) of Khachen. Around 1273 the Georgian lord Sargis Jaqeli also received *inju* status. During the same decade the cities of Kars, Telavi, Belakan, "and many other lands" were separated from royal Georgian control and given by the Mongols to their favorite, Sadun Artsruni/Mankaberdeli.

During the thirteenth century the Mongols managed successfully to keep the lords divided and frequently absent from the area entirely. Dividing the lords was never difficult. The Mongols were adroit at exploiting antagonisms existing within branches of the same family. Thus to punish Avag Zakarian (ca. 1243), his lands were given to his more loyal cousin Shahnshah. The Georgian royal Bagratid dynasty was another family neutralized. Eventually sanctioning two monarchs, the Mongols effectively divided the kingdom and the royal treasury, expropriating one-third of it for themselves (1250s). In the 1260s and 1270s the Mongols furthered the territorial and political ambitions of the Orbelians and Artsrunis at the expense of the Zakarids and the Georgian Bagratid dynasty. Finally, at the end of the thirteenth century and the beginning of the fourteenth century, the Mongols elevated a Jaqeli to the Georgian throne. In addition to the manipulation of *nakharar* precedence, the Mongols were able to divide the lords by creating conflicts of loyalty. With the aim of destroying the ties that had existed between the lords and the Georgian court, the Mongols incorporated certain prominent *nakharars* into their own court and administration. This is especially visible after 1256, the year in which Hulegu became Il-Khan in Iran, when Caucasian nobles were actually given symbolic offices within Hulegu's court. Cooptation of allegiance was furthered by intermarriage between the Mongols (or officials in the Il-Khanid administration in Iran) and the Caucasian nobility. The Christian Caucasian literary sources mention eight examples of this, and the Cilician sources mention a number of Cilician Armenian notables who had Mongol spouses.

The absence of prominent lords from the Caucasus resulted from two Mongol requirements. First was the obligation of the two- to three-year journey to their capital, Kara Korum, in Mongolia, and later to Tabriz in Iran, which the Mongols insisted on for important lords. Throughout the thirteenth century, prominent Armenian lords frequently were traveling to the East. Often trips were undertaken voluntarily to advance personal interests or to resolve some local business. In any case, the effect was the removal from Armenia of the most powerful (and potentially the most dangerous) lords. In the absence of certain grandees, other lords could and did attempt to encroach upon the lands and rights of their rivals. The absence of Armenian lords from their native habitats also resulted from the obligation of the lords to participate with their cavalry in Mongol campaigns. Usually forced to fight as advance attackers, the Caucasian troops had a simple choice facing them: life and the spoils of victory, or death from defeat or attempted desertion. The lords and their troops were taken on campaigns all over the Middle East, North Africa, and Asia. The stringent requirements involved in participating in Mongol campaigns were a major cause of the princes' rebellion of 1259 to 1261. It is true that the Mongols placed considerable trust in certain Armenian lords, such as *amirspasalar* Shahnshah's son Zakare and Prosh Khaghbakian, who aided in the capture of Baghdad (1258). The honors bestowed upon the noted military man Tarsayich Orbelian by Abaqa Khan are also noteworthy. However, often the Caucasians suffered decimation. In 1261 many Armenian and Georgian warriors died when the Mongol general Kitbuqa's army in Egypt was wiped out. Prince Sevada Khachentsi was killed in the battle for Mayyafarikin. In 1261-1262 the young prince Burtel Orbelian died in the North Caucasus, fighting Hulegu's enemy, Berke. Caucasians died in the war between Arghun Khan and Baraq in the mid-1260s in Central Asia. In the late 1270s Caucasians suffered dreadful losses during the Mongols' ill-conceived campaigns in Gilan, on the southern shore of the Caspian Sea. Participation in Mongol campaigns resulted in more than the deaths of thousands of men. In the absence of the *nakharar* warlords, the Caucasus was left without committed defenders to protect it from the persistent raids and sorties of Mongol, Turkmen, and local rebels.

Despite the serious shortcomings of life under the Mongols, for most of the thirteenth century Armenian culture developed freely. This was due as much to the generally free status of the church as to the largesse of the lords and merchants. In the thirteenth and early fourteenth century, there were a number of large monastic complexes where clerics were educated and where the many manuscripts surviving from this period were written, copied, and illuminated. Among the flourishing monasteries were Ayrivank, Sanahin, Haghbat, Nor Getik (Goshavank), Khoranashat, Kayenadzor, Khor Virap, Kecharuyk, and Gladzor. This last institution was founded by a student of the historian Vardan Areveltsi in the 1280s, and is described as a "university" in a colophon dating from 1321. Possessing at least nine professors and some fifteen lecturers, Gladzor's rise and decline followed that of its patrons, the Proshians and Orbelians.

The Collapse of the Il-Khans

The reign of Ghazan Khan (1295-1304) is regarded by scholars as a watershed, during which important changes took place in the Mongol Empire. Some changes, such as fiscal reforms, did not take root among Ghazan's successors. Others, such as the Islamization of the Mongols, were of a permanent nature. A fundamental problem was that the economic system of the nomads was incompatible with the agricultural and mercantile economy of Armenia. In the thirteenth century the Mongols had expropriated for their own use vast tracts of land across the Armenian highlands, taking certain choice farming areas for summer and winter pasturage for their herds. The slopes of the Aragats Mountains, and the areas of Vayots Dzor, parts of the plain of Ayrarat, and areas around Karin/Erzerum, Van, Berkri, and Baghesh/Bitlis became summer *yaylas,* while Vaspurakan, the Ayrarat plains, and the Kharberd/Kharpert region were used for wintering places. Formerly these areas had been under intensive agricultural development, but increasingly in the late thirteenth and in the fourteenth century they became semidesert. Parts of southern and western Armenia were used almost solely for animal husbandry. The Mongols and Turkmen nomads used the area between Erzinjan, Baiburt, and Sebastia/Sivas, and areas around Van and in Diarbekir for these purposes also. Not only was good farmland allowed to desiccate, but with the mass enslavings and deportations of whole villages, there were fewer farmers; and with the theft of livestock, remaining farmers often were deprived of their only source of power for pulling the plow.

The severity of Mongol tax policies had been responsible for both Armenian rebellions of the thirteenth century. Not only was the rate of taxation high, but the manner in which taxes were collected was brutal. Beyond the difficulties posed by "legal" taxes were the problems of the illegal exactions. Such extraordinary taxes demanded by local Mongol officials and/or rebels included money and goods. The billeting of Mongol couriers and envoys in Armenian villages was another draining abuse decried in the sources. Ghazan attempted to stem the deterioration of the central government's control over its officials, but by the early fourteenth century, it was too late. The last Il-Khan, Abu Sa'id (1316-1335), futilely attempted to forbid the practices that were destroying the population and the countryside. A revealing inscription of this khan, carved on the wall of Ani's Manuche mosque, describes the situation: "[In the past] taxes were collected and force was used . . . the place started to become deserted, men from among the common people scattered, the elders of the city and of the province because of the taxes . . . abandoned their possessions real and movable and their families, and went away."

The breakdown of economic life in the early fourteenth century was accompanied by increasing religious intolerance. With the Islamization first of Ahmad Khan (1282-1284) and then with Ghazan's conversion to Islam, Christianity quickly passed from the status of a favored religion to that of a tolerated religion. Anti-Christian persecutions began almost at once. Though checked during part of Ghazan's reign, they became the rule rather than the exception under his intolerant successors. In the Caucasus, anti-Christian persecution was launched with the plundering and killing expeditions of the fanatical Muslim zealot Nauruz (1295-1296) during the reign of Ghazan Khan. Although Nauruz eventually was hunted down and executed at Ghazan's command, with Christian Caucasians gleefully participating, the situation never reversed itself. Religious persecution intensified during the second part of the reign of Ghazan's successor, his brother Muhammad Khuda-Banda (1304-1316). In 1307 Khuda-Banda resumed collection of the *jizya,* or head tax on non-Muslims, something Ghazan had tried but was obliged to discontinue. The sources report that even month-old children were registered for payment of the *jizya.* In the 1320s Grigor, bishop of Karin/Erzerum, was killed after refusing to convert. In 1334 Christians were obliged to wear special blue badges as a visible indicator of their subordinate status. The requirement of the blue badge, kerchief, or hat to set the Christians apart from Muslims was observed by the Bavarian captive Johann Schiltberger around 1400, and so was a feature of the entire fourteenth century.

Following the death of Abu Sa'id in 1335, nine years of internecine warfare broke out among various nomadic elements vying for power. Between 1335 and 1344 no less than eight khans were enthroned, only to be deposed or murdered shortly afterward. But the collapse of the Il-Khans, far from signaling freedom from oppressive rule for the Armenians, meant only that their land now became the theater of warfare for the various new contenders. During the first part of the fourteenth century, the first set of new contenders consisted of two nomadic clans, the Jalayirids and the Chobanids. As a result of warfare between these tribes, parts of southwestern Armenia were ravaged. The Chobanid Malik Ashraf turned his wrath on the remnants of the once-great Armenian noble houses in Ani and Bjni, decimating them in the early

1350s. The rule of the Chobanids was ended by another northern invasion, from Khan Jani Beg of the Golden Horde (1357). The latter part of the fourteenth century was occupied by warfare between two new contenders, the Kara Koyunlu Turkmens and the Ottomans. The Ottomans were part of the Oghuz tribesmen who had first come into Asia Minor in the eleventh century, but greatly increased with new arrivals during the thirteenth century. By the beginning of the fourteenth century, the Ottoman entity had emerged as the strongest of the many small states to arise on the ruins of the Sultanate of Rum. Throughout the fourteenth century the Ottomans continued to expand at the expense of other Turkmen principalities. Toward the end of the century, they controlled areas of western Armenia, such as Sebastia/Sivas, Erzinga/Erzinjan, and Melitene/Malatia.

The confused situation thus created in the Caucasus and Asia Minor did not go unnoticed by Khan Tokhtamysh of the Golden Horde. In 1385, with an army of 50,000, he invaded Azerbaijan via Darband and Shirvan. After taking Tabriz, his marauding army divided into sections, one group going via Marand to Nakhichevan and Siunik, which was plundered from south to north. Khan Tokhtamysh's divided army reunited in Karabagh and then returned north via Shirvan. With them went 200,000 slaves, including tens of thousands of Armenians from the districts of Parskahayk, Siunik, and Artsakh.

The Timurid Invasions

In 1386-1387, 1394-1396, and 1399-1403, Armenia was subjected to what were perhaps the most brutal invasions yet. These were led or directed by the lame warlord Timur (Tamerlane) and constituted the last major invasions of the Armenian highlands from Central Asia. During the first Timurid invasion of 1386-1387, Nakhichevan was captured and the fortress of Ernjak was besieged (though it did not surrender until 1401). The towns and fortresses of Karbi, Bjni, Garni, Surmari, and Koghb fell, and the districts of Ayrarat and Lesser Siunik were devastated. Tiflis was taken and sacked. After wintering in Mughan in Azerbaijan, Timur's generals crossed into the Kajberunik and Chapaghjur districts of southern and southwestern historical Armenia, where they fought unsuccessfully against the Kara Koyunlu Turkmens. Some Timurid detachments reached as far north as Karin/Erzerum, looting, pillaging, and taking slaves as they went. In 1387 Timur besieged the

emir Ezdin at Van. When he took the citadel after a month's besiege-
ment, the women and children were enslaved, while some 7,000 males
of all faiths were killed by being hurled from the walls. After Timur left
Asia Minor in 1387, severe famine ensued. Due to the disruptions he
had caused, crops were not planted, and now there was nothing to
harvest. Cannibalism was reported in some areas.

In 1394 Timur returned. Entering western historical Armenia from
northern Mesopotamia, he took Erzinjan, parts of Basen district, and
Avnik fortress. Kars, Surmari, Koghb, Bagaran, and Ayrarat were
ravaged, and the Kara Koyunlu Turkmen areas, centered at Arjesh north
of Lake Van, were attacked. At this point Timur turned upon Khan
Tokhtamysh of the Golden Horde, who had been raiding Shirvan. The
Timurids defeated Tokhtamysh and sacked his principal cities of Astrakhan and Sarai. Timur appointed Miran, his half-mad son, as governor
of Iran, Iraq, Armenia, and other parts of the Caucasus. In 1396 Miran
continued operations against Ernjak in the south and expanded warfare
against the Kurdish emir of Bitlis. In 1397 southern Vaspurakan was
ravaged and Ani in the north fell. Strangely, all powers of resistance had
not been completely broken by the Timurids. In 1399 King Giorgi VII
of Georgia attacked the Timurid besiegers of Ernjak fortress, temporarily freeing those inside from the thirteen-year siege. But when Timur
learned about this, he left Samarkand and headed for the Caucasus. In
revenge, he attacked northeastern Armenia and southern Georgia, killing, destroying, and taking slaves. More than 60,000 Caucasians were
led into slavery this time (in 1400), and many districts in northern
Armenia were depopulated. Subsequently, Timur headed for western
historical Armenia, where he took Sebastia/Sivas and Melitene/Malatia
from his archenemies, the Ottomans. After conquering Aleppo, Damascus, Mardin, and Baghdad, Timur decisively beat and captured the
Ottoman sultan, Sultan Bayazid II, in 1402. The next year Georgia was
invaded again and its king finally submitted to Timur. During 1403-
1404 Timur wintered in Karabagh before returning to Samarkand, where
he died in 1405.

By the end of the fourteenth century, the condition of the Armenians of central and eastern Asia Minor was bleak. Information on this
period derives from the *History* of Tovma Metzopetsi (d. 1446), from
colophons, and from the accounts of foreign travelers. Hamd Allah
Mustawfi Qazvini, the accountant-general of Iran, noted the decline of
the cities and towns in Caucasia and across the Armenian highlands in
his day (1340). Speaking of Georgia and Abkhazia, he stated that

"revenues in the time of their native kings amounted to near 5,000,000 dinars of the present currency; but in our times the government only obtains 1,202,000 dinars." About Rum, which embraced western historical Armenia, he said: "Its revenues at the present day amount to 3,300,000 dinars as set down in the registers; but during the time of the Seljuks they were in excess of 15,000,000 dinars of the present currency." The walls of Sebastia/Sivas were in ruins; Avnik was in ruins; Baiburt "was a large town; it is now but a small one"; Mush, "in former times a large city, but now a ruin"; Berkri, "a small town, that was a large place formerly." Khlat "is the capital of this province [Greater Armenia] and its revenues in former days amounted to near 2,000,000 dinars of the present currency; but now the total sum paid is only 390,000 dinars" (Qazvini, 1919). Until the Seljuk invasions, Siunik had some 1,000 villages, while at the end of the thirteenth century the figure had declined to 677 villages. According to Samvel Anetsi and Matthew of Edessa, the former Artsruni kingdom in Vaspurakan had over 4,000 villages, but thirteenth- and fourteenth-century authors speak of that area with distress, as if describing a desert. Furthermore, in the 1350s the trade routes shifted away from the northern cities of Ani and Kars, to the southern cities of Khlat, Mayyafarikin, and Arjesh, helping to impoverish northeastern Armenia.

Toward the end of the fourteenth century, the Armenian Church and especially its hierarchy was under attack. In 1387-1388, Stepanos, archbishop of Sebastia/Sivas, was executed for refusing to convert to Islam. His monastery of St. Nshan was transformed into a dervish sanctuary, and other churches were demolished. In 1393-1394, Catholicos Zakaria of Aghtamar and Teodoros, the catholicos of Sis, both were executed. Between 1403 and 1406, according to the Spanish ambassador Clavijo, Timur demolished the churches of Erzinjan and Bekarich. In addition to attacks from without, the Armenian Church was suffering from internal division at the end of the fourteenth century. The influence of Roman Catholicism, which had been growing on the Cilician Armenian clergy during the thirteenth century, led to a break between Echmiadzin and Sis during the tenure of Catholicos Hakob of Sis (1327-1341, 1355-1359). But by midcentury the Dominicans had won over to Catholicism the influential Hovhannes Krnetsi of southern Siunik, who began attracting to Catholicism his former classmates. The fight against the Armenian Catholics of Krna preoccupied the Armenian Church leadership for much of the fourteenth century. During the reign of Catholicos Hakob, matters had deteriorated to the point that the

Cilician catholicos supported Krna's efforts against Echmiadzin. Another source of jurisdictional conflict in the fourteenth century was the catholicosate (or anticatholicosate) of Aghtamar.

At the end of the fourteenth and the beginning of the fifteenth century, a few small Armenian principalities still existed. These were in the same areas that had withstood previous invaders and owed their semiautonomy to the forbidding mountainous terrain: areas of Vayots Dzor, Siunik, Artsakh, Gugark, Rshtunik, Mokk, Sasun, and Mush. The Timurids preserved the Orbelians in Siunik, the Dopians in Tsar, the Proshians in Vayots Dzor and Shahapunik. However, the circumstances of the Armenian lords were far from easy. Most were under constant pressure to convert to Islam. Tovma Metzopetsi as well as foreign travelers described the plight of the remaining lords:

> During the first year of his reign [Umar, Timur's grandson], he forcibly made to apostatize three princes of our people who had remained like a tiny cluster of grapes among us: the son of Ivane and grandson of Burtel, Burtel, *ter* of Orotan, of the Orbelian family; his brother Smbat whom they took with his family to Samarqand (but subsequently, through divine mercy and their prayers they returned to their patrimony); the ter of Eghegis named Tarsayich, son of Gorgon they caused to apostatize; the ter of Maku they detached from the false and diophysitic [beliefs] of Aghtarmayutiun [Roman Catholicism], and the son of an azat named Azitan from Aghtsuats village in the Ayraratian district. Later, however, they repented and became true Believers in Christ and heirs of the Kingdom. (Tovma Metzopetsi, 1987)

The same sources refer to Crypto-Christianity, the observance of Christianity in secret. Other lords converted. Clavijo and Tovma Metzopetsi both mention the Armenian prince Taharten, governor of Erzinjan. His son by a daughter of the emperor of Trebizond was a Muslim and (perhaps because of his faith) Timur's governor of the same city. Another probable Armenian lordly convert to Islam is the emir Ezdin of Van, whom Tovma Metzopetsi described as being "of the line of King Senekerim," that is, of some Artsruni background (1987).

As a result of the unsettled, unsafe times, some lords of completely impregnable fortresses, unable to maintain themselves in any other way, turned to banditry. Prime sources of loot were the increasingly rare caravans passing over the bandits' lands, or even booty captured from

Timurids and Turkmens. Sometimes bandit lords operated alone, sometimes in alliance with others, Christian or Muslim. Tovma Metzopetsi speaks of one such mixed group of Kurdish Muslim and Armenian Christian brigands from Sasun and Khut that looted a Timurid camp in southwestern Armenia in the early 1390s. The Spanish ambassador Clavijo encountered Caucasian bandits both en route to Erzinjan from Trebizond in 1403, and on his return, again in northwestern Armenia and southwestern Georgia: "for though they are Armenians and profess to be Christians, all are robbers and brigands; indeed they forced us, before we were let free to pass, to give a present of our goods as toll for right of passage" (Clavijo, 1928).

Despite the extremely bleak situation across the Armenian highlands at the end of the fourteenth century, the sources still report a few instances of secular and clerical Armenian lords enjoying some influence with the Timurids. Among the secular rulers belong the unnamed woman ruler of Igdir castle mentioned by Clavijo and the Armenian lord of Bayazit. Another such lord was the Roman Catholic Nur ad-Din, mentioned earlier. Among the clerical lords enjoying some influence with the Timurids belong the director of Metop monastery, Hovhannes, and the noted intellectual, *vardapet* Grigor Tatevatsi (Gregory of Tatev), who was a confidant of Timur's son, Miran.

FOR FURTHER INFORMATION

For the sources of, or more information on, the material in this chapter, please consult the following (full citations can be found in the Bibliography at the end of this volume).

Aristakes Lastiverttsi, 1973, 1985.   Minorsky, 1953a.

Clavijo, 1928.   Tovma Metzopetsi, 1860, 1892, 1987.

Kirakos Gandzaketsi, 1961, 1986.

11

CILICIAN ARMENIA

Ani Atamian Bournoutian

The Cilician period, culminating in the establishment of the king-dom of Cilicia in about 1199, represents something of a break in Armenian history. For the first time, major events in the history of the Armenian people were played out in territories that were never part of the ancestral Armenian homeland and where Armenians probably did not even constitute a majority of the population. It is also the first period since that of the Roman Empire in which the concerns of Western Europe—represented by the Crusader states—and the Roman Catholic Church had a major impact on events affecting the Armenian people. Moreover, the number and variety of the many contemporary European, Armenian, Greek, and Arabic sources, while by no means providing a complete narrative, supply rich detail on specific events and personali-ties of Cilicia, and imbue it with a more "modern" flavor than previous periods of Armenian history.

Early History

The early history of the Armenians in Cilicia is that of the efforts of two Armenian families over the course of many generations to extend their control over a region of distinct and varied geographical features. Lower Cilicia is a broad plain in Asia Minor that borders the Mediterranean Sea. It is ringed by three mountain chains: the Taurus Mountains to the northwest, the Anti-Taurus Mountains to the northeast, and the Amanus Mountains to the east. In addition to the economic potential of access to the sea, the western half offered a more secure situation, as the mountain passes through the Taurus, particularly the major pass, known as the Cilician Gates, are long and narrow and easily defended. Because of the coastline and navigable inland rivers, this was also a region of trade and cities: to the west, Adana and Tarsus, and farther east, Mamistra (Mopsuestia, Misis). The upper, eastern diagonal of the plain borders on the Amanus Mountains and Syria to the east. Its mountainous character and remoteness made it a less prosperous region and a less secure one, as the Amanus passes, notably the Amanus Gates, are wider and shorter and, therefore, less easily defended against invaders than those of the Taurus.

Cilicia and its environs, populated in this period by Greeks, Arabs, and Jews as well, had been home to Armenians since the eleventh century. After the fall of the Bagratid kingdom, the Byzantine Empire, which had controlled Cilicia since the mid-tenth century, assigned many imperial military officials of Greater Armenia to lands farther west, in and around the Cilician plain. Other Armenians emigrated there on their own initiative. All brought with them their households and, those who had them, their troops. Although the generals or chieftains in Byzantine service were assigned to protect the region from Seljuk incursions, they sought as well to establish new principalities for themselves. Being far from the center of Byzantine authority, they were able to achieve a level of semi-independence in their territories.

During the second half of the eleventh century, the most powerful Armenian in the region was Philaretus, a general of the Byzantine emperor Romanus IV Diogenes. Philaretus controlled a wide and strategic region from Antioch to Melitene (Malatia), but his territory was eventually broken by Seljuk attacks. Upon Philaretus's death in 1092, his Armenian lieutenant, Gogh Vasil ("Basil the Robber"), inherited his holdings in Raban and Kesum and his position as the most powerful Armenian chieftain in Cilicia.

Along the Anti-Taurus Mountains in the late eleventh and early twelfth centuries were other lieutenants of Philaretus, such as Tatul of Marash, Gabriel (in some Armenian sources, Khoril) of Melitene, and Toros of Edessa (Urfa, Urha). Like many Armenian imperial officials, Tatul, Gabriel, and Toros held to the Greek Orthodox faith. The area of Tarsus was controlled by a member of the Artsruni house, Abul-Gharib. East of Mamistra, in the fortress of Gobidara, was Ruben, a former

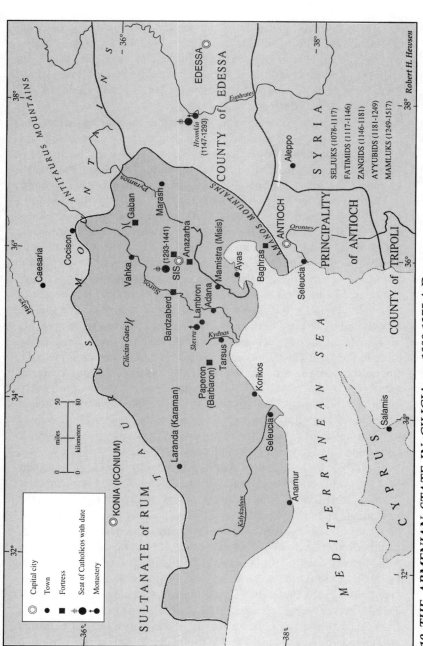

10. THE ARMENIAN STATE IN CILICIA, c. 1080-1375 A.D.

Robert H. Heusen

Capital city
Town
Fortress
Seat of Catholicos with date
Monastery

SELJUKS (1078-1117)
FATIMIDS (1117-1146)
ZANGIDS (1146-1181)
AYYUBIDS (1181-1249)
MAMLUKS (1249-1517)

SYRIA

COUNTY of EDESSA

EDESSA

Euphrates

Hromkla
(1147-1293)

Aleppo

PRINCIPALITY
of ANTIOCH

ANTIOCH

Orontes

PRINCIPALITY
of ANTIOCH

COUNTY of TRIPOLI

ANTITAURUS MOUNTAINS

Caesaria

Halys

Cocison

Gaban

Marash

Pyramos

Vahka

SIS
(1293-1441)

Anazarba

Mamistra (Misis)

Sihun

Bardzaberd

Lambron

Adana

Skevra

Ayas

Baghras

Seleucia

AMANOS MOUNTAINS

MOUNTAINS

Cilician Gates

Paperon
(Barbaron)

Tarsus

Kydnos

Korikos

Laranda (Karaman)

SULTANATE of RUM

KONIA (ICONIUM)

Seleucia

Kalykadnos

Anamur

M E D I T E R R A N E A N   S E A

C Y P R U S

Salamis

miles
kilometers
0   50
0   80

38°
36°
34°
32°

38°
36°
34°
32°

Armenian Byzantine official in the service of King Gagik II, who migrated west after the fall of the Bagratid kingdom. To the far western edge of the Cilician plain, in the area of the Cilician Gates, was King Oshin, an Armenian official of the Byzantine Empire, who, upon Abul-Gharib's death, was granted the strategic fortresses of Lambron and Baberon to defend the gates against the Turks.

Despite their probable lack of numerical superiority, Armenians came to dominate key positions in Cilicia. Among these many chieftains, two houses maintained their dominance and, by the early twelfth century, rivaled each other for control of the plain. They have come to be known as the Rubenids or Rubenians, after Ruben, and the Hetumids, or Hetumians, after King Oshin's son Hetum. Unlike the Rubenids, the Hetumids remained loyal vassals of Byzantium, and they retained the fortresses of Lambron and Baberon as the secure center of their power. The Rubenids, after the death of Gogh Vasil in about 1112, came to control the upper, mountainous region around the fortress of Vahka. Some later chroniclers identify Ruben as a relative of King Gagik Bagratuni. There is no historical basis to this claim, but it is no doubt based on accounts that Ruben's grandson, Toros, avenged Gagik's death by killing the late king's assassins. However, the fact that these accounts of Toros's revenge appear about the time of Gogh Vasil's death make it likely that, fabricated or true, the Rubenids proclaimed their tie to the Bagratid dynasty in order to legitimize their ascendancy and territorial ambitions in the region. These ambitions consisted of aggressively extending their control southward to the lower plain with its principal trade routes and ports. This expansion naturally brought the Rubenids into conflict with the Hetumids, who, as loyal imperial vassals, defended Byzantine Cilician territory from Rubenid incursions.

At the same time that the Rubenids were beginning to enlarge their holdings in Cilicia, European forces had entered Asia Minor as part of the First Crusade of 1095. There is some debate as to whether the Armenians and other Christians in Cilicia actually saw the Crusaders, or "Franks," as they were called, as welcome "liberators" from Seljuk control. Rather, some historians assert that the Seljuk ascendancy in Asia Minor after the battle of Manzikert (Malazgerd, Manazkert) in 1071, in fact, helped to provide some stability in the region and filled a vacuum in authority left by ineffectual Byzantine rule. Cleaning out the "infidel" Turk, however, provided a powerful justification for the Crusaders to enter Asia Minor. For Cilician history, the establishment of Crusader states at nearby Edessa and Antioch meant that Europe's desire to carve out independent principalities in the region became a major political and military factor with which all of the Armenian chieftains of Cilicia had to reckon. The history of Cilician Armenia was thus not made, nor can it be told, in isolation, as its course was inevitably affected by that of the Muslim, Byzantine, and Crusader states that neighbored it.

The Crusades and Armenia

From the first, the Crusaders—who included among their numbers clergy and merchants as well as military men—sought out Armenians as guides, purveyors of supplies, and soldiers. As the strongest Christian military leaders in the region, the Cilician Armenian lords became frequent and valuable allies. Armenian, Muslim, and Crusader leaders alike, however, saw in each other a lack of unity, internal rivalries, and territorial ambition, and frequently played one against another. An example is the fall of Toros of Edessa. Soon after the arrival of the Crusaders, Toros requested the assistance of Baldwin of Boulogne, a French Crusade leader in maintaining control of Edessa, which Toros had recently taken from the Seljuks. Baldwin agreed, but only after Toros had promised to make him heir to Edessa by formally adopting the Frenchman as his son. When another raid of Baldwin's against the Turks endangered the safety of the area, the Armenians there, who bore little love for the Greek Orthodox Toros, rose up to overthrow him. Baldwin refused any aid to his "father" and let events run their course. The result was Toros's death by an Armenian mob and Baldwin's assumption of the title of Count of Edessa.

The Armenian chieftains were frequently principal players— sometimes allies, sometimes targets—in the struggle among the Crusade leaders for control and expansion of the two Crusader states of the County of Edessa and the Principality of Antioch. By the year 1118, the territories of Gogh Vasil's successors and the lands of Abul-Gharib and other Armenian chieftains, whose holdings lay east of the Cilician plain, were conquered by Baldwin of Boulogne and his heirs and incorporated into the County of Edessa. This left the Rubenids and the Hetumids, who were more removed from the immediate vicinity of Crusader ambitions, as the only strong and semi-independent Armenian chieftains left in the region.

One of the earliest important Rubenid gains was made by Toros (period of leadership, 1102-1129), the grandson of Ruben, when he captured from the Byzantines the two fortresses of Bardzberd and Anazarba. The latter, rising to a height of 700 feet, became a center of the Rubenids and was probably the strongest of the Armenian fortresses in Cilicia. The Rubenids continued expanding their holdings in the midst of shifting frontiers and alliances. Toros was succeeded by his brother Levon (period of leadership, 1129-1140). Levon became known as "Leo" or "Leon" to the Europeans and, as evidence of growing Rubenid power, dubbed by Western sources as "Prince Leo of the Mountains." By the year 1135, he had succeeded in extending his holdings to the Mediterranean by capturing, for a short period, the key cities of Mamistra, Adana, and Tarsus. This he was able to accomplish largely thanks both to internal fighting among the Muslims, engineered by the Turkish commander of Aleppo, Zangi, and to the deflection of Byzantium's attention to problems with the Serbs and Magyars. By 1137, however, Emperor John Comnenus was able to direct his troops to Asia Minor. His immediate concern was the Crusader principality of Antioch, which, ever since its founding, was to have been turned over to Byzantine rule. As the Rubenid holdings were literally a wedge driven between imperial territories in western Asia Minor and Antioch, John lost no time in invading and reimposing Byzantine rule in his Cilician territories, happily assisted in this task by his Hetumid allies. Tarsus, Adana, and Mamistra quickly fell, and soon after, the key Rubenid fortresses of Vahka and Anazarba. Levon was taken captive to Constantinople, along with his wife and two of his sons, Ruben and Toros. Levon, his wife, and Ruben, all died in captivity; young Toros, however, managed to escape and returned to Cilicia. Military-political events soon provided favorable circumstances for the Rubenids, now led by a grown Toros (period of leadership, 1144-1169), to restore their power in the region. In 1143 John Comnenus died. The next year Zangi captured the County of Edessa. This was a calamitous event for the Crusades, marking their first major defeat, and sparked the Second Crusade. For the many Armenians in Edessa, it meant evacuation to the nearby Crusader state of Antioch and into Cilicia proper. A significant consequence came of the fall of Edessa, however. In 1146 Edessa's former ruler, Count Joscelin II, died after an unsuccessful and bloody attempt to recapture it, during which Zangi's forces killed hundreds of Armenians and other Christian civilians. Joscelin's wife, Beatrice of Saone, sold to the Byzantines many of the fortresses that her husband had controlled. She kept one, however, the stronghold of Hromkla, or Rum Qalat, on the Euphrates River and granted it to the Armenian catholicos. Hromkla became and remained for the next one hundred years the seat of the catholicosate, despite the fact that for most of this period it was deep in Muslim-held territory.

Meanwhile, Toros was proving himself an able leader. By 1148, the year of the Second Crusade, the Rubenids had recaptured Vahka from the Byzantines and had reestablished Rubenid power in Anazarba and other areas. At the same time, the growing power of Zangi's son, Nur al-Din, particularly after the latter's capture of Damascus in 1154, forced the Crusader states into a closer alliance with Byzantium. Reginald of Chatillon, prince of Antioch, agreed to retake the Cilician cities on the coast for the Greeks (Byzantines), but then failed to hand over the territory to Byzantium. When the Greeks subsequently refused payment for the attack, Reginald sought and received Toros's cooperation in seeking retribution, and, in one of the least glorious and most wasteful episodes of the Crusades, the two leaders combined forces in raiding and looting the Greek island of Cyprus. A short time later the emperor Manuel Comnenus counterattacked and marched through Cilicia, took Toros by surprise, and reduced the area to its already legal status of Byzantine vassal state. It was for but a short period, however. Baldwin, king of the Crusader state of Jerusalem, now allied through marriage with Manuel, mediated on Toros's behalf, probably as thanks for Toros's military aid the previous year, and the Armenian leader soon regained control—albeit under nominal Byzantine suzerainty—over Cilicia.

Toros succeeded in keeping on generally cordial terms with both the Seljuks and the Crusaders. He made what appears to be the first attempt to ally the two dominant Cilician Armenian families, by marrying his daughter to the son of the Hetumid leader, though the bride was later repudiated. Most important, he created over a period of years the beginnings of an Armenian Rubenid state, coming to peaceful terms with the Byzantines and receiving limited Byzantine recognition of his position in Cilicia. He was an active participant in regional military affairs. He established friendly relations with Prince Bohemond III of Antioch by helping him gain the throne against the claims of Bohemond's mother. In 1164 Toros joined a combined force of Crusader and Byzantine troops against Nur al-Din and later helped negotiate the release of Bohemond and the Byzantine commander from Muslim capture. Toros's consolidation of land and his prestige were such that one contemporary Western source referred to Cilicia as "the land of King Toros."

Toros died in 1169, at a critical time for all of Asia Minor and Palestine. Saladin (Salah al-Din) had by that date conquered Egypt and allied it with Syria, creating a formidable Muslim force that literally encircled the Crusader states and threatened Cilicia. A struggle for Toros's position immediately began among his brothers. One of them, Mleh, who had converted to Islam, killed Toros's son to assure the legality of his own succession and allied himself with Nur al-Din, still the most powerful Muslim leader. Backed by Nur al-Din's forces, Mleh invaded the Rubenid holdings, took possession of all Byzantine fortresses there, and held control for several years, much to the dismay of the other Rubenid nobility. When Nur al-Din died in 1174, the Rubenid leadership lost no time in ousting Mleh and choosing Toros's nephew, Ruben (period of leadership, 1175-1187), as his successor.

Ruben continued his family's traditional struggle against the Hetumids. The Hetumids, however, enlisted the help of Prince Bohemond III of Antioch, who was now himself a Byzantine vassal, and despite the assistance that the Rubenids, under Toros, had lent him, allied with his fellow vassals against Ruben. In 1183 Bohemond invited Ruben to Antioch for talks, purportedly aimed at reconciling the two Armenian houses, and promptly took Ruben captive. It was a brief captivity, but it gave Ruben's brother Levon an opportunity to exert his considerable skills as interim ruler of the house. It also developed in Levon a deep-seated animosity toward Antioch. Soon after his release, Ruben placed the leadership of the house in the able hands of his brother and retired to a monastery near Sis, where he died one year later.

Levon (period of leadership and reign, 1187-1219) took full advantage of the favorable circumstances now facing his territory. Byzantine power in Asia Minor had all but been broken by their defeat at the hands of the Turks at the battle of Myriocephalon, near Phyrgia, in 1176. Saladin had dealt the Europeans the most crushing blow of the Crusades when he captured Jerusalem in 1187, the culmination of a powerful Muslim counterattack against the Crusades. The fall of the Holy City launched the Third Crusade, which, while it recaptured the key city of Acre, failed in retaking Jerusalem itself. With the cornerstone of the Crusader states now lost, European strength was confined to the Mediterranean coastal states of Antioch, Tripoli, and Tyre.

The Kingdom of Cilicia

In the eyes of the Crusaders, Cilicia now assumed a new strategic importance as a major Christian enclave. Evidence of this is a letter written in 1189 by Pope Clement III both to Catholicos Grigor IV Tgha and Levon, formally requesting their military and financial assistance to the Crusading forces. Levon was both wise and ambitious enough to see that the circumstances were ripe to win once and for all official recognition of his position in the region. As early as 1190, Western chroniclers were referring to Levon as "duke," and "prince," but Levon's goal was a royal crown. He had hoped to receive it from the German Holy Roman Emperor, Frederick Barbarossa, probably as a condition for further Rubenid assistance to the Crusade effort. Unfortunately for Levon, Frederick drowned while in Asia Minor in 1190. Finally, in either 1198 or 1199—the date is disputed, though there is firmer evidence for the latter—Levon received not one but two crowns, one from a representative of the new German emperor, Henry VI, and one from the Byzantine emperor. Chroniclers recount Levon's coronation as King of Armenia at the Cathedral of Tarsus on January 6 as a grand and ceremonious event, with nearly fifty members of both the Rubenid and Hetumid nobility, as well as numerous members of the clergy and representatives from Europe and the Crusader states.

During Levon's long reign Cilicia reached its greatest geographical extent and the apex of its power. Armenians finally had secure control of the coastal plain and their Mediterranean port cities. King Levon succeeded in the long Rubenid quest of breaking Hetumid power in western Cilicia. From his new capital at Sis he established alliances through his own, his daughter's, and his niece's marriage to the houses of Cyprus, Antioch, and Byzantium, respectively.

Levon's reign was marked, however, by two major crises. Levon's grand plan was to extend his control by uniting Cilicia to the powerful neighboring state of Antioch. It was a design that had occupied most of his reign, both before and after his coronation. Upon succeeding Ruben, Levon had made an uneasy peace with Bohemond III of Antioch, his brother's captor. When Saladin invaded Bohemond's principality, in about 1190 or 1191, Levon had made no attempt to aid his neighbor. Rather, as soon as Saladin had withdrawn from the strategic Antiochene fortress of Baghras (Gaston), which had been granted to the Order of the Knights Templar, Levon had seized it and refused to give it up. He had then plotted with Bohemond's wife, who wanted to assure the Antiochene succession of her line and, turning the tables, captured Bohemond during an invitation for talks on the Baghras question. Levon's terms for Bohemond's release was Cilician suzerainty over Antioch. The Antiochene nobility, many of whom had Armenian blood, were ready to accept the terms, but the citizenry, particularly the largely Italian commercial interests, who feared Armenian competition, rebelled and established a commune to govern the principality. Levon had obviously lost the first round of his fight for Antioch.

Levon had managed, however, shortly before his coronation, to marry his niece Alice to Bohemond's son, Raymond. Soon after the birth of their son, Raymond Ruben, the boy's father died. Given Bohemond's advanced age, Antioch was sure to be governed by an Armenian regency if Raymond Ruben was upheld as heir, against his uncle, the Count of Tripoli. A protracted struggle ensued, with the pope and German emperor, the recent supporters of Levon's elevation to kingship, committed to the child's claim, and the Count of Tripoli, allied with Antioch's Pisan and Genoese merchants and the still-disgruntled Templars, against him. Even had Levon been willing to restore Baghras to the Templars as the pope requested, the popular sentiment in Antioch against the Armenians was too strong. The war of the Antiochene succession dragged on for the next quarter of a century. Old Bohemond of Antioch died in 1201, but Levon was too distracted by Seljuk raids into Cilicia to press the Armenian claim. Eventually, the Count of Tripoli, Bohemond's younger son, succeeded his father, thereby ending Levon's hopes of uniting the two states.

Levon's second and, for Cilicia itself, more serious crisis arose as a direct result of his coronation and was to plague the kingdom until its fall. This was the question of doctrinal and liturgical unity with the Roman Catholic Church, which the papacy had attempted to impose since the First Crusade. In granting Levon a royal crown with the consent and blessing of the pope, the German emperor as well as Rome expected acknowledgment of the pope as the head of Christendom. Whether Levon had agreed to such acknowledgment beforehand is unknown, but once crowned, he tried to allay the fears and anger of the Armenian clergy by requiring them only to make minor changes in the Armenian liturgy and only to concede a "special respect" to the pope as the successor of St. Peter. An early and apolitical Armenian supporter of unity with Rome was Nerses of Lambron, Bishop of Tarsus, but the cause found no leadership among the Cilician clergy after his death in 1199 and no widespread support at any time. As the thirteenth and fourteenth centuries wore on, the conflict over unity caused a serious rift not only between the Armenian crown and clergy but between the clergy of Greater Armenia and of the Cilician kingdom as well. The dispute over ecclesiastical unity with Rome became an issue that was exploited by the papacy and the Crusaders as the Muslim counteroffensive against Cilicia later gained strength.

Cilician Society and Economy

The nature of the kingdom created in Cilicia by Levon and his successors differed greatly from that of the Bagratid dynasty and was, due to a century of close contact with the Crusaders, a decidedly Armenian-Western hybrid in certain respects. The relationship of the king to the nobility was essentially a Western feudal one of sovereign to vassal, rather than the earlier *nakharar* system of "first among equals." This relationship did not develop immediately or completely. As late as 1215, certain Cilician nobles still reserved the right to levy trade duties on foreign merchants, despite royal agreements of exemption, and throughout the life of the kingdom, the nobility had a voice in the question of succession. Western feudal law, specifically the *Assizes* of Antioch (which has survived only in its Armenian translation), was used to judge cases involving the court and nobility. Armenian nobles were knighted in the European tradition, and jousts and tournaments, unknown in Greater Armenia, became popular sport. Latin and French terms of nobility and office were used in place of Armenian equivalents: "paron" ("baron") rather than *nakharar,* and "gonstapl" ("constable") rather than *sparapet.* The alphabet itself was extended to accommodate certain new sounds introduced by Western languages, thus the Armenian letters o and f. French and Latin became secondary languages at the royal court. The nobility, as surviving manuscript illuminations and chroniclers' descriptions reveal, also adopted Western feudal dress. European, particularly French names, such as Raymond, Henri, Etien, Alice, Isabelle, and Melisende, became popular among members of the royal court. This was an age where alliances and agreements were often sealed by marriages, and the amount of intermarriage with the Cilician nobility, primarily Armenian noble women, meant that there were those of Armenian blood in the courts of every Crusader state, in Byzantium, and even in European noble families. Frequently, in order to facilitate these marriage alliances, Armenian nobles converted to Catholicism and the Greek Orthodox faith.

On the level below that of nobility, Cilicia was a heterogenous society, where the Armenian dealt with European, Greek, Jew, Eastern Christian, and Muslim on a daily basis. While there exists very little information on the "average" Cilician Armenian of the commercial class, it is probable that intermarriage and the degree of "Frankishness" were on a smaller scale here than among the nobility; and among tradesmen and the peasantry, who made up the majority of the Armenian population, probably not at all. Certainly the clergy did its best, in the face of pressure from the throne, to keep its Eastern, Armenian character intact.

The fortunes of geography placed Cilicia at a strategic point in several important trade routes linking Central Asia and the Persian Gulf to the Mediterranean, routes that carried, among other goods, the lucrative spice trade from India and Southeast Asia to Europe. Cilicia itself was a prosperous land and exported livestock as well as hides, wool, and cotton. Its goat-hair cloth had long been renowned for its strength. Timber from the mountains was traded as well as grain, wine, raisins, and raw silk. As was widespread in the period, there was also a profitable trade in Christian and Muslim slaves. During and after Levon's reign, the port of Ayas on the Gulf of Alexandretta, always an important stopover for European and oriental merchants, underwent a revitalization as the center of East-West commerce in Asia Minor. Ayas was a market center as well as a port, and its bazaars sold dyes, spices, silk and cotton cloth, carpets, and pearls from all over Asia, and finished cloth and metal products from Europe. Early in his reign Levon signed agreements with the Italian city-states of Genoa, Venice, and Pisa, and later with the French and the Catalans, granting their merchants tax exemptions and other privileges in return for their trade. Thus, there was in Ayas, Tarsus, Adana, and Mamistra a thriving European merchant community, dominated by the Italians, which was allowed by treaty its own trading houses, churches, and courts of law. As French became the secondary language of the Cilician court, Italian became the secondary language of Cilician commerce.

Coins were struck by Cilician leaders as early as the second Rubenid leader, Toros, in the mid-twelfth century. During the period of the kingdom, gold and silver coins, called *dram* and *tagvorin,* were struck at the royal mints at Sis and Tarsus. In trade, all other coins of the period were used as well, such as the Italian *ducat, florin,* and *zecchino,* the Greek *besant,* the Arab *dirham,* and the French *livre.*

With the catholicosate at distant Hromkla on the Euphrates until the turn of the thirteenth century, the catholicos was assisted in administering the Armenian Church in Cilicia by fourteen bishops during the reign of Levon, and even more appear to have been named in later years.

Sis, Tarsus, Lambron, Anazarba, and Mamistra were the seats of archbishops. Sources list up to sixty monastic houses in Cilicia, though the location of many of these remains unknown.

The Rule of the Hetumids

King Levon I died in 1219, after one of the longest rules in Cilicia. Asia Minor and Palestine had a far different political configuration at his death than at the beginning of his rule. The Crusaders, led by the Venetians, had invaded the center of Christian power in the East, Constantinople, in 1204, forcing the Byzantine emperor to set up an empire-in-exile in Nicea. Farther east, Saladin's united Syria and Egypt was the stronghold of Muslim power in the region and an equal, if not greater, threat to Cilicia than the Seljuks. Europe recognized that threat to their own status in the region and sent the Fourth Crusade in 1215, which tried but failed to invade Egypt and check Saladin's power.

Levon at his death named his only child, Zabel (Isabelle), as his heir, but his grandnephew, Raymond Ruben of Antioch, with papal support, seized the throne. The Armenian nobility ousted and imprisoned Raymond Ruben and installed the young Zabel on the throne, with Constantine, a Hetumid noble, as regent, an action that marked the beginning of Hetumid rule in Cilicia. With the Seljuks occupying the western Taurus Mountains and threatening another invasion, Constantine sought an alliance with Antioch and arranged for Philip, the son of the Prince of Antioch, to marry Zabel, insisting, however, that the groom become a member of the Armenian Church. Whatever Zabel's feelings about her new husband, the Armenian nobility were not pleased. Philip seemed to disdain Armenian customs—it is said that he refused even to grow a beard—and was in Antioch more than in his adopted country. In 1224 he was arrested and poisoned in prison. Constantine saw an opportunity to consolidate Hetumid influence in Cilicia and married his own son, Hetum, to the widowed Zabel, then only fourteen years of age and three years Hetum's senior. Queen Zabel is one of the few female personalities mentioned by sources on Cilicia, and certainly the strongest. Upon her first husband's murder, she fled to the protection of the Knights Hospitaller rather than remain in Cilicia, and she refused for several years to live with her new husband. By 1230 she relented and the two were crowned at Sis, thus officially giving an equal share in governing the kingdom to the Hetumids.

Hetum I (1226-1270) enjoyed a reign of forty-four years, the longest of any Cilician king, and was fortunate during that time to have the wise counsel and support of his brother Smbat, the High Constable, or *sparapet,* of Cilicia, who has left the *Chronicle of Smbat,* a valuable source of that period (Der Nersessian, 1959). The reign of Hetum and Zabel is usually characterized as a "flowering of the arts," but it was as marked by as much warfare as any other in Cilicia's history. The Seljuks invaded again in both 1233 and 1245, demanding high tributes and inflicting terrible damage; the Ayyubids with their Mamluk army in Egypt were an ever-growing threat; and now, a new force appeared on the scene, the Mongols. Moving westward from the steppes of Central Asia, the Mongols had attacked the Seljuks in Anatolia and established a stronghold north of Syria. The Mongols were not Muslim but shamanists and had a common enemy with the Christians of the area in the Seljuks and Mamluks. The papacy, the Crusaders, and the Armenians all made great efforts at an alliance with the Mongol leaders, even hoping for their conversion to Christianity.

King Hetum, wisely, lost no time in approaching the Mongols. In 1247 he sent his brother Smbat to the Mongol court in the distant city of Kara Korum, and several years later he traveled there himself, to seal an alliance with the Great Khan Möngke against the Muslim powers threatening Cilicia. Upon his return to Cilicia, Hetum traveled through Greater Armenia, the first and only Cilician leader since the first generation of Rubenids and Hetumids to see the Armenian homeland.

The Mongol alliance was initially of great benefit to Cilicia and to the Mongols themselves in holding back the Seljuks and the Mamluks. Armenians fought side by side with Mongols and Antiochenes to defeat the Mamluk army at Aleppo and Damascus. The alliance was beneficial to the Armenians, however, only as long as the Mongols remained strong in the region around Cilicia. In 1260 the Mediterranean Crusader states, feeling their own security threatened by growing Mongol power, allowed Mamluk troops to march through Latin Palestine against a combined Mongol and Armenian force. The result was a crushing defeat by the Mamluks at Ayn Jalut, a victory that saved Egypt from the Mongols and encouraged the Muslims of Damascus, Aleppo, and other cities of Syria to rise against their Mongol conquerors. The Mongols were thus pushed back and contained in Iran, too distant to help Cilicia against renewed Mamluk and Seljuk attack.

While Hetum traveled again to the Mongol court, now at Tabriz, to seek more military aid, the Mamluk leader Baybars sought to punish

Cilicia's alliance with the Mongols against Egypt. For twenty days the Mamluks devastated the country, killing thousands, taking thousands more as prisoners and slaves, and setting fire to the cathedral at Sis and looting its treasury. The port of Ayas was destroyed, with serious consequences for the Cilician economy. The Armenians under Smbat the Constable fought as best they could, but they were hopelessly outnumbered. Hetum returned to find his country in ruins and retired to a monastery, abdicating in 1269 in favor of his son, Levon II (1270-1289).

Levon's reign was marked by a wave of invasions into Cilician territory by the Mamluks and by Turkmen and Kurdish bands. Levon was forced to sign a ten-year treaty with the Mamluks, requiring him to pay a high annual tribute in return for the safety of his people. Levon died in 1289, leaving the oldest of several sons, Hetum, to succeed him.

At a time when strong leadership was needed, Hetum II's reign, or rather series of reigns (1289-1293; 1295-1297; 1299-1307) marks the nadir of Cilician rule, checkered with fractious family and factional strife that was to characterize the kingdom's political history until its fall. Despite Levon II's treaty, the Mamluk threat still loomed, and in 1292, Hromkla was invaded, the catholicosate and its reliquaries and treasury looted, and the catholicos, Stepannos IV, taken captive. Hetum abdicated in favor of his brother, Toros (1293-1294) and, a devout convert to Catholicism, entered a Franciscan monastery. He was persuaded to resume the throne two years later. During his second reign, he married his sister to Amaury (Amalric) de Lusignan, brother of the king of Cyprus, whose children would later inherit the Cilician throne. Hetum traveled to Iran to reforge an alliance with the Mongols and from there went to Constantinople to do the same with Byzantium. Upon his return, he found that his brother Smbat I (1297-1299, not to be confused with the High Constable) had seized the throne. Hetum and his brother Toros were imprisoned, the latter strangled, and Hetum partially blinded. Another brother, Constantine I (1299), overthrew Smbat, declared himself king, and released Hetum. One year later Hetum had gathered enough support to retake the throne and exiled both Smbat and Constantine to Constantinople.

Hetum's strongly and openly pro-Roman sentiments no doubt were a factor in his overthrow. It was characteristic of the Cilician period that it was the kings, rather than the catholicoses, who controlled the course of Armenian-Roman church relations, and with distant Hromkla sacked in 1292, Hetum took the opportunity to move the catholicosate to Sis, the political capital, where this control could be better exercised. In this period those dismayed with Cilicia's "Romanizing" tendencies, particularly those in Greater Armenia, found a leader in Stepanos Orbelian (d. 1304), the metropolitan bishop of Siunik. His poem *Voghb,* or "Lament," reflects his sentiments on the pro-papacy direction of the catholicosate in Cilicia.

Shortly before Hetum abdicated for the final time to enter a monastery and left his throne to his nephew Levon III (1305-1307; co-ruler since 1301), the Mongol leadership dealt the Christian world a devastating blow by declaring its conversion to Islam. Still uncertain if this meant the end of hopes for alliance against the Mamluks, Hetum, now as a Franciscan friar, King Levon III, and about forty Cilician noblemen visited the Mongol emir at Anazarba. Their question of an alliance was answered when all were treacherously put to death.

More civil strife ensued. The throne passed to another of Hetum II's brothers, King Oshin (1307-1320). In a bid for European military assistance, two Armenian church councils were held, at Sis in 1307 and at Adana in about 1316, at which a number of Armenian clergy and nobles formally agreed to conform to Roman liturgical and doctrinal practice, including recognition of the pope. There rose to the surface intense anti-Roman sentiment, which soon became a general anti-Western reaction. King Oshin was poisoned in 1320. When his son and successor Levon IV (1320-1341) had both his own wife and stepfather killed and married the widowed queen of Cyprus, the Cilician nobility saw it as evidence of Levon's pro-European policy and rose up and murdered him in 1341.

The Lusignans

This chain of events left few living and legitimate contenders for the Cilician throne. The only ones left, in fact, were the nephews of Hetum II, the children of Amaury de Lusignan. Thus it was that the Cilician throne passed from a series of Armenian kings who were pro-Western in sentiment to a line that was European in culture and upbringing, and not at all popular with the Armenians. The first Lusignan king, Guy (1342-1344), in an effort to please his Armenian subjects, assumed the more Eastern, though Greek, name of Constantine. He reigned for a brief two years before being murdered. It is a significant indication of the political chaos in Cilicia at this time that there are no reliable Armenian sources and few sources of any kind relating to events of this period. Constantine was succeeded by a cousin, another Constantine (1344-1362), who is frequently identified with yet another cousin Constantine (1367-1373). During the interim, it is unclear as to who was on the throne. An illegitimate Lusignan nephew, Levon (later Levon V), is said by some sources to have held power from 1363 to 1364. In any event, King or the Kings Constantine considered it more realistic to undertake a policy of appeasement to the Mamluks, by ceding to them pieces of the kingdom, in return for the safety of its inhabitants. The last Constantine, sensing the desperateness of his country's situation, went so far as to sign a treaty surrendering rule of the kingdom, providing that the safety of the Armenians would be honored. The Armenian nobility opposed this treaty and murdered him in 1373. After a one-year regency by Constantine's widow, the Lusignans were recalled to the throne, and Levon V (1374-1375) and his wife, Margaret of Soisonns, were crowned at Sis (Rudt-Collenberg, 1980).

It was a short and unhappy reign. The Mamluks dealt their final, crushing blow to Cilicia in 1375; the royal family was taken captive to Cairo and Cilicia came under Mamluk domination. Levon was ransomed and went to Europe, traveling from court to court to enlist Europe's aid in recapturing his kingdom. He died in 1393 in Paris and was given the honor of burial in the church of St. Denis, the traditional medieval resting place of the kings of France, where his tomb can still be seen today.

Though the Cilician kingdom was at an end, the Mamluks did not hold Cilicia for long, and the Armenians who remained there came under Turkic domination around the turn of the century. Those Armenians who could fled the area, many eastward to Iran and Greater Armenia; some, particularly merchant families, westward, to found or add to the Armenian communities of the diaspora in France, the Netherlands, Italy, Spain, and Poland. By the early sixteenth century, all of Cilicia, as all of Asia Minor, had passed to Ottoman Turkish control. A few semi-autonomous mountainous principalities such as Hadjin and Zeitun survived until the nineteenth century.

What tangibly remains of the Cilician kingdom are written records (few translated into English) and works of art. All important sources on the period have been printed and many translated. Cilicia had what came to be a distinctive dialect from that of Greater Armenia, and some linguists trace the origins of modern Western Armenian to the language of the Cilicians. The works of art that have survived include fine examples of silver and other metalwork and coins, but especially manuscript illuminations. Toros Roslin, who headed the scriptorium at Hromkla in the thirteenth century, revitalized the Armenian art of illumination; his work was filled with the details of daily life and displayed a less stylized form than that of his predecessors.

Something less tangible that remained of Armenian Cilicia was the kingly title. This passed to Levon V's relative, John I, King of Cyprus, who had also inherited the equally meaningless Crusader title of "King of Jerusalem." Through John's descendants it passed to the House of Savoy, so that as late as the nineteenth century, the prince of Savoy claimed, among his other titles, that of "King of Armenia."

FOR FURTHER INFORMATION

For the sources of, or more information on, the material in this chapter, please consult the following (full citations can be found in the Bibliography at the end of this volume).

Bedoukian, 1962.   Hetoum, 1988.
Boase, 1978.   Maalouf, 1984.
Dostourian, 1993.   Mutafian, 1993.
Edwards, 1987.   Setton, 1969-1990.

Cilician Armenia Dynasties

Lords

Ruben, d. 1095

Constantine, 1095-1102

Toros, 1102-1129

Constantine, 1129

Levon, 1129-1140

Toros, 1144-1169

Ruben, 1169-1170

Mleh, 1170-1175

Ruben, 1175-1187

Levon, 1187 to 1199 (as lord)

Kings

Levon I, 1199-1219

Queen Zabel (Isabelle), 1219-1223 (co-ruler with Philip of Antioch to 1223, co-ruler with Hetum to 1252)

Hetum I, 1226-1270 (co-ruler with Queen Zabel [Isabelle] until her death in 1252)

Levon II, 1270-1289

Hetum II, 1289-1293

Toros, 1293-1294

Hetum II, 1294-1297 (second reign)

Smbat, 1297-1299

Constantine, 1299

Hetum II, 1299-1307 (third reign)

Levon III, 1301-1307 (co-ruler with Hetum II)

Oshin, 1307-1320

Levon IV, 1320-1341

Constantine II (Guy de Lusignan), 1342-1344

Constantine III, 1344-1362

Levon V (Lusignan), 1363-1364

Constantine IV, 1364-1373 (considered a usurper by some; sources mention a Queen Mary as regent from 1369-1374)

Levon V, (Lusignan) (second reign) 1374-1375

12

MEDIEVAL ARMENIAN LITERARY AND CULTURAL TRENDS

(Twelfth–Seventeenth Centuries)

Peter Cowe

The period under consideration, though rather less studied than other periods of Armenian history and culture, not only provides an important transition from the classical to the modern eras of Armenian civilization, but offers much of intrinsic interest. Its cultural trends largely follow the contours of political, economic, and military events. This results in a characteristic curve peaking at both ends of the spectrum with a series of troughs in the middle, especially during the first half of the sixteenth century in consequence of protracted Ottoman-Safavid border disputes, after which there is a marked recovery, establishing the infrastructure for and prefiguring some of the forms of the most significant developments of the next period.

Set geographically on one of the major thoroughfares between east and west, Armenia was always quick to be affected by demographic movements. From the eleventh century onward it underwent a phase of unprecedented flux due to successive migrations of Turkic peoples to settle in the Near East and the counterpoise of increased Western

European involvement in the region beginning with the Crusades. One impact of this was the creation of a permanent Armenian diaspora in Cappadocia, Cilicia, and the north and west coasts of the Black Sea, establishing communities that subsequently played a role in cultural enrichment. In view of these factors, Armenians were composing in French, Arabic, Persian, and Turkish in addition to their native language. An increasing number of foreigners were conversant in Armenian as well. One might cite Hetum of Korikos's *La Flor des Estoires de la Terre d'Orient* (1529) and Abu Salih's Arabic *History of the Churches and Monasteries of Egypt and Some Neighboring Countries* (1895).

Eastward Trends in Armenian Genres

Previously Armenia's closest literary and artistic contacts had been with Byzantium and Jacobite or West Syrian Christianity. At one time the Armenians even protected the Syrian patriarch Michael in the catholicosal residence at Hromkla. However, as these Christian communities became increasingly subject to new Muslim administrations, a greater Eastern influence becomes apparent on Armenian genres and aesthetic. Similarly, whereas Byzantine models had been seminal in the development of the Armenian prose tradition, a partial shift in emphasis emerges toward the recultivation of poetry for narrative, didactic, and other functions, as had been the case before the invention of the script and was still maintained by the oral bards *(gusans)*.

This transition is already visible in the eleventh century and is well exemplified by the career of Grigor (Magistros) Pahlavuni, a learned prince of the Pahlavuni family. He gained his title as a Byzantine official with jurisdiction over the region of Mesopotamia and shared Hellenophile interests with the then-catholicos Petros Getadardz, with whom he was in regular correspondence. Moreover, he was the only premodern Armenian writer to elaborate his private letters for publication according to classical practice. These he composed with studied Byzantine obscurity of style and fascination with ancient mythological lore (Magistros, 1910).

At the same time, as he demonstrates in his grammatical compilation, he became enamored with Arabic and exercised himself to learn the language in order to become acquainted with its literature. Thus, finding himself in Constantinople in discussion with an Arab named Manuche who denigrated the Bible for not being in verse, he undertook to fashion a metrical version of scripture. His version runs to over a thousand lines and was completed in three days, according to the prose foreword. The salient new feature it incorporates is monorhyme, a characteristic of the Arabic epic genre of *qasida* that had also begun to influence Persian courts. Grigor wisely selected a rhyme in *-in,* which maximized the possibilities for grammatical diversity in Armenian and hence facilitated stylistic variation throughout his *tour de force.* The verse he employed *(tagh)* was made up of isosyllabic lines contrasting with the irregular meters of earlier times, but this development (which may derive from Syriac prototypes) had already been gaining currency for some centuries. In *tagh* poems the individual line usually represented a semantic unit. This paradigm (although having little in common with Greek prosody) was termed Homeric meter *(homerakan chap).* Although Armenian has the potential for quantitative verse, this was never developed and so we find no imitation of the Arabo-Persian *aruz* meters as in Ottoman divan literature.

Magistros's achievement became a standard of emulation up to the end of the seventeenth century for long narrative poems. Subsequently, as Persian formed the literary medium of the Seljuk and Il-Khanid states, its impact on their Armenian communities is also observable. Indeed Kostandin Erznkatsi (Constantine of Erzinka) mentions being entertained by recitations from the *Shah-name,* while Armenians were later to produce their own version of the epic *(Rustam Zal)* replete with characters and episodes culled from the *Daredevils of Sasun.* Similarly, the thirteenth-century trend toward composing shorter lyric pieces is reminiscent in some respects of the *ghazel* (lyric form). Instead of the formal colophon with invocation of the trinity and full description of the circumstances of writing, poets of this genre adopted the latter's final self-reference *(takhallus),* eliciting their response to the composition. Such poems sometimes feature the *ghazel*'s couplets, but are more commonly arranged in rhyming four-line stanzas. Often the typical rhyming patterns of Turkish folk poetry are utilized, and occasionally Turkish dialogue is found, as in Hovhannes Erznkatsi's (John of Erzinka) "Hovhannes and Asha," which treats of love between a Christian and Muslim.

Another poetic form with Persian parallels is the quatrain. A large number of such pieces that have been transmitted under the name of the sixteenth-century singer Nahapet Kuchak may in fact be reworkings of earlier *gusan* compositions. They are known as *hayren* and consist of lines of fifteen syllables, as in Greek popular verse. The style was maintained into more modern times in the folk songs of the Armenian community of Agn. Predominantly devoted to the theme of love, they treat this in a direct and often humorous vein, either representing the lover's address to his beloved or an exchange between them. They were intended to be sung to the accompaniment of stringed instruments.

In contrast to these, lyric poems in a higher poetic register would be sung unaccompanied, as in Persian. Moreover, the importance of the melody to the overall effect is frequently stressed by writers on style. Thus Vardan Areveltsi (d. 1271) comments: "The melody of the *tagh* song should be suitably composed so that it moves sweetly and modulates at an appropriate point in the proper way . . . when verses' words, melody, thought and metre cohere, then the *tagh* is most apt and fitting" (Areveltsi, 1981, pp. 198-99).

In many instances an attractive melody would be reutilized by later poets and might then serve as the nucleus of the compositional process to which apposite lyrics would be devised. Unfortunately, few such melodies have survived from this period.

This raises the more general question of transmission. Whereas the *gusan* poems were composed orally and handed down by word of mouth, these others were created by literate poets (sometimes referred to as *kertogh,* a calque on the Greek *poietes*) and circulated in collections known as *tagharan,* which were transcribed along with most prose works in monastic scriptoria and reflected the tastes of this more educated class to which many of the poets belonged. Copyists employed a utilitarian aesthetic according to which a rigid distinction was usually made between what was useful *(pitani)* or of general moral edification and what was viewed as ephemeral or of local or individual interest and hence less likely to be preserved. This accounts for the largely religious nature of most of the medieval Armenian material. However, from about the sixteenth century, some collections start to admit *hayren* compositions as well.

Literary Language

Another major development of this period was the emergence of a new literary idiom. The provision of a script in the fifth century and the inception of grammatical instruction tended to inhibit linguistic change, yet, since the majority of the population was illiterate, the disparity between the written and spoken media only continued to widen. As Latin was retained in Western Europe as the language of church and scholarship, so in Armenia *grabar* (the written or literary form) coexisted along with the various spoken dialects. The strain required to maintain the distinction between them is evident where scribes have deviated from older texts by substituting a more familiar regional form. With the establishment of a state in Cilicia came the necessity of training a secular bureaucracy and judiciary unskilled in *grabar*. Various chancellery documents in this idiom still survive, such as the commercial privilege granted by Levon II to the Genoese in 1288 or the chrysobull from 1331 of Levon IV bestowing other privileges on the Sicilians. These employed a register closer to current speech patterns characterized by the addition of the particle *ku* in forming continuous verbal tenses. However, this middle Armenian idiom never became fully normative. As the medical writer Mkhitar Heratsi (Mekhitar of Her), personal physician to Catholicos Nerses Shnorhali (Nerses the Gracious) (d. 1173), states in one of his treatises, "I wrote this in the free, colloquial language so as to be accessible to all readers" (Heratsi, 1971, p. 248). The colloquial language was not constrained by the precise rules that governed correct usage in *grabar*.

Meanwhile, textbooks for the intellectual elite of the monastic academies that flourished throughout much of this period adhered to a more classical medium, as upheld by Grigor Tatevatsi (Gregory of Tatev) in the colophon to his "Book of Questions" of 1397: "The solution to these questions . . . was not adapted to the unrefined lay vernacular, but was merely concerned [to present] what was beneficial *(pitani)* to the church and issues of faith edifying for vardapets of acute precision and impeccable understanding" (1729, p. 772). However, with the increasing isolation of Armenian communities and the weakening of central religious authority, the need for basic guidelines on standards of Christian conduct, administration of the sacraments, and so on, to disseminate to parishes became increasingly pressing. Consequently, a number of such collections, such as Hovhannes Erznkatsi's "Advice to Ordinary Christians" of 1289, were compiled in a very simple style for a wide readership. This sort of register was probably also applied in ordinary preaching. Later it came to be known by the term *kaghakakan* (civil) and was also employed in written collections of homilies, such as those of Ghukas Loretsi (d. ca. 1551).

Legal Texts

Canon law had been an early Armenian preoccupation. Pronouncements of various earlier church councils were translated in the fifth century and combined with later indigenous statutes by Catholicos Hovhannes Odznetsi (John of Odzun) in the early eighth century. Thereafter, the collection *(kanonagirk)* continued to expand, acquiring *inter alia* important provisions on fasting, communion, and veneration of icons attributed to Gevorg Erznkatsi (d. 1416). Most of the remaining materials, many rather extraneous to the original conception of the compilation, were inserted by Azaria Sasnetsi (Azaria of Sasun) into his edition first copied at Constantinople in 1609.

In this period a rather different manual was produced by Davit Gandzaketsi (d. ca. 1140) offering advice to priests on how to hear confession and apportion penance. Based largely on the Levitical code, its ninety-seven canons are in many respects rather conservative, requiring public acts of contrition for misdemeanors. Yet in other cases they can be more enlightened, such as denying that menstruation should be considered unclean, since it is a natural phenomenon and thus part of God's creation. Moreover, penalties vary in gravity depending on the age of the party involved, whether they are clergy or lay in status, and their intentions in committing the act. The work also offers a valuable insight into interethnic and interfaith relations in the region—Armenian women living with Kurds, suckling Muslim children, parents selecting a Muslim godfather for their children, and priests baptizing those outside the Church. Though it touches on more civil crimes, its Christian humanity is manifest in cases such as commending resort to lies and bribes in order to cover the retreat of an escaped slave.

Gradually the codification of Islamic law impacted Armenian developments in the same sphere. The area around Gandzak had been ruled by a Kurdish emirate of Shaddadids but came under Seljuk rule in the last quarter of the eleventh century. Questions of legal jurisdiction naturally arose in suits involving Christians and Muslims, yet it seems clear that Armenians would appeal to the Muslim legal system on occasion for redress in disputes arising within their community. One factor behind this practice was the lack of a written codification of Armenian customary law. With the extinction of the Arsacid line, there had been no impetus toward drawing up such a document, while the Bagratid kingdom was not favorable to its formulation because of its fragmentation into smaller realms.

The inadequacies of the current situation were patent to Mkhitar Gosh (d. 1213), another native of Gandzak, who readily acquiesced to the behest of his ecclesiastical superior to put together a manual *(Girk datastani)* to assist judges assess the cases that came before them. His compilation of 251 articles was completed in 1184. About the same time complaints came to the Catholicos Grigor Tgha (1173-1193) from various localities stating that Muslim officials did not accept the Armenian form of justice and therefore insisted that cases be tried in their courts. When a thorough inventory of the library at Hromkla failed to uncover a civil code, a learned Syrian priest named Theodos was commissioned to translate the Syro-Roman Law Code, while Nerses Lambronatsi (Nerses of Lambron) translated the Mosaic Law, the codes of Constantine and Leo, and military regulations from Greek. These latter collections seem to have had rather limited practical effect; however, Gosh's manual laid the foundation for all subsequent Armenian legal thought in our period.

Gosh regarded his task as synthesizing the main legal corpora of his day, punctuating them with his own insights and reflections. Structurally he closely follows the *kanonagirk* and Davit's penitential. The third written source he employed is the Bible, especially the legal sections of the Old Testament, which he quotes verbatim with comment, usually to mitigate the severity of punishments imposed. For example, in the case of settling up the wages for orchard workers, he notes that this should be done justly, despite regional variations. However, if any cheating should occur, the thief is to repay double the amount, not four times as in the Mosaic law. However, perhaps the most valuable facet of his presentation is his citations of oral customary law, for example, with regard to adultery: "If the guilty party had remorse after separation and the couple wished, they could remarry—we speak as we have heard" (Gosh, 1975, p. 40).

Although Gosh did not envisage himself as a lawgiver or his work as a law code in the sense of the Code Napoléon, offering a systematic treatment of legal issues based on first principles, nevertheless, certain precepts are discernible in shaping its provisions. As a cleric and monastic, it was natural for him to seek to ensure the monasteries' well-being against encroachment by neighboring landlords. Hence, for example, if someone bequeathed land to the church during ill health and then recovered, that codicil in his will could not be altered. He also desired to protect the peasantry from abuse by putting a ceiling on taxes and prohibiting usury, which could ruin farmers in a series of bad harvests. Moreover, where possible, he strove to eradicate regional differences, supplanting these with others of more general application. It is also significant that Gosh regarded Muslims as legally equal to Christians and hence opposed levying a religious tax.

Within the next century Gosh's formulation was twice redacted to take account of changed sociopolitical conditions. Whereas the original had only envisaged bishops administering justice, civil matters were now placed under the jurisdiction of the local prince in the second, while the king was endowed with greater prerogatives in the third. The second simplifies Gosh's style and separates the ecclesiastical matter from the secular. The third is at once clearly dependent on both the earlier versions and very distinct from them. Composed in much more popular language, it abbreviates a lot of the religious material, but adds statutes from customary law. In several respects it adopts a more liberal approach, for example, with regard to a serf's rights of mobility or the rejection of an owner's rights to bring back a runaway slave, which form part of the other two recensions.

This latter in turn served as the primary source for the manual's more thoroughgoing accommodation to the conditions of the Armenian state in Cilicia by Smbat (1208-1276), brother of King Hetum I, high constable of the realm and architect of his Mongol diplomacy. This version, which appeared in 1265, introduced order and more systematic arrangement into the structure of the individual articles and consistency in their groupings such as befitted a law code. The work follows social stratification, commencing with ordinances concerning the king and nobility (indicating the impact of West European nomenclature on court offices), before embracing military and ecclesiastical affairs and then discussing marriage law, inheritance, mercantile regulations, issues relating to serfs, and payment of damages. Similarly, by rendering the text in the Cilician vernacular, Smbat facilitated its implementation by the lay justices. He significantly curtailed Gosh's long introduction and biblical citations, concentrating, as he tells us, on the "heart of the matter." Where appropriate, he nevertheless incorporated Byzantine and Franco-Norman data (Karst, 1905).

His debt to the latter source is further indicated by his translation in the same year of the *Assizes* (law code) of Antioch, ironically almost on the eve of that Crusader state's destruction by the Mamluks. This fact renders the Armenian translation all the more important since the Old French original has not survived. It betrays certain broad parallels in organization with Smbat's law code, beginning with seventeen articles on relations between the monarch and his vassals, followed by twenty-one on marital and family questions, property, bequests, creditor-debtor concerns, and criminal law.

Subsequently Gosh's manual spread to the Armenian colonies to regulate their community life. One of the best-documented instances is that of Poland, where the manual was already in use in the fourteenth century. As Armenian commerce expanded its significance and won special concessions from the crown, protests started to be lodged and disputes arose with local merchants in centers such as Lvov. The upshot was cases involving murder or physical injury, damage to property, and theft were to be tried at the city tribunal; the rest were to be tried by the local judge along with the Armenian elders on the basis of Armenian law. Because of suspicions concerning the precise nature of Armenian law, which was inaccessible to the local judiciary, the collection was translated into Latin for King Sigmund I in 1519. Upon review, it was approved with certain changes. Soon afterward this version was translated into Polish, the earliest manuscript dating from 1523. Later in the same century the document passed from Polish into Kipchak, an extinct Turkic dialect, most of whose literature was created by Armenians in their own script as they lost facility in the Armenian language itself. Thereafter, it was employed by the Armenian colonies of Astrakhan and Nor Nakhichevan within the Russian Empire and in India, as well as elsewhere. In the mid-nineteenth century, the Indo-Armenian writer Avdall mentions that the British courts there still referred questions of hereditary bequests and wills to the Armenian bishops for clarification (1841, p. 247).

Medicine

Another tradition largely utilizing the vernacular, as we have seen, was medicine. Armenian contributions to the field had tended to be of a practical nature. Greater systematization was gradually introduced in our period by figures such as Mkhitar Heratsi. In the introduction to his work "The Consolation of Fevers" *(Jermants mkhitarutiun)* of 1184, he informs us:

> I was trained in the writings of the Arabs, Persians and Greeks. I saw in the writings they have that they possess the art of medicine full and complete according to the first wise men (Galen, Hippocrates, etc.) i.e. diagnosis, which is the wisdom and teaching of the art of medicine. But among the Armenians I did not find the instruction and wisdom of diagnosis at all, but only treatment and that not systematic and comprehensive, but brief and eclectic, compiled from various sources. (1971, p. 247)

His survey deals with two hundred diseases giving rise to fever, including typhoid and malaria, on the basis of several Greek and Arab authorities.

Apart from facilities attached to monasteries, it is known that Queen Zabel (Isabelle) established a hospital in the Cilician capital of Sis in 1241. There are also contemporary translations of parts of Avicenna's Medical Canon and Abu Sa'id's anatomy as well as a veterinary tract entitled "Concerning the Horse and Other Beasts of Burden." In the next century Grigor Kiliketsi compiled a medical dictionary composed of 330 entries regarding drugs and their preparation and a second portion devoted to various conditions and their treatment. However, the major contribution to the advancement of Armenian medicine was made by the fifteenth-century writer Amirdovlat Amasiatsi (Amirdovlat of Amasia), most of whose autograph copies are preserved in the Matenadaran Institute of Manuscripts, Erevan.

Taken together, Amasiatsi's works form an Armenian version of Avicenna's great collection. One of his first treatises, the *Akhrapatin* of 1459, parallels the fifth book of the canon, treating pharmacology in twenty-five chapters. Number twenty-three provides a table with the appropriate terms listed in Armenian, Greek, "Frankish," and Persian. His "Utility of Medicine" *(Ogut bzhshkutian)* of 1469, based on books one, three, and five of the canon, concentrates on anatomy and pathology. Among the over 200 ailments treated, twenty chapters are given over to eye disease (1940). Five years later he produced another study devoted to vital signs, which considers techniques for drawing blood. His most extensive work, however, encompassing 3,700 entries, is a medical dictionary *(Angitats anpet)* similar to Avicenna's second book in which Arabic, Turkish, and Latin are added to the arsenal of languages employed in his earlier treatise (1926).

His impact on the subsequent development of medicine is clear from Buniat Sebastatsi's (Buniat of Sebastia) redaction of his "Utility of Medicine" in 1626. Sebastatsi produced a work of his own, the "Book of Medicine" *(Girk bzhshkutian tomari)* four years later in fifty chapters, in which he directs special attention to psychological and nervous disorders (1644). His contemporary Asar Sebastatsi had produced a similar account of practical medicine some years previously entitled "On the Medical Art" *(Girk bzhshkakan arhesti)* in 140 chapters (1993). Thereafter, increasingly Armenians were exposed to Western medical approaches. Thus, for example, Giorgio Baglivi (1668-1707), an orphan adopted by an Italian doctor, studied at Salerno, Padua, and Bologna and became professor of anatomy and surgery at Rome.

As in related cultures, along with the clergy, Armenian doctors were also interested in alchemy, again largely under Arabic influence. References to the "arcane arts" are extant from the twelfth century, and the translations are preserved from the next. A Persian treatise was rendered for King Hetum I, while later in the century the indefatigable *vardapet* Hovhannes Erznkatsi notes the views of Arab scientists on minerals, acids, and gases. Indigenous texts concerning the transmutation of base metals into gold are ascribed to the sixteenth-century practitioner Daniel Abegha, among others. Gradual exposure to European thought led to the translation of works by Domenicus Auda and Richard de Fournival and thereafter to the debate between alchemy and chemistry. Metallurgic experimentation facilitated a number of Armenian crafts such as goldsmithery, glass fabrication, pottery, and the production of inks and paints.

Although the target of ecclesiastical condemnation since the creation of the Armenian alphabet and inception of literature in the eighth century A.D., astrology remained another very popular pseudoscience. Several writings, particularly translations of Arabic and Persian works, are known from manuscript collections. The interesting obstetrics treatise "Secrets of Women" by Archbishop Hovhannes, alongside scientific questions such as malformations, contraceptive methods, and so on, and religious issues such as the relation of the soul to birth, also indulges in speculation on topics such as the influence of the planets on the embryo. The demand for such materials can easily be gauged from the fact that two of the earliest Armenian printed books of 1512-1513 are devoted to the topic. The *Akhtark* contains horoscopes, calendars, and dream interpretation, while the *Urbatagirk* (lit. "Friday Book") concentrates on the prophylactic aspect, offering prayers of St. Cyprian against demons, wizards, and sects, others for protection, and a treatment of the evil eye. The prevalence of such concerns is also observable from the many prayer scrolls *(hmayil)* extant from the seventeenth century with prayers and readings over the sick and for the aversion of negative influences.

Monastic Life

The true repositories of Armenia's intellectual history were, however, the monasteries, which, though themselves intermittently subject to destruction and dissolution, nevertheless represented the culture's one enduring institution from the twelfth to the seventeenth century. Endowed in perpetuity with lands, villages, mills, and oil presses as a memorial to the donors' piety and hence of prime economic importance, they are often resplendent vehicles for artistic expression. Apart from Cilicia, few Armenian castles have been preserved, and consequently churches and monastic complexes form the culture's major architectural structures.

There is abundant literary evidence to indicate the existence of monasticism in Armenia already in the fourth century, yet Armenian monasticism maintained a significant eremitic character. Consequently, only in the tenth century do large edifices in stone emerge. There follows a period of consolidated expansion into the fourteenth century with the addition of belfries (such as the very attractive example at Haghpat of 1245), libraries, and large halls *(gavit)* for assembly, teaching, and so on. Thereafter, a broad hiatus ensues until the renewal of the seventeenth century, as has been stated. In addition to successfully solving the architectural problems, Armenian monastic churches presented the opportunity for figural composition around the drum of the dome, as at Gandzasar, or for higher relief sculpture on the facade, as on the impressive west front of Amaghu Noravank. Moreover, a number of churches still reveal signs of the glorious frescoes that originally covered the interior wall space (e.g., Tatev and Saghmosavank). They would further be adorned with altar curtains, like the one for Gosh's monastery prepared by Arzu-khatun and her daughters. Of it the historian Kirakos Gandzaketsi (Kirakos of Gandzak) remarks:

> It was a marvel to those who beheld it . . . dyed with diverse colors and illustrated with images very precisely executed as if they had been carved, depicting the Savior's incarnation and [lives] of other saints . . . Those who saw it would praise God for granting women the wisdom to produce tapestries and the genius of embroidery. (1961, pp. 215-16)

Monasteries also increasingly became patrons of literature. Whereas most works of the early period, and especially history, were composed by bishops, often at the request of the local dynasty, by the twelfth to the seventeenth century this role was assumed by the *vardapet* or teacher at one of the monastic academies at the behest of one of his colleagues or pupils. This development had an impact on the very conceptualization and approach to the genre. Moreover, frequently bishops themselves resided in monasteries, as in the Jacobite tradition, while the sociopolitical relationship between secular and religious authority was gradually transformed. Previously it was not uncommon for the episcopacy to be held by a younger scion of the princely house. Now under Muslim suzerainty it was deemed prudent to reverse the process by presenting the family property as a religious *waqf* administered by a hereditary higher clergy. Examples of such "prince-bishops" were found throughout the Armenian lands, in Erznka, Aghtamar, Maku, and Caucasian Albania.

Historiography

The demise of the old aristocratic houses meant that historiography was viewed even more as an ecclesiastical discipline (except for a few texts from Cilicia, such as the annals of Hetum II, spanning the years 1076 to 1296). Individual works often were commissioned by a catholicos who wished to preserve a record of contemporary events. However, building on the tradition of Movses Khorenatsi (Moses of Khoren), it became the norm to preface this main portion with an epitome of earlier history, traced back to the country's Christianization by Kirakos, to the origin of the human race by most practitioners of the genre, and to creation itself by Vardan Areveltsi. The chronographic approach was much cultivated during the twelfth-seventeenth centuries, from large undertakings such as Samvel Anetsi's (Samuel of Ani) work, which extended until 1180, to the widespread band of largely anonymous continuators who expanded the original chronicle sometimes for centuries by recording events of more local significance. Along with manuscript colophons, these are particularly important for the sixteenth century, as there is no major treatment from the conclusion of Tovma Metzopetsi's (Thomas of Metzop) "History of Leng Timur" (1385-1440) until those of Grigor Daranaghtsi and Arakel Tavrizhetsi (Arakel of Tabriz) covering the years 1602-1662. In addition to national history, one work by the local metropolitan, Stepanos Orbelian, concentrates on the region of Siunik. It is unusual in the amount of archival and inscriptional documentation it provides.

Granted the breadth of Armenia's international contacts, it is hardly surprising that an effort was made to acquaint Armenian readers with neighboring cultures. Thus Vardan Areveltsi translated the chronicle of the Syrian patriarch Michael (d. 1199) with the assistance of the priest Ishokh. Almost contemporaneously, an early version of the Georgian chronicle was rendered, circulating under the name Juansher. In the fourteenth century Nerses Paliants, the Latin archbishop of Manazkert, translated a chronicle of the Pole, Fra Martinus. Despite their diversity, they are all loose renderings, those responsible appropriating their sources to various degrees by inserting material of direct Armenian interest. Developing the ethnographical excursus on the Turks in Michael's work, a thirteenth-century epitomator added a new section discussing the Mongols, or "Nation of Archers." The latter theme was also explored by Hetum of Korikos, constable of Cilicia from 1294 to 1305, in his *La Flor des Estoires de la Terre d'Orient,* which he wrote for Pope Clement V.

Scribal Arts

Book arts also flourished throughout the twelfth-seventeenth centuries within a monastic setting. While valuable liturgical items such as gospel books were copied in uncial *(erkatagir)* script on parchment with rich textual illumination into the thirteenth century, scholarly materials were usually produced in paper with minimal adornment. Moreover, since the development of a minuscule hand *(bolorgir)* in about the ninth century, the amount of material that could be comfortably contained within a normal book increased vastly. This in turn facilitated the scholastic movement toward the greater codification and synthesis of knowledge, creating a number of compendia, such as the full Bible, which were now accessible *i mi tup* (within one cover). Whereas provincial scribal practice in the preceding period is rather erratic, it was raised to a high degree of consistency in Cilicia, where in centers such as Grner, Drazark, and especially Skevra a small, finely wrought script was perfected. The last school was particularly influential through the line of teacher-pupils Nerses Lambronatsi, Grigor Skevratsi, Aristakes Grich, and Grigor Skevratsi (nephew of Grigor). Aristakes and Gevorg contributed manuals on the important practical issues of orthography and syllabication; the latter's exemplars were highly sought after as models.

While all students were schooled in scribal skills, a rigorous training in illumination was much less common. Although some laymen, such as Toros Roslin, were trained, many painters derived from the ranks of the higher clergy. Armenian miniature of the twelfth century as elaborated in gospels and other liturgical books betrays significant Byzantine influence in subject and treatment. Increasingly Western motifs gained popularity, especially in the atelier of the catholicate at Hromkla, as illustrated by Roslin's Lady Keran gospel of 1265. Much attention focused on the canon tables tabulating the passages evangelists hold in common. A uniquely Armenian genre of commentaries developed in which the various flora and fauna that adorn the tables are ' accorded allegorical significance. In contrast, the schools of Greater Armenia preserve greater continuity with the past, those from Khachen and Artsakh perpetuating strikingly primitive traits. While several schools in the north and east maintained a rather tenuous existence, those in the Van region flourished under relatively peaceful and prosperous conditions. These display more Persian influence and are characterized by a highly abstract approach, dispensing with most of the architectural framing of scenes to concentrate more dramatically on the figures themselves, against a backdrop of floral embellishment.

Higher Education

It is sometimes suggested that the model of contemporary European universities is an appropriate analogy to these Armenian academies, yet surely the monastic school offers a closer parallel. Quite apart from the similarity of setting, the Armenian institutions lacked the stability of university foundations, on the one hand reflecting the broader political situation of the region, but also being heavily dependent on the quality of the teaching staff to draw students. When figures such as Vanakan Vardapet or Grigor Tatevatsi moved to a different location, their pupils would generally follow suit. Moreover, despite secondary references to the seven liberal arts, the mathematical quadrivium (arithmetic, music, geometry and astronomy) received comparatively little attention. The greatest involvement with the last of these arose from practical considerations relating to the date of Easter pursued by such scholars as Hakob Ghrimetsi (ca. 1350-1426). Their results (often embracing several centuries) were usually tabulated in works known as *parzatumar* (calendrical explanation). Music was studied mainly for performance in the liturgy and office, not generally for its theoretical aspects. In the course of time the precise tradition of how the various chants were executed diversified in different parts of the country, as is exemplified by the contrasting practice of the major centers of Echmiadzin, Jerusalem,

Constantinople, and New Julfa until more recent times. Moreover, interest in numerology focused on symbolic significance rather than calculation or measurement. Instead, from the bulk of the production of the *vardapets* associated with the academies, there can be no doubt that scripture formed the principal focus of their inquiry. This emphasis thus maintains continuity with the Armenians' early formation in the School of Edessa.

Meanwhile, the *artakin* (lit. external, i.e., nonreligious) fields of grammar, rhetoric, and logic provided the basic tools ancillary to that task. The procedure was to write a commentary *(meknutiun)* on texts regarded as authoritative within a given discipline, in the course of which the thought of pagan authors such as Dionysius Thrax (ca. 170–ca. 90 B.C.: grammar), and Aristotle and Porphyry (logic) became increasingly Christianized. These were supplemented by the *nurb griank* (subtle writings) of Christian authors incorporating the works of the Cappadocian Fathers, Psuedo Dionysius the Areopagite, Evagrius of Pontus, and the philosopher David "the Invincible." Using the minuscule script, all the primary texts on the syllabus might be collected in one volume, such as Mkhitar Ayrivanetsi's (Mekhitar of Ayrivan) famous homiliary of about 1282, which well symbolizes the fundamental aspiration to reconcile divine revelation with human inquiry.

Brief introductions to the various textbooks for student needs were provided by Grigor Abasian in his *Patjarats girk* (Book of Synopses). These were supplemented for more advanced classes by detailed investigations *(lutsmunk)* of problematic passages in the texts, such as those of Davit Kobayretsi (d. ca. 1220) on the Cappadocians and Dionysius and Hovhannes Orotnetsi (d. 1387) and Grigor Tatevatsi (d. 1409) on Aristotle. In the mid-sixth century, the Armenians had been introduced to the dogmatic florilegium, tabulating excerpts from church Fathers in favor of or in opposition to a certain proposition, in Timothy Aelurus's refutation of the Christological definition of the Council of Chalcedon (451). From the eleventh century the form was exploited to gather together the varied interpretations of commentators on a particular work, thus offering a conspectus of the status quaestionis and facilitating the resolution of their viewpoints. Armenians were also unique in developing a commentary tradition on the exegetical and philosophical writings of the Hellenistic Jewish author Philo of Alexandria (ca. 25 B.C.–ca. 45 A.D.), whose ideas had little influence on Byzantium and who does not seem to have even been translated in Syriac. Yet his views on cosmology and divine providence were the subject of keen debate in Armenia over several centuries, stimulating the development of indigenous thought on those issues.

Scholarly discussions resulted in compilations of question and answer *(hartsmunk ev pataskhanik)* on specific topics, the most celebrated being that of Vanakan Vardapet (d. 1251). More wide-ranging discussion with his royal patron, Hetum I, during the 1240s initiated Vanakan's pupil Vardan's encyclopedic work *Zhghlank* (lit. conversations), which employs the same format to present a fascinating kaleidoscope of the questions provoking intellectual curiosity at the time. It well articulates the contrast between the empirical Syriac and Arabic approach to natural philosophy and the more speculative position adopted by the Armenians, who lacked access to Aristotle's physical and biological treatises. Nevertheless, the Armenians' speculative position gradually diversified over the next two centuries through closer contacts with those traditions, the effects of which are already visible on Vardan's historical compilation of 1267. It benefits from the Syrian Ishokh's "Book Concerning Nature" *(Girk i veray bnutian)*. Undoubtedly the most comprehensive treatment of this type is Grigor Tatevatsi's "Book of Questions" *(Hartsmants girk)*. Subdivided into ten chapters, his magnum opus proceeds systematically from a consideration of non-Christian and heretical propositions to an expositions of his own tradition. Beginning with a detailed review of Psuedo Dionysius's teaching on the angelic realm, Tatevatsi treats in turn creation, the composition of man, biblical and ecclesiastical history, the church and its worship and sacraments, culminating in eschatological issues of the afterlife.

From the information available, it seems that monastic life was increasingly regulated by St. Basil's provisions, while Nerses Lambronatsi also translated St. Benedict's rule, which he had seen applied in Latin monasteries on the Black Mountain near Antioch. Once again *vardapets* composed most of the hymns *(sharakan, tagh, gandz,* etc.) for feasts of the saints and other celebrations. Throughout this period musical execution preserved an important extempore quality. Consequently, the notation *(khaz)* employed was elaborated from the basic pointing of texts such as the gospel to give guidance in chanting and declamation. Beginning as a reminder of certain initial and codal melismas, the system of signs became increasingly more complex between the twelfth and fifteenth centuries, after which it gradually fell into abeyance. Since no comprehensive key has been preserved, musicologists are still unsure of the significance of several of its forms.

Poetry

In addition to the rhetorical study of the Bible and other texts, students were also trained in poetic composition. To assist beginners, word lists of appropriate synonyms for use in verse were prepared. Although many did not aspire to lofty lyric accomplishments, they nevertheless utilized the skill they attained in composing colophons to the manuscripts they copied in which a verse component became increasingly popular. Apart from meditating on liturgical hymns, particularly since Grigor Narekatsi's (Gregory of Narek) "Book of Lamentation" *(Matian voghbergutian),* poetry became an integral part of monastic spirituality. Side by side with the more intellectual tradition represented by Evagrius and the commentaries written on his corpus by such figures as Grigor Skevratsi (d. ca. 1230), Kirakos Erznkatsi (d. 1355), and Matteos Jughayetsi (Matthew of Julfa) (d. ca. 1412) was a more affective strain emphasizing contrition and tears of compunction.

Some poems, such as those of Grigor Tgha, seek to emulate Narekatsi's verse. His uncle Shnorhali designated his major poem *Hisus Vordi* (Jesus the Son) a *voghbergutiun* (elegy/lamentation) like the *matian.* Each point in the retelling of sacred story is punctuated by reflections on the state of the soul, the awareness of sin and alienation, and prayer for reconciliation for appropriation in private devotions. Many ecclesiastical poets cultivated the genre of the personal lament *(voghb)* as a means of self-examination and confession. At times this becomes a psychomachia, utilizing the age-old form of a dialogue between the two opposing principles in the human composition of flesh and spirit. When the latter, according to Khachatur Kecharetsi (Khachatur of Kechar) (d. 1331), poses the question of how the flesh had misled it into a shallow accommodation with this transient life, it receives the sobering response:

> I am a horse, and you the horserider,
> I am a servant, and you the master,
> When you have a wish, I put it into effect.
> Why do you blame me, the earthborn? (1958, p. 152)

An indication of the deep bond between master and pupil in this period is the frequency with which the latter would write his mentor's life. In addition to a prose *vita,* poetic treatments were also common. At first these were eulogistic laments on their teachers' passing, praising their physical as well as spiritual attributes as an angel in the flesh. Sometimes they included a ritual search for the *vardapet* culminating in a vision of his inauguration into the angelic ranks of paradise. Subsequently, panegyrics tended to be written as tokens of respect during the teacher's life as well.

Religion

Religiously Armenia was a very pluralistic society. Vestiges of Zoroastrianism lingered on particularly in the group referred to as *arevordik* ("children of the sun"). One community of *arevordik* near Samosata was received into the Armenian Church in the 1170s through the good offices of Nerses Shnorhali, while others in the neighborhood of Amida continued well into the nineteenth century. Additionally there were strong colonies of Armenian Chalcedonians in various parts of the Byzantine Empire (especially in Cappadocia and Trebizond) as well as along the Georgian border. Often they engaged in polemic against the main body of the Armenian Church, such as in the missive the rhetor Theopistes, secretary to Prince Aaron of Balu, sent to his counterpart of Sasun, provoking a detailed apology from the theologian Poghos Taronetsi in 1101. Apart from this they were very active in translating from Greek and Georgian into their own language up to the eighteenth century. Naturally they rendered all the Byzantine service books for their own use. Other works, however, entered immediately into the Armenian mainstream. Ivane Zakarian had adopted a Chalcedonian confession at the turn of the thirteenth century and sponsored a monastery of his coreligionists at Pghndzahank. There the monk Symeon occupied himself with renderings from Georgian. One of the earliest copies of his translation of the Neoplatonic Proclus's *Elements of Theology* was incorporated into Mkhitar Ayrivanetsi's homiliary, while in 1363 Hovhannes Vorotnetsi commissioned a copy of Symeon's version of St. John of Damascus's *Source of Knowledge* in Tiflis. In collaboration with a colleague, Minas, he also rendered St. John Climacus's *Ladder of Spiritual Ascent,* which gained wide currency in a revised version of 1290 from Cilicia.

Cilicia had been in intermittent contact with Latin Christianity during the twelfth century, which led to the establishment first of Franciscan houses and then of Dominican ones by the middle of the thirteenth century. As a result, several Western motifs are observable in the art of the period. Moreover, whereas philosophical pursuits were generally advanced in Greater Armenia, the only important philosopher of the Cilician state was Vahram Rabuni (d. ca. 1290), secretary to Levon II, who showed openness to European trends in nominalism. Enlarging the scope of reader's aids in scriptural study, Stephen Langton's Vulgate chapter divisions were inserted into Armenian Bibles of the end of the century. By the 1230s Latin monastics had also arrived on the Armenian plateau and subsequently entered into dialogue with the scholars of Gladzor and Tatev. Centered in the monastery of Krna, they in turn initiated a significant series of translations from Latin with the aid of Armenian converts who were soon to be established as the Fratres Unitores.

Their work was supervised by the missionary Bartolomeo di Bologna who became first archbishop of Atrpatakan in a hierarchical line that reached to 1766. Together with Hovhannes Tsortsoretsi, a former pupil of Esayi Nchetsi, in 1321 he rendered Aquinas's sacramental theology from the *summa*, which later influenced Grigor Tatevatsi's eclectic eucharistic formulations. Nevertheless, many of the dogmas they introduced were impugned by their Armenian counterparts. Vardan Areveltsi queried the understanding of purgatory and Mkhitar Skevratsi the basis for papal supremacy in the primacy of Peter. However, unlike their neighbors, the Byzantines and Syrians, it was characteristic of the Armenians not to instigate acrimonious exchanges with proponents of other religious views. On the contrary, ecclesiastics such as Gosh and Vardan Aygektsi argued pragmatically that rather than insisting on uniformity in belief and practice, affairs should be governed by confessional tolerance and interethnic entente. In like vein, the poet Frik advocates greater cooperation of all Christian peoples against their common enemies. At the same time, the expansion in hymnography eulogizing St. Gregory the Illuminator and other early hierarchs and saints related to the area (such as St. Sargis) in this period gives clear expression to the distinctiveness of the Armenian Christian tradition.

As in art, so in literature, Armenian borrowings from the West more usually impacted form and methodology rather than content. Previously the main genre for the discursive exposition of a theme, often evolving from a biblical citation, was the homily *(jar)*. Now this was largely supplanted by the *karoz* (sermon, cf. Latin *praedicatio,*) which, while treating fundamentally the same subject matter, was typified by the more rigorous use of logic. Characteristically it proceeds by subdividing the main theme into its constituent elements and defining each in turn with supporting arguments so as to arrive at a more comprehensive understanding of the topic under discussion. One of the first collections was authored by Hovhannes Tsortsoretsi, while that of Bishop Bartolomeo, translated from Latin by Hakob Krnetsi in 1331, was one of the most influential. Its proverbial illustrations, in particular, were so appealing that they frequently infiltrated compilations ascribed to indigenous writers. As a whole the genre offers a wide range of information on contemporary social mores.

In addition to movements advocating union either with Byzantine Orthodoxy or Roman Catholicism, heretical sects such as the Tondrakites preserved a folk religion beyond the penumbra of the church's sacraments. Although their cult center had been destroyed by Grigor Magistros, the devotees continued to maintain a marginal existence. That their ideas persisted is well demonstrated by the case of a sectarian Tomas, who is recorded to have appeared in New Julfa in 1642 espousing similar beliefs. They were propagated into modern times. A manual known as the *Key of Truth* is related to the movement and was confiscated in Anatolia only in 1837.

Laments

Earlier it was mentioned that religious poets sometimes composed personal laments as a spiritual exercise. Communally the lament became a popular social and political genre that came to terms with major disasters, such as the devastation of large cities by war. Thus there are extant treatments of the fall of Edessa to the Turk Zangi in 1144, Jerusalem to Salah al-Din (Saladin) in 1187, as well as a series tracing Ottoman expansion encompassing Constantinople (1453), Crimea (1455), Nicosia (1570), Tabriz (1585), and the Safavid removal of the population of Julfa to Isfahan in 1604. Whereas later examples tend to be fairly short, simple narratives by lower clergy, the earlier practitioners are generally taken from the upper echelons and demonstrate their skill in longer works in a high poetic style employing the devices of personification and apostrophe to intensify the pathos. The city is invoked as an orphaned widow after the manner of the biblical book of Lamentations, addressing her scattered and deceased children. The extent of the cataclysm is heightened by inclusion of the natural forces. Hence, as Hovhannes Makuetsi (John of Maku) states, when Julfa was breached, "All the hills entered mourning, the seas and rivers were moved to weeping" (1969). Moreover the contrast with its prosperous, illustrious past underlines the city's present plight, painted in somber hues. Often this is accompanied by poignantly reiterated rhetorical questions as by Nerses Shnorhali on the cessation of festivities:

> Where now is the crown you were embellished with or your
>   magnificent fillet ?
> Where are the adornments of the lady, bride of the king's son?
>   (1973, p. 33)

Successor to the teeming multitudes, the image of a loan owl perched on the ruins frequently symbolizes the utter desolation of the place. Usually also the question of theodicy is broached and resolved with reference to the former population's sinfulness. In the final portion a note of optimism for the future is often sounded for the readers' consolation. As Simeon Aparanetsi (Simeon of Aparen) writes in an allusion to the book of Daniel:

> It is not right to break the thread of hope
> Any more than Israel in Babylon,
> But to take [as models of] hope the young men in the fire
> And to sing their songs. (1969, p. 238)

Significantly, this final element is lacking in treatments like the lament of the cathedral of Echmiadzin by Stepanos Orbelian (d. 1304). By not offering comfort, this category more closely resembles the tone of the funeral oration. As the author's focus concentrates on the decline of the Armenian plateau since the departure of the royalty and many of the noble houses to Cilicia, this strategy is adopted to apply psychological pressure on the conscience of nobles to return and reestablish an Armenian state there.

Other Poetic Genres

For those who had gone to foreign parts, whether in pursuit of trade or as a result of expulsion, the motherland continued to exert a gravitational pull on their emotional allegiance. Their feelings of yearning and loss are eloquently channeled into another genre, the song of the exile *(pandukht, gharib)*. These regularly lament the émigré's alienation, lack of rights, and vulnerability in a place where neither he nor his worth receives recognition. His quandary is often depicted by a different bird motif, as in the following excerpt from Mkrtich Naghash, archbishop of Amida (d. ca. 1469):

> The exile in a foreign land is indeed extremely wretched.
> Like a fowl separated from its flock. Going off course it finds rest
>   nowhere,
> But continues to wander until it reaches its place. (1965, p. 165)

The opposite genre, a celebration of the joys of merriment and good company *(tagh urakhutian),* is also widely found. Sitting around a table laden with choice delicacies, the assembled gathering is to enjoy the plenty and take relief from responsibility and care while young men ply them with wine and entertain them with song and dance to the accompaniment of the saz and santur. Indeed, as alcoholic beverages were illicit under Islam, Armenians and other Christians had a monopoly on the wine trade in the Middle East. With the emphasis on fun, good humor, and harmonious interaction, sometimes the poems are explicit on the etiquette expected, discouraging drunkenness, rowdiness, and pique. As was noted earlier of the oral tradition, love is one of the most widespread themes to receive poetic treatment. It is also handled in many different ways. Under the influence of sufic texts such as *'Attar's Mantiq at-tayr* (Conference of the Birds), figures such as Kostandin Erznkatsi (thirteenth century) composed religious allegories around the theme of the rose and nightingale to express their mystical love for Christ. In St. John's Gospel (15:11-12) Jesus tells the disciples, "I have spoken thus to you, so that my joy may be in you, and your joy complete. This is my commandment: love one another, as I have loved you." To this Kostandin offers his own commentary, utilizing the theme of inebriation to convey ecstasy:

> Today . . . we should be intoxicated with love, we who are united
>   together.
> The rose is adorned with beauty and has given us the command.
>   (Erznkatsi, 1962, pp. 132-33)

Aware that the universe is permeated by divine love, the poet employs settings of spring and dawn to emphasize the exhilaration that he experiences in his vision of the divine light of the "Sun of righteousness." Other poets employ the rose and nightingale motif in a fascinating range of contexts unexplored by surrounding cultures.

Songs of earthly love are usually divided into two categories, one eulogizing the physical attributes of the beloved woman *(govasank)*, the other the outpouring of the poet's unrequited love *(gangat)*. The former follows a broad Middle Eastern pattern of cataloging the young woman's external attractions in an extremely stylized sequence (sometimes in an alphabetic acrostic) with increasingly elevated similes. Finally the poet is forced to confess her beauty absolutely peerless and incomparable. A typical example is provided by Hovhannes Tlkurantsi (John of Tlkuran):

> I saw a beautiful image
> Like the sun which gives light,
> I saw eyes like seas,
> Eyebrows thicker than cloud and sea.
> A pale forehead and lush mouth,
> Plaits and braid that would pluck out your soul,
> Her bosom was filled with dazzling white roses,
> Her waist and back more supple than a willow. (1958, p. 13)

As this excerpt indicates, no reference is made to the woman's qualities of character and intellect. In fact, the poet Naghash Hovnatan (1661-1722) devotes one of his works to women's "shortwittedness." There he articulates the marked distinction between women's exterior and interior aspects very succinctly in the opening lines, drawing the parallel between women's minds and their pot plants. The latter may develop into a large yellow clump of good height. But color is their only attraction, they emit no fragrance. He then jocularly proceeds to justify the censure by citing their fundamental weakness, namely that they pay no heed to men's advice, but prefer their own false talk and customs in a spirit of mutual appreciation. Moreover, this proclivity becomes more ingrained with every generation. If the mother is bad, the daughter is ten times worse. It is not until the Enlightenment that appreciation is shown of women's mental and emotional capabilities. The only exception to this is the Virgin Mary, who besides representing beauty and purity is portrayed as the embodiment of maternal affection and strength.

Baghdasar Dpir (1683-1768) is a good representative of the more sophisticated taste of the upper echelons of Armenian society in Constantinople. His treatment of the lover's plaint is chaste and restrained.

His beloved is so elusive that his soul wanders over hill and dale like a dervish in search of her. Gradually a note of melancholy insinuates itself into the tone, especially when he compares himself to the nightingale lamenting the absence of its rose. In urging the petals to open it is pierced by the thorns. In contrast, Naghash Hovnatan is more direct and earthy in his expression, as in his attempt to woo a widow who, he complains, displays unnecessary coquetries to tease him.

> Come, let's send each other a writ,
> Let's stop being so abusive.
> It's cold, come let's huddle together
> To keep warm.
> Let's get drunk.
> Quince will do fine for starters,
> Then let's unclasp your bosom. (Hovnatan, 1983, pp. 40-41)

Another aspect of poetic activity consisted of social criticism. One of the main exponents is the thirteenth-century writer Frik. He inveighs against the vices of dishonesty, exploitation, and immorality in a type of verse similar to what the contemporary scholars described as popular comedy, or what we might call satire. For example, in his attack on adultery and drunkenness, he adopts the catalogue approach of the *govasank* from head to toe, only this time draws attention to the abuse the various bodily parts have suffered as a result of such sybaritic excesses.

> Your heart is filled with deceit like a beast or wolf:
> You should have shown yourself merciful to the poor and
>   orphaned. . .
> Your stomach you've let sag loosely like a horse or mule:
> You should have behaved with self-restraint and been moderate in
>   consuming food. (Frik, 1952, p. 305)

The message he purveys with effective bluntness is of the transience of life and the future reckoning of judgment where the inequalities of this life are not replicated and the criterion is honest dealing and care for others. In fact, some of his poems closely resemble the counsel of his contemporary Hovhannes Erznkatsi to the wealthy merchant class of his city, underlining their shortcomings in community welfare, avoiding almsgiving, negligence in hospitality to wayfarers, defrauding widows as well as unconcern for piety. In at least two of his poems ("Complaint to Christ" and "Against Fate"), Frik insightfully pursues his criticism beyond the human factor to voice his incomprehension of the world order itself and the possibility of reconciling this with the workings of providence. Here too the power of his appeal is located in the vivid contrastive vignettes he juxtaposes, allowing the accumulation of instances to overwhelm the easy certainties of audience and reader alike, as on the question of preserving one's family line in his *gangat* to Christ:

> One is given twenty sons and daughters,
> One is barren and does not have a single child.
> He lives as a captive under miserable conditions
> And has no way to be remembered on the earth. (Frik, 1952, p. 544)

With the publication of the first (partial) edition of Frik's poems in 1930, these works became a cause célèbre for the now-discredited Soviet scholarship on the subject. Their notoriety was conditioned by the notion that they offer a novel iconoclastic attitude toward organized religion; in fact, these poignant appeals mark no new departure, but arise out of a well-established medium in the Judeo-Christian tradition already embodied in the Psalter, at once the most basic and widespread primer in forming morals and piety.

This period is associated with some of the great Persian romances, such as Layla and Majnun, Vis o-Ramin, and Varqeh o-Golshah. Although there existed analogs in neighboring Georgia, such as Rustaveli's "The Knight in the Panther's Skin," there is no reflection of this trend in Armenia. As these works were essentially court creations, the instability of Armenia's statehood and demise of its royal house did not offer a suitable environment for that genre to thrive. However, we find a variety of tales (*zruyts*) of eastern origin circulating in Armenian, sometimes in multiple recensions. Alongside ancient gnomic material such as Akhikar, there are versions of the "Youth and the Maiden" and "King Pahlul" deriving from Arabic and the "Counsels of Nushirvan" translated from Persian in the thirteenth century. These indicate the Armenians' love of enigmas, parables, and aphorisms, which is also visible in the indigenous collections of Mkhitar Gosh and Vardan Aygektsi (d. 1235) as well as Nerses Shnorhali's set of puzzles, apparently originally intended for the guards on duty at the catholicosal residence of Hromkla to while away the long night watches.

Another group of stories illustrating Indian spirituality in the renunciation of this world in favor of a life of ascetic purity adapted well to the atmosphere of Armenian monasticism. (Indeed the earlier type also developed distinctly Christian themes in the course of transmission.) One originally describing the Buddha's enlightenment, the tale of Barlaam and Ioasaph (i.e., Bodhisattva), became only partially metamorphosed, preserving its fundamental teaching of a sage elder persuading a young prince to forsake his wealth and status in exchange for prayer and solitude. Its popularity is demonstrated by the number of prose versions. Later it was versified appropriately by the hero's namesake, Hovasap Sebastatsi.

Another of this type of tale, the "City of Bronze," rendered from an Arabic intermediary in the tenth century, appears in a different form in the "Thousand and One Nights." In the process of its appropriation, it was embellished with verses termed *kafa* (from an Arabic root), which comment on the preceding scene, heightening its emotional impact. These verses are usually composed in monorhymed quatrains and cast in the *hayren* meter. Hence they probably derive from popular practice in the narrative presentations of the *gusans*. In "City of Bronze" they form laments, as the following which the hero recites on reaching the city of his destination only to find it abandoned and empty, allegorically pointing to the vanity of human glory:

> Alas for you, fair city, that there is no one alive in you.
> All have turned to dust: there is no owner in these well-stocked stores.
> Would that we had never seen such bewildering things.
> Woe on us too if we should become like them—pitiable and fit for
>   tears. (Akinian, 1958, p. 21)

The Alexander Romance attributed to Pseudo Callisthenes had been translated into Armenian in the fifth century, but in its turn was regarded as too pagan in spirit. Hence Khachatur Kecharetsi appended his own commentary in the same *kafa* style and an epilogue in which he expounds an elaborate typology by which the events of the Macedonian king's life prefigured the coming of Christ. As the former defeated Darius, the latter overcame Satan. The former penetrated deserts and places infested with wild beasts, while Christ tamed our nature. Alexander's image was reverenced as a god by the Greeks, but Christ is worshiped by those in heaven and on earth. Subsequently, the poetic accretions continued with Grigoris Aghtamartsi and his pupil

Zakaria Gnunetsi in the sixteenth century. At the same time they built on Khachatur's illuminations of the battle scenes, making the cycle one of the richest and most developed of nonreligious topics in Armenian art.

The genre of punctuating a prose narrative with poetic passages enjoyed wide popularity thereafter in both elevated and folk contexts. A good example of the former is Eremia Chelebi's description of the great fire of Constantinople in 1660, where, in addition to laments, the *kafas* offer appropriate paraphrases from scripture and moral advice. In the folk idiom the form was exploited by the *ashugh* (from the Arabic term *ashik,* for "lover") successor to the *gusan,* who appears first in the Armenian community in the figure of Nahapet Kuchak and a larger group from New Julfa in the next century, presumably under the patronage of the merchant *(khodja)* class.

The prototype of this kind of poet is found at the end of the fifteenth century significantly at the Safavid court. There rivals such as Kurbani and Kureni brought Azeri folk meters such as the *qoshma* to new levels of accomplishment. Their prose romances *(hikaye)* were interspersed with various verses of the sort we have already seen in praise of beauty, heroism, social criticism, and moral advice. This same pattern is also observable in the Armenian cycle of the *Sasna Dzrer* (Daredevils of Sasun), especially the third phase centering on Sasuntsi Davit (David of Sasun), who is not only a warrior but also a singer and poet. Another of the genres describing significant military or political events *(destan)* has had a long history; it even was utilized by contemporary folk poets to describe atrocities committed against the Armenian population of Sumgait and Baku in the last few years. A number of the Armenian practitioners studied under Turkish masters. As many made a livelihood by going on tours of eastern Anatolia and Caucasia, like the most famous of them, Sayat Nova (1712-1795), they composed a large part of their compositions in Azeri Turkish, the lingua franca of the region. As a result of these contacts, Armenian variants developed on the tale of the Robin Hood figure, Köroğlu and his band, loosely based on historical events surrounding the Jelalian revolt at the turn of the seventeenth century. The Armenian *ashughs* held a special devotion toward Surb Karapet (St. John the Baptist), the *murazatu* (bestower of desires), and organized annual competitions in their art during the pilgrimage to celebrate his feast day at his shrine in Mush.

Printing

The rise of the Armenian merchant class had a significant cultural impact. Figures such as Tigran Honents at Ani in the thirteenth century had already assumed the traditional aristocratic patronage of dedicating churches. Their interests and superstitions were obviously to a large extent behind the early experiment in printing by Hakob Meghapart at Venice in 1512-1513, and their financing supported the later presses, which sprang up in Constantinople (1567), Lvov (1616), New Julfa (1638), Amsterdam (1660), Livorno (1670), and in India later. They are thus the nucleus of the modern reading public. Moreover, at New Julfa they established their own school where, as in the case of the poetry they encouraged, the medium of instruction was the colloquial vernacular *(ashkharhabar)*. Textbooks such as Ghukas Vanandetsi's *Gandz chapoy* (Treasury of Measures: Amsterdam, 1699) catered to their needs, offering a conspectus of the weights, measures, and monetary units in use all over the world as well as interesting details about the national characteristics of the Europeans with whom they would be doing business. Moreover, their account books provide fascinating insights into economic conditions in Central Asia where they were active. Their presence in cities like Milan and Amsterdam aroused the interest of local scholars in their language and culture and laid the foundations of modern Armenology through publications such as Francesco Rivola's Armeno-Latin dictionary (1621) and grammar (1624) and Johann Joachim Schröder's more encompassing *Thesaurus linguae Armenicae* (1711). Their artistic patronage was an important conduit in the transmission of Western styles and motifs, as in the Bible of Ghazar Baberdatsi (Lazar of Baberd) (MS. no. 351 in the Matenadaran, Erevan), which was commissioned in Lvov in 1619, employing the iconography of many of the illustrations of the De Bry Bible of 1609 from Mainz. Thereafter the style spread to New Julfa, where it became very popular. Similarly, the celebrated first printing of the Armenian Bible by Oskan Erevantsi at Amsterdam in 1666 has a series of woodcuts inspired by Dürer.

Crafts

Although there is less information regarding artisans and tradesmen, indications are that they thrived in several urban settings. One such is

Erznka, which for a long time was primarily an Armenian city whose bazaars and wares (fabrics, copper utensils, and lampstands, etc.) were extolled by the Arab traveler Ibn Battuta on his visit in 1333. The indefatigable cleric Hovhannes drew up an interesting set of statutes for its confraternity in 1280 to promote mutual self-help and raise the moral tone of the community. Subsequently, more specifically guild structures emerged regulating the conduct of particular professions, including the *ashughs,* some of whose regulations are preserved from the eighteenth and nineteenth centuries. Special mention must be made of the Armenian pottery in Kutahia, which gained priority over Isnik in the seventeenth century. Among the churches and mosques adorned with its craftsmanship is the Monastery of St. James in Jerusalem. Status symbols of many gospels commissioned by merchants are the books' elaborate gilt and silver covers. The covers testify to the skill of goldsmiths in such major centers as Constantinople and New Julfa, which attracted artisans from all over the Armenian world. Metal objects from Tokat and Erzerum also attained a high degree of finesse by the seventeenth century.

Seventeenth-Century Revival

Merchant influence and capital also underlay the revamping of the catholicate of Echmiadzin, particularly under the active tenure of Pilippos Aghbaketsi (1632-1655). After a period of monastic decadence vividly portrayed by Grigor Daranaghtsi (1576-1643) in his contemporary history, the seeds of reform were sown by a group of four committed ecclesiastics who traveled to Egypt and Palestine to reacquaint themselves with the monastic movement's roots. On their return they established the Mets Anapat (great "desert," or *skete*) at the turn of the century. The momentum was maintained by reformers such as Asar Sebastatsi, who sought to found new monasteries and prefigured the work of his compatriot Mkhitar Sebastatsi (Mekhitar of Sebastia) (1676-1749) at San Lazzaro in the next century. As the latter discovered, at that time only in Europe could the necessary conditions be found for a monastic and scholarly community to survive.

Subsequently the attempt was made to raise the standard of clerical education and hence to return to the old curriculum. However, the Philohellene works which already required commentaries that began by simply paraphrasing the text in Hovhannes Vorotnetsi's time were now completely incomprehensible and hence required a totally new translation. A number of these were effected by Stepanos Lehatsi (Stephen of Poland) (d. 1689). Lehatsi had been brought up in Lvov, where he received a good training in Polish and Latin, which formed the basis of his renditions of Pseudo Dionysius, Josephus, Proclus, Aristotle's Physics, and the Quran. In addition, he produced a shortened version of the Grand Miroir edited in 1605 by Johann Maior under the title *Hayeli varuts* (Mirror of Conduct), criticizing the vices and foibles of different social classes. Other textbooks on grammar and logic were prepared by Simeon Jughayetsi (d. 1657).

Armenian religious renewal followed the Counter Reformation in the Roman Catholic Church in the aftermath of the Council of Trent (1545-1563), which led to renewed interest in proselytism throughout the Middle East to be directed by the Congregation for the Propagation of the Faith. The congregation was provided with a polyglot press from which issued a range of materials to foster mission among the Armenians. Moreover, the Jesuit order established itself officially in Constantinople in 1609 and about thirty years later was settled in New Julfa. In the course of the next century, a variety of priests, especially from France and Italy, were dispatched to pursue this task. Some of them became quite knowledgeable about Armenian culture in the process.

Perhaps the most outstanding was Clemens Galanus (1610-1666), who participated in the Theatine mission in Tiflis, opened a school in Constantinople, and spent the last portion of his life in Lvov, where a preliminary acceptance of papal supremacy had already been achieved in 1635. His great three-volume work *Conciliationis Ecclesiae Armenae cum Romana* (Rome, 1650-1690) is extremely important for presenting the European public with a detailed exposition of Armenian history and refutation of the bizarre heresies with which Armenians often were charged in popular tracts. Galanus's successor at the Theatine school in Lvov, Louis Marie Pidou, is also important for his theatrical talents in composing the earliest extant Armenian tragedy, "The Martyrdom of St. Hripsime" of 1668. Only the titles of his other compositions have survived. "The Martyrdom" follows the norms of neoclassical drama and, following local convention, includes Polish intermedia for the benefit of the wider audience. Its propaganda value is fully exposed in the epilogue in which the saint's spirit appears and promises to intercede for the Armenians as long as they remain faithful to the church of her homeland. It seems also to have had some influence on later Armenian plays on the same theme.

While this missionizing movement provoked quite a heated riposte in some quarters, such as New Julfa, where Tatevatsi's "Book of Questions" received its first printing and the Armenian position was defended anew by such scholars as Hovhannes Mrkuz (1643-1715), others were more sympathetic to Roman arguments. The reading of the last gospel at the conclusion of the divine liturgy is a ubiquitous memorial to this openness to Western practice. Similarly, Voskan compared the Armenian text of the Bible with the Vulgate before publication and altered certain passages of the New Testament accordingly. Moreover, the catholicos of the time, Hakob Jughayetsi (Hakob of Julfa) (1655-1680), died on his way to Europe to pledge his acceptance of papal claims in return for assistance in liberating his homeland.

Others actually transferred their affiliation, paving the way for the creation in 1742 of an Armenian Catholic patriarchate with a seat in Lebanon. Some of these, like the Fratres Unitores, were involved in valuable translation activities, though executed in a style and expression characteristic of the Latin originals from which they predominantly derived. One of the most prolific in this endeavor was Hovhannes Holov (1635-1691). Alongside renderings of such classics of popular piety as Thomas à Kempis's "Imitatio Christi" and the "Giardino Spirituale" and more weighty expositions of Roman doctrine, he pointed the way to Armenian classicism in a treatise on rhetoric of 1674, while making a case for the development of the vernacular as a literary medium in one of his final works.

Thus the dynamism of Armenian culture that had dissipated in the middle of the period from the twelfth to the seventeenth centuries is revived in the seventeenth century and redirected toward goals that were to gain increased importance in the ensuing era. Particularly notable are the cultural significance of the merchant class, their network of international contacts, initiatives in creating a secular educational curriculum, and impact on the transformation of book production from the largely cloistered scribe to the greater flexibility and accessibility of the printing press. Gradually the study of history again becomes a source of stimulation, fostering in the subsequent generations the aspiration of reattaining statehood by constructing a patriotic army. Finally, underpinning a number of these changes, there is the multifaceted impact of reestablishing regular contacts with Europe, which result in ever greater integration of the educated classes intellectually and culturally in the next two centuries.

FOR FURTHER INFORMATION

For the sources of, or more information on, the material in this chapter, please consult the following (full citations can be found in the Bibliography at the end of this volume).

Cowe, 1989.

Der Nersessian, 1978.

Mathews and Sanjian, 1991.

Mkhitar Sasnec'i, 1993.

Nersissian, 1984.

Russell, 1987a.

Thomson, 1989.

BIBLIOGRAPHY FOR VOLUMES I AND II

Abovian, Khachatur. 1858. *Verk Hayastani* (Wounds of Armenia). Tiflis.

Abrahamian, A. G. 1964. *Hamarot urvagids hai gaghtavaireri patmutian* (Concise Outline of the History of Armenian Expatriate Communities). Erevan.

Abu, Salih. 1865. *The Churches and Monasteries of Egypt and Some Neighbouring Countries.* Trans. B. T. A. Evetts. Oxford.

Acoghic. See Stepanos Asoghik (Taronetsi).

Adontz, Nicholas. 1970. *Armenia in the Period of Justinian.* Trans. and Comm. by Nina Garsoïan. Lisbon.

Aftandilian, Gregory. 1981. *Armenia: Vision of a Republic: The Independence Lobby in America.* Boston.

(Agathangelos). 1970. *The Teaching of Saint Gregory: An Early Armenian Catechism.* Trans. and comm. R. W. Thomson. Cambridge, MA.

Agathangelos. 1976. *Agathangelos, History of the Armenians.* Trans. and Comm. R.W. Thomson. Albany, NY.

Ahmad, Feroz. 1969. *The Young Turks.* Oxford.

Ahmed Emin (Yalman). See Emin (Yalman), Ahmed.

Ajarian, Hrachia. 1942-1962. *Hayots andznanunneri bararan* (Dictionary of Armenian Personal Names). 5 vols. Erevan.

Akinian, Nerses. 1958. "Zruits bghndze kaghaki" (The Tale of the City of Bronze). *Handes Amsorya.*

al-Baladhuri. 1968. *The Origins of the Islamic State.* Trans. Ph. K. Hitti. 2 vols. New York. Originally published in 1916.

Alboyadjian, Arshak. 1941, 1955, 1961. *Patmutiun hay gaghtakanutian* (History of Armenian Emigrations). 3 vols. Cairo.

Alishan, Ghevond (Leonce M.). 1888. *Léon le Magnifique.* Translated from Armenian. Venice.

Alishan, Ghevond. 1893. *Sisakan.* Venice.

Allen, W.E.D., and Paul Muratoff. 1953. *Caucasian Battlefields.* Cambridge, UK.

Amasiatsi, Amirdovlat. See Amirdovlat Amasiatsi.

Amirdovlat Amasiatsi. 1459. *Akhrapatin.* Preserved in Matenadaran Institute of Manuscripts, no. 8871.

Amirdovlat Amasiatsi. 1926. *Angitats anpet.* Ed. K. V. Basmajian. Vienna.

Amirdovlat Amasiatsi. 1940. *Ogut bzhshkutian* (Utility of Medicine). Ed. St. Malkhasian. Erevan.

Ammiani Marcellini res gestae libri qui supersunt. Ed. and trans. R.C. Rolfe. 3 vols. Loeb Classical Library.

(Anania Shirakatsi) (Anania of Shirak) Anania Širakac'i. 1964. "Autobiographie d'Anania Sirakac'i." Trans. H. Berbérian. *Revue des études arméniennes,* n.s. 1.

(Anania Shirakatsi) (Anania of Shirak) Ananias of Širak. 1992. *The Geography of Ananias of Širak (Ašxarhac'oyc'): The Long and the Short Recensions.* Trans. R. H. Hewsen. Beihefte zum Tübinger Atlas des Vorderen Orients. Reihe B, 77. Wiesbaden.

Ananian, Paolo. 1961. "La data e le circonstanze della consecrazione di S. Gregorio Illuminatore." *Le Muséon* 74. Original Armenian version published in *Pazmavep* (1959-1960).

Ananias of Širak. See Anania Shirakatsi.

Ananun, Davit. 1926. *Rusahayeri hasarakakan zargatsume* (The Social Development of the Russian Armenians). Vol. 3, *1901-1918.* Venice.

Anasian, Hakob. 1957. *Haykakan aghbiurnere Biuzantiayi ankman masin* (Armenian Sources on the Fall of Byzantium). Erevan. English trans. in A. K. Sanjian (Cambridge, MA, 1969), and with commentary in *Viator* 1 (1970).

Anasian, Hakob. 1961. *XVII dari azatagrakan sharzhumnern arevmtian Hayastanum* (The Seventeenth Century Freedom Movements in Western Armenia). Erevan.

Anderson, M. S. 1966. *The Eastern Question, 1774-1923.* London.

Andreasyan, H. D. 1964. *Polonyali Simeon'un seyahatnâmesi, 1608-1619.* Istanbul.

Aparantsi, Simeon. See Simeon Aparantsi.

Appian. "The Mithridatic Wars." *Appian's Roman History.* Ed. and trans. Horace White. Vol 2. pp. 240/1-476/7. Loeb Classical Library.

Appian. "The Syrian Wars." *Appian's Roman History.* Ed. and trans. Horace White. Vol 2. pp. 104/5-236/7. Loeb Classical Library.

Arakel Tavrizhetsi (Arakel of Tabriz). 1896. *Patmutiun* (History). Vagharshapat.

Arakelian, A. 1964. *Hay zhoghovrdi mtavor mshakuiti zargatsman patmutiun* (The History of the Development of the Intellectual Culture of the Armenian People). Vol. 2, *XIV-XIX Centuries.* Erevan.

Areveltsi, Vardan. See Vardan Arevelsi.

Aristakēs Lastivertc'i. See Aristakes Lastiverttsi.

(Aristakes Lastiverttsi) (Aristakes of Lastivert) Aristakes de Lastivert. 1973. *Aristakes de Lastivert. Récit des malheurs de la nation arménienne.* Trans. M. Canard and H. Berbérian. Brussels.

(Aristakes Lastiverttsi) Aristakēs Lastivertc'i. 1985. *History*. Trans. R. Bedrosian. New York.

Arkomed, S. T. 1929. *Pervaia gruppa revoliutsionerov armian na Kavkaze*. Tiflis.

Arlen, Michael J. 1975. *Passage to Ararat*. New York.

Armenian Academy of Sciences. 1971-1984. *Hay zhoghovrdi patmutiun* (History of the Armenian People). Vols. 1-4. Erevan.

Armenian Assembly. 1975. *Directory of Armenian Scholars*. Washington, D.C.

"An Armenian Catholic Bishop of Nakhichevan." 1837. *Journal Asiatique* (March).

Armenian Delegation. 1919. *Réponse au mémoire de la Sublime-Porte en date du 12 février 1919*. Constantinople.

Armstrong, John A. 1976. "Mobilized and Proletarian Diasporas." *American Political Science Review* 70, no. 2 (June).

Arrian. *Anabasis Alexandri*. Ed. and trans. E. I. Robson. 2 vols. Loeb Classical Library.

Arutjunova-Fidanjan, A. 1986-1987. "Some Aspects of the Military-Administrative Districts and of Byzantine Administration in Armenia during the 11th Century." *Revue des études arméniennes*, n.s. 20.

Arutyunian, N. V. 1970. *Biainili (Urartu): Voenno-politicheskaia istoriia i voprosy toponimiki* (Biainili [Urartu]: Military-Political History and Questions of Place-Names). Erevan.

Asar Sebastatsi (Asar of Sebastia). 1993. *Girk bzhshkakan arhesti* (Book on the Medical Art). Ed. D. M. Karapetian. Erevan.

Asdourian, P. 1911. *Die politischen Beziehungen zwischen Armenien und Rom vom 190 v. Chr. bis 428 n. Chr.* Venice. Armenian edition (1910).

Asoghik, Stepanos. See Stepanos Asoghik.

Avakian, Arra. 1977. "Armenians in America: How Many and Where." *Ararat* 18, no. 1 (Winter).

Avdall, Johannes. 1841. "On the Laws and Lawbooks of the Armenians." *Journal of the Royal Asiatic Society of Bengal* 111.

Aydenian, Arsen. 1866. *Critical Grammar of Ashkharhabar or the Modern Armenian Language* (in Armenian).

Azarpay, Guitty. 1968. *Urartian Art and Artifacts: A Chronological Study*. Berkeley.

Baberdatsi, Ghazar. See Ghazar Baberdatsi.

Bakalian, Anny. 1993. *Armenian-Americans: From Being to Feeling Armenian*. New Brunswick, NJ.

Balcer, J. M. 1984. *Sparda by the Bitter Sea*. Chico, CA.

Baldwin, Oliver. 1926. *Six Prisons and Two Revolutions*. London.

Baltrusaitis, Jurgis, and Dickran Kouymjian. 1986. "Julfa on the Arax and Its Funerary Monuments." In *Armenian Studies/Etudes Arméniennes: In Memoriam Haïg Berbérian*, ed. Dickran Kouymjian. Lisbon.

Barkan, O. L. 1958. "Essai sur les données statistiques des registres de recensement dans l'Empire ottoman aux XVe et XVIe siècle." *Journal of the Economic and Social History of the Orient*. Vol. 1.

Barsoumian, Hagop. 1982. "The Dual Role of the Armenian Amira Class with the Ottoman Government and the Armenian *Millet* (1750-1850)." In vol. 1 of *Christians and Jews in the Ottoman Empire*, eds. B. Braude and B. Lewis. New York.

Barton, James L. 1930. *Story of Near East Relief, 1915-1930*. New York.

Basmadjian, Garig. 1971. "Armenian Poetry: Past and Present." *Ararat* (Spring).

Bauer-Manndorff, Elizabeth. 1984. *Das Frühe Armenien*. Vienna.

Bedoukian, Kerop. 1978. *The Urchin: An Armenian's Escape*. London. Published in the U.S. under the title *Some of Us Survived* (New York, 1979).

Bedoukian, P. 1978. *Coinage of the Artaxiads of Armenia*. London.

Bedoukian, P. Z. 1962. *Coinage of Cilician Armenia*. New York.

Bedrosian, Margaret. 1991. *The Magical Pine Ring: Armenian-American Literature*. Detroit.

Berbérian (Perperean), Haïg. 1965. *Niuter K. Polsoy hay patmutian hamar* (Material for the History of the Armenians in Constantinople). Vienna. Originally published as a series of four articles in *Handes Amsorya*.

Beylerian, Arthur. 1983. *Les grandes puissances: L'Empire Ottoman et les Arméniens dans les archives françaises, 1914-1918*. Paris.

Boase, T. S. R. 1978. *The Cilician Kingdom of Armenia*. Edinburgh, New York.

Boase, T. S. R. 1979. *The Cilician Kingdom of Armenia*. 2nd ed. Danbury, CT.

Borian, B. A. 1929. *Armeniia, mezhdunarodnaia diplomatiia i SSSR*. Vol. 2. Leningrad.

Borisov, A. A. 1965. *Climates of the U.S.S.R.* Trans. R. A. Ledward. Chicago.

Bournoutian, George A. 1983. "The Ethnic Composition and the Socio-Economic Conditions of Eastern Armenia in the First Half of the Nineteenth Century." In *Transcaucasia: Nationalism and Social Change*, ed. R. Suny. Ann Arbor.

Bournoutian, George A. 1992. *The Khanate of Erevan under Qajar Rule, 1795-1828*. Costa Mesa, CA.

Bournoutian, George A., trans. 1994. *A History of Qarabagh*. Costa Mesa, CA.

Brosset, M. F. 1874. *Collection d'historiens arméniens*. Vol. 1. St. Petersburg.

Buniat Sebastatsi (Buniat of Sebastia). 1644. *Girk bzhshkutian tomari* (Book of Medicine). Preserved in Matenadaran Institute of Manuscripts no. 1023.

Busse, H., ed. and trans. 1972. *History of Persia under Qajar Rule*. New York.

Buxton, Noel and Harold. 1914. *Travels and Politics in Armenia*. London.

Cahen, Claude. 1968. *Pre-Ottoman Turkey*. London.

Cambridge History of Iran. 1983, 1985, 1991. Vol. 2, *The Median and Archaemenian Periods*, ed. Ilya Gershevitch. Vol. 3, *The Seleucid, Parthian, and Sasanid Periods*, ed. Ehsan Yarshater. Vol. 7, *From Nadir Shah to the Islamic Republic*, ed. Peter Avery et al. Cambridge, UK.

Campbell, George Douglas (Duke of Argyll, 8th Duke). 1896. *Our Responsibilities for Turkey*. London.

Carswell, John. 1968. *New Julfa, The Armenian Churches and Other Buildings*. Oxford.

Cartwright, John. 1611. *The Preacher's Travels . . . through Syria, Mesopotamia, Armenia, Media, Hircania, and Parthia. . . .* London.

Çebesoy, Ali Fuat. 1955. *Moskova hâtıraları* (21/11/1920-2/6/1922) (Moscow Memoirs [November 21, 1920–June 2, 1922]). Istanbul.

Chamchian, Mikayel. 1784-1786. *Hayots patmutiun* (Armenian History). 3 vols. Venice.

Charny, Israel W. 1983. *International Conference on the Holocaust and Genocide*. Book I, *The Conference Program and Crisis*. Tel Aviv.

Chaumont, M. L. 1982. "Tigranocerte: Données du problème et état des recherches." *Revue des études arméniennes*, n.s. 16.

Chelebi, Evliya. See Evliya Chelebi.

Chronicles of the Chaldean Kings (626-556 B.C.). 1961. Trans. D.J. Wiseman. London.

La Chronique attribuée au Connétable Smbat. Trans. G. Dédéyan. 1980. Paris.

Chronique de Matthieu d'Edesse: Bibliothèque historique arménienne. 1858. Trans. E. Dulaurier. Paris.

Clavijo. 1928. *Embassy to Tamerlane, 1403-1406*. Trans. G. Le Strange. London.

Commission of the Churches on International Affairs. 1984. *Armenia: The Continuing Tragedy*. Geneva.

Cook, M. A. 1972. *Population Pressures in Rural Anatolia, 1450-1600*. London.

Cowe, S. P. 1989. "An Allegorical Poem by Mkrtich Naghash and Its Models." *Journal of the Society for Armenian Studies* 4.

Current Digest of the Soviet Press. 1991. 43, no. 18. (5 June).

Dadrian, Vahakn N. 1975. "The Common Features of the Armenian and Jewish Cases of Genocide: A Comparative Victimological Perspective." *Victimology* 4.

Dadrian, Vahakn N. 1986. "The Naim-Andonian Documents on the World War I Destruction of the Ottoman Armenians." *International Journal of Middle East Studies* 8, no. 3 (August).

Dadrian, Vahakn N. 1986a. "The Role of Turkish Physicians in the World War I Genocide of Ottoman Armenians." *Holocaust and Genocide Studies* 1, no. 2.

Dadrian, Vahakn N. 1989. "Genocide as a Problem of National and International Law: The World War I Armenian Case and Its Contemporary Legal Ramifications." *Yale Journal of International Law* 14, no. 2 (Summer).

Dadrian, Vahakn N. 1991. "The Documentation of the World War I Armenian Massacres in the Proceedings of the Turkish Military Tribunal." *International Journal of Middle East Studies* 23, no. 4 (November).

Dadrian, Vahakn N. 1992. "The Role of the Turkish Military in the Destruction of the Ottoman Armenians." *Journal of Political and Military Sociology* 20, no. 2 (Winter).

Dadrian, Vahakn N. 1993. "The Role of the Special Organisation in the Armenian Genocide during the First World War." In *Minorities in Wartime,* ed. Panikos Panayi. Oxford, UK, Providence, RI.

Dandamaev, M. A. 1990. *Political History of the Achaemenid Empire.* Leiden.

Dandamaev, M. A., and V. Lukonin. 1988. *Culture and Social Institutions of Ancient Iran.* Cambridge.

Daranaghtsi, Grigor. See Grigor Daranaghtsi.

Darbinjan, M. O. 1965. *Simeon Lekhatzi, Putevye zametki.* Moscow.

Dashian, Hagovpos, and Kerope Sbenian. 1898. *Study of the Classical Armenian* (in Armenian).

Dasxuranc'i, Movsēs. See Movses Daskhurantsi.

David. 1983. *Definitions and Divisions of Philosophy.* Trans. Bridget Kendall and Robert W. Thomson. Atlanta.

Davis, Leslie A. 1989. *The Slaughterhouse Province.* New Rochelle, NY.

de Lusignan, Levon V. *Chronique d'Arménie.* 1906. In *Recueil des Historiens des Croisades: Documents arméniens,* vol. 2. Paris.

Dédéyan, Gérard. 1996. "Les princes arméniens de l'Euphratès et l'Empire byzantin (fin XIe-milieu XIIIe s.)." *L'Arménie et Byzance.* Paris.

Dédéyan, Gérard, ed. 1982. *Histoire des Arméniens.* Toulouse.

Dekmejian, R. Hrair. 1975. *Patterns of Political Leadership: Egypt, Israel, Lebanon.* Albany, NY.

Dekmejian, R. Hrair. 1976. "The Armenians: Historical Memory, Consciousness and the Middle East Dispersion." *Middle East Review* (April).

Der Nersessian, Sirarpie. 1945. *Armenia and the Byzantine Empire.* Cambridge, MA.

Der Nersessian, Sirarpie. 1959. "The Armenian Chronicle of the Constable Smpad'." *Dumbarton Oaks Papers.* No. 13.

Der Nersessian, Sirarpie. 1962. "The Kingdom of Cilician Armenia." In Vol. 2, *A History of the Crusades,* ed. K. M. Setton. Philadelphia.

Der Nersessian, Sirarpie. 1969. *The Armenians.* London.

Der Nersessian, Sirarpie. 1978. *Armenian Art.* London.

Diakonoff, I. M. 1985. *Prehistory of the Armenian People.* Delmar, NY.

Diakonoff, I. M., and V.P. Neroznak. 1985. *Phrygian*. Delmar, NY.

Dio's Roman History. Ed. and trans. E. Cary. 9 vols. Loeb Classical Library.

Djemal Pasha (Jemal Pasha). 1922. *Memories of a Turkish Statesman, 1913-1919*. London.

"Documents: The State Department File." 1984. *Armenian Review* 37/1 (Spring).

Dostourian, A. E. 1993. *Armenia and the Crusades: The Chronicle of Mathew of Edessa*. Boston.

Drasxanakertc'i, Yovhannēs. See Hovhannes Draskhanakerttsi (Yovhannēs Drasxanakertc'i).

Earle, E. M. 1935. *Turkey, the Great Powers and the Bagdad Railway*. New York.

Edwards, R. W. 1987. *The Fortifications of Armenian Cilicia*. Washington, D.C.

Egan, Eleanor Franklin. 1919. "This To Be Said for the Turk." *Saturday Evening Post* 192, 20 December.

Ełišē. See Eghishe.

(Eghishe) Ełishe. 1982. *History of Vardan and the Armenian War*. Trans. R.W. Thomson. Harvard Armenian Texts and Studies, 5. Cambridge, MA.

Elliott, Mabel E. 1924. *Beginning Again at Ararat*. New York.

Emin, Joseph. 1792. *The Life and Adventures of Joseph Emin, an Armenian*. London.

Emin, Joseph. 1918. *Life and Adventures of Joseph Emin, 1726-1809*. 2 vols. Calcutta.

Emin (Yalman), Ahmed. 1930. *Turkey in the World War*. New Haven.

Encyclopaedia of Islam. 1960. 2nd ed. Leiden. See especially, "Armīniya," "Kara-Koyunlu," and "Enwer Pasha."

Erznkatsi, Kostandin. See Kostandin Erznkatsi.

Etmekjian, James. 1964. *The French Influence on the Western Armenian Renaissance, 1843-1915*. New York.

Eudin, Xenia Joukoff, and Robert C. North. 1957. *Soviet Russia and the East, 1920-1927: A Documentary Survey*. Stanford.

Evliya Chelebi. 1896-1928. *Seyahatname* (Travel Account). 10 vols. Istanbul. Partial English trans. Joseph von Hammer-Purgstall, under the title *Travels of Evliya Chelebi*, 2 vols. (London, 1834-1846). Partial Armenian trans. in Safrastian, vol. 3 (Erevan, 1967).

Eznik. 1959. *Eznik, De Deo*. Trans. L. Mariès and C. Mercier. (Patrologia Orientalis. XXVIII 3-4), Paris.

Faroghi, S. 1984. *Towns and Townsmen of Ottoman Anatolia*. Cambridge.

Fontenrose, Joseph. 1959. *Python: A Study of Delphic Myth and Its Origins*. Berkeley.

Forbes, Thomas B. 1983. *Urartian Architecture*. BAR International Series, 170. Oxford.

Frik. 1952. *Frik Divan*. Ed. Archbishop Tirair. New York.

Galanus, Clemens. 1650, 1690. *Conciliationis Ecclesiae Armenae cum Romana.* 2 vols. Rome.

Gandzaketsi, Kirakos. See Kirakos Gandzaketsi.

Garitte, G. 1952. *La Narratio de Rebus Armeniae.* Louvain.

Garsoïan, Nina. 1967. *The Paulician Heresy.* The Hague and Paris.

Garsoïan, Nina. 1984-1985. "The Early Medieval Armenian City: An Alien Element?" *The Journal of Ancient Near Eastern Studies* 16-17.

Garsoïan, Nina. 1985. *Armenia Between Byzantium and the Sasanians.* London.

Garsoïan, Nina. 1994. "Reality and Myth in Armenian History." In *The East and the Meaning of History.* Rome.

Garsoïan, Nina. 1997. "The Armenian Church between Byzantium and the East." *Morgan Library Symposium* (1994). New York.

Garsoïan, Nina G., T. F. Mathews, and R. W. Thomson, eds. 1982. *East of Byzantium: Syria and Armenia in the Formative Period.* Washington, D.C.

Genocide: Crime against Humanity. 1984. Special issue of *Armenian Review* 37, no. 1 (Spring).

Georgia. 1919. *Dokumenty i materialy po vneshnei politike Zakavkaz'ia i Gruzii.* Tiflis.

Ghazar Baberdatsi (Ghazar [Lazar] of Baberd). n.d. Bible. Preserved in Matenadaran Institute of Manuscripts, no. 351. Erevan.

(Ghazar Parpetsi) Ghazar P'arpec'i. 1985. *History of the Armenians.* Trans. R. Bedrosian. New York.

(Ghazar Parpetsi) Łazar P'arpec'i. 1991. *The History of Łazar P'arpec'i.* Trans. and Comm. R. W. Thomson. Atlanta.

(Ghevond) Lewond. 1982. *The History of Lewond.* Trans. Z. Arzoumanian. Philadelphia.

Ghukas Vanandetsi. 1699. *Gandz chapoy, kshroy, tvoy, ev dramits bolor ashkharhi* (Treasury of Measures, Weights, Numeration, and Currency from All Over the World). Amsterdam.

Gidney, James B. 1967. *A Mandate for Armenia.* Kent, OH.

Gilbert, Charles K., and Charles T. Bridgeman. 1921. *Foreigners or Friends.* New York.

Girk Tghtots (The Book of Letters). 1994. Jerusalem.

Graves, Philip. 1941. *Briton and Turk.* London.

Great Britain. Foreign Office. 1916. *The Treatment of Armenians in the Ottoman Empire. See* Toynbee, Arnold J., ed. 1916.

Great Britain. Foreign Office. 1928. *British Documents on the Origins of the War, 1898-1914.* Eds. G. P. Gooch and Harold Temperley. Vol. 5. London.

Great Britain. Parliament. 1878. *Sessional Papers.* Vol. 83, c. 1973, Turkey no. 22.

Great Britain. Parliament. 1878a. *Sessional Papers.* Vol. 83, c. 2083, Turkey no. 39.

Great Britain. Parliament. 1895. *Sessional Papers.* Vol. 109, c. 7894, Turkey no. 1.

Great Britain. Parliament. 1896. *Sessional Papers.* Vol. 95, c. 7923, Turkey no. 1.

Great Britain. Parliament. House of Commons. 1917. *The Parliamentary Debates.* 5th series. London.

Great Britain. Public Record Office. Classes 371 and 424.

Grégoire de Narek. See Grigor Narekatsi.

Gregorian, V. 1972. "The Impact of Russia on the Armenians and Armenia." In *Russia and Asia,* ed. W. S. Vucinich. Palo Alto.

Gregory, J. S. 1968. *Russian Land, Soviet People: A Geographical Approach to the U.S.S.R.* New York.

Griboedov, A. S. 1953. "Proekt uchrezhdeniia Rossiiskoi Zakavkazskoi kompanii." In *Sochineniia,* ed. V. Orlov. Moscow.

Grigor Daranaghtsi (Grigor of Daranagh). 1915. *Zhamanakagrutiun* (Chronology). Jerusalem. French trans. M. F. Brosset in vol. 1 of *Collection d'historiens arméniens* (St. Petersburg, 1874).

Grigor Magistros (Gregory the Magister) Pahlavuni. 1910. *Grigor Magistrosi Tghtere* (The Letters of Grigor Magistros). Ed. K. Kostaniants. Alexandropol.

Grigor Narekatsi (Gregory of Narek) (Grégoire de Narek). 1961. *Grégoire de Narek: Le Livre de Prières.* T. Kéchichian. Paris.

Grigor Tatevatsi (Grigor of Tatev). 1729. *Girk hartsmants* (Book of Questions). Constantinople.

Hachakhapatum. 1927. "Ausgewählte Reden aus dem Hatschachapatum vom hl. Mesrop." Trans. S. Weber and E. Sommer. In *Ausgewählte Schriften der armenischen Kirchenväter,* ed. S. Weber, vol. 1. Munich.

Hairapetian, S. 1995. *A History of Ancient and Medieval Armenian Literature.* Delmar, NY.

Hakobian, H. 1932. *Ughegrutiunner* (Travel Accounts). Vol. 1, *1253-1582.* Erevan.

Hakobian, V. A. 1951, 1956. *Manr zhamanakagrutiunner XIII-XVIII dd.* (Minor Chronicles, XIII-XVIII Centuries). 2 vols. Erevan.

Hakobian, V., and A. Hovhannisian. 1974. *Colophons of Seventeenth Century Armenian Manuscripts.* Vol. 1, *1601-1620.* Erevan.

Halasi-Kun, T. 1963. "The Caucasus: An Ethno-Historical Survey." *Studia Caucasica* 1. The Hague.

Hammer-Purgstall, Joseph von. 1827-1835. *Geschichte des Osmanischen Reiches.* 2nd ed. 10 vols. Pesht. French trans. J. J. Hellert under the title *Histoire de l'Empire ottoman,* 18 vols. (Paris, 1835-1841).

Hammer-Purgstall, Joseph von, trans. 1834-1846. *Travels of Evliya Chelebi.* 2 vols. London.

Harney, Robert F., Anne McCarthy, and Isabel Kaprielian, eds. 1982. "Armenians in Ontario." *Polyphony* 4, no. 2 (Fall/Winter).

Harvard Encyclopedia of American Ethnic Groups. 1980. Stephan Thernstrom, Ann Orlov, and Oscar Handlin, eds. Cambridge, MA.

Haykakan Sovetakan Hanragitaran (Armenian Soviet Encyclopedia). 1974-1986. 12 vols. Erevan.

Hekimian, Kim. 1990. "Armenian Immigration to Argentina: 1909-1939." *Armenian Review* 43, no. 1/169 (Spring).

Heratsi, Mkhitar. See Mkhitar Heratsi.

Herodotus. 1954. *The Histories.* Trans. Aubrey De Selincourt. London.

Herodotus. Trans. A. D. Godley. 4 vols. Loeb Classical Library

Hertslet, Edward. 1891. *The Map of Europe by Treaty.* Vol. 4. London.

Hetoum. 1988. *A Lytell Cronycle.* Toronto.

Hetum of Korikos. 1529. *La Flor des Estoires de la Terre d'Orient.* Paris.

Hewsen, Robert H. 1978-1979. "Introduction to Armenian Historical Geography: The Nature of the Problem." *Revue des études arméniennes,* n.s. 13.

Hewsen, Robert H. 1983. "Introduction to Armenian Historical Geography: II. The Boundaries of Achaemenid Armenia." *Revue des études arméniennes,* n.s. 17.

Hewsen, Robert H. 1984. "Introduction to Armenian Historical Geography: III. The Boundaries of Orontid Armenia." *Revue des études arméniennes,* n.s. 18.

Hewsen, Robert H. 1992. *The Geography of Ananias of Shirak: Introduction, Translation and Commentary.* Wiesbaden.

Hofmann, Tessa. 1985. "German Eyewitness Reports of the Genocide of the Armenians 1915-16." In *A Crime of Silence: The Armenian Genocide,* Permanent People's Tribunal. London.

Hourani, Albert H. 1947. *Minorities in the Arab World.* London.

Housepian, Marjorie. 1972. *Smyrna 1922: The Destruction of a City.* London.

Hovannisian, Richard G. 1962. "The Armenian Communities of Southern and Eastern Asia." *Armenian Review* 15 (Autumn).

Hovannisian, Richard G. 1967. *Armenia on the Road to Independence, 1918.* Berkeley, Los Angeles.

Hovannisian, Richard G. 1971-1996. *The Republic of Armenia.* 4 vols. Berkeley, Los Angeles, London.

Hovannisian, Richard G. 1974. "The Ebb and Flow of the Armenian Minority in the Arab Middle East." *Middle East Journal* 28, no. 1 (Winter).

Hovannisian, Richard G. 1991. "Altruism in the Armenian Genocide of 1915." In *Embracing One Another,* eds. Samuel and Pearl Oliner. New York.

Hovannisian, Richard G. 1993. "The Armenian Diaspora and the Narrative of Power." In *Diasporas in World Politics,* eds. Dimitri C. Constas and Athanassios G. Platias. London.

Hovannisian, Richard G. 1994. "The Etiology and Sequelae of the Armenian Genocide." In *The Conceptual and Historical Dimensions of Genocide,* ed. George J. Andreopoulos. Philadelphia.

Hovannisian, Richard G. 1994a. "Historical Memory and Foreign Relations: The Armenian Perspective." In *The Legacy of History in Russia and the New States of Eurasia,* ed. S. Frederick Starr. Armonk, NY, and London.

Hovannisian, Richard G., ed. 1980. *The Armenian Holocaust: A Bibliography Relating to the Deportations, Massacres, and Dispersion of the Armenian People, 1915-1923.* Cambridge, MA.

Hovannisian, Richard G., ed. 1986. *The Armenian Genocide in Perspective.* New Brunswick, NJ.

Hovannisian, Richard G., ed. 1992. *The Armenian Genocide: History, Politics, Ethics.* London, New York.

(Hovhannes Draskhanakerttsi) Yovhannēs Drasxanakertc'i. 1987. *Yovhannēs Drasxanakertc'i, History of Armenia.* Trans. K. H. Maksoudian. Atlanta.

Hovhannes Makuetsi (Yovhannēs Makuec'i) (Hovhannes of Maku). 1969. "Oghb Hayastanay Ashkharhi Erevanay ev Jughayu" (Lament on the Land of Armenia, Erevan, and Julfa). In *Hay mijnadarian patmakan oghber* (Medieval Armenian Historical Laments), ed. P. M. Khachatrian. Erevan.

(Hovhannes Mamikonian) Yovhannēs Mamikonean. 1993. *Pseudo-Yovhannēs Mamikonean, The History of Tarōn (Patmutiwn Tarōnoy): Historical Investigation, Critical Translation and Historical and Textual Commentaries.* Trans. Levon Avdoyan. Atlanta.

(Hovhannes Mandakuni) Johannes Mandakuni. 1927. "Reden des armenischen Kirchenvaters Johannes Mandakuni." Trans. J. Blatz and S. Weber. In *Ausgewählte Schriften der armenischen Kirchenväter,* ed. S. Weber, vol. 2. Munich.

(Hovhannes Odznetsi) Johannis Ozniensis. 1834. *Johannis Ozniensis Opera.* Trans. J. Aucher. 2 Vols. Venice.

Hovhannes Tlkurantsi (Hovhannes of Tlkuran). 1958. *(Khev) Hovhannes Tlkurantsi Taghagirk* (Book of Tagh Poems by [Crazy] Hovhannes of Tlkuran). Ed. N. Bogharian. Jerusalem.

Hovhannisian, Ashot, comp. 1926. *Hayastani avtonomian ev Antantan: Vaveragrer imperialistakan paterazmi shrdjanits* (Armenia's Autonomy and the Entente: Documents from the Period of the Imperialistic War). Erevan.

Hovnatan, Naghash. 1983. *Tagher* (Tagh Poems). Ed. A. Mnatsakanian. Erevan.

Hudson, Michael C. 1968. *The Precarious Republic: Political Modernization in Lebanon.* New York.

Hughes, Byron O. 1939. "The Physical Anthropology of Native Born Armenians." PhD. diss., Harvard University. Published as "Occasional Paper no. 6 of the Society for Armenian Studies." Photocopy (1986).

Ibn Ḥawḳal. 1964. *Configuration de la terre.* Trans. J. H. Kramers and G. Wiet. 2 vols. Paris.

Inglisian, V. 1963. "Die armenische Literatur." In *Armenisch und kaukasische Sprachen,* ed. G. Deeters (Handbuch der Orientalistik, 1, 7).

İslam Ansiklopedisi. 1945-88. 1st ed. See especially "Ak-Koyunlu" and "Kara-Koyunlu," Vladimir Minorsky. Istanbul.

Jahukian, G. B. 1987. *Hayots lezvi patmutiun: Nakhagrayin zhamanakashrjan* (The History of the Armenian Language: The Pre-Literate Period). Erevan.

Jennings, R. 1976. "Urban Population in Anatolia in the Sixteenth Century: A Study of Kayseri, Karaman, Amasya, Trabzon and Erzurum." *International Journal for Middle Eastern Studies* 7.

Johannes Mandakuni. See Hovhannes Mandakuni.

Johannis Ozniensis. See Hovhannes Odznetsi.

Kapoïan-Kouymjian, Angèle. 1988. *L'Egypte vue par les Arméniens.* Paris.

Kaprielian, Isabel. 1987. "Migratory Caravans: Armenian Sojourners in Canada." *Journal of American Ethnic History* 6, no. 2 (Spring).

Karakashian, Madatia. 1895. *Critical History of the Armenians* (in Armenian).

Kardashian, Ardashes. 1943. *Niuter Egiptosi Hayots patmutian hamar.* (Materials for the History of the Armenians of Egypt). Cairo.

Karst, J., ed. 1905. *Armenisches Rechtsbuch.* 2 vols. Strassburg.

Katerdjian, Hovsep. 1849, 1852. *Tiezerakan Patmutiun* (Universal History). 2 vols. Venice.

Kayaloff, Jacques. 1973. *The Battle of Sardarabad.* The Hague.

Kazemzadeh, Firuz. 1951. *The Struggle for Transcaucasia, 1917-1921.* New York, Oxford.

Kazemzadeh, Firuz. 1974. "Russian Penetration of the Caucasus." In *Russian Imperialism from Ivan the Great to the Revolution,* ed. Taras Hunczak. New Brunswick, NJ.

Kazhdan, A.P. 1975. *Armiane v sostave gospodstvuiushchego klassa Vizantiiskoi Imperii v XI-XII vv.* Erevan.

Kecharetsi, Khachatur. See Khachatur Kecharetsi.

Kerr, Stanley E. 1973. *The Lions of Marash: Personal Experience with American Near East Relief, 1919-1922.* Albany, NY.

Kevorkian, Garo. 1954-67/68. *Amenun taregirke* (Everyone's Almanac). Beirut.

Khachatur Kecharetsi (Khachatur of Kecharis). 1958. *Khachatur Kecharetsi xiii-xiv dd.* Ed. T. Avdalbegian. Erevan.

Khachikian, Levon. 1950. *Colophons of Fourteenth Century Armenian Manuscripts* (in Armenian). Erevan.

Khachikian, Levon. 1955, 1958, 1967. *Fifteenth Century Armenian Manuscript Colophons* (in Armenian). 3 vols. Erevan. Partial English trans. A. K. Sanjian. Cambridge, MA, 1969.

Khachikian, Levon. 1972. In *Hay zhoghovrdi patmutiun* (History of the Armenian People), Armenian Academy of Sciences, vol. 4. Erevan.

Khatisian, Alexandre. 1930. *Hayastani Hanrapetutian dsagumn u zargatsume* (The Creation and Development of the Republic of Armenia). Athens.

(Khatisian, Alexandre) Khatissian, Alexander. 1950. "The Memoirs of a Mayor, Part IV." *The Armenian Review* 3, no. 2 (Summer).

Khorenatsi, Movses. See Movses Khorenats'i.

Kirakos Gandzaketsi (Kirakos of Gandzak). 1961. *Patmutiun hayots* (History of the Armenians). Ed. K. A. Melik-Ohanjanian. Erevan.

Kirakos Gandzaketsi. 1986. *History of the Armenians.* Trans. R. Bedrosian. New York.

Kiuleserian, Babgen. 1939. *Patmutiun katoghikosats Kilikioy (1441-en minchev mer orere)* (History of the Catholicosate of Cilicia [from 1441 to Our Days]). Antelias.

Kiumurjian, Eremia Chelebi. 1913, 1932, 1939. *Stampoloy patmutiun* (History of Istanbul). 3 vols. Vienna.

Kloian, Richard D., comp. 1985. *The Armenian Genocide: News Accounts from the American Press, 1915-1922.* 3rd ed. Berkeley.

Knapp, Grace H. 1915. *The Mission at Van.* New York.

Knik Havatoy (The Seal of Faith). 1974. Louvain

Koriun. 1964. *The Life of Mashtots.* Trans. B. Norehad. New York. Reprinted 1985 in the *Delmar Classical Armenian Text Series.* New York.

Kostandin Erznkatsi (Constantine of Erzinka). 1962. *Tagher* (Tagh Poems). Ed. A. Srapian. Erevan.

Kouymjian, Dickran. 1975. "The Canons Dated 1280 A.D. of the Armenian Akhî-Type Brotherhood of Erzinjan." In part I, vol. 2 of *Actes du XXIXe congrès international des orientalistes, Paris, 1973.* Paris.

Kouymjian, Dickran. 1982. "L'Arménie sous les dominations des Turcomans et des Ottomans (X^e-XVIe siècles)." In *Histoire des Arméniens,* ed. Gérard Dédéyan. Toulouse.

Kouymjian, Dickran. 1983. "Dated Armenian Manuscripts as a Statistical Tool for Armenian History." In *Medieval Armenian Culture,* T. Samuelian and

M. Stone, eds. University of Pennsylvania Armenian Texts and Studies, vol. 6. Chico, CA.

Kouymjian, Dickran. 1988. "A Critical Bibliography for the History of Armenia from 1375 to 1605." *Armenian Review* 41/1 (Spring).

Kouymjian, Dickran. 1994. "From Disintegration to Reintegration: Armenians at the Start of the Modern Era, XVIth-XVIIth Centuries." *Revue du monde arménien* 1.

Krikorian, Mesrob K. 1978. *Armenians in the Service of the Ottoman Empire, 1860-1908.* London.

Kuper, Leo. 1982. *Genocide: Its Political Use in the Twentieth Century.* New Haven, London.

Kurat, Y. T. 1967. "How Turkey Drifted into World War." In *Studies in International History,* K. Bourne and D. C. Watt, eds. London.

Kurkjian, Vahan M. 1958. *A History of Armenia.* New York.

Landau, Jacob M. 1981. *Pan-Turkism in Turkey: A Study of Irridentism.* London.

Lang, David Marshall. 1981. *The Armenians: A People in Exile.* London.

Lang, David Marshall, and Christopher J. Walker. *The Armenians.* Minority Rights Group, no. 32 (revised). London.

Lastivertc'i, Aristakēs. See Aristakes Lastiverttsi.

Laurent, J. 1919. *L'Arménie entre Byzance et l'Islam.* Paris. Revised and enlarged edition by M. Canard (Lisbon, 1980).

Łazar P'arpec'i. See Ghazar Parpetsi.

Lazian, Gabriel. 1957. *Hayastan ev hai date* (Armenia and the Armenian Question). Cairo.

Le Strange, Guy. 1939. *Lands of the Eastern Caliphate.* Cambridge, UK.

Le Strange, Guy, ed. and trans. 1926. *Don Juan of Persia, A Shi'ah Catholic, 1560-1604.* New York, London.

Lebon, J. 1929. "Les citations patristiques du Sceau de la foi." *Revue d'histoire ecclésiastique* 5.

Lehatsi, Simeon. See Simeon Lehatsi.

Lepsius, Johannes. 1897. *Armenia and Europe: An Indictment.* London.

Lepsius, Johannes. 1916, 1919a. *Der Todesgang des armenischen Volkes.* Potsdam.

Lepsius, Johannes, ed. 1919. *Deutschland und Armenien, 1914-1918.* Potsdam.

Lewis, Bernard. 1968. *The Emergence of Modern Turkey.* 2nd ed. London, New York.

Lockhart, L. 1938. *Nadir Shah.* London.

Lockhart, L. 1958. *The Fall of the Safavid Dynasty and the Afghan Occupation of Persia.* Cambridge, UK.

Luckenbill, Daniel David. 1989. *Ancient Records of Assyria and Babylonia.* 2 vols. Reprint, London.

Lydolph, P. E. 1970. *Geography of the U.S.S.R.* 2nd ed. New York.

Lynch, H. F. B. 1901. *Armenia: Travels and Studies.* 2 vols. London.

Lynch, H. F. B. 1990. *Armenia: Travels and Studies.* 2 vols. London, 1901. Reprint, New York.

Maalouf, A. 1984. *The Crusades Through Arab Eyes.* New York.

Magistros, Grigor. See Grigor Magistros (Grigor the Magister) Pahlavuni.

Mahé, J.-P. 1993. "L'Eglise arménienne de 611 à 1066." In *Histoire du christianisme,* vol. 4, ed. J.-M. Mayeur et al. Paris.

Maksoudian, Krikor. 1988-1989. "The Chalcedonian Issue and the Early Bagratids: The Council of Širakawan." *Revue des études arméniennes* 21.

Makuetsi, Hovhannes. See Hovhannes Makuetsi.

Mallory, J. P. 1989. *In Search of the Indo-Europeans: Language, Archaeology and Myth.* London.

Mamikonean, Yovhannēs. See (Hovhannes Mamikonian) Yovhannēs Mamikonean.

Manandian, Hakob. 1963. *Tigrane II et Rome.* Lisbon. Original Armenian edition, Erevan, 1940.

(Manandian) Manandyan, Hakob. 1965. *The Trade and Cities of Armenia in Relation to Ancient World Trade.* Trans. and ed. Nina Garsoïan. Lisbon.

Mandakuni, John (Johannes). See Hovhannes Mandakuni.

Mandelstam, André. 1917. *Le sort de l'empire Ottoman.* Paris, Lausanne.

"Manifest H. H. Dashnaktsutian" (Manifesto of the Armenian Revolutionary Federation). 1958. In *Droshak: Hai Heghapokhakan Dashnaktsutian Organ, 1890-1897* (n.p.)

Mariès, L. 1924. "Le De Deo d'Eznik de Kolb. Etude de critique littéraire et textuelle." *Revue des études arméniennes* 4.

Mathews, T. F., and A. K. Sanjian. 1991. *Armenian Gospel Iconography: The Tradition of the Glajor Gospel.* Dumbarton Oaks Studies, 29. Washington, D.C.

Mathieson, R. S. 1975. *The Soviet Union: An Economic Geography.* New York.

Matossian, Mary Kilbourne. 1962. *The Impact of Soviet Policies in Armenia.* Leiden.

Meillet, Antoine. 1936. *Esquisse d'une grammaire comparée de l'arménien classique.* 2nd ed. Vienna.

Mekhitar, Abbot. 1749. *Dictionary of the Armenian Language* (in Armenian).

Mekhitar, Abbot. 1985. *Grammar in Armeno-Turkish* (in Armenian).

Melson, Robert F. 1992. *Revolution and Genocide: On the Origins of the Armenian Genocide and the Holocaust.* Chicago, London.

Metzopetsi, Tovma. See Tovma Metzopetsi.

Mikayelian, V. A. 1960. *Hayastani giughatsiutiune Sovetakan ishkhanutian hamar mghvads paikari zhamanakashrdjanum (1917-20)* (The Peasantry of Armenia during the Period of Struggle for Soviet Power, [1917-1920]). Erevan.

Minorsky, Vladimir. 1953. *Studies in Caucasian History.* London.

Minorsky, Vladimir. 1953a. "Thomas of Metsop on the Timurid-Turkman Wars." In *To Professor M. Shafi.* Lahore.

Minorsky, Vladimir. 1958. *A History of Sharvān and Darband.* Cambridge and London.

Mirak, Robert. 1980. "Armenians." In *Harvard Encyclopedia of American Ethnic Groups,* Stephan Thernstrom, Ann Orlov, and Oscar Handlin, eds. Cambridge, MA.

Mirak, Robert. 1983. *Torn Between Two Lands: Armenians in America, 1890 to World War I.* Cambridge, MA.

Mkhitar, Gosh. 1975. *Girk datastani* (Judicial Manual). Ed. Kh. Torosian. Erevan.

Mkhitar Heratsi. 1832. *The Consolation of Fevers* (in Armenian). Venice.

Mkhitar Heratsi (Mekhitar of Her). 1971. In *Hay groghner* (Armenian Writers). Jerusalem.

(Mkhitar Sasnetsi) Mxit'ar Sasnec'i (Mekhitar of Sasun). 1993. *Theological Discourses.* Trans. S. P. Cowe. Vol. 21 (in Armenian), and vol. 22 (in English) of *Corpus Scriptorum Christianorum Orientalium.* Louvain.

Mkrtich Naghash. 1965. *Mkrtich Naghash.* Ed. E. D. Khondkarian. Erevan.

Morgenthau, Henry. 1918. *Ambassador Morgenthau's Story.* Garden City, NY.

Mouradian, Claire. 1979. "L'immigration des Arméniens de la diaspora vers la RSS d'Arménie, 1946-1962." *Cahiers du Monde russe et sovietique* 20, no. 1 (January-March).

Mouradian, Claire. 1990. *De Staline à Gorbachev: Histoire d'une République sovietique. l'Arménie.* Paris.

(Movses Daskhurantsi) Movsēs Dasxuranc'i. 1961. *The History of the Caucasian Albanians.* Trans. C.J.F. Dowsett. London.

(Movses Khorenatsi) Moses Khorenats'i (Moses of Khoren). 1978. *History of the Armenians.* Trans. and Comm. Robert W. Thomson. Cambridge, MA.

Mserlian, Kevork. 1947. *Akanavor hayer Ekibtosi medj* (Distinguished Armenians in Egypt). Cairo.

Mutafian, Claude. 1993. *Le royaume arménien de Cilicie, XIIe-XIVe siècle.* Paris.

Naghash, Mkrtich. See Mkrtich Naghash.

Nalbandian, Louise. 1963. *The Armenian Revolutionary Movement.* Berkeley, Los Angeles.

Nalbandian, Mikayel. 1940-1948. *Erkeri liakatar zhoghovatsu* (Complete Collection of Works). 4 vols. Erevan.

Nassibian, Akaby. 1984. *Britain and the Armenian Question, 1915-1923.* London.

Nerses Shnorhali (Nerses the Gracious). 1973. *Oghb Edesioy* (Lament on Edessa). Ed. M. Mkrtchian. Erevan.

Nersissian, V. 1984. "Medieval Armenian Poetry and Its Relation to Other Literatures." In *Armenia: Annual Volume Review of National Literatures,* ed. Vahé Oshagan, vol. 13. New York.

Nève, F. 1861. "Exposé des guerres de Tamerlane et de Schah-Rokh dans l'Asie occidentale, d'après la chronique arménienne inédite de Thomas de Medzoph." In *Académie royale des sciences, des lettres et des beauxarts de Belgique: Mémoires, couronnés,* vol. 11/4. Brussels.

Niepage, Martin. 1975. *The Horrors of Aleppo.* London, 1917. Reprint, New York.

Olmstead, A. T. 1948. *History of the Persian Empire.* Chicago.

Orbelian, Stepanos. 1859. *History of the Region of Sisakan by Stepanos Orbelian, Archbishop of Siunik'* (in Armenian). Ed. K. Shahnazariants. Paris.

Orbelian, Stepanos. 1864. *Histoire de la Siounie par Stépannos Orbelian.* Trans. M.-F. Brosset. St. Petersburg.

Ormanian, Malachia. 1912, 1914, 1927. *Azgapatum* (National History). Vols. 1-2, Constantinople. Vol. 3, Jerusalem.

Ormanian, Malachia. 1955. *The Church of Armenia.* Trans. Marcar Gregory. 2nd ed. London.

Oshagan, Vahé. 1982. *The English Influence on West Armenian Literature in the Nineteenth Century.* Cleveland.

Oshagan, Vahé. 1986. "Literature of the Armenian Diaspora." *World Literature Today,* 60.2.

Oshagan, Vahé, ed. 1984. *Armenia: Annual Volume Review of National Literatures.* Vol. 13. New York.

Pahlavuni, Grigor. See Grigor Magistros (Gregory the Magister).

P'arpec'i, Łazar. See Ghazar Parpetsi.

Papazian, H. 1972. In *Hay zhoghovrdi patmutiun* (History of the Armenian People), Armenian Academy of Sciences. Vol. 4. Erevan.

Papikian, Hakob. 1909. *Adanayi egherne* (The Adana Calamity). Constantinople.

Pavstos Buzand P'awstos Buzand. 1989. *The Epic Histories: Attributed to P'awstos Buzand (Buzandaran Patmut'iwnk').* Trans. and comm. N. G. Garsoïan. Harvard Armenian Texts and Studies, 8. Cambridge, MA.

Pechevi. 1961. *Ta'rikh* (History). In *Contemporary Turkish Sources on Armenia and the Armenian* (in Armenian), ed. A. Safrastian, vol. 1. Erevan.

Perikhanian, A. 1967. "Une inscription araméenne du roi Artašēs trouvée à Zanguézour (Siwnik')." *Revue des études arméniennes,* n.s. 3.

Permanent People's Tribunal. 1985. *A Crime of Silence: The Armenian Genocide.* London.

Piotrovsky, B. B. 1967. *Urartu: The Kingdom of Van and Its Art.* Trans. P. Gelling. London. Originally Published as *Vanskoe tsarstvo (Urartu)* (Moscow, 1959).

Pipes, Richard. 1964. *The Formation of the Soviet Union.* Cambridge, MA.

Pitcher, D. E. 1972. *An Historical Atlas of the Ottoman Empire.* Leiden.

Pliny. *Natural History.* Trans. H. Rackham. 10 vols. Loeb Classical Library.

Plutarch. "Crassus." *Lives.* Trans. B. Perrin. Vol. 3. pp. 314/5-422/3. Loeb Classical Library.

Plutarch. "Lucullus." *Lives.* Trans. B. Perrin. Vol. 2. pp. 470/1-610/1. Loeb Classical Library.

Plutarch. "Pompey." *Lives.* Trans. B. Perrin. Vol. 5. pp. 116/7-324/5. Loeb Classical Library.

Polybius. *The Histories.* Trans. W. R. Patron. 6 vols. Loeb Classical Library.

Procopius. "Buildings." *Works.* Trans. H.B. Dewing. Vol. 7. Loeb Classical Library.

Procopius. "The Gothic War." *Works.* Trans. H.B. Dewing Vols. 3-5. Loeb Classical Library.

Procopius. "The Persian War." *Works.* Trans. H.B. Dewing Vol. 1. Loeb Classical Library.

Pseudo-Sebeos. See Sebeos.

Qazvini. 1919. *The Geographical Part of the Nuzhat-al-Qulub of Hamd-Allah Mustawfi of Qazvin.* Trans. G. Le Strange. London.

Recueil des Historiens des Croisades: Documents arméniens. 1906. Vol. 2. Paris.

Renfrew, Colin. 1987. *Archaeology and Language: The Puzzle of Indo-European Origins.* New York.

Renoux, C. 1993. "Langue et littérature arméniennes." In *Christianismes Orientaux,* ed. M. Albert et al. Paris.

Res Gestae Divi Augusti. Ed. and trans. F. W. Shipley. Loeb Classical Library.

Rudt-Collenberg, W. H. 1963. *The Rupenides, the Hethumides, and Lusignans.* Paris.

Russell, James R. 1982. "Zoroastrian Problems in Armenia: Mihr and Vahagn." In *Classical Armenian Culture,* ed. T. J. Samuelian. University of Pennsylvania Armenian Texts and Studies, vol. 4.

Russell, James R. 1984. "Pre-Christian Armenian Religion." In *Aufsteig und Niedergang der Römischen Welt,* II.18.4, ed. W. Haase and H. Temporini.

Russell, James R. 1987. "A Mystic's Christmas in Armenia." *Armenian Review* 40, no. 2-158 (Summer).

Russell, James R. 1987a. *Yovhannēs T'lkuranc'i and the Medieval Armenian Lyric Tradition.* Atlanta.

Russell, James R. 1987b. *Zoroastrianism in Armenia.* Harvard Iranian Series, 5. Cambridge, MA.

Russell, James R. 1989. "The Craft and Mithraism Reconsidered." *Proceedings of the American Lodge of Research* (Masonic), New York.

Russell, James R. 1993. "Tork' and Tarkhu." *Proceedings,* Second International Conference on the Armenian Language, Erevan, September 1987.

Russia, Ministerstvo Inostrannykh Del SSSR. 1924. *Razdel Aziatskoi Turtsii po sekretnym dokumentam b. ministerstva inostrannykh del.* Ed. E. A. Adamov. Moscow.

Russia, Ministerstvo Inostrannykh Del SSSR. 1957. *Dokumenty vneshnei politiki SSSR.* Vol. 1. Moscow.

Sachar, Howard M. 1969. *The Emergence of the Middle East, 1914-1924.* London.

Safrastian, A. 1961, 1964, 1967, 1972. *Contemporary Turkish Sources on Armenia and the Armenians* (in Armenian). 4 vols. Erevan.

Sanjian, Avedis K. 1965. *The Armenian Communities in Syria under Ottoman Dominion.* Cambridge, MA.

Sanjian, Avedis K. 1969. *Colophons of Armenian Manuscripts, 1301-1480: A Source for Middle Eastern History.* Cambridge, MA.

Sarkissian, A. O. 1938. *History of the Armenian Question to 1885.* Urbana, IL.

Sarkissian, Karekin. 1965. *The Council of Chalcedon and the Armenian Church.* London.

Sasnec'i, Mkhitar. See Mkhitar Sasnetsi.

The Scriptores Historiae Augustae. Ed. and trans. D. Magie. 3 vols. Loeb Classical Library.

Sebastatsi, Asar. See Asar Sebastatsi.

Sebastatsi, Buniat. See Buniat Sebastatsi.

Sebeos. 1904. *Histoire d'Heraclius.* Trans. F. Macler. Paris.

Setton, K. M., ed. 1969-1990. *A History of the Crusades.* 6 vols. Madison, WI.

Shalian, A. 1964. *David of Sassoun.* Athens, OH.

Shiragian, Arshavir. 1976. *The Legacy.* Boston.

Shirakatsi, Anania. See Anania Shirakatsi.

Shirinian, Lorne. 1990. *Armenian-North American Literature: A Critical Intro-duction.* New York.

Shnorhali, Nerses. See Nerses Shnorhali.

Simeon Aparantsi (Simeon of Aparan). 1969. "I veray arman Tavrizoy" (On the Capture of Tabriz). In *Hay mijnadarian patmakan oghber* (Medieval Armenian Historical Laments), ed. P. Khachatrian. Erevan.

Simeon Lehatsi (Simeon of Poland). 1936. *Ughegrutiun* (Travel Journal). Ed. Nerses Akinian. Vienna. Russian trans. M. Darbinjan (Moscow, 1965). Partial Turkish trans. H. Andreasyan (Istanbul, 1964). Partial French trans. Angèle Kapoïan-Kouymjian, *L'Egypte vue par les Arméniens* (Paris, 1988). Partial Polish trans. Zbigniew Kosciow (Warsaw, 1991).

Siurmeian, A. 1935. *Tsutsak hayeren dzeragrats Halepi* (Catalogue of Armenian Manuscripts of Aleppo). Jerusalem.

Sommer, Ernst. 1919. *Die Wahrheit über die Leiden des armenischen Volkes in der Türkei während des Weltkrieges*. Frankfurt.

Soviet Armenia. 1972. Moscow.

Sprengling, M. 1953. *Third Century Iran: Sapor and Kartir*. Chicago.

(Stepanos Asoghik) Acoghic. 1883. *Etienne Acoghic de Daron, Histoire Universelle*. Trans. E. Dulaurier. Books 1 and 2. Paris.

(Stepanos Asoghik) Asołik. 1917. *Etienne Asołik de Taron, Histoire Universelle*. Trans. F. Macler. Book 3. Paris.

Strabo [of Amasia]. 1961. *The Geography*. Ed. and trans. H. L. Jones. Loeb Classical Library.

Strom, Margot Stern, and William S. Parsons. 1982. *Facing History and Ourselves: Holocaust and Human Behavior*. Watertown, MA.

Sue, Eugene. 1991. *The Wandering Jew*. Dedalus European Fiction Classics Series. New York.

Suleiman, Michael W. 1967. *The Political Parties in Lebanon: The Challenge of a Fragmented Culture*. Ithaca, NY.

Suny, Ronald Grigor. 1972. *The Baku Commune, 1917-1918*. Princeton.

Suny, Ronald Grigor. 1983. *Armenia in the Twentieth Century*. Chico, CA.

Suny, Ronald Grigor. 1993. *Looking Toward Ararat: Armenia in Modern History*. Bloomington, IN.

Surmelian, Leon Z. 1946. *I Ask You, Ladies and Gentlemen*. London.

Swietochowski, Tadeusz. 1985. *Russian Azerbaijan, 1905-1920: The Shaping of National Identity in a Muslim Community*. Cambridge, MA.

Synodicon Orientale, ou Receueil des synods nestoriens. 1902. J. B. Chabot. Paris.

Tacitus. *Annales*. Ed. and trans. J. Jackson. 3 vols. Loeb Classical Library.

Taft, Elise Hagopian. 1981. *Rebirth*. Plandome, NY.

Tallon, M., trans. 1955 "Livre des Lettres. Ier Groupe: Documents concernant les relations avec les Grecs" (Book of Letters). *Mélanges de l'Université de S. Joseph*. 32, fasc. 1. Beirut.

Tatevatsi, Grigor. See Grigor Tatevatsi.

Tavrizhetsi, Arakel. See Arakel Tavrizhetsi.

Ter Ghewondian, A. 1976. *The Arab Emirates in Bagratid Armenia*. Trans. Nina Garsoïan. Lisbon.

Ter Minassian, Anahide. 1973. "Le mouvement révolutionnaire arménien, 1890-1903." *Cahiers du monde russe et sovietique* 14, no. 4 (October-December).

Thierry, J. M., and P. Donabedian. 1989. *The Art of the Armenians*. Paris.

Thomas Artsruni. See Tovma Artsruni.

Thomson, R. W. 1988-1989. "The Anonymous Story-Teller (also known as Pseudo-Šapuh)." *Revue des études arméniennes*, n.s. 21.

Thomson, R. W. 1994. *Studies in Armenian Literature and Christianity*. Variorum. Aldershot, UK.

Thomson, R. W. 1995. *A Bibliography of Classical Armenian Literature to 1500 AD*. Turnhout.

Tlkurantsi, Hovhannes. See Hovhannes Tlkurantsi.

Toumanoff, Cyril. 1963. *Studies in Christian Caucasian History*. Washington, D.C.

Toumanoff, Cyril. 1966. "Armenia and Georgia." In *Cambridge Medieval History*, vol. 4, 2nd ed.

Toumanoff, Cyril. 1969. "The Third-Century Arsacids: A Chronological and Genealogical Commentary." *Revue des études arméniennes*, n.s. 6.

Toumanoff, Cyril. 1976. *Manuel de généalogie et de chronologie pour l'histoire de la Caucasie chrétienne*. Rome.

Tournebize, François. 1910. "Léon V de Lusignan dernier roi de l'Arméno-Cilicie." *Etudes publiées par des pères de la Compagnie de Jésus* 122 (Paris).

Tournebize, François. 1910a. *Histoire politique et religieuse de l'Arménie*. Paris.

(Tovma Artsruni) Thomas Artsruni. *History of the House of the Artsrunik'*. Trans. and Comm. R. W. Thomson. Detroit 1985.

Tovma Metzopetsi (Thomas of Metzop). 1860. *Patmutiun Lank Tamuray ev hadjordats iurots* (History of Timur Lang and His Successors). Paris. Partial French trans. F. Nève (Brussels, 1861).

Tovma Metzopetsi (Thomas of Metzop). 1892. *Colophon*. Tiflis.

(Tovma Metzopetsi) T'ovma Metsobets'i. 1987. *History of Tamerlane and His Successors*. Trans. R. Bedrosian. New York.

Toynbee, Arnold J. 1915. *Armenian Atrocities: The Murder of a Nation*. London.

Toynbee, Arnold J. 1917. *Turkey: A Past and a Future*. London.

Toynbee, Arnold J. 1922. *The Western Question in Greece and Turkey*. London.

Toynbee, Arnold J., ed. 1916. *The Treatment of Armenians in the Ottoman Empire 1915-16: Documents Presented to Viscount Grey of Fallodon, Secretary for Foreign Affairs*. London.

Türk Devrim Tarihi Enstitüsü. 1964. *Atatürk'ün tamim, telgraf ve beyannameleri* (Ataturk's Circulars, Telegrams, and Declarations). Vol. 4, *1917-1938*. Ankara.

Turkey. 1919. *Memorandum of the Sublime Porte Communicated to the American, British, French and Italian, High Commissioners on the 12th February 1919*. Constantinople.

Ukhtanes. 1985, 1988. *Bishop Ukhtanes of Sebastia: History of Armenia*. Trans. Z. Arzoumanian. 2 Parts. Fort Lauderdale, FL.

United States vs. Cartozian. 1925. 6 Federal Reporter, 2nd Series, 919 (District Court of Oregon).

United States. Department of State. 1943, 1946. *Papers Relating to the Foreign Relations of the United States 1919: The Paris Peace Conference.* Vols. 3-4, 6. Washington, D.C.

United States. National Archives. Record Group 59.

Uratadze, G. I. 1956. *Obrazovanie i konsolidatsiia Gruzinskoi Demokraticheskoi Respubliki.* Munich.

Ussher, Clarence D. 1917. *An American Physician in Turkey.* Boston.

Vanandetsi, Ghukas. See Ghukas Vanandetsi.

Vardan Areveltsi. 1981. In *Hay grakan knnadatutian krestomatia* (Chrestomathy of Armenian Literary Criticism), ed. Zh. A. Kalantarian. Erevan.

(Vardan Areveltsi) Vardan Arewelc'i. 1989. "The Historical Compilation of Vardan Arewelc'i." Trans. R. W. Thomson, in *Dumbarton Oaks Papers.* 43, pp. 125-226.

Velleius Paterculus. *Compendium of Roman History.* Ed. and trans. F. W. Shipley. Loeb Classical Library.

Vratzian, Simon. 1928. *Hayastani Hanrapetutiun* (The Republic of Armenia). Paris.

Vryonis, Speros. 1971. *The Decline of Medieval Hellenism in Asia Minor and the Process of Islamization from the Eleventh through the Fifteenth Century.* Berkeley, Los Angeles, London.

Waldstreicher, David. 1989. *The Armenian Americans.* New York.

Walker, Christopher J. 1980. *Armenia: The Survival of a Nation.* London, New York.

Walker, Christopher J., ed. 1991. *Armenia and Karabagh: The Struggle for Unity.* London.

Wheeler-Bennett, John W. 1938. *Brest Litovsk: The Forgotten Peace, March 1918.* London.

Winkler, G. 1994. *Koriwns Biographie des Mesrop Mastoc'* (Orientalia Christiana Analecta, 245), Rome.

Woods, John. 1976. *The Aq-Quyunlu: Clan, Confederation, Empire, A Study in 15th/9th Century Turko-Iranian Politics.* Minneapolis.

Wyszomirski, M. J. 1975. "Communal Violence: The Armenians and Copts as Case Studies." *World Politics* 27, no. 3 (April).

Xenophon. *Anabasis.* Ed. and trans. C. L. Brownson. 2 vols. Loeb Classical Library.

Xenophon. *Cyropaedia.* Ed. and trans. W. Miller. 2 vols. Loeb Classical Library.

Yovhannēs Drasxanakertc'i. See Hovhannes Draskhanakerttsi.

Yovhannēs Mamikonean. See Hovhannes Mamikonian.

Yuzbashian, K. 1975-1976. "L'administration byzantine en Arménie aux Xe et XIe siècles." *Revue des études arméniennes,* n.s. 10.

Yuzbashian, K. 1988. *Armianskie gosudarstva epokhi Bagratidov i Vizantiia IX-XI vv.* Moscow.

Zarbhanalian, Garegin. 1905. *Patmutiun hayeren dprutian* (History of Armenian Literature). Vol 2. 2nd ed. Venice.

Zulalian, M. K. 1959. "*'Devshirme'-n* (mankahavake) osmanian kaysrutian medj est turkakan ev haikakan aghbiurneri [The *'Devshirme'* (Child-Gathering) in the Ottoman Empire According to Turkish and Armenian Sources]." *Patma-Banasirakan Handes* (Historical-Philological Journal), nos. 2-3. Erevan.

Zulalian, M. K. 1966. *Jalalineri sharzhume* (The Jelali Movement). Erevan.

NOTES ON THE CONTRIBUTORS

ANI ATAMIAN BOURNOUTIAN received her Ph.D. from Columbia University and is currently Assistant Dean at Barnard College. She has contributed several articles on Armenia in the *Dictionary of the Middle Ages.*

ROBERT BEDROSIAN is a specialist in the history and cultural anthropology of eastern Asia Minor. He has translated into English several of the Armenian classical historians and chroniclers. He currently works as a computer programmer in New York City.

PETER COWE taught Armenian language and literature at Columbia University for several years before joining the UCLA Department of Near Eastern Languages and Cultures as a visiting associate professor. His recent publications include translations of Mkhitar Sasnetsi's *Theological Discourses* (1993) and *A Catalogue of the Armenian Manuscripts in the Cambridge University Library* (1994).

NINA G. GARSOÏAN was the first holder of the Gevork Avedissian Chair in Armenian History and Civilization at Columbia University. She also served for two years as the Dean of the Graduate School of Princeton University. She has written and translated many works on Armenian history and culture, including *The Paulician Heresy* (1967), *Armenia between Byzantium and the Sasanians* (1985), *The Epic Histories Attributed to P'awstos Buzand* (1989), and *L'église arménienne et le Grand Schisme d'Orient* (1997/98). She is the recipient of numerous awards and honors.

ROBERT H. HEWSEN is Professor of History at Rowan University in New Jersey. He is a specialist in the historical geography of Armenia and has contributed several large scale maps to the Tübingen Atlas of the Middle East. He has translated and published the geography attributed to

Anania of Shirak (1992) and is currently completing a historical atlas of Armenia.

RICHARD G. HOVANNISIAN is the Holder of the Armenian Educational Foundation Chair in Modern Armenian History at the University of California, Los Angeles. He is the author of *Armenia on the Road to Independence* (1967) and *The Republic of Armenia*, 4 vols. (1971-1996), and he has edited three volumes on the Armenian genocide. A Guggenheim Fellow, he was elected to the National Academy of Sciences of Armenia in 1991 and awarded an honorary doctorate from Erevan State University in 1994.

JAMES RUSSELL is Mashtots Professor of Armenian Studies at Harvard University and has also taught at the Hebrew University of Jerusalem. He has published a monograph on the Zoroastrian influence in ancient Armenia and is a frequent contributor to the *Revue des études arméniennes*, *Le Muséon*, and the *Journal of the Society for Armenian Studies*.

ROBERT W. THOMSON is the Calouste Gulbenkian Professor of Armenian Studies at Oxford University. He was the first Mashtots Professor at Harvard University (1969-1992) and served as Director of Dumbarton Oaks (1984-1989). His major research interest is classical and medieval Armenian literature, and he has translated with introduction and commentary several major Armenian historians.

INDEX